Generative AI-Powered Data Architectures:

From Governance to Autonomous Analytics

Bahaa Eddine Elbaghazaoui
https://orcid.org/0000-0002-3206-5162
Sultan Moulay Slimane University, Morocco

Mohamed Amnai
Ibn Tofail University, Morocco

Noreddine Gherabi
https://orcid.org/0000-0002-2020-249X
Sultan Moulay Slimane University, Morocco

IGI Global
Scientific Publishing
Publishing Tomorrow's Research Today

Vice President of Editorial	Melissa Wagner
Director of Acquisitions	Mikaela Felty
Director of Book Development	Jocelynn Hessler
Production Manager	Mike Brehm
Cover Design	Jose Rosado

Published in the United States of America by
IGI Global Scientific Publishing
701 East Chocolate Avenue
Hershey, PA, 17033, USA
Tel: 717-533-8845 | Fax: 717-533-7115
Website: https://www.igi-global.com E-mail: cust@igi-global.com

Library of Congress Cataloging-in-Publication Data

Names: Elbaghazaoui, Bahaa Eddine, 1996- editor. | Amnai, Mohamed, 1974- editor. | Gherabi, Noreddine editor.
Title: Generative AI-powered data architectures : from governance to autonomous analytics / edited by Bahaa Eddine Elbaghazaoui, Mohamed Amnai, Noreddine Gherabi.
Description: Hershey, PA : IGI Global Scientific Publishing, [2026] | Includes bibliographical references and index. | Summary: "This book aims to bridge the gap between data architecture and AI advancements by exploring how generative technologies can influence data modeling, orchestration, privacy, and ethics"-- Provided by publisher.
Identifiers: LCCN 2025029853 (print) | LCCN 2025029854 (ebook) | ISBN 9798337356167 hardcover | ISBN 9798337356174 paperback | ISBN 9798337356181 ebook
Subjects: LCSH: Artificial intelligence--Data processing.
Classification: LCC Q336 (print) | LCC Q336 (ebook)
LC record available at https://lccn.loc.gov/2025029853
LC ebook record available at https://lccn.loc.gov/2025029854

British Cataloguing in Publication Data
A Cataloguing in Publication record for this book is available from the British Library.

Table of Contents

Preface xiii

Chapter 1
Conceptual Understanding of Generative AI in the Modern World 1
Aryan Vasa, Ajeenkya D.Y. Patil University, India
Aditya Shrivastav, Ajeenkya D.Y. Patil University, India
Sunil Sankathala, Ajeenkya D.Y. Patil University, India
Kashvi Chaturvedi, Ajeenkya D.Y. Patil University, India
Susanta Das, Ajeenkya D.Y. Patil University, India

Chapter 2
Generative Artificial Intelligence: Evolution, Applications, and Ethical Considerations 27
Aditya Shrivastav, Ajeenkya D.Y. Patil University, India
Sunil Sankathala, Ajeenkya D.Y. Patil University, India
Kashvi Chaturvedi, Ajeenkya D.Y. Patil University, India
Krutika Patre, Ajeenkya D.Y. Patil University, India
Susanta Das, Ajeenkya D.Y. Patil University, India
Rizwan Shaikh, Dr. D.Y. Patil Institute of Management and Entrepreneur Development, India

Chapter 3
Generative AI as an Accelerator for Data Engineering 57
N. Rajkumar, Alliance School of Advanced Computing, Alliance University, India
C. Viji, Alliance School of Advanced Computing, Alliance University, India
Balusamy Nachiappan, Prologis, USA
A. Mohanraj, Sri Eshwar College of Engineering, India
Judeson Antony Kovilpillai, Amity University, India
Oswalt Manoj S., Alliance School of Advance Computing, Alliance University, India

Chapter 4
Generative Adversarial Networks in Feature Engineering: An Unsupervised Approach 83
Rohini Vijay Tarade, Ajeenkya D.Y. Patil University, India
Sneha Ashish Shirke, Ajeenkya D.Y. Patil University, India
Pooja Dehankar, Ajeenkya D.Y. Patil School of Engineering, India
Susanta Das, Ajeenkya D.Y. Patil University, India

Chapter 5
GENALYTICS: A Deep Dive Into Real-Time Insights via Generative AI 105
Monika Dandotiya, Poornima University, Jaipur, India
Nikhil Kumar Goyal, Poornima University, Jaipur, India
Priyanka Yadav, Swami Keshvanand Institute of Technology, Management, and Gramothan, Jaipur, India
Kriti Sankhla, Poornima University, Jaipur, India
Monika Kumari, Poornima University, Jaipur, India

Chapter 6
AI-Integrated Data Governance Frameworks for Real-Time, Scalable, and Ethical Data Architectures 135
Rituraj Jain, Marwadi University, India
Adalbert Musengamana, Marwadi University, India

Chapter 7
Autonomous Data Orchestration With Generative AI: Redefining Pipelines for Intelligent Analytics 165
Muhammad Usman Tariq, Abu Dhabi University, UAE & University College Cork, Ireland

Chapter 8
A New Approach for Federated, Shared, and Collaborative Learning via a SAN Storage Network 193
Saad Mahmoudi, Computer Science Research Laboratory, Ibn Tofail University, Kenitra, Morocco
Mohamed Amnai, Computer Science Research Laboratory, Ibn Tofail University, Kenitra, Morocco
Tarik Elmouden, Computer Science Research Laboratory, Ibn Tofail University, Kenitra, Morocco

Chapter 9
Generative AI for Fake News Detection in Data Architectures: From Literature to Challenges and Future Directions 215
Bahaa Eddine Elbaghazaoui, National School of Applied Sciences, Sultan Moulay Slimane University, Beni Mellal, Morocco
Tarik el Moudden, Computer Science Research Laboratory, Faculty of Science, Ibn Tofail University, Kenitra, Morocco
Khalid Benabbes, ENS, Moulay Ismail University, Meknès, Morocco.

Chapter 10
Securing the Imagination: Security and Privacy Challenges in Generative AI Systems 239
Nikhil Kumar Goyal, Poornima University, Jaipur, India
Kapil Gulati, Poornima University, Jaipur, India
Ashish Avasthi, Poornima University, Jaipur, India
Sumit Kumar Kapoor, Poornima University, Jaipur, India
Bright Keswani, Poornima University, Jaipur, India
Sangita Gupta, Poornima University, Jaipur, India

Chapter 11
Exploring the Potential of Generative AI in Financial Information Control and External Audit 267
Souad Garawit, Hassan II University, Casablanca, Morocco
Leila El Gnaoui, Hassan II University, Casablanca, Morocco

Compilation of References 291

About the Contributors 325

Index 335

Detailed Table of Contents

Preface... xiii

Chapter 1
Conceptual Understanding of Generative AI in the Modern World 1
Aryan Vasa, Ajeenkya D.Y. Patil University, India
Aditya Shrivastav, Ajeenkya D.Y. Patil University, India
Sunil Sankathala, Ajeenkya D.Y. Patil University, India
Kashvi Chaturvedi, Ajeenkya D.Y. Patil University, India
Susanta Das, Ajeenkya D.Y. Patil University, India

Generative AI, an innovative subset of Artificial Intelligence, is revolutionizing industries including business, healthcare, education, and the arts. This article examines the origins of GenAI, critical technologies and foundational concepts (such as GANs, VAEs, Diffusion Models, and Transformers), and well-known tools like DALL·E and ChatGPT. It describes how GenAI produces realistic text, graphics, code and audio and how it's used to businesses, software, design, and learning. Along with examining issues like hallucinations, abuse, and inexplicability, the review also examines important societal issues including trust, bias, ethics, transparency and environmental effect. It also covers how GenAI fosters productivity, creativity, and human-AI cooperation. Through case studies and research analysis, it demonstrates how GenAI development is quickly transforming the fields like business, logistics, education, design, engineering, etc. In order to ensure that GenAI advances humankind without endangering it, it ends by urging a responsible, transparent, and moral approach to its use.

Chapter 2
Generative Artificial Intelligence: Evolution, Applications, and Ethical Considerations.. 27
Aditya Shrivastav, Ajeenkya D.Y. Patil University, India
Sunil Sankathala, Ajeenkya D.Y. Patil University, India
Kashvi Chaturvedi, Ajeenkya D.Y. Patil University, India
Krutika Patre, Ajeenkya D.Y. Patil University, India
Susanta Das, Ajeenkya D.Y. Patil University, India
Rizwan Shaikh, Dr. D.Y. Patil Institute of Management and Entrepreneur Development, India

Generative Artificial Intelligence (GAI) is a technical term used to designate elaborate machine learning algorithms that allow the creation of human-like output text, images, audio, and biomedical data. Such methods as Generative Adversarial Networks (GANs), Variational Autoencoders (VAEs), and diffusion models led to making GAI an initiative that promotes innovation in other fields such as healthcare, education, and creative fields. Yet with its fast development, one must wonder about algorithm bias as well as data privacy issues, misinformation, and control over AI-based content. The chapter delves into the history of the development of GAI, its theoretical background, and its fundamental implementation. It presents a bibliometric analysis to point out the interdisciplinary dynamics of GAI study. It looks at ethics implications, legal implications as well as social implications and necessity of responsible innovation. The chapter winds up with highlighting the challenges that persist and proposing future steps toward transparent and responsible use of generative technologies.

Chapter 3
Generative AI as an Accelerator for Data Engineering 57
N. Rajkumar, Alliance School of Advanced Computing, Alliance University, India
C. Viji, Alliance School of Advanced Computing, Alliance University, India
Balusamy Nachiappan, Prologis, USA
A. Mohanraj, Sri Eshwar College of Engineering, India
Judeson Antony Kovilpillai, Amity University, India
Oswalt Manoj S., Alliance School of Advance Computing, Alliance University, India

The exponential growth of data in the digital era has heightened the importance of efficient data engineering practices. Traditional approaches to data ingestion, cleaning, transformation, and governance often require significant manual intervention, domain expertise, and development time, leading to bottlenecks in analytics and decision-making. By leveraging natural language prompts, contextual learning, and synthetic data generation capabilities, GenAI can facilitate code generation for data pipelines, improve data quality, enhance metadata documentation, and support intelligent decision-making in real-time environments. This chapter explores the integration of Generative AI into data engineering workflows, providing a comprehensive review of relevant technologies, conceptual frameworks, industrial applications, and challenges. Several case studies highlight the tangible benefits of this synergy, including improved productivity, reduced operational costs, and higher data accuracy.

Chapter 4
Generative Adversarial Networks in Feature Engineering: An Unsupervised Approach.. 83
Rohini Vijay Tarade, Ajeenkya D.Y. Patil University, India
Sneha Ashish Shirke, Ajeenkya D.Y. Patil University, India
Pooja Dehankar, Ajeenkya D.Y. Patil School of Engineering, India
Susanta Das, Ajeenkya D.Y. Patil University, India

The process of collecting & choosing features from unprocessed data is made much easier in ML because of the breakthrough work of GANs. GANs are ideal for unsupervised feature engineering as they are composed of a generator & discriminator that participate in adversarial training. This allows the discovery of hidden patterns without the need for predetermined labels. GANs improve datasets & strengthen models by boosting diversity & decreasing overfitting. They help to reduce dimensionality, which reduces computational expenses & simplifies model complexity. GANs increase model accuracy in many domains (computer vision, NLP, healthcare, etc). However, some obstacles are there (challenging training, problems with synthetic data quality, expensive computing, & moral dilemmas). It is imperative to make advancements in training procedures, integrate them with other ML paradigms & establish ethical norms for the usage of synthetic data. This chapter aims to review GANs in unsupervised feature engineering, examining their theoretical underpinnings, real-world applications, & prospects.

Chapter 5
GENALYTICS: A Deep Dive Into Real-Time Insights via Generative AI 105
Monika Dandotiya, Poornima University, Jaipur, India
Nikhil Kumar Goyal, Poornima University, Jaipur, India
Priyanka Yadav, Swami Keshvanand Institute of Technology, Management, and Gramothan, Jaipur, India
Kriti Sankhla, Poornima University, Jaipur, India
Monika Kumari, Poornima University, Jaipur, India

With today being an age of hyper-connected systems and real time decision-making, it is no wonder that real time analytics have emerged as the key to organizations looking to draw actionable intelligence out of constantly changing data streams. Lastly, the chapter talks about the issues of implementation, ethical concerns, and legal issues involved with real-time generative systems. Future directions are explained, such as the changes towards federated learning, autonomous analytics, and quantum-assisted generative AI. The chapter will also be a conceptual guide and practical road map to the researcher, practitioners and industry professionals, whether the landscape of intelligent real-time analytics is playing out according to the initial expectations or not.

Chapter 6
AI-Integrated Data Governance Frameworks for Real-Time, Scalable, and Ethical Data Architectures 135
Rituraj Jain, Marwadi University, India
Adalbert Musengamana, Marwadi University, India

In the context of modern big data environments, this chapter explores how data governance reshapes the portrayal and management of data—an essential factor in maintaining data quality, security, and compliance. This underlines the fact that data has not only become a record-keeping asset, but also a strategic driver of insights and decisions. Against the volume, velocity, variety, and veracity challenges that characterize big data, this chapter surveys flexible, integrated, adaptive governance frameworks based on a core reflection of elements of compliance, real-time access, data stewardship, and security. It analyzes practical issues, such as no architecture, no visibility of the data, and no sponsorship, and develops solutions for automation, balancing accessibility with security, and promoting data literacy. Firms, such as Airbnb, Uber, and GE Aviation, provide tangible examples of good governance. Finally, the chapter discusses future trends, such as AI, NLP, and hybrid cloud innovations, that would create sustainable data-driven ecosystems.

Chapter 7
Autonomous Data Orchestration With Generative AI: Redefining Pipelines for Intelligent Analytics 165
Muhammad Usman Tariq, Abu Dhabi University, UAE & University College Cork, Ireland

Orchestration of autonomous data using generated AI transforms traditional analytics pipelines by introducing intelligent automation, context-related decision-making, and adaptive data workflows. This ambitious paradigm leverages the capabilities of large-scale models and basic AI systems to dynamically manage the absorption, transformation, integration, and delivery of data, eliminating the need for constant human supervision. Generated AI enables the system to interpret metadata, understand the data's intent, and optimize the pipeline itself based on power metrics or actual time analysis requirements. In contrast to the traditional static architecture, autonomous orchestration introduces continuous learning, enabling the pipeline to evolve further and adapt to changing business requirements and data ecosystems. Enhance agility, eliminate operational bottlenecks, and enhance accessibility for advanced analytics. This shift redefines the role of data engineers, focusing on governance, monitoring, and strategic design while minimizing manual intervention in pipeline operations.

Chapter 8
A New Approach for Federated, Shared, and Collaborative Learning via a SAN Storage Network 193
Saad Mahmoudi, Computer Science Research Laboratory, Ibn Tofail University, Kenitra, Morocco
Mohamed Amnai, Computer Science Research Laboratory, Ibn Tofail University, Kenitra, Morocco
Tarik Elmouden, Computer Science Research Laboratory, Ibn Tofail University, Kenitra, Morocco

The exponential emergence of IoT devices in a smart city generates significant data traffic on the network. This traffic can be affected by changes in the values exchanged between IoT devices and the aggregation server, which further guarantees the lack of parameter integrity, leading to unreliable learning. For this reason, we propose a new approach to protecting the private and confidential data of IoT devices required for federated learning of an AI model. Our approach aims to improve accuracy of learning model predictive values based on Fiber Channel technology, which adjusts the sharing and storage of learning parameters over the network, ensuring a reliable connection between IoT devices and storage arrays. This technology accelerates the AI model training phase while reducing latency.

Chapter 9
Generative AI for Fake News Detection in Data Architectures: From Literature to Challenges and Future Directions 215
Bahaa Eddine Elbaghazaoui, National School of Applied Sciences, Sultan Moulay Slimane University, Beni Mellal, Morocco
Tarik el Moudden, Computer Science Research Laboratory, Faculty of Science, Ibn Tofail University, Kenitra, Morocco
Khalid Benabbes, ENS, Moulay Ismail University, Meknès, Morocco.

The proliferation of fake news threatens data integrity and public trust, challenging the foundations of modern data-driven systems. This chapter explores how Generative AI, particularly large language models (LLMs), can enhance fake news detection and support trustworthy data architectures. We review key techniques in misinformation detection and analyze the emerging role of GenAI in enabling automated content validation, explanation generation, and credibility assessment. The integration of these models into data pipelines introduces new opportunities but also raises concerns such as hallucinations, bias propagation, and ethical risks. We outline the main challenges and propose future research directions to design autonomous, explainable, and resilient systems capable of mitigating misinformation in real time while upholding transparency and data governance principles.

Chapter 10
Securing the Imagination: Security and Privacy Challenges in Generative AI Systems 239
Nikhil Kumar Goyal, Poornima University, Jaipur, India
Kapil Gulati, Poornima University, Jaipur, India
Ashish Avasthi, Poornima University, Jaipur, India
Sumit Kumar Kapoor, Poornima University, Jaipur, India
Bright Keswani, Poornima University, Jaipur, India
Sangita Gupta, Poornima University, Jaipur, India

Generative Artificial Intelligence (AI) has rapidly become a mainstream technology capable of autonomously producing realistic and diverse media content, including text, images, video, music, and code. As models like GPT, DALL·E, and Stable Diffusion transform industries such as entertainment, marketing, education, and software development, they also introduce a complex landscape of security and privacy risks. This chapter, per the authors, explores critical vulnerabilities such as prompt injection, adversarial attacks, data poisoning, and model inversion, which can lead to unethical outputs and exposure of sensitive training data. It further examines threats arising from large-scale data scraping, copyright violations, and lack of user consent, while also addressing ethical issues tied to misinformation, deepfakes, and surveillance. The chapter reviews technical safeguards including differential privacy, federated learning, watermarking, adversarial training, and secure deployment methods like sandboxing and real-time monitoring.

Chapter 11
Exploring the Potential of Generative AI in Financial Information Control and External Audit 267
Souad Garawit, Hassan II University, Casablanca, Morocco
Leila El Gnaoui, Hassan II University, Casablanca, Morocco

Today's technology advancements provide innovative support to oversight mechanisms through operational capacities. This study explores how artificial intelligence (AI), and in particular generative AI, can be integrated into financial information control with the objective of improve its quality. It analyses the challenges posed by information asymmetry and conflicts of interest, and highlights how AI enhances financial reporting through anomaly detection and the acceleration of control procedures, providing timely decision support. The methodological approach relies on a documentary analysis, supported by a framework assessing the integration of AI into corporate governance mechanisms. Particular attention is given to external audit processes, where AI can strengthen audit quality by reducing risks to an acceptable level and issuing an audit opinion on the financial statements, while fostering more innovative governance models. The objective is to provide research-based insights and recommendations for the sustainable and ethical deployment of these technologies.

Compilation of References 291

About the Contributors 325

Index 335

Preface

OVERVIEW OF THE SUBJECT MATTER

In the rapidly evolving digital landscape, Generative Artificial Intelligence (GenAI) has emerged as one of the most transformative forces in data-driven innovation. While traditional AI focused primarily on prediction and classification, generative models have introduced new capabilities in content creation, data synthesis, pipeline automation, and decision orchestration. This paradigm shift redefines how data is generated, processed, governed, and leveraged across industries.

The book *Generative AI-Powered Data Architectures: From Governance to Autonomous Analytics* explores how GenAI can reshape the entire data lifecycle, from ingestion and engineering to governance, analytics, and autonomous decision-making. It brings together a set of cutting-edge research contributions, each addressing critical aspects of building resilient, ethical, and intelligent data architectures that harness the generative power of AI.

RELEVANCE AND CONTEXT IN THE MODERN WORLD

The advent of Large Language Models (LLMs), Generative Adversarial Networks (GANs), and Autonomous Agents has enabled enterprises and researchers to rethink traditional data systems. Modern organizations face unprecedented challenges in data volume, heterogeneity, privacy, and compliance, all while seeking faster insights and automation. GenAI provides a bridge, allowing systems not only to process data but to augment and reason about it creatively.

In this context, the convergence between data engineering, AI governance, and ethical intelligence is no longer optional, it defines the foundation of next-generation digital ecosystems. This book positions itself at that intersection, offering theoretical insights, technical frameworks, and applied use cases that reflect the future of data-driven innovation.

TARGET AUDIENCE

This book is designed for a wide spectrum of readers:

- Researchers and Academics exploring novel architectures that integrate AI-driven automation and governance.
- Data Engineers and Architects seeking scalable frameworks for real-time, intelligent pipelines.
- AI Practitioners and Data Scientists interested in applying generative models for data augmentation, governance, and analytics.
- Policy Makers and Industry Leaders focusing on the ethical and regulatory implications of autonomous data systems.

The contributions within this volume are interdisciplinary by design, bridging computer science, information systems, data ethics, and intelligent automation, to serve both theoretical exploration and practical implementation.

CHAPTER SUMMARIES AND CONTRIBUTIONS

1. Conceptual Understanding of Generative AI in the Modern World

This chapter lays the theoretical foundation for the volume by introducing the conceptual underpinnings of generative AI. It examines the evolution from rule-based intelligence to probabilistic and neural generative models, establishing a framework for understanding how GenAI differs from traditional AI paradigms. It provides the necessary vocabulary and context for subsequent chapters.

2. Generative Artificial Intelligence – Evolution, Applications, and Ethical Considerations

This contribution offers a comprehensive historical and ethical lens, tracing the journey of generative AI technologies. It explores key breakthroughs such as GANs, transformers, and diffusion models, while addressing the ethical dilemmas associated with content authenticity, data bias, and societal impact. This chapter sets the ethical baseline for deploying GenAI responsibly.

3. Generative AI as an Accelerator for Data Engineering

Here, the authors discuss how generative models are transforming data engineering workflows, from synthetic data generation to schema inference and ETL automation. The chapter highlights GenAI's ability to reduce human intervention in repetitive data tasks and foster intelligent, adaptive data pipelines.

4. Generative Adversarial Networks in Feature Engineering – An Unsupervised Approach

This chapter delves into unsupervised feature extraction and representation learning using GANs. It provides methodological depth on how adversarial architectures can enhance data quality, uncover latent structures, and improve downstream machine learning models, particularly in domains with limited labeled data.

5. GENALYTICS – A Deep Dive into Real-Time Insights via Generative AI

The "GENALYTICS" framework introduces a fusion of real-time analytics and generative intelligence, enabling systems that not only analyze but anticipate trends. The chapter presents a reference architecture for continuous insight generation, illustrating how GenAI can enhance situational awareness in sectors like finance, logistics, and cybersecurity.

6. AI-Integrated Data Governance Frameworks for Real-Time, Scalable, and Ethical Data Architectures

This work focuses on data governance enhanced by AI, presenting frameworks that balance scalability, compliance, and transparency. It discusses metadata automation, policy generation through large language models, and the role of GenAI in ethical auditing, defining a vision for AI-augmented governance systems.

7. Autonomous Data Orchestration with Generative AI – Redefining Pipelines for Intelligent Analytics

This chapter explores autonomous orchestration, where data pipelines become self-configuring and self-optimizing through GenAI agents. The authors propose an architecture where GenAI modules monitor, adapt, and repair pipelines dynamically, leading toward the era of self-driving data systems.

8. A New Approach for Federated Shared and Collaborative Learning via a SAN Storage Network

In this contribution, the focus shifts to distributed and federated architectures. It demonstrates how storage-area-network (SAN) infrastructures can support collaborative learning without compromising data privacy. This model promotes secure, multi-institutional AI collaboration and contributes to the vision of decentralized intelligence.

9. Generative AI for Fake News Detection in Data Architectures – From Literature to Challenges and Future Directions

Addressing a timely societal issue, this chapter investigates how GenAI can aid in misinformation detection and content verification. Through a detailed literature review and experimental insights, it outlines challenges and proposes future directions for integrating GenAI into trustworthy data ecosystems.

10. Securing the Imagination – Security and Privacy Challenges in Generative AI Systems

This chapter presents an in-depth discussion on the security vulnerabilities and privacy concerns inherent to generative models. It covers adversarial attacks, model inversion, and data leakage risks, proposing countermeasures and governance strategies for building secure generative ecosystems.

11. Exploring the Potential of Generative AI in Financial Information Control and External Audit

The closing chapter connects GenAI with financial data governance and auditing, showing how generative systems can improve fraud detection, automate report generation, and enhance compliance analytics. It underscores how generative intelligence can drive accuracy and transparency in highly regulated environments.

CONCLUSION – IMPACT AND CONTRIBUTION TO THE FIELD

This book positions Generative AI as a cornerstone of the next generation of data-centric architectures. By merging theory, technical innovation, and ethical awareness, it provides a blueprint for AI-driven data ecosystems that are self-learning, trustworthy, and adaptive.

Beyond technology, this collection stimulates a new dialogue about responsible automation and human-machine collaboration in the age of generative intelligence. The insights presented here will guide researchers, practitioners, and policymakers in designing data architectures that are not only powerful but also sustainable and ethically aligned with the evolving digital society.

Chapter 1
Conceptual Understanding of Generative AI in the Modern World

Aryan Vasa
Ajeenkya D.Y. Patil University, India

Aditya Shrivastav
https://orcid.org/0009-0000-8461-8171
Ajeenkya D.Y. Patil University, India

Sunil Sankathala
https://orcid.org/0009-0004-7809-7647
Ajeenkya D.Y. Patil University, India

Kashvi Chaturvedi
https://orcid.org/0009-0005-3192-3400
Ajeenkya D.Y. Patil University, India

Susanta Das
https://orcid.org/0000-0002-9314-3988
Ajeenkya D.Y. Patil University, India

ABSTRACT

Generative AI, an innovative subset of Artificial Intelligence, is revolutionizing industries including business, healthcare, education, and the arts. This article examines the origins of GenAI, critical technologies and foundational concepts (such as GANs, VAEs, Diffusion Models, and Transformers), and well-known tools like

DOI: 10.4018/979-8-3373-5616-7.ch001

DALL·E and ChatGPT. It describes how GenAI produces realistic text, graphics, code and audio and how it's used to businesses, software, design, and learning. Along with examining issues like hallucinations, abuse, and inexplicability, the review also examines important societal issues including trust, bias, ethics, transparency and environmental effect. It also covers how GenAI fosters productivity, creativity, and human-AI cooperation. Through case studies and research analysis, it demonstrates how GenAI development is quickly transforming the fields like business, logistics, education, design, engineering, etc. In order to ensure that GenAI advances humankind without endangering it, it ends by urging a responsible, transparent, and moral approach to its use.

1. INTRODUCTION

Artificial Intelligence has been growing as a trending topic among researchers, analysts, industrialists and even the general public. Everyone is fascinated and interested to learn about it and use it as a technology to basically make the work easier. Artificial Intelligence has eventually become a popular choice as a smart investment for many people as well as industries. However, Artificial Intelligence is a broad field comprising different types and subsets and one of it's subsets has rapidly expanded in terms of use or applications in daily life recently. That subset of AI is Generative AI. It is becoming more and more popular because of its accessibility and capacity to generate realistic and imaginative outcomes. It has an impact on a variety of industries, including software development, marketing, education, medicine, and the arts and music. The field of generative artificial intelligence (GenAI) grew rapidly in late 2022, enabling a large audience to produce realistic images, music, and texts that resembled those of a human. This strategy has broad results for a number of domains, including content creation, which is itself a rising field. With the introduction of programs like ChatGPT, DALL·E, and Midjourney, the use of AI in content production has advanced significantly. These applications have made powerful Large Language Models (LLMs) accessible to the general public, enabling anyone without technical knowledge to produce writing, images, and even music that is human-like. The field of AI has a lot complex-language terms which everyone may not be familiar with and it may become difficult to understand, hence it would be better to understand the foundation of AI and Generative AI. According to Sakıın and Kusuma (2023), generative AI encompasses various models such as GANs, VAEs, diffusion models, and transformers, all of which are intended to produce realistic content by identifying patterns in data. Hence, understanding what generative AI actually means and how content creation operated prior to the widespread availability of these tools is crucial before delving into the specifics of the technology. Examining this can help us understand why generative AI has become so popular. The ability to create is what the term "generative" refers to. All AI models could be broadly referred to as generative since they generate outputs such as rules or predictions. Due to unlike data-driven predictions or analyses, "generative AI" refers to models that produce entirely new and unique content based on the data they have been trained on, such as text, images, or music that sounds human. Beyond computations, these models produce interactive and consumable content (García-Peñalvo & Vázquez-Ingelmo, 2023).

Before understanding and going deep into conceptual understanding of the foundational basics of AI and Generative AI, it is crucial to know about its origins. Learning about the history of AI and Generative AI can help us build the foundation for its complete timeline as well as grasp abstract ideas and terms/ concepts. The idea behind artificial intelligence (AI) was to create machines that could think, learn, and make decisions just like people do. When Alan Turing questioned whether machines were capable of thinking in the 1950s, it became well-known. With applications in image analysis, language translation, speech recognition, and decision-making tools, artificial intelligence has developed into a broad field over time. The 1970s and 1980s saw a slowdown in AI development because of limited computing power and practical results; this period is referred to as the "AI winter." However, new training methods became successful as technology advanced in the early 2000s. AI has become more effective and approachable for regular people thanks to generative AI, which produces content that is natural and human-like. Although the idea of Generative AI started in the late 1950s, it gained attention when the idea of Generative AI was implemented and applied to create ChatGPT, a popular example of AI and Generative AI, which in turn started around November 2022 and became popular in early 2023. Platforms such as ChatGPT and DALL·E have made generative AI, a technology that has transformed different industries like education, healthcare, marketing, and communication, accessible. However, the use of it raises ethical concerns due to its growth (Corchado et al., 2023).

The potential of AI to revolutionize human-machine interaction has long existed, and new developments have brought this vision closer to reality than before. Generative Artificial Intelligence (GenAI), which includes models that can independently produce new digital content like text, images, audio, code, and even synthetic datasets, is one of the most disruptive and extensively discussed subsets of AI today (Sakirin & Kusuma, 2023; Kalota, 2024). Replicating the data distribution they are trained on allows generative systems to simulate outputs that are remarkably human-like, in contrast to traditional AI models that concentrate on classification or prediction (Feuerriegel et al., 2023; García-Peñalvo & Vázquez-Ingelmo, 2023). According to Sakirin and Kusuma (2023), the term is typically used by researchers to refer to powerful systems that are capable of producing realistic and detailed content, such as GANs, VAEs, Diffusion Models, and Transformers. In common speech, however, people may refer to any AI that creates something new, such as text, images, or music, as "generative AI," even if the underlying technology isn't actually generative (García-Peñalvo & Vázquez-Ingelmo, 2023). One of the most revolutionary developments in AI, generative artificial intelligence (GenAI) has gained the attention of the public as well as researchers and developers because of its capacity to create content that is human-like, including text, images, audio, and video (García-Peñalvo & Vázquez-Ingelmo, 2023; Banh & Strobel, 2023). In other words, a technological revolution that transcends automation to content creation, generative artificial intelligence (GenAI) redefines human-machine interaction by producing generative outputs that resemble people, including text, graphics, and music (Wood & Moss, 2024).

The adoption of ChatGPT, DALL·E, Midjourney, and Copilot has been further accelerated by their recent proliferation, showcasing capabilities that were previously believed to be unique to human creativity (Feuerriegel et al., 2023). Nevertheless, the precise definition of "Generative AI" is still up for debate, despite the field's quick advancement and societal influence. The way the term is understood in popular discourse and how it is used in scholarly literature differs noticeably (Bianchini, 2025). These subjects generally refer to the fundamental fields that you must comprehend and hone in order to collaborate with generative AI systems. Beyond merely being able to write code, these serve as the cornerstone for creating, utilizing, and innovating GenAI technologies (Fathi et al., 2025b). According to Akolekar et al. (2025), the incorporation of AI tools into mechanical engineering education has demonstrated encouraging outcomes by providing design support and interactive learning simulations that closely mirror real-world applications. Analogously, frameworks that emphasize the use of generative AI to address conceptual gaps in STEM education (El Fathi et al., 2025) and for culturally responsive assessment in science (Nyaaba et al., 2024) mirror the larger trend toward inclusive and customized learning experiences. Meanwhile, the ethical and social implications of generative AI are receiving more attention, particularly with regard to how it affects perception, biases, and equity in content creation. Hence this review article tries to explain the basic concepts, applications and social implications of generative AI, which gives the readers a practical perspective on its radical prowess as well as the current challenges.

2. FOUNDATIONS OF GENERATIVE AI

They look for patterns in the distribution and structure of the data itself. They get trained and adapted at identifying patterns in the data to produce original, comparable examples. A generative model might produce new text, images, or data points that appear to be from the original set. In contrast to the more prevalent discriminative modelling used in traditional machine learning, generative modelling is a mathematical technique that forms the foundation of generative AI (Nyaaba et al., 2024). In simple words, discriminative models concentrate on learning how to classify data. In terms of mathematics, their goal is to determine P(Y|X), or the likelihood that a label Y will be assigned to an input X. In a classification task, for instance, such a model learns to determine whether an email is spam or not based on its content (X), attempting to predict Y as either 0 or 1 (Nyaaba et al., 2024). On the other hand, generative models go further: they attempt to learn the data's complete distribution, including the joint probability P(X, Y) or even just P(X). This indicates that they not only comprehend the category to which a sample belongs, but they also model the generation of the data. Thus, generative models are capable of producing completely new samples that are similar to the original data, which is a very powerful capability. As we know Generative AI is rapidly growing field, it comprises lot of complex terms and concepts. In this quickly developing technology, computers that can independently produce new results are replacing conventional data-driven artificial intelligence. AI is now a co-creator in fields ranging from language and visual arts to coding and scientific discoveries, thanks to this creative shift made possible by deep learning and enormous datasets. In general, computer systems that mimic human cognitive processes including learning, reasoning, and perception are referred to as artificial intelligence (AI) (Kalota, 2024). Machine learning (ML), a branch of artificial intelligence, uses data to identify patterns instead of explicit programming to help systems perform better on tasks over time (Feuerriegel et al., 2023). A branch of machine learning called deep learning (DL) uses multi-layered neural networks to handle high-dimensional data and identify intricate correlations and features. Since it makes it possible to simulate the complex data distributions required for content creation, DL is especially important to GenAI (Janiesch et al., 2021; LeCun et al., 2015). We can now concentrate on generative AI after learning the fundamentals of AI, machine learning, and deep learning. "Generative" simply means to produce or create. Therefore, technology that can produce new content, such as text, images, music, videos, or even computer code, is referred to as generative AI.

Generative AI has existed over time, but ChatGPT attracted much attention following its release in the end of 2022. To better understand how such tools as ChatGPT work, we should also learn about some significant notions, including the large language models (LLMs), generative pre-trained transformers (GPTs), and natural language processing (NLP) (Kalota, 2024).

A. Natural Language Processing (NLP): Natural language processing (NLP) is a research field within artificial intelligence that empowers computers to attain a very rudimentary understanding of human language and the ability to communicate with humans in the same language. There will be the creation of machines that read, comprehend, and even write language in the manner that human beings find easy to use. This will allow computers to have a dialogue with us and learn things based on our talk and help researchers who dare to study what language really is. Overall, NLP makes possible the following technologies: chatbots, voice assistants, language translators (Kalota, 2024).

B. Large Language Model (LLM): A computer tool that helps a computer to predict the word that is likely to come first on a sentence. It does it by using the probability of words appearing together, as they usually do. As a model knows, there are higher chances of the use of the word, are, after the word, is, is used in the beginning of a sentence written with the words, they. This kind of technology enables such capabilities as automatically filling in an email or a text. Transformer: A transformer is a kind of artificial intelligence model that transforms input into a useful output, frequently in a different format. Giving it a written prompt, for instance, can be transformed into an entire essay, email, picture, or even sound. It can comprehend and produce various kinds of content, much like a clever converter (Kalota, 2024).
C. Generative Pretrained Transformer (GPT): Generative Pretrained Transformers (GPTs) are AI models that can produce text, code, and other content in response to inputs you enter (referred to as prompts). Several iterations of GPT have been developed, including GPT-1, GPT-2, GPT-3, and GPT-4. ChatGPT is one of the most popular programs that makes use of GPT. An artificial neural network and large language models are used by ChatGPT, a generative AI chatbot, to comprehend a prompt and provide a thorough response. For human-like dialogue, it integrates artificial intelligence (AI), natural language processing (NLP), and robust language models (Kalota, 2024).
D. Artificial Neural Networks (ANNs): ANNs are computer programs that mimic the functioning of the human brain. The layers that comprise an ANN are an input layer, an output layer, and multiple hidden layers between them. Every hidden layer receives information, processes it, and then forwards the outcome to the subsequent layer. The final product, which could be a prediction, response, or choice, is produced after this methodical process is completed (Kalota, 2024).

3. APPLICATIONS OF GENERATIVE AI

Here, applications of Generative AI are discussed in two ways, one is based on the overview of the different output and result methods generative by any Generative AI model and the other is the wide range of applications in terms of distinct fields.

The application of generative artificial intelligence (GAI) involves converting input from one format to another, such as text to image, video, code, or audio. Tools like ChatGPT help with content creation, produce responses that seem human, and help create unique text for tasks like customer service or sales. Models like Stable Diffusion generate images from text prompts, which is helpful in fields like medical training, design, and advertising. In domains such as engineering and the visual arts, generative AI is now being utilized as a creative partner, stimulating the creative process and assisting with idea generation and prototyping (Chen et al., 2025; Thoring et al., 2023). The following is a general overview of the outputs and results generated by Generative AI:

A. Code: By converting instructions from natural language into functional code, generative AI is revolutionizing the way software developers write code. CodeBERT and GraphCodeBERT are two examples of tools that can produce code from written descriptions or models because they are specifically trained on programming languages. Even general AI models that have been trained on a lot of data, including code, can help with coding. In order to assist programmers, platforms such as GitHub Copilot offer code snippet suggestions, finish incomplete code, write tests, identify duplicate code, and fix bugs. In addition to accelerating development, this also increases productivity, promotes testing more quickly, and raises the caliber of software solutions (Banh & Strobel, 2023).
B. Audio: Creating realistic sound, such as human-like speech and music, is the main goal of generative AI in audio. They are developing technologies such as text-to-speech and speech-to-speech to support accessibility tools, training videos, audiobooks, digital assistants, and customer service. High-end models, like Microsoft's VALL-E, can generate incredibly realistic voices for a more captivating user experience. Generative models such as MusicLM are also utilized in the production of music, allowing users to describe a melody or mood and obtain original musical compositions (Banh & Strobel, 2023). These tools save time and money when compared to traditional methods by enabling businesses to create custom audio for marketing, movies, or games while also assisting musicians in igniting their creativity (Chen et al., 2025; Thoring et al., 2023).
C. Other: Beyond merely producing text, images, videos, code, or audio, generative AI is also significantly advancing specialized fields. To help scientists with drug

development and bioengineering, for instance, programs like AlphaFold and OpenBioML can predict and design new protein structures. AI 3D modelling tools like DreamFusion, GET3D, and Point-E are capable of producing realistic and intricate 3D models. These make the creative process faster, simpler, and more accessible in fields like virtual reality, architecture, product design, and gaming (Banh & Strobel, 2023).

Generative AI has immense applications such that is can be used almost in majority of the fields. Everyone individuals, companies, and organizations—is anticipated to be impacted by generative AI. It can help people in many ways and increase productivity, even though it might replace some human tasks. It presents fresh chances to assist employees and enhance organizational performance (Chen et al., 2025; Thoring et al., 2023). At the moment, major tech firms like Amazon, Google, IBM, Microsoft, and OpenAI are spearheading the creation of these tools. Some real-world applications of Generative AI are explained below:

I. Business

Generative AI uses in business are numerous and include marketing, customer service, healthcare, human resources, entertainment, and more. Personalized messages can be generated for customers based on its ability to predict when they might make a purchase. An estimated 30% of marketing messages will be produced by AI by 2025. Generative AI also speeds up innovation by lowering the cost and speed of ideation and prototyping. Over 30% of new drugs could be found by 2025 using generative AI, and AI models are even being used in medicine to create new antibodies. Through collaboration, idea refinement, questioning of expert opinions, and new ways of thinking, generative AI can increase human creativity. It can swiftly generate a large number of concepts that people can evaluate and expand upon. Research has indicated that while AI tools such as Chatbots and DALL·E can produce innovative ideas that are on par with or occasionally superior to those of inexperienced humans, the best human ideas can still be competitive. This demonstrates that generative AI is a helpful auxiliary tool rather than a substitute for human creativity (Kalota, 2024; Musa & Kakudi, 2025).

II. Education

For more than four decades, artificial intelligence (AI) has been utilized in education to support teaching, student support, administration, and intelligent tutoring. In educational settings, GenAI is being used more and more to support activities like intelligent tutoring and individualized feedback, which improves learning results and student engagement (El Fathi et al., 2025). By providing equal access to information, generative AI tools such as ChatGPT can assist educators in developing educational resources and tests while simultaneously advancing equity. These tools still have drawbacks, such as factual errors and the inability to customize content for specific students, but they can help with student work evaluation and instructional strategy improvement. Even students gain from this. According to one study, medical students thought AI was a good teaching tool. More individualized learning experiences could result from the use of tools like ChatGPT, which would improve intelligent tutoring systems. However, some universities have banned these tools or are revising their academic policies due to their potential for misuse by students. Since some universities now view the use of AI as academic misconduct, they are redesigning assessments to be more resistant to AI help, either by reverting to pen-and-paper exams or utilizing multimedia (Kalota, 2024; Musa & Kakudi, 2025).

III. Software Engineering

Software developers and entrepreneurs can benefit greatly from generative AI, particularly those engaged in contracts for software development, maintenance, or updates. It facilitates the writing of code, the discovery and correction of bugs, and the creation of documentation, among other phases of the software development process. This is true of all digital products, including websites, apps, and stand-alone software. OpenAI Codex, Tabnine, CodeT5, Polycoder, and ChatGPT are a few of the well-known tools. Globally, generative AI is being adopted by businesses in nations like the USA and the UK. Utilizing this technology helps businesses increase sales and achieve greater success. Not only does this boost business performance, but it also stimulates economic growth. Generative AI is becoming increasingly important in helping industries work more efficiently and produce better results, as evidenced by its growing use (Musa & Kakudi, 2025).

IV. Healthcare and Drug Related Applications

In several ways, recent developments in generative AI particularly transformer-based models like ChatGPT are beginning to have a big impact on healthcare:

i. Customised Treatment Plans: By examining a patient's medical history, genetic makeup, and way of life, generative AI can assist clinicians in developing customised treatment regimens. This improves the effectiveness and personalization of treatments (Chen et al., 2025; Thoring et al., 2023).
ii. Discovery and Development of Drugs: Conventional drug development is expensive and time-consuming. Through the analysis of chemical data, generative

AI expedites the process of identifying and designing possible drug candidates. Predicting the behavior of molecules can also help cut down on the time and expense of introducing new medications to the market. Examples include programs like Chemputer, AlphaFold, and DeepChem (Chen et al., 2025; Thoring et al., 2023).

iii. Medical Imaging: AI can accurately analyze medical scans, such as MRIs or X-rays, assisting physicians in making better decisions and identifying diseases early (Musa & Kakudi, 2025).

iv. Medical Chatbots: Chatbots which can give the patients medical advice, answer questions, and help them manage symptoms and prescriptions are driven by generative artificial intelligence. An example of this type of a chatbot is Babylon Health that offers personalized aid to patients (Chen et al., 2025; Thoring et al., 2023).

v. Medical Research: Generative AI is able to create synthetic (fake yet realistic) patient data. It encourages new medical knowledge and assists medical researchers to study medical patterns keeping the information about patients confidential (Chen et al., 2025; Thoring et al., 2023).

vi. Generative AI is transforming medical documentation as it helps doctors write more detailed patient notes faster and more accurately. It can automate routine chores in addition to indicating a relevant piece of information and ensuring the consistency of the language and formatting. Moreover, its capability to interpret unstructured data of patient records enables its use in extracting key information in the process of making diagnosis and planning the treatment. This enhances more knowledgeable clinical decisions as well as patient care besides making the documentation process faster. Healthcare workflows in documentation are already being enhanced with the help of generative AI due to the organizations, such as Meditech, HCA Healthcare, and BayerPharma (Musa & Kakudi, 2025).

Conclusively, generative AI has become a powerful tool that can be used in increasing research, education, and the provision of healthcare. There are also some applications of Generative AI in terms of other various fields, like Video game development, Art and Graphic Designing, Robotics and Machine Learning, Technological advancements and Product development, etc (Kalota, 2024; Musa & Kakudi, 2025).

4. SOCIETAL IMPLICATIONS

It is crucial to look beyond generative AI's technical capabilities and consider how it impacts individuals, communities, and the entire world as it becomes more prevalent in our daily lives. Although the technology creates new opportunities, it also makes us as a society wonder how we will responsibly adjust to and handle these changes. Beyond merely altering the way that content is taught, generative AI is forcing teachers and students to reconsider what it truly means to produce, evaluate, and work with machine-generated knowledge (Hsu & Hsu, 2025). Initially, opinions regarding ChatGPT's use in the classroom were divided. Some perceived it as a danger, believing that students might use it to evade actual education, which could result in the dissemination of false information. On the other hand, opinions started to change as big businesses like Google and Microsoft started developing their own versions of these tools and incorporating them into popular platforms. With more people realizing the potential advantages of generative AI in education, attitudes toward it have grown more open and optimistic over time (Hsu & Hsu, 2025).

The potential of generative AI to produce fresh and diverse content has both advantages and drawbacks. One significant problem is its effect on the environment because it takes a lot of energy to train and operate these sophisticated models. Trust among the public is another issue. Concerns about job loss and misuse, such as disseminating false information, are growing as AI gets better, particularly in automating human tasks. Its future will be shaped by how society perceives and embraces this technology, both generally and on a personal level. Differentiating between real and artificial intelligence-generated content is becoming more difficult as generative AI advances. Focusing on responsible and explainable AI is therefore even more crucial. According to research, people frequently view AI-generated content with suspicion and are reluctant to believe it. By imitating human behaviour, social chatbots like Replika can forge emotional connections with users, demonstrating how some generative AI tools are made to foster trust. In order to improve the user experience and build trust over time, other tools try to help users in a helpful and consistent manner (Hsu & Hsu, 2025).

Generative AI is also revolutionizing the banking and finance industry by enhancing decision-making, fostering innovation, and streamlining operations. In crucial domains like risk management, fraud detection, providing individualized financial services, and algorithmic trading support, GenAI is being used with the help of big datasets and intelligent algorithms. The ability to detect fraud is one of its most crucial functions (Hsu & Hsu, 2025).

By improving, supporting, and automating numerous tasks, generative AI has the potential to revolutionize industries like marketing, the arts, and online services. However, acknowledging and resolving its issues is just as crucial. Problems such as erroneous results (hallucinations), inadequate data quality, and the possibility of abuse underscore the necessity for researchers and experts to make diligent and continuous efforts. To ensure that generative AI is applied responsibly and constructively, we need to actively look for answers and pose important queries about how the technology, its surroundings and the data it uses can be enhanced. The way we address generative AI's effects on society through thoughtful planning, responsible application and open discussion will ultimately determine whether it has potential advantages or disadvantages. It is crucial to strike the right balance between innovation and responsibility to ensure that generative AI actually enhances and supports human life rather than destructively replacing or disrupting it (Banh & Strobel, 2023; Bonde, 2024; Şahin & Karayel, 2024).

5. LIMITATIONS OF GENERATIVE AI

Although generative AI systems are incredibly powerful, they are limited by a number of basic issues that prevent them from being widely used and trusted in practical situations. The training process and the fact that current models produce results based on probabilistic reasoning rather than deterministic logic are primary reasons for these limitations. These models frequently function as intricate "black boxes", which in simple words means that, we only know and understand the input given to the model and the output it produces, but we don't know from where, how and why it generated the particular output from the given input. This happens because the AI models are made up of lots of parameters, which the models learn and implement during training. People are unable to see how decisions are made, which raises questions about control, transparency, and accuracy. Furthermore, broader systemic problems like bias, legal difficulties, and environmental costs still affect generative AI and influence the practical and ethical limits of its use. Since they have a direct impact on the security, reliability, and equity of generative AI applications in various fields, it is imperative to comprehend these model-level flaws (Banh & Strobel, 2023; Bonde, 2024). Some of the important limitations of the current Generative AI are discussed below:

A. Hallucinations

A significant drawback of generative AI is its propensity to generate hallucinations, or outputs that appear extremely certain and realistic but are factually inaccurate or nonsensical. This occurs as a result of generative models' reliance on probabilistic techniques for content generation, which means they produce answers based on presumptions based on training rather than facts. While researchers investigate the underlying causes of hallucinations, they note that training data frequently consists of a combination of contradictory, fictional, and factual content. Models may produce results that are not accurate as a result of this diversity in input. Closed-source models exacerbate the issue by providing no transparency regarding their training data, making it more difficult to identify or manage the source of errors (Banh & Strobel, 2023; Bonde, 2024).

Hallucinations can happen when creating images as well as when reading text. Some AI-generated images of people, for instance, contain anatomical errors, demonstrating the imprecision of visual outputs. Errors can occur even in simple tasks like basic arithmetic, demonstrating the limitations of current models in terms of precision and reasoning. These are particularly difficult to detect automatically because the generated content frequently sounds and looks realistic. Although there are a few statistical and model-based techniques for assessing hallucinations, they are frequently insufficient when compared to manual human review and are not always dependable. Human oversight is therefore still necessary to guarantee the precision and potential of generative AI outputs (Banh & Strobel, 2023; Bonde, 2024).

B. Bias

The quality of the data used to train generative AI systems is crucial by design. Consequently, bias is a significant drawback that may result in unfair, deceptive, or discriminatory results in practical applications. Training and inference are the two main phases where these biases manifest. Children can learn about algorithmic bias in a practical and efficient way by using generative AI tools, such as text-to-image programs, to develop their understanding of AI at a young age (Vartiainen et al., 2024). To guarantee responsible use, bias in generative AI is ultimately a complicated problem that requires careful planning, ongoing observation, and deliberate intervention (Vartiainen et al., 2024).

C. Transparency

As we know the Generative AI models are said or know to be working as "Black Boxes", the researchers, governments, individuals, analysts, etc. have rising demand for clear explanations and higher transparency for generating suitable outputs. Although generative AI explainability is still in its infancy, it is already thought to be essential, particularly for high-impact applications like customer support, business platforms, or healthcare. For instance, it is extremely dangerous for users to follow inaccurate or deceptive recommendations when generative AI is used to provide medical advice or product recommendations without knowing how they were created. In these situations, making a mistake can have major repercussions, such as selecting the incorrect product or even taking the wrong prescription. Even though models like ChatGPT do surprisingly well on standardized tests (like medical exams), they don't truly understand context, which is crucial for making decisions in the real world. This demonstrates the significance of understanding not just what a model produces, but also how and why it produces a particular result. Explainability and supervision are crucial in business contexts, particularly when generative AI is employed in vital systems or communicates directly with users. By meeting stakeholder expectations and ensuring safety, they assist businesses in establishing trust. If ability of explaining is lacking, users might be left wondering if the AI's recommendations or results are reliable. Open-source versus closed-source model debates is another facet of transparency. Many proprietary GAI models do not disclose the source of their data, even though they are trained on enormous datasets that are scraped from the internet. Regarding copyright and intellectual property in particular, this presents ethical and legal issues. Open-source models and datasets are becoming more and more significant because they support legal compliance, make data sources visible, and enable safer and more confident GAI system deployment for businesses (Vartiainen et al., 2024).

Basically, as generative AI becomes more popular, it is not only a technical necessity but also a social, legal, and ethical imperative to make these systems more transparent and understandable.

D. Misuse

Generative AI tools open up new creative and automation opportunities for both individuals and businesses by making it easier than ever to produce highly realistic content. `However, the same instruments can also be employed in ways that are detrimental. The surge of deepfakes, or incredibly lifelike fake media that mimic real people like politicians or celebrities, is a serious worry. For example, false photos of Donald Trump's arrest have gone viral and deceived a lot of people. This misuse includes identity theft, fraud, scams, and phony websites, which facilitates the deception of the public and the influence of the media or political figures. Generative AI being easily accessible, criminals can take advantage of these technologies in new ways. These systems are prohibitively expensive to develop and maintain, which prevents smaller organizations from using them. The increasing prevalence of automation raises concerns about job displacement, particularly in creative and content-based industries. Concerns regarding security, privacy, environmental sustainability, and economic accessibility are brought up by generative AI in addition to its fundamental technical limitations. These issues must be resolved to guarantee responsible and fair implementation (Feuerriegel et al., 2023; Banh & Strobel, 2023).

6. FUTURE DIRECTIONS AND CHALLENGES

Generative Artificial Intelligence (GenAI) is expected to transform many areas of business, technology, and even life as we know it in the next several years. More likely, researchers and specialists, in Business Information System and Engineering (BISE), will explore several possible future paths in which GenAI can open up new opportunities when it comes to creativity, productivity, and value. The following section describes key areas in which GenAI developments in the future are likely to open up important potential. In the future of Education 2030, it is known that generative AI will dominate classrooms by providing more flexible, creative, and child-centred resources that would support the global aims of enhancing education (Sandhu et al., 2024). It is believed that GenAI will have an immense contribution not only in content creation and generation but also in business analytics, decision-making, process design and development, it will also help the IT and Data Science sector for handling and working with data, it is also predicted to be enhancing human-computer interaction and contributing to engineering technology in many ways / fields. Even the economy is said to be changing drastically due to Generative AI. Through more efficient content delivery, reduced needless repetition, and experience customization to meet individual needs, generative AI promotes sustainability in both, the industries as well as education (Baskara, 2024; Şahin & Karayel, 2024). Some of the advanced development methods due to Generative AI for the future are explained below:

A. Business Process Management

The way in which companies manage and enhance their internal procedures will be completely transformed by generative AI. In the near future, businesses will probably use GenAI to automate monotonous tasks, enhance customer and employee satisfaction, and inspire innovative process improvements. Teams could learn more about and improve workflows by using GenAI models, for instance, to automatically create process descriptions. Generative tools can be used by businesses to improve current workflows or come up with innovative ideas for re-engineering operations without having to start from scratch. GenAI models that are based on natural language will also assist in extracting process details from emails, text records, and unstructured documents, thereby decreasing the need for human input. Proactive decision-making and process outcome forecasting will also probably be aided by GenAI-powered advanced predictive and simulation tools. In the near future, GenAI will help robotic process automation (RPA) by substituting more intelligent, adaptive automation that can be retrofitted into legacy systems for strict rules. The creation of next-generation process guidance systems is anticipated in the long run. These will be driven by massive language models that can learn from organization-wide data and provide contextual, real-time support across various digital touchpoints, including chat interfaces, emails, manuals, and wikis (Baskara, 2024; Şahin & Karayel, 2024).

B. Decision Analytics and Data Science

GenAI will become more advanced in its capacity to facilitate data-driven decision-making as it develops. One significant future path will be tailoring GenAI for particular fields, such as finance, law, or medicine, using context-rich data to increase accuracy and usability. This will require new safe customization methods that increase accuracy while safeguarding confidential data. By using stronger algorithms and more user-centred design, researchers will also concentrate on lowering hallucinations, which are false or misleading outcome. Providing evidence or citations, making AI-generated content easier to understand, and enabling users to check outputs before acting on them are some examples of how to do this. Additionally, GenAI will automatically produce human-friendly explanations of analytics and decisions, thereby bridging the gap between technical modelers and business users. Simple summaries of sophisticated tools like SHAP or LIME may be incorporated into future systems, increasing the transparency and accessibility of analytics for all decision-makers (Baskara, 2024; Şahin & Karayel, 2024).

C. Digital Business Management and Leadership

Generative AI has the potential to revolutionize how companies lead, innovate, and function. It will probably lead to previously unthinkable new goods, services, and even business models in the future. On the inside, it will alter the way group's function, interact, and reach decisions. Increasingly, AI-based assistants will handle jobs like resource planning, social media management, and scheduling, freeing up human workers to concentrate on strategic and high-level thinking. GenAI will have an impact on management structures and leadership philosophies as it becomes more integrated into enterprises. In order to accommodate AI's potential and constraints, managers and executives will need to embrace new theories and frameworks. The nature of work itself will also change; many workers will communicate with intelligent, speech-based systems, and the capacity to create compelling prompts and decipher AI responses will become a useful ability. It's probable that new positions like prompt engineers or AI interaction designers will appear (Baskara, 2024; Şahin & Karayel, 2024).

Knowledge management will benefit from GenAI's ability to facilitate automated content discovery, multilingual documentation, dynamic training recommendations, and user-specific learning resource delivery.

D. Economics of Information Systems

GenAI is believed to boost efficiency and productivity, it will have a big impact on the world economy. A large number of tasks, including content writing, coding, translation, and customer service, will be automated. In numerous sectors, this will lower operating expenses and open up new growth prospects. BISE researchers will probably investigate these changes by evaluating the effects of GenAI on performance through field research. They could assess whether programmers improve their efficiency with GenAI tools or whether artists become more imaginative with AI support, similar to how AlphaGo improved human Go players' performance (AlphaGo, developed by Google's DeepMind, is a AI-based computer program that defeated professional human Go players, including world champion Lee Seedol) (Baskara, 2024; Şahin & Karayel, 2024).

Whole sectors might experience disruptions. Artificial intelligence (AI)-generated content may complement or even replace user-generated content on platforms like Shutterstock or Stack Overflow. Future studies will examine how competition, access, and innovation are affected by open-source versus closed-source development. Additionally, policymakers will need to reconsider regulations. Job roles, educational models, copyright protection, and data ownership will all be impacted by GenAI. Data monopolies could be a problem, particularly if only a few big businesses have access to the user interaction data required to train GenAI systems that perform well. Should this concentration of power not be addressed by careful economic and digital policy, it may impede innovation and fair competition (Baskara, 2024; Şahin & Karayel, 2024).

There are even more ways or fields in which GenAI will be used, which may change or develop the fields' environment. E-commerce and marketing will also undergo change. AI will enable businesses to produce emotional messaging, modify content for accessibility or mobile use, and develop tailored campaigns based on user behavior and characteristics. Human creatives will be able to concentrate on strategy and innovation as tasks like news summarization, thumbnail creation, and voiceover production are automated. Beyond marketing, recommender systems will advance in sophistication, employing language models to further tailor content. Generative AI will enhance information delivery in domains such as journalism and law while promoting accessibility for instance, by transforming content into audio or Braille formats. Nevertheless, Generative AI is anticipated to transform the way research and design projects are carried out. AI will have the capacity to extract and arrange design knowledge for future use, which is currently dispersed throughout documents or locked into tools. This implies that researchers and designers can collaborate more readily and work more quickly (Baskara, 2024; Şahin & Karayel, 2024).

As a co-designer in the creative and innovation space, AI will help produce concepts, prototypes, and even early-stage software based on straightforward user input. This will improve learning and increase productivity while designing. The use of AI as a creative collaborator will be advantageous for developers, artists, and UX designers. In general, the potential of generative AI extends beyond its ability to replace manual labor. It will be a potent instrument to enhance human creativity, better decision-making, and the efficiency and inclusivity of digital systems. It will have an impact on a variety of industries, including public service, design, education, and business, changing our perspectives on innovation and human-machine cooperation (Feuerriegel et al., 2023).

Though all of these implications seem innovative technological advancements and it may sound really interesting, we should not forget that AI and Generative AI are not perfect. There are certain challenges to be faced in terms of Generative AI development. The development of generative AI has sparked major ethical and equitable questions in various spheres of society. As AI is becoming so popular, there is a lot of concern that these systems may manipulate and propagate prejudices based on gender, race, or a Western viewpoint. Concerns have also been raised regarding whether or not content produced by AI is actually original and who should be given credit as the true author. Even though GenAI may result in new job opportunities, people who find it difficult to adjust to the changes may lose their jobs as a result. The impact of this technology on student learning and whether or not students are being informed of its more profound effects and consequences are the main concerns in the field of education (Baskara, 2024; Şahin & Karayel, 2024).

These concerns will cut across the fields of technology, ethics, law, and society, necessitating proactive approaches and close attention. The following is a list of some concerns and challenges to be faced in the future related to Generative AI:

(a) The uneven allocation of resources will be a significant obstacle, potentially preventing smaller companies from participating in the generative AI market. Large companies will probably continue to be the only ones with access to expert talent, big datasets, and high-performance computing. Emerging players may find it challenging to enter or remain in the market as a result of monopolistic practices, in which large companies limit access to their language models or datasets. Such dynamics could undermine innovation and competition if policy-level interventions are not made (Baskara, 2024; Şahin & Karayel, 2024).
(b) The inability of AI systems to be explained will be a major issue as well. Due to the growing use of generative AI tools in high-stakes domains like healthcare,

law, and defence, people who are not highly technical, like government officials or doctors, will need to comprehend the reasoning behind AI-generated decisions. In order to make AI outputs more comprehensible and reliable, Explainable AI is becoming more and more necessary. To achieve true transparency, however, cooperation between fields such as cognitive science, AI, and human-computer interaction will be necessary (Baskara, 2024; Şahin & Karayel, 2024).

(c) Concerns about ethics are anticipated to grow even more prominent. Additionally, as students increasingly use AI to finish assignments without acknowledgment, academia may struggle to maintain academic integrity. Mechanisms for educational assessment and integrity will need to be rethought in light of this. Intellectual property and legal issues will also arise as generative AI becomes more prevalent. Copyright cases involving data scraping are among the legal disputes that are already arising and are probably going to get worse. Since AI models store or reuse user input, organizations may also unintentionally expose sensitive information. As a result, businesses might start forbidding or restricting the use of generative AI platforms in their ecosystems more strictly (Baskara, 2024; Şahin & Karayel, 2024).

(d) Cybersecurity risks related to generative AI will keep increasing. It is possible for these systems to be used for system manipulation, illegal access, or data theft. Malicious actors may get around security measures and recover private information by employing methods like AI jailbreaking. Many workers will be vulnerable to these vulnerabilities as more industries incorporate generative AI into their daily operations (Baskara, 2024; Şahin & Karayel, 2024).

(e) A less obvious but no less significant worry is the excessive reliance on artificial intelligence tools. It is possible that human cognitive abilities, including creativity, critical thinking, and problem-solving, will decline as users become used to delegating thinking tasks to machines. In classrooms, students who consume a lot of AI-generated content may struggle to express themselves or think critically when participating in oral discussions or solving real-world problems (Baskara, 2024; Şahin & Karayel, 2024).

(f) Sustainability will be a big problem. Massive electricity and water consumption are required to train large-scale AI models, which degrades the environment. The training of GPT-3, for example, used hundreds of thousands of litres of freshwater and more than 1.2 gigawatt-hours of energy. Although AI has the potential to increase energy efficiency in other areas, a more environmentally friendly AI future depends on carefully controlling the ecological costs of developing and maintaining such systems (Creely & Janssen, 2025; Kalota, 2024).

7. BIBLIOMETRIC ANALYSIS

To consider the thematic correlations and study trends in the dataset, a bibliometric co-occurrence network was built with the help of VOSviewer according to the keyword occurrence in the Lens.org database (Figure 1). The visual representation gives clear clustering of research themes whereas each node refers to a keyword and the size of the node reveals how frequently a keyword occurs in a corpus. Closeness of nodes is associated with the intensity of co-occurrence relationships.

The red cluster mostly focuses on microbiology and phylogenetics so one may find such words as phylogeny, soil microbiology and 16S rRNA. The green cluster has its focus on genomics and molecular biology with key words such as molecular sequence data, base sequence, and genetic linkage. Blue cluster revolves around the study of animals and experimental physiology of the body with important words being mice, rats, animals, and cultured cells. The purple cluster explains the studies on human health and clinical outcomes, adult, middle aged, biopsy, and chronic diseases. Finally, the yellow cluster lies within the area of immunology and cellular biology with the examples of such words as T-lymphocytes, immunity, and dendrites.

In this network map, robust cross-disciplinary connections between genomics, microbiome research, animal modelling, and clinical research can be observed, providing the prospective of combined landscape of the biological and biomedical sciences.

Figure 1. Keyword co-occurrence network of Gen AI

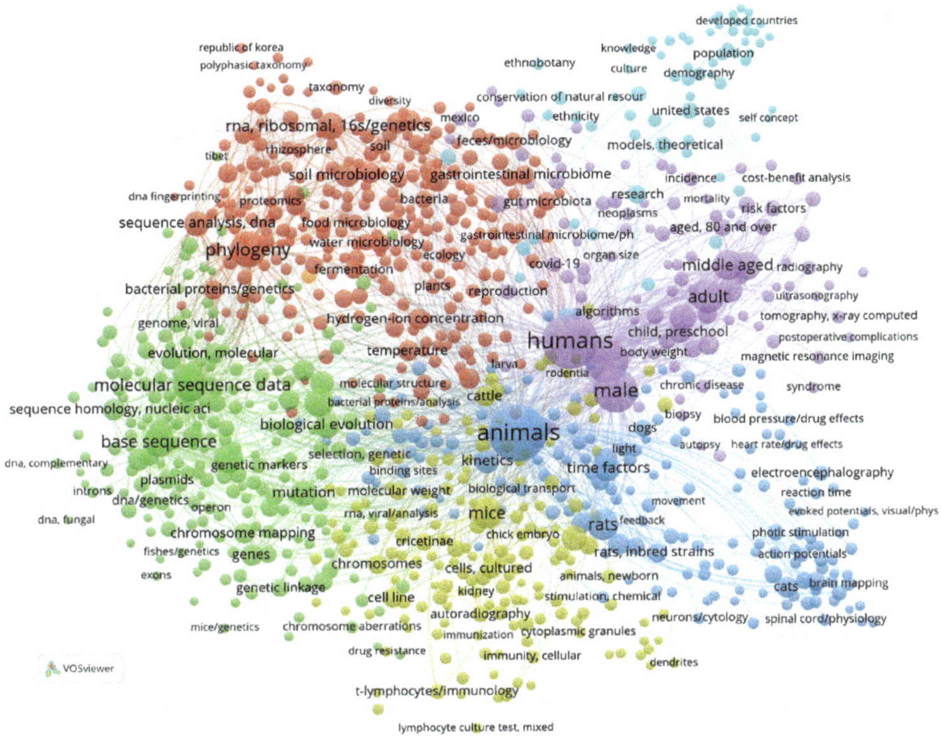

(Source: Lens Database; created using VOSviewer) (The Lens, 2025; Nees & Waltman, 2019).

Figure 2 represents a choropleth map with the distribution of research contributions (or counts) in countries. The data is graphically represented in form of gradation of color where the size of the hues (more towards the yellow hue) shows more number of publications, and vice versa (the color is more towards the blue hue) lower counts of publication numbers. Germany has an advantage over the other countries like the United States, the Netherlands, Italy, and the United Kingdom with an entry of over 10000. The countries with limited entries have been classified in the dark blue and some are located in Africa, South America and Southeast Asia. The given map will help describe the global trends in the research and various publication rates..

Figure 2. Choropleth map showing the distribution of publication counts across countries

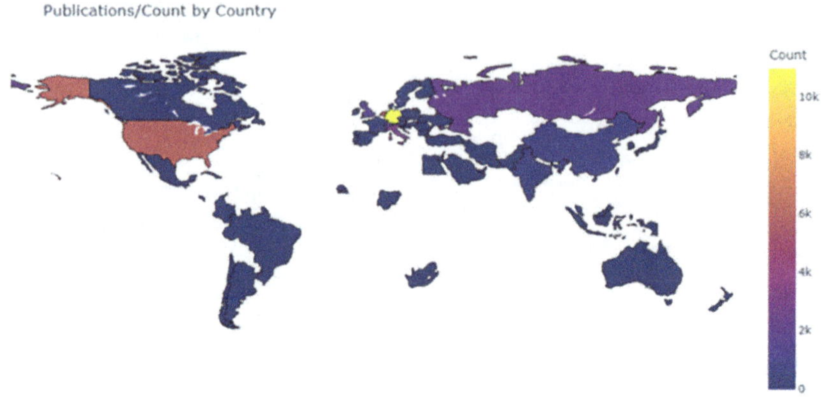

(The Lens, 2025).

8. CONCLUSION

Gen AI is one of the 21st century's most revolutionary technologies, changing the way we work, learn, create, and think. Its capacity to create original, superior content on its own, including text, images, music, code, and synthetic data, marks a significant departure from conventional AI that was primarily concerned with classification or prediction. GenAI has evolved from academic labs into common-place tools that impact industries, education, communication, and even our sense of creativity thanks to models like GANs, VAEs, Diffusion Models, and especially Transformer-based Large Language Models like GPT. The dual nature of GenAI as a technological advancement and a conceptual challenge makes it especially intriguing. It is not conceptually clear and it becomes harder to implement, govern, address it ethically, and to incorporate it into education, nonetheless GenAI has demonstrated enormous potential in virtually every industry. It brings efficiency, innovation and cost saving to business and industry but also drawbacks which include job loss, bias in algorithms, and regulatory lapses. It has the ability to enable schools to limit the production of personal learning situations, automate administrative duties, and co-produce collectively, but merely in case they develop vital, hard-out models to oversee its usage. Philosophical and pedagogical changes involved to co-exist, in order to co-exist with GenAI systems demand a novel type of literacy, not merely literacy as knowledge on how to utilize these tools but literacy as knowledge on how to use them cogently and vicariously. GenAI is just a reflection of our ideals, our suppositions about smartness and our utopias, it is not simply a technological breakthrough. With the continued evolution of this field we can see a clear need of interdisciplinary collaboration and ethical oversight as well as greater conceptual grounding. Next time, regulating its risks and ensuring it does not harm the general population, we can make everything that is creative about GenAI.

REFERENCES

Akolekar, H., Jhamnani, P., Kumar, V., Tailor, V., Pote, A., Meena, A., Kumar, K., Challa, J. S., & Kumar, D. (2025). The role of generative AI tools in shaping mechanical engineering education from an undergraduate perspective. *Scientific Reports*, *15*, 9214. Advance online publication. DOI: 10.1038/s41598-025-93871-z PMID: 40097637

Banh, L., & Strobel, G. (2023). Generative artificial intelligence. *Electronic Markets*. Advance online publication. DOI: 10.1007/s12525-023-00680-1

Baskara, F. X. R. (2024). Generative AI as an enabler of sustainable education: Theoretical perspectives and future directions. *Bulletin of Journal of Teaching and Educational Pedagogics*, *3*(3), 9. DOI: 10.32996/bjtep

Bianchini, F. (2025). Generative artificial intelligence: A concept in progress. *Ethics and Information Technology*. Advance online publication. DOI: 10.1007/s13347-025-00875-8

Bonde, L. (2024). A conceptual design of a generative artificial intelligence system for education. *International Journal of Research and Innovation in Applied Science*, *9*(4), 457–469. DOI: 10.51584/IJRIAS.2024.904034

Chen, L., Song, Y., Guo, J., Sun, L., Childs, P., & Yin, Y. (2025). How generative AI supports human in conceptual design. *Design Studies*. Advance online publication. DOI: 10.1017/dsj.2025.2

Corchado, J. M., López, S., Núñez, J. M., Garcia, R., & Chamoso, P. (2023). Fundamentals. *Advances in Distributed Computing and Artificial Intelligence Journal*, *12*(2), 139–146. DOI: 10.14201/adcaij.31704

Creely, E., & Janssen, K. (2025). Onto-epistemological understandings of generative artificial intelligence in education. *International Journal of Changes in Education*, *2*(2), 55–65. DOI: 10.47852/bonviewIJCE52024380

El Fathi, T., Saad, A., Larhzil, H., Lamri, D., & Al Ibrahmi, E. M. (2025). Integrating generative AI into STEM education: Enhancing conceptual understanding, addressing misconceptions, and assessing student acceptance. *Smart Learning Environments*, *12*, 25. Advance online publication. DOI: 10.1186/s43031-025-00125-z

Feuerriegel, S., Zschech, P., Hartmann, J., & Janiesch, C. (2023). Generative AI. *Business & Information Systems Engineering*, *65*(6), 561–565. DOI: 10.1007/s12599-023-00834-7

García-Peñalvo, F. J., & Vázquez-Ingelmo, A. (2023). What do we mean by GenAI? A systematic mapping of the evolution, trends, and techniques involved in generative AI. *International Journal of Interactive Multimedia and Artificial Intelligence*, *8*(4), 7–16. DOI: 10.9781/ijimai.2023.07.006

Hsu, T.-C., & Hsu, T.-P. (2025). Teaching AI with games: The impact of generative AI drawing on computational thinking skills. *Education and Information Technologies*. Advance online publication. DOI: 10.1007/s10639-025-13624-3

Kalota, F. (2024). A primer on generative artificial intelligence. *Education Sciences*, *14*(2), 172. DOI: 10.3390/educsci14020172

Musa, Z. M., & Kakudi, H. A. (2025). Exploring the concept of generative artificial intelligence: A narrative review. *International Journal of Latest Technology in Engineering* [IJLTEMAS]. *Management & Applied Science*, *14*(4), 1–7. DOI: 10.51583/IJLTEMAS.2025.140400001

Nees, J. V., & Waltman, L. (2019). *VOSViewer Manual.* https://www.vosviewer.com/documentation/Manual_VOSviewer_1.6.11.pdf

Nyaaba, M., Zhai, X., & Faison, M. Z. (2024). Generative AI for culturally responsive assessment in science: A conceptual framework. *Preprint.* https://doi.org/DOI: 10.20944/preprints202409.1276.v2

Şahin, O., & Karayel, D. (2024). Generative artificial intelligence (GenAI) in business and industry: A systematic review on the threshold of transformation. *Journal of Smart Systems Research*, *5*(2), 156–175. DOI: 10.58769/joinssr.1597110

Sandhu, R., Cheema, G. S., Channi, H. K., Kaur, M., & Ghai, D. (2024). An introduction to generative AI tools for education 2030. In *Emerging Technologies and Globalization of Education* (p. 1). IGI Global., DOI: 10.4018/979-8-3693-2440-0.ch001

The Lens. (2025). *Search results for "Generative AI"*. Retrieved July 11, 2025, from https://www.lens.org/lens/search/scholar/list?q=Generative%20AI

Thoring, K., Huettemann, S., & Mueller, R. M. (2023). The augmented designer: a research agenda for generative AI-enabled design. *Proceedings of the Design Society*, *3*, 3345–3354. DOI: 10.1017/pds.2023.335

Vartiainen, H., Kahila, J., Tedre, M., López-Pernas, S., & Pope, N. (2024). Enhancing children's understanding of algorithmic biases in and with text-to-image generative AI. *New Media & Society*. Advance online publication. DOI: 10.1177/14614448241252820

Wood, D., & Moss, S. H. (2024). Evaluating the impact of students' generative AI use in educational contexts. *Journal of Research in Innovative Teaching & Learning*, *17*(2), 152–167. DOI: 10.1108/jrit-06-2024-0151

Chapter 2
Generative Artificial Intelligence:
Evolution, Applications, and Ethical Considerations

Aditya Shrivastav
https://orcid.org/0009-0000-8461-8171
Ajeenkya D.Y. Patil University, India

Krutika Patre
https://orcid.org/0009-0001-7969-4409
Ajeenkya D.Y. Patil University, India

Sunil Sankathala
https://orcid.org/0009-0004-7809-7647
Ajeenkya D.Y. Patil University, India

Susanta Das
https://orcid.org/0000-0002-9314-3988
Ajeenkya D.Y. Patil University, India

Kashvi Chaturvedi
https://orcid.org/0009-0005-3192-3400
Ajeenkya D.Y. Patil University, India

Rizwan Shaikh
https://orcid.org/0009-0005-5689-7640
Dr. D.Y. Patil Institute of Management and Entrepreneur Development, India

ABSTRACT

Generative Artificial Intelligence (GAI) is a technical term used to designate elaborate machine learning algorithms that allow the creation of human-like output text, images, audio, and biomedical data. Such methods as Generative Adversarial Networks (GANs), Variational Autoencoders (VAEs), and diffusion models led to making GAI an initiative that promotes innovation in other fields such as healthcare, education, and creative fields. Yet with its fast development, one must wonder about algorithm bias as well as data privacy issues, misinformation, and control over AI-based content. The chapter delves into the history of the development of GAI, its theoretical background, and its fundamental implementation. It presents a bibliometric analysis to point out the interdisciplinary dynamics of GAI study. It looks at ethics implications, legal implications as well as social implications and necessity

DOI: 10.4018/979-8-3373-5616-7.ch002

of responsible innovation. The chapter winds up with highlighting the challenges that persist and proposing future steps toward transparent and responsible use of generative technologies.

1. INTRODUCTION

Generative Artificial Intelligence (Generative AI or GAI) is a type of artificial intelligence system that can generate new content autonomously with a statistical distribution which is equal to its training data (He et al., 2025). Using contemporary machine learning algorithms such as generative adversarial networks (GANs), variational autoencoders (VAEs), diffusion models, and large language models (LLMs) such systems are able to produce realistic and varied synthetic outputs in the form of images, language, audio, video, and molecules (Chen & Esmaeilzadeh, 2024; He et al., 2025; Sengar et al., 2024). Generative models, in contrast to discriminative models, are trained on the joint probability distribution of input features, rather than on a classification or prediction task, thus are able to produce data that is not only realistic, but can often be nearly indistinguishable to real-world samples (Chen & Esmaeilzadeh, 2024; Gupta et al., 2024).

Generative AI is a development in concept which began more than 50 years ago, with the creation of rule-based systems during the middle of the 20 th century (He et al., 2025). The first line of generative work was based on heuristics determined by experts and symbolic reasoning. The later development of probabilistic modeling and neural networks provided the basis of the current paradigms of machine learning. A key turning point came in the 2010s when deep generative models, in particular GANs (2014) and VAEs (2013) emerged that were capable of high-resolution, high-fidelity data generation (He et al., 2025; Sengar et al., 2024). This push was also fuelled by the subsequent invention of transformer-based architectures, and the generation of foundation models, such as the Generative Pre-trained Transformer (GPT) family, which displayed these kinds of capabilities, unheard of previously, in language generation, and multi-modal understanding (Gupta et al., 2024; Sengar et al., 2024). Developments in recent years have brought generative AI into contact with reinforcement learning, cross-modal synthesis, and ethical AI frameworks, as such developments have a broadening technical and social imprint (Sengar et al., 2024; Sun et al., 2024).

The domination of generative AI in academic and industrial spheres is raising the need to review it thoroughly as the body of knowledge grows fast. Growing usage of GAI has since infiltrated key sectors such as healthcare to support improvements in the area of diagnostics, treatment and drug research and development, education, artistic industry and scientific research (Chen & Esmaeilzadeh, 2024; Arowosegbe et al., 2024). The fact that the number of publications in peer-reviewed journals since 2017 is exponentially increasing demonstrates the maturing of the field and its potential to change the paradigms of knowing and creating solutions (Gupta et al., 2024; Sengar et al., 2024). Yet, the fast rate of innovation also presents thorny ethical, legal and social issues, such as data privacy, algorithmic bias, misinformation, and control of artificial content (Chen & Esmaeilzadeh, 2024; Arowosegbe et al., 2024). Thus, systematic and critical review needs to be conducted not only to trace the intellectual and technological history of generative AI but also to discover emerging research trends, important contributions, and outstanding issues (Chen & Esmaeilzadeh, 2024; Gupta et al., 2024; Sun et al., 2024). This review serves as a reference point to researchers, practitioners, and policymakers who have to walk through the promises and pitfalls of the transformative technology.

2. THEORETICAL FOUNDATIONS OF GENERATIVE ARTIFICIAL INTELLIGENCE

Generative AI has been based upon a combination of probabilistic models, deep learning models, and powerful neural models capable of synthesizing data with specific statistical structure in order to match desired real world distributions. In principle, the overall purpose of Generative AI is to learn complicated data-generating mechanisms and simulate them using algorithmic frameworks inside of which models could create surprising novel data that is still plausible. The following three major families of generative models have helped develop the field: generative adversarial networks (GANs), variational autoencoders (VAEs), and families based on the stochastic differential equation-enabled diffusion approach, which provide different ways to consider probabilistically-motivated data generation, representation learning, and probabilistic inference (He et al., 2025; Bond-Taylor et al., 2021).

GANs, are constructed out of the basis of the adversarial relationship between a generator and a discriminator, where the former is expected to generate a fake data and the latter is expected to guess whether a sample is real or artificial. This game theoretically founded as a minimax game and gives an optimum equilibrium with the distribution generated converging towards data distribution. Although GANs have made realism and resolution in images their benchmark, they are hampered by concerns like mode collapse and unstable training dynamics, mostly influenced to a great extent by the need to set a fine balance between generator and discriminator updates (He et al., 2025; Bond-Taylor et al., 2021). VAEs are, instead, posed in the context of the Bayesian inference paradigm. They learn to encode an input into continuous latent space and decode it in latent space to take it back to the original input data and optimizing a variational lower bound called Evidence Lower Bound

(ELBO). This framework offers principled way to generative modeling which has tractable inference and regularized latent representations. Though VAEs are prone to provide more diverse outputs, they are likely to incur poorer perceptual quality since the underlying latent space is limiting its smoothness (Bond-Taylor et al., 2021). To mitigate these drawbacks, hybrid models incorporating the expressive representation of GANs and structured latent representation of VAEs, e.g. VAE-GANs have introduced to reconcile these drawbacks (Bond-Taylor et al., 2021).

Recently, diffusion models have appeared as an alternative to GAN, radically different in a generative approach. These models characterize a forward corrupted-noise process that adds noise to data gradually and a reverse denoising process learnt using a neural network. The generating process essentially is an evolutionary chain of stochastic corrections, mathematically described by stochastic differential equations and optimal transports theory. By doing so, fine-grained distribution learning of diffusion models is possible and they are more stable in training and less prone to mode collapse than GANs (Bond-Taylor et al., 2021; Alonso, 2025; Chen et al., 2024). The quality and diversity of samples generated by diffusion models has steered them into generative research limelight, particularly, in the visual and audio generation related fields (Alonso, 2025; Chen et al., 2024). All these setup models are supported by the deep learning frame work which is the computational backbone needed to learn in a high dimensional, non-linear data distribution. The deep neural networks can be used as a function approximator that can capture the complex pattern and structure in the data. Generative neural networks CNNs, enabled generative tasks in the visual domain, and RNNs structured text. The development of transformer-based architectures however has changed this altogether. Transformers are a self-attention-based model that enables the dynamic weighting of the input features relative to the global context and lead to a massive enhancement of the model capacity to memorize long-range dependencies and semantic relationships (He et al., 2025; Palaniappan, 2025). It has played a crucial role in leading to the creation of scaled generative models, numerous examples of which include the GPT series and DALL·E, with impressive performance in tasks related to language, vision and multimodal synthesis (Palaniappan, 2025).

Transformers can be trained formidably scalable, highly data-efficient and parallel, displacing traditional architectures as the de facto standard foundation models. They can be extended to vision tasks, through vision transformers, which can model image data (all the token representation) as sequence of tokens and simultaneously maintain the structural information (with the flexibility of the transformer via attention mechanisms). Adding transformers to generative frameworks previously developed based on transformers, e.g. transformer-based VAEs and diffusion models, makes them more expressive and allows synthesizing multi-modal data. Incorporating these hybrid systems, these technologies take advantage of the strength of the classical generative models and map capabilities of transformers to split the boundaries of what generative AI is capable of (Alonso, 2025). Nevertheless, despite such progress, training of generative models is still a tough task. The GANs need to be tuned well so that the adversarial imbalances do not occur nor another form of catastrophic forgetting does not arise. VAEs have to compromise between reconstruction quality and latent space regularization, and generally, need to alter the ELBO objective. Robust diffusion models require thousands of iterative processes, making them computationally intensive and time consuming to train. The most recent developments have overcome these problems in the form of optimization and architectural innovations. GAN methods like the Wasserstein loss have enhanced faster convergence and reduced mode collapse, and memory-efficient diffusion algorithms and latent diffusion models have made training diffusion models in a large scale possible (Alonso, 2025; Chen et al., 2024).

Even after the optimization stage, architectural advancements are an ongoing factor in progress. Adding attention mechanisms to GANs and VAEs allows a greater focus on global dependencies and increases generative quality. The newer versions of the transformer, including Transformer-XL and Funnel-Transformer, present enhancements in long-context modeling and computationally efficient (Chen et al., 2024). Latent diffusion models can work with much smaller spaces with much fewer resources, yet with high fidelity. In addition, the curriculum learning techniques that add complexity over time have increased training stability and pretraining without supervision has allowed the models to generalize on the task, which they have learned using huge unlabelled datasets. As we have seen, multi-modal and multi-task learning has also allowed generative models to use diverse data types as inputs and their output to cover a broad spectrum of fields, such as images and audio, structured documents and molecular graphs (Chen et al., 2024; Singh, 2024).

In short, the generative AI theoretical background will be based on the relationship between probabilistic systems, deep learning models, and constantly improving training strategies. The benefits and trade-offs of GANs, VAEs, and diffusion models are different, and transformer-based systems allow flexibility patterns to be considered unlike any other. These models grow up, and training, optimization, and integration techniques evolve accordingly, and the training, optimization and integration of generative AI are at the cutting edge of machine learning and cross-disciplinary research (He et al., 2025; Alonso, 2025).

3. APPLICATIONS OF GENERATIVE AI

Generative AI is having a juicy moment of immense breakthroughs along with the year 2020, triggering bio-mimetic breakthroughs across a wide swath of disciplines. The generative models have been used in more diverse applications than generative natural language processing to include biomedical research where they have demonstrated unmatched performance in producing logically conscious and creative output (Chang et al., 2024; Kumar et al., 2025). Transformer-based large language models (LLMs) have achieved a breakthrough in the field of text generation and natural language processing with the emergence of GPT-3, GPT-4, and ChatGPT, which have broken new grounds in machine-generated language. Trained on massive and diverse corpora, these models have proved incredibly effective at creating coherent and contextually relevant text in a wide variety of applications such as conversational agents, summarization, translation and question-answering. Chang et al. (2024) also highlight the transformative power of these models in changing language technologies, whereas Kumar et al. (2025) evaluate the revolutionized effect of such models on chatbot interactions by mentioning that they can create tailored, context-specific responses that foster user interest in using chatbots. Nonetheless, both articles also emphasize the ethical issues regarding bias, misinformation, and opacity of the large models. A methodological overview of applying generative to different NLP tasks, such as robot operation using language, is outlined in Strippoli (2023) and Baliga et al. (2023). An exponentially increasing number of studies also discuss and examine the role of ChatGPT and similar models in the field of education, medical care, and research, although it is also warned that such tools entail perils linked to data privacy and excessively blind faith in the results produced by an AI program (Chang et al., 2024).

Generative models in visual tasks have made it possible to create photorealistic, high-fidelity images using models based on Generative Adversarial Networks (GANs), diffusion models, and models such as DALL·E, based on transformers. The models have been effectively used in fields including design, media, medical imaging, and autonomous navigation (He et al., 2025).

Advancing on generation of images, recent development has moved generation to video aperture. Newer solutions such as Sora and Runway AI use spatial-temporal encoding techniques with deep learning techniques of frame prediction to produce realistic video material that captures time consistency. These models help in storytelling, simulation, learning and entertainment. Despite being resource-heavy, the initial share of these models demonstrated their effectiveness and potential, along with the necessity of scaling the architecture that ensures consistency over different periods of time (He et al., 2025).

It is also the use of generative AI that has contributed greatly to the development of software with generative models like OpenAI Codex, GitHub Copilot, Google Gemini and are used to automate processes like code generation, bug fixes, test cases and documentation. These systems are conditioned to huge codebases and can convert natural language instructions into executable code. Actual experiments achieve 20-50% increases in productivity, and there has been significant improvement in the efficiency of developers and software maintenance (Dakhel et al., 2024; Baduge et al., 2022; Tembhekar et al., 2023). Nonetheless, quality and security of AI-generated code remains a source of concern especially in view of strengths and weaknesses, copyright, and ownership. Scientists propose to combine human control and effective audit tools to guarantee trustworthiness of the production infrastructure (Dakhel et al., 2024).

Generative models are transforming creative processes in the creative industries where artistic production can be generated automatically, either in images, music, or design. GANs, VAEs and transformer techniques are being used now in the creation of original visual art, music composition, and as concept designers. According to the works by Zhou and Lee (2024), Ardeliya et al. (2024), and Kanbach et al. (2023), not only do tools like Midjourney, DALL-E, and Stable Diffusion allow more people to be productive in their creativity, but they also make access to advanced design technology technically available to everyone. Starting with music application, MuseNet and Flow Machines examples produce melodies, harmony, and complete pieces of music (in different styles). Although such trends increase the realm of creativity, they also pose ethical concerns regarding authorship and artistic originality and the influence of artificial intelligence on the creative community of the population. However, the most common opinion in the literature makes generative AI a co-creator, enhancing the human imagination but not taking their place (Ardeliya et al., 2024).

Generative models are being used in the biomedical field to speed the discovery of drugs and the creation of personalized medicine. GANs or VAEs and graph-based generation methods are used to model molecules, liposomes, protein-drug interactions, and to produce synthetic biomedical data. With these models, it is possible to have a quick prediction of drug response, estimation of treatment effects, identification of biomarkers, and stratified therapy designs. Although Mishra et al. (2025) and Paul et al. (2020) offer a thorough assessment of the value of generative frameworks in expeditious, cost-efficient drug development pipelines, they also challenge the research on the topic. Moreover, as mentioned by Hillary et al. (2024) and Singh (2025), these models would help individualize a specific pharmaceutical according to their genome, thus contributing to further developing personalized treatment. Nevertheless, there are still limitations regarding the use of generative AI in clinical workflows regarding validation, explainability, and systemic bias. There are requests to restrict the validations to several centers, considering the necessity of results to collaborate with researchers of other disciplines (Hillary et al., 2024).

Although generative AI is currently impacting many aspects of our life, including language and vision, software development, artistic creation, and health innovations, the most profound changes have happened between 2020 and 2025. LLM and multimodal generative models capabilities have established an improved performance standard and increased human work output, and opened the possibilities of new collaborative human-machine modes. Nevertheless, it is essential to mention that with the further penetration of these systems in the work of society there is an urgent need to deal with the long-standing issues of moral management, just inequality, responsibility, and access. The further development will require not just technical innovations but also ethically responsible integration with the guiding process of cross-disciplinary research and policy system approach (Chang et al., 2024; Kumar et al., 2025; Hillary et al., 2024).

4. BIBLIOMETRIC ANALYSIS

To further investigate the topics in development and cross-disciplinary scope of Gen AI research, a keyword co-occurrence network was created based on bibliography data obtained using Lens.org and visualized in VOSviewer (The Lens, 2025; Nees & Waltman, 2019). The obtained network map reflects the conceptual map of the generative AI research field, where nodes are the keywords assigned by their authors, and edges reflect the number of times they are found in other lines. The clusters, based on color-codes are related to different thematic groups through co-citation strength and semantic relatedness (Figure 1). The centrality of the network brings forward the concept of humans, recognizing the prevalence of interest in human-related generative AI applications, especially in medical health and psychological behavior and decision-making areas. Frequently used related words like female, adult, middle aged and young adult denote use of generative systems in diverse categories such as demographic. Also, such keywords as mental recall, social perception, and reaction time are the calls to be interested in the cognitive science and the research of behavior with references to the AI technologies. Keywords in the lower central region produce a dense cluster, including such words as generative AI, large language models, ChatGPT, LLM, and artificial intelligence/ethics, which suggests another wave of interest in the transformer-based language models and their impact on society.

Figure 1. Keyword co-occurrence network of generative AI

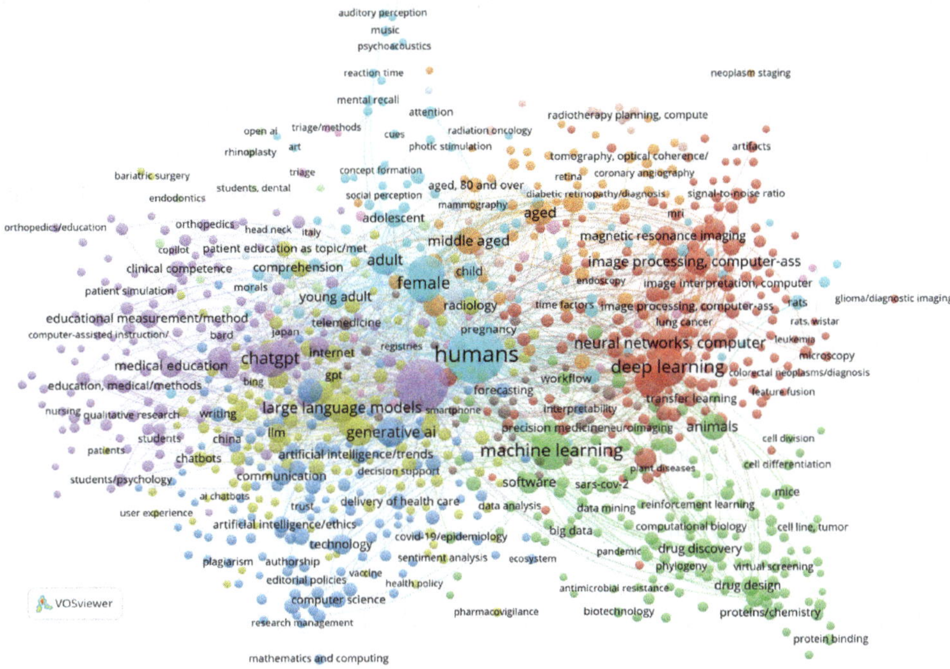

(Source: Lens Database; created using VOSviewer) (The Lens, 2025; Nees & Waltman, 2019).

Next to the central cluster in figure 1, there is a very purple area which is dominated by educational topics, keywords including medical education and clinical competence and student simulation. It means that a solid literature exists regarding pedagogical embedding generative AI, especially in clinical education, curriculum enrichment, and online learning spaces. The higher right corner of the map bears the big red mass with the terms like deep learning, neural networks, computer, image processing, computer-assisted, and radiology. The area encompasses the methodology and practical development of AI generative in the means of diagnostic imaging, signal analysis and pattern recognition and connects to such terms as MRI, tomography, and coronary angiography. The related terms such as, the interpretability, workflow, and transfer learning propose the parallel emphasis on the model transparency and the clinical flexibility. The green group in the bottom right corner is where life sciences and drug discovering combine with AI. Such keywords like drug design, virtual screening, protein binding, and computational biology, indicate the developments of the generative models in the precision medicine, molecular forecast, and bioinformatics.

In the network, seminal studies can be summarized in the form of repetitive words such as machine learning, software, mathematics and computing, and computer science, demonstrating the technical origins of generative systems. Among them, the words ethics, technology, and health policy seem to be interconnected with generative AI, indicating the development of the body of literature in the field of responsible innovation, governance patterns, and the ayment to the regulations.

To achieve a better understanding of the inner conceptual landscape of generative artificial intelligence a zoomed-in version of the keyword co-occurrence network was investigated to show the most central and commonly co-occurring keywords. This subnetwork shows the structural core of the ongoing research in generative AI and it demonstrates that all concepts produced in this research area like e.g. the concepts of artificial intelligence, generative AI, large language models and ChatGPT are semantic tools that bridge the gap between research areas (Figure 2). In this visualization, the dominance of the term related to the artificial intelligence is the result of its role as a key concept out of which both the technical and applied subfields are stemmed. Correlations among such terms as artificial intelligence, generative AI, large language models, reflect the overwhelming position of transformer-based architectures and neural language models as leading the innovations in recent years.

Figure 2. Zoomed-in keyword co-occurrence subnetwork visualized

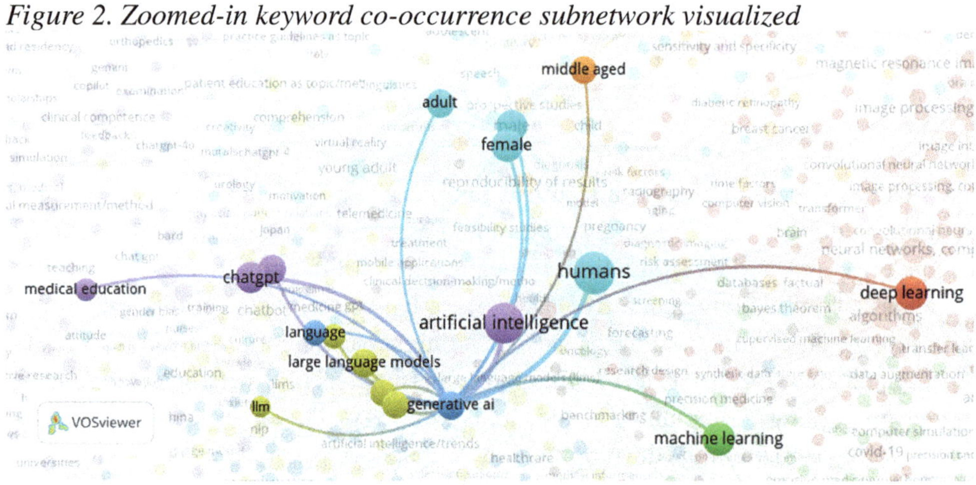

(Source: Lens Database; created using VOSviewer) (The Lens, 2025; Nees & Waltman, 2019). (See also Figure 1).

The blue cluster in figure 2 including the terms such as humans, female, middle aged, adult signifies the human-centered and demographic aspect of generative AI research. The right side green and red clusters show the correspondence of technical convergence with machine learning and deep learning respectively. They are also closely related to the main node which confirms the fact that generative AI cannot exist without other areas supported under data-driven model training, and representation learning. In the meantime, a separate node dedicated to the study of the field of medical education appears in "medical education/ChatGPT," which indicates the interest boom in generating models in education.

On a more detailed level, an analysis of the directional relations between research prevailing themes shows the gradual occurrence of generative AI approaches within the subdomains of biomedical and technological application (Figure 3). This chart highlights the interconnected pathways that establish deep learning as the hub connective part of the generative AI scholarship ecosystem. Small learning Deep learning cuts across everyone and, as shown in Figure 3, has the best prominent hub whose relational vectors point to various directions, including drug discovery, animal, covid-19, and computer assisted image processing. The red cluster is still in the compact, central group of primary, fundamental methods like those known as the neural networks, computer vision, transfer learning, and the convolutional neural networks, but taking expansion to the practical level and applications like the magnetic resonance imaging and also the diagnostic imaging, the vital areas of present-day clinical diagnostics. It is especially noteworthy that the connection between deep learning and the green cluster has been extended, with especially dense integration with the terms, generative AI, drug design, and drug discovery, which suggests growing practices in applying generative AI in drug innovation. The purple cluster, with its hub of, relatedly to "ChatGPT, large language models, and artificial intelligence, has well-defined bidirectional sentiment to early humans and machine learning, indicating that user-centered applications (e.g., decision support, education, health communication) are, in turn, taking their place in improving and refining the core predictive AI. Additional evidence of the assumed increase in the role of generative AI in patient-facing technologies and individualized digital therapeutics growth comes in the form of demographic markers, which includes reference to women, middle-aged, and adults. Additionally, the bridging keyword: artificial intelligence, and machine learning, and humans serve as semantic portals on the interdisciplinary synergy of the algorithm development and social application.

Figure 3. Zoomed in-keyword co-occurrence subnetwork

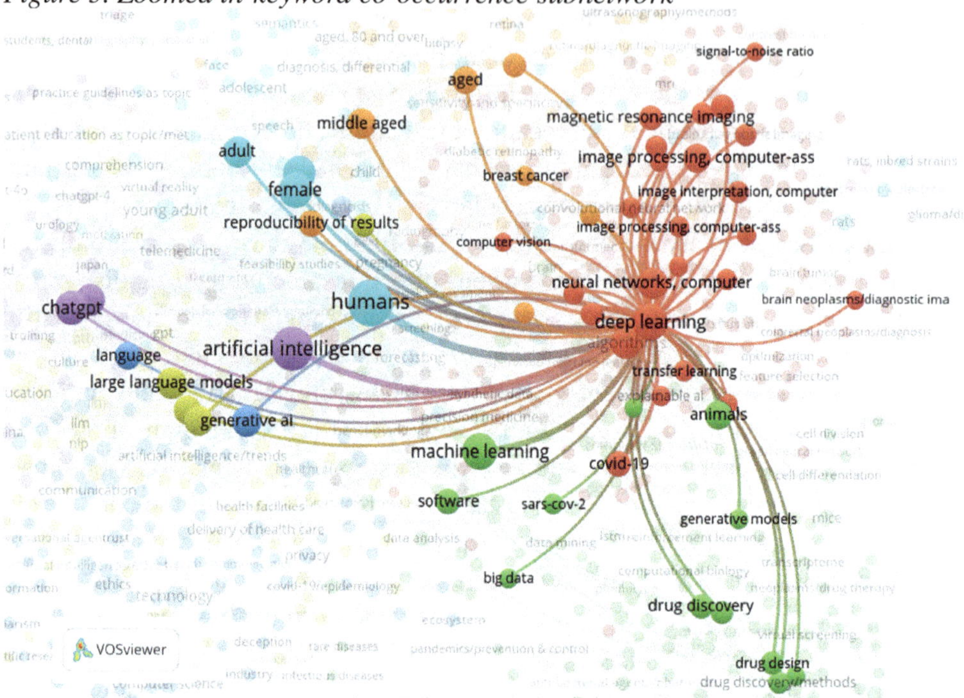

(Source: Lens Database; created using VOSviewer) (The Lens, 2025; Nees & Waltman, 2019). (See also Figure 1).

Still further tightening the path that generative AI takes in biomedical sphere, Figure 4 shows a keyword co-occurrence network highlighting the dominant role of machine learning as a semantics and conceptual connection across the field. The green well spreading over the machine learning is the evidence of its deep connection to health-related spheres, including to the topics of drug discovery, drug design, covid-19, and animals. The proliferation of machine learning into these areas of biomedicine shows its applicability in the development of data-driven, outbreak modeling, and translational medicine. The yellow cluster around generative AI, large language models, and chatGPT demonstrates still notable close connections both to the field of artificial intelligence and to language. This shows the rising anxiety about the implementation of AI in such areas as the sphere of health care, where the domains of ethics, communication, and technology meet. The fact that the terms like medical education, clinical competence, and telemedicine are found in the purple and blue clusters means that the direction toward AI-facilitated training, and simulation, has become rather tangible.

Figure 4. Zoomed in-keyword co-occurrence subnetwork

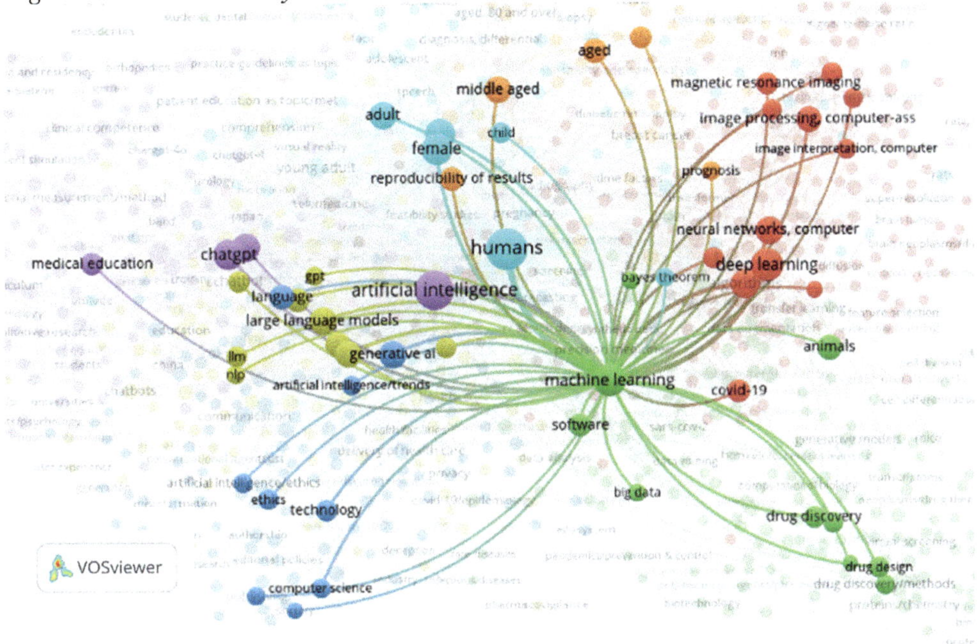

(Source: Lens Database; created using VOSviewer) (The Lens, 2025; Nees & Waltman, 2019). (See also Figure 1).

There is one more zoomed-in visualization, which generalizes the macroscopic perspective of the scholarly landscape with the nucleus of the domain, where "artificial intelligence" takes the central thematic position from which all other spheres revolve. As indicated in Figure 5, the name of the concept artificial intelligence occupies the focal area of the network with thick, multicolored connections leading to the different subfields in th symbolizing its role by integrating modern biomedical and technological research. The purple cluster, with the dominance of such terms like the title, and behind AI, we can see such key terms as ChatGPT, language, students, education, and curriculum that underlines the increasing role of AI in medical education and training.

In the meantime, the green cluster that is centered at the machine learning and is connected with drug discovery, covid-19, precision medicine, and big data represents the biomedical and pharmaceutical use of AI approaches. It is particularly interesting that this figure identifies privacy, ethics, and communication as the aspects well incorporating into the discussion (blue and yellow clusters), which also confirms that AI in health is not only a matter of computational power any more, but also has to be facing societal, legal, and moral challenges. The red group is also highly visible being built on deep learning and associated with the topic of image processing, but linked closely to neural networks and diagnostic methods like magnetic resonance imaging. The cluster still serves as the technological core of AI-based diagnostic imaging, but it is well enmeshed in the larger AI system.

Figure 5. Zoomed in-keyword co-occurrence subnetwork

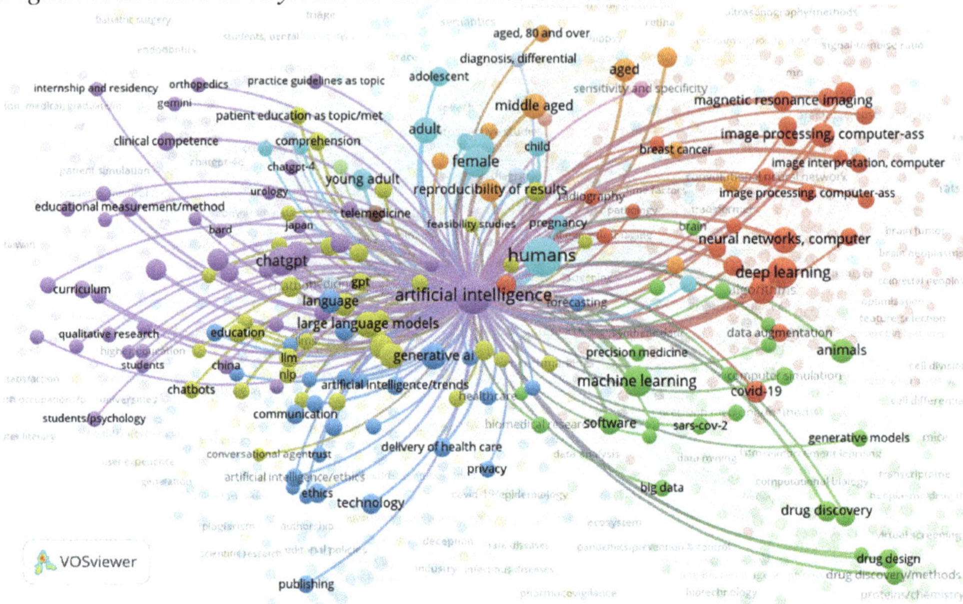

(Source: Lens Database; created using VOSviewer) (The Lens, 2025; Nees & Waltman, 2019). (See also Figure 1).

5. ETHICAL, LEGAL, AND SOCIAL IMPLICATIONS

Between 2022 and 2025, ethical, legal, and social implications (ELSI) of generative AI have become a key topic of scholarly discussion regarding the fast development of the generative model's field in terms of challenging issues connected to fairness, intellectual property, and governance. Figure 6 shows the pros and cons of Generative AI. Other significant vulnerabilities are algorithmic bias, algorithmic fairness and algorithmic transparency in generative systems. In recent research, it has been emphasized that just through the use of large language models and generative adversarial networks (GANs), biases present in society can be passed on, not to mention the intensification of already existing biases through models of training data (Lin & Losavio, 2025; Ferrara, 2023). This is most explicit in the sphere of healthcare, i.e., biased training data can deliver models that underperform in terms of certain ethnic or gender groups, thus enforcing structural disparities (Marchesi et al., 2025). These biases have varied origins which include unbalanced data sets, untransparent algorithm development and a lack of enough human supervision. Generative models are also reinforcing stereotypes because they produced results that adhere to prejudices accepted in society and, therefore, continue to negatively affect trust in AI systems (Lin & Losavio, 2025; Ferrara, 2023). The measures that can be undertaken in order to reduce these problems are the creation of adversarial training techniques, data augmentation, and fairness-aware algorithmic procedures (Lin & Losavio, 2025). The recent methods based on synthetic data, especially in the medical sector, have potential in improving the representational balance and model performance without compromising privacy and data authenticity (Marchesi et al., 2025). At the same time, the emphasis on transparency and accountability is emerging in both academic and policy discourses, and there is an increasing agreement on how the details regarding the dataset of used to train models, the architecture of the models, and the generative process should be disclosed to make that process of oversight and trust possible (Lin & Losavio, 2025). However, achieving actual algorithmic fairness is an unattainable objective that requires continuous cross-functional partnership and regulatory abidance (Lin & Losavio, 2025; Ferrara, 2023).

Figure 6. Pros and Cons of Gen AI

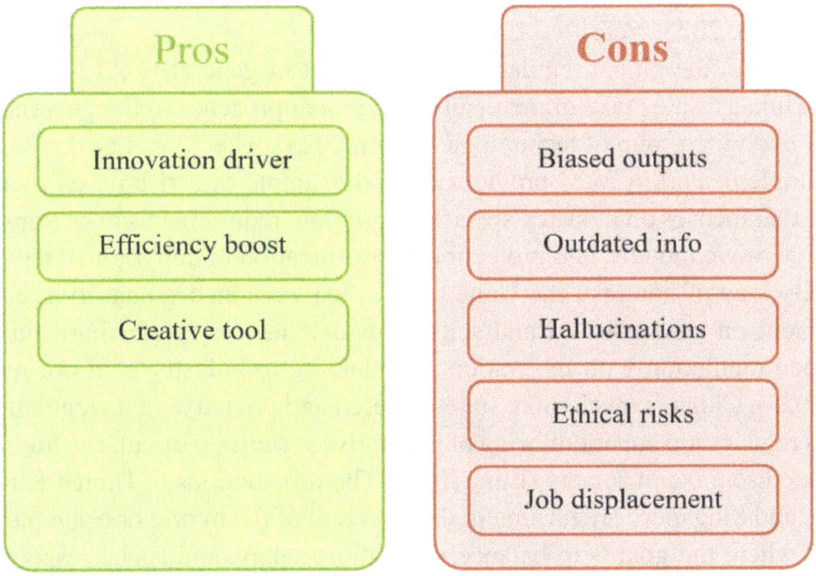

Simultaneously, the spread of generative AI has come with an increased discussion of the intellectual property (IP) rights and ownership of data, including AI-generated content copyright and the legality of the usage of a copyrighted data set to train an AI model (Lim, 2025; Vebritha, 2024). The legal frameworks of most jurisdictions, such as the United States and the European Union, still fail to put copyright works created independently by AI under the protection, arguing that the requirement is the significant human contribution in the creation of a work (Wyczik & Wieczerzak, 2024). However, new case law shows that there is an increasing departure, with an authoritative court like the Beijing Internet Court acknowledging the copyright status of AI-aided works in cases where there was enough human input (Lim, 2025). In the meantime, the so-called AI-owner solution, based on patent jurisprudence, is becoming increasingly popular, according to which the controller or owner of the AI-system can obtain rights to its results, but it creates new ethical and policy issues (Matulionyte & Lee, 2022). It is in the grey area to be used to train generative models of copyrighted content. In the United States, such an action is commonly justified through fair use doctrine, and the EU AI Act proposed in 2024 will ensure transparency and eventually might enforce licensing models to training data (Lim, 2025). Listed among possible regulatory solutions are collective licensing models, digital watermarking, and contractual mechanisms of clarification between rights and duties of interested parties (Lim, 2025). Ethically, there is fear about unauthorized use of data, the authoritative source of the dataset, and the overall consequences of Artificial Intelligence generated content to negatively impact the humanity through squandering human creativity, labor markets, and incentive systems necessitating creation (Lim, 2025; Vebritha, 2024).

Meanwhile, the global regulatory environment of generative AI is in the very state of flux, as states take dramatically different approaches to the governance of this fast-evolving group of technologies (Lim, 2025). The AI Act of the European Union implemented in 2024 provides a good example of a risk-based regulation strategy that focuses on industry-specific regulation, requirements to be transparent about generative models, and protection over utilization of copyrighted data (Lim, 2025). By way of contrast, the United States has remained reliant to a relatively large extent on market-based and self-regulatory devices, preferring to displace prescribed regulation with innovation and yielding to industry codes of morality (Lim, 2025). China is much more state-centered and proactive in its regulation and requires registration and monitoring of generative systems, particularly those which affect the discourse in society (Lim, 2025). The jurisdictions of United Kingdom, Canada, and Singapore are turning in the direction of the hybrid or principle-based systems where the goal is to balance innovation, safety, and social responsibility (Remolina, 2023). The absence of international harmonization is considered one of the fundamental barriers, which does not facilitate adequate cross-border monitoring and cooperation (Lim, 2025). The contemporary scholarship favors such adaptive approaches to governance as resilience, preparedness, and responsive regulation, as these can help manage the quick turn of events and the rapid evolution in what can and cannot be done with generative AI and thus how it needs to be regulated

(Remolina, 2023). In any jurisdiction, the perceived necessity to promote not only the trust of society but also the responsible development and harnessing of generative AI technologies had the consent that multi-stakeholder engagement, public transparency, and ethical governance processes are key to the process (Lim, 2025).

6. LIMITATIONS OF BASIC GENERATIVE MODELS AND THE ROLE OF ADVANCED VARIANTS

Mode collapse is one of the most reported constraints in the GANs where generator generates limited diversity output hence not capturing the complete variability in the training data. This is a problem caused by the game- theoretic nature of adversarial min-max optimization: the generator can specifically target the limitations of the discriminator and map large numbers of latent codes to one or a few outputs to minimize the adversarial loss without learning the true data distribution (Li et al., 2020; Goodfellow et al., 2014). In essence, this is the case because adversarial loss function does not overtly punish the generator in the event that it misses on some data modes, in other words, the generator would have no incentive to do better in the event the discriminator ignores such omissions. Because of it, GANs tend to be affected by so-called mode dropping, which occurs when the synthetic distribution will only sample a part of the actual data structure (Li et al., 2020; Goodfellow et al., 2014). Empirically, mode collapse has been proven quantitatively to be an issue that reduces output diversity and increases Frche Inception Distance (FID), which implies incomplete coverage of data (Li et al., 2020; Goodfellow et al., 2014).

Although Variational Autoencoders (VAEs) were much more stable to train, the tendency to optimize on the Evidence Lower Bound (ELBO) optimization criterion results in blurry sample images. ELBO optimizes a trade-off between reconstruction fidelity and regularization of latent space by Kullback-Leibler (KL) divergence term (Bredell et al., 2023; Kingma & Welling, 2013). The reconstruction target, usually induced as a pixel wise loss, will favor output mean-taking, in particular, when the decoder is not expressive. At the same time, the KL divergence does not allow the latent space to exceed a prior distribution say an isotropic Gaussian, and this too constrains the capacity of the model to produce sharp detailed outcomes. This trade off makes VAE average across a set of outputs that are plausible given a given input and this results in a noticeably blurry generations. An empirical example acts in line with this observation: standard VAEs always attain greater reconstruction error rates and worse FID results when compared to GANs, which highlights the characteristic to blur (Bredell et al., 2023; Kingma & Welling, 2013).

Generative models are normally assessed in terms of well-known empirical measures. Frechet Inception distance (FID) is a metric that quantifies the distance between the distributions of feature vectors of generated and real images based on the activations of an Inception network. The smaller the FID scores, the more similar are the resulting data with the real data in their quality and diversity (Chong & Forsyth, 2020). Inception Score (IS) measures the overall generative quality of generated images by determining whether generated images can be both categorized and varied using a degree of classification and categorization; higher IS scores indicate better generator quality. At the same time, reconstruction error which is often used in the case of VAEs is a measurement of the perceptual or pixel-wise difference between a given input and its reconstruction. Fidelity is represented by lower reconstruction error (Bredell et al., 2023). Although FID and IS are the most broadly utilized estimators, they are not devoid of limitations; recent studies have indicated biases created by finite sample size and are trying to recommend bias-free estimators to enhance robustness and reliability (Chong & Forsyth, 2020).

In countering the weaknesses inherent in typical models, a number of innovative types have come on board. Wasserstein GANs (WGANs) instead of the Jensen-Shannon divergence, the GAN loss function contains the Wasserstein distance, therefore, provides smoother optimization landscape and more stabilities during the training process. Training robustness is then added by introducing a gradient penalty (WGAN-GP) which advances on the convergence behavior (Gulrajani et al., 2017). Experimental tests prove that WGANs are much more effective in diminishing mode collapse and lowering FID scores with a high output diversity (Gulrajani et al., 2017).

With VAEs specifically, the β-VAE variant adds to the model a hyperparameter (which is written as a 88 euroidget; in the case of VAEs, an added hyperparameter (designated 88 euro¥ kitipe advantageous disentangled latent representations. The increased beta will involve more emphasis on the independence among latent dimensions at the cost of reconstruction accuracy. Nevertheless, it comes at the cost of simpler disentanglement, but this has been proven to lead to more structured and interpretable latent representations and quantitatively assessed with disentanglement metrics (Higgins et al., 2017).

Conditional generative models take both GANs and VAEs a step further, to use external information in the generation process, e.g. the class label. Conditional GANs and VAEs have been able to condition the generator and discriminator (or encoder and decoder) together, allowing generating control over generative specific types of data (Yang et al., 2025). The model has shown better consistency with conditioning variables and sample diversity, as has been supported by the evaluation markers such as conditional FID and class-conditional accuracy (Yang et al., 2025).

The generative modeling has recently grown stronger with the introduction of the Transformer-based architectures, which has brought a self-attention mechanism. In contrast to recurrent or convolutional ones, self-attention permits every position in a sequence to dynamically attend all others, and is capable of flexibly and efficiently modeling long-range dependencies (Wahid et al., 2023; Sohl-Dickstein et al., 2015). In this mechanism, each similarity score between tokens is calculated as the model employs learned query and key projections. The scores can be normalized through softmax function to give attention weights, which are then passed onto a set of value vectors giving contextually aggregated representation of each position. This type of formulation allows the model to combine world context in one computational step (Wahid et al., 2023; Sohl-Dickstein et al., 2015).

More importantly, the mechanisms of the recurrence and the convolution are folded into self-attention. In contrast to RNNs that sequentially pass information and fail to achieve adequate performance when faced with long-range dependencies, self-attention provides a direct interaction between any two input positions independently of their distance (Tang et al., 2018). Likewise, against CNNs to capture local patterns by their receptive fields, self-attention is more flexible in that its receptive field adjusts according to content, thereby it can make use of local and global structures (Tang et al., 2018; Sohl-Dickstein et al., 2015). It was also recently demonstrated that the shape of attention matrices during training does indeed change over time, developing meaningful aspects like symmetry and directional bias, which optimize performance on tasks that mean semantic comprehension (Tang et al., 2018; Sohl-Dickstein et al., 2015).

7. CHALLENGES AND FUTURE DIRECTIONS OF GENERATIVE AI

Since 2022, generative artificial intelligence has exploded in innovation, as it has seen the rise and popularization of large language models and multipurpose systems that can now generate coherent and creative texts, images, and other mediums. But this impressive development also has shown that there are still some challenges related to technical, ethical, and governance aspects that need to be solved so that generative AI technologies are implemented safely, fairly, and in the social good (Gwon et al., 2025). One of the most burning technical problems is the hallucination issue when the generative models give some outputs that seem true but inaccurate or misinformed in reality. Such issue is highly disturbing in critical sectors like medical profession, law-based thinking, and journalism where facts cannot be compromised. There is a variety of reasons why hallucinations occur, such as poor or biased training data, overparameterization, inadequate incorporation into known sources of evidence, or the likelihood of error through extended generation itself (Gwon et al., 2025). Such outputs are commonly presented with an unwarranted level of certainty, making them more prone to the wrong interpretation and being perceived as veracious information which discredits user trust and makes the process of validation difficult to perform. Mitigation measures like retrieval-augmented generation (RAG), domain-specific fine-tuning, reinforcement learning through human feedback (RLHF), adversarial training, and human-in-the-loop verification demonstrated limited success, however. Hallucination is an open research topic. The existing efforts are being conducted to enhance scalable detection strategies, produce taxonomies, and come up with standard evaluation benchmarks native to both textual and multimodal outputs (Gwon et al., 2025; Joshi, 2025).

Besides hallucination, generative AI models still have persistent problems with control and generalization. The more size and dimensions of these systems grow, the less understandable their internal dynamics and their phenomena, being harder to control them, particularly in an agentic or semi-autonomous environment. The resultant opacity is of grave concern, primarily on the possibility of adversarial manipulation, the challenge of taking back the system after malfunctions, and the behavior of new or adversarial scenarios. Even these vulnerabilities are aggravated by the increased utilization of multimodal and agent-based generative models, which initiate broader operational conditions and multi-layered interactions with surroundings and users (Taeihagh, 2025; Michel-Villarreal et al., 2023). Adding to these, is the limited capacity of the existing generative models to be able to extend to different or out-of-distribution data, such that their performance becomes unreliable in the general setting and thus limit their application in real-world scenarios. The focus of research has turned to study stronger architectures and adaptive learning systems to enhance generalization and robustness (Michel-Villarreal et al., 2023).

In order to mitigate these shortcomings, the development of trustful and interpretable generative AI systems has become the subject of an impressive amount of research. Explainability is taking centre stage in AI design especially in situations that require transparency, accountability and trust. Recent work formalizes core principles of explainable AI, such as faithfulness, plausibility, completeness, minimality, and robustness that may apply when evaluating explainable AI systems, in addition to interpretability of inner-mechanics. Self-explaining models, dynamic explanation systems, and model-agnostic intelligibility systems are the other directions that are increasing in traction when tackling the promise of making opaque systems more understandable and transparent (Sadiq & Aqib, 2023). According to the empirical evidence, the more transparent the generative AI technologies will be, the more transparent they might seem, the less cognitive friction can be experienced, and the systems of credits connected to the processes of collaboration between a human user and AI agent in the framework of some organizational practices or decision-making processes can be considerably weightier (Bragazzi & Garbarino, 2024).

However, technical advancements by themselves are not enough to know that generative AI will evolve safely and ethically. The broader societal consequences of the technologies that concern bias amplification, data privacy breaches, misinformation, asymmetries of power, and possible displacement of human labor are also gaining more attention (Janssen, 2025). Critical theorists note that regulating generative AI needs responsive, co-regulatory policies, rooted in theories of complex-sensitive governance. The recommendations refer to the consideration of the concern of public values during AI design, interchangeable data provenance, internal systems of accountability in organizations and the shared responsibility of developers, deployers, and users of AI systems (Taeihagh, 2025). Defensive measures in layers, the technological means of generative AI such as algorithmic monitoring, outside supervision, and life-long learning systems, are essential to address the risk of dynamicity (Taeihagh, 2025; Janssen, 2025). On the policy-making side, there has been an apparent convergence about the fact that multi-stakeholder, cross-sectoral generative AI governance should be multi-dimensional and combine legal, technical, ethical, and societal aspects. Recent policy literature has put forward policy frameworks that encourage the use of adaptive regulatory mechanisms, such as sandbox, iterative rule-making, and innovation units in the public sector to test and refine regulatory responses under real-time conditions. Collaboration among countries is also crucial, especially in light of the fact that the risks and the benefits that can be brought about by generative AI cut across all borders. Researchers believe that existing streams of voluntary self-regulation are insufficient in the era of profound market concentration and urge a need to have more public supervision, antitrust policy, and participatory regulation as evidence against the control by a handful of technology giants (Taeihagh, 2025; Thirunagalingam, 2025; Gandhi et al., 2025). The use of ethical design models based on the principles of fairness-by-design, inclusive AI development, and stakeholder-based governance is also picking up steam as the model of future regulatory practice (Thirunagalingam, 2025).

Finally, the evolution of generative AI between 2022 and 2025 has been defined by severe issues associated with hallucination, model control, and generalization. Although the technical solutions, especially RLHF, RAG and explainability framework, provide encouraging avenues, they should be combined with societal governance and policy controls to be able to have safer, equitable, and transparent deployment. Generative AI advances should follow an interdisciplinary path with continuous observation and a flexible form of governance bound together by ethical and public interest values (Bragazzi & Garbarino, 2024; Taeihagh, 2025; Thirunagalingam, 2025; Gandhi et al., 2025).

8. CONCLUSION

GAI is fast becoming a revolutionary technology in most spheres of human activity, including medicine and scientific research, art, design, and media. Spurred by the innovation of machine learning frameworks, including GANs, VAEs, and diffusion models, GAI has turned down the previously imposed limits of computational creativity and solution-finding. Such models do not only improve automation and innovations, even including new forms of human and machine interaction and content creation. With the rise of powers, the GAI poses an intricate mixture of ethical, legal, and social dilemmas. Issues of algorithmic fairness, intellectual property, data privacy and truthfulness of created content are getting more pressing. Unless carefully regulated, the introduction of such technologies could further the inequities existing or create a whole new set of evils. The following issues raise the need to build a multidisciplinary approach that should close the gap between technical development and ethical research, legality, and social political concern.

Comprehensive and prospective governance of GAI is the crucial issue. Flexible regulatory systems, algorithmic explainability, and accountability, and open discussion are essential to making sure that the biggest positives of GAI will be shared with as many people as possible; that the potential risks will take a place second to none. GAI will base its value to societal needs not just on the complexity of the technology used but also on how well it upholds the mechanisms of integration systems. Responsible innovation has to be kept as the focus of the global agenda, whereby GAI should be able to ensure that it plays a significant role in advancing the world and not negating the elements of equity, accountability, and trust.

REFERENCES

Alonso, M. N. I. (2025). The Mathematics of Modern Generative Modeling: Normalizing Flows, Autoregressive and Diffusion Models. *SSRN*. https://doi.org/DOI: 10.2139/ssrn.5089573

Ardeliya, V. E., Taylor, J., & Wolfson, J. (2024). Exploration of artificial intelligence in creative fields: Generative art, music, and design. *International Journal of Cyber and IT Service Management*, *4*(1), 40–46. DOI: 10.34306/ijcitsm.v4i1.149

Arowosegbe, A., Alqahtani, J. S., & Oyelade, T. (2024). Perception of generative AI use in UK higher education. *Frontiers in Education*, *9*. Advance online publication. DOI: 10.3389/feduc.2024.1463208

Baduge, S. K., Thilakarathna, S., Perera, J. S., Arashpour, M., Sharafi, P., Teodosio, B., Shringi, A., & Mendis, P. (2022). Artificial intelligence and smart vision for building and construction 4.0: Machine and deep learning methods and applications. *Automation in Construction*, *141*, 104440. DOI: 10.1016/j.autcon.2022.104440

Baliga, S., Murthy, H. K., Sadhale, A., & Upadhyaya, D. (2023). Advanced applications of generative AI and natural language processing models. In *Advances in computational intelligence and robotics book series* (pp. 69–86). https://doi.org/DOI: 10.4018/979-8-3693-0502-7.ch004

Bond-Taylor, S., Leach, A., Long, Y., & Willcocks, C. G. (2021). Deep Generative Modelling: A comparative review of VAEs, GANs, normalizing flows, Energy-Based and autoregressive models. *IEEE Transactions on Pattern Analysis and Machine Intelligence*, *44*(11), 7327–7347. DOI: 10.1109/tpami.2021.3116668 PMID: 34591756

Bragazzi, N. L., & Garbarino, S. (2024). Toward Clinical Generative AI: Conceptual framework. *JMIR AI*, *3*, e55957. DOI: 10.2196/55957 PMID: 38875592

Bredell, G., Flouris, K., Chaitanya, K., Erdil, E., & Konukoglu, E. (2023). Explicitly minimizing the blur error of variational autoencoders. *arXiv (Cornell University)*. https://doi.org//arxiv.2304.05939DOI: 10.48550

Chang, Y., Wang, X., Wang, J., Wu, Y., Yang, L., Zhu, K., Chen, H., Yi, X., Wang, C., Wang, Y., Ye, W., Zhang, Y., Chang, Y., Yu, P. S., Yang, Q., & Xie, X. (2024). A survey on evaluation of large language models. *ACM Transactions on Intelligent Systems and Technology*, *15*(3), 1–45. DOI: 10.1145/3641289

Chen, M., Mei, S., Fan, J., & Wang, M. (2024). Opportunities and challenges of diffusion models for generative AI. *National Science Review*, *11*(12). Advance online publication. DOI: 10.1093/nsr/nwae348 PMID: 39554240

Chen, Y., & Esmaeilzadeh, P. (2024). Generative AI in Medical Practice: In-Depth Exploration of privacy and Security challenges. *Journal of Medical Internet Research, 26*, e53008. DOI: 10.2196/53008 PMID: 38457208

Chong, M. J., & Forsyth, D. (2020). Effectively unbiased FID and inception score and where to find them. *2022 IEEE/CVF Conference on Computer Vision and Pattern Recognition (CVPR)*, 6069–6078. https://doi.org/DOI: 10.1109/cvpr42600.2020.00611

Dakhel, A. M., Nikanjam, A., Khomh, F., Desmarais, M. C., & Washizaki, H. (2024). Generative AI for Software Development: A Family of Studies on Code Generation. *Generative AI for Effective Software Development*, 151–172. https://doi.org/DOI: 10.1007/978-3-031-55642-5_7

Ferrara, E. (2023). Fairness and Bias in Artificial intelligence: A brief survey of sources, impacts, and mitigation strategies. *Sci*, *6*(1), 3. DOI: 10.3390/sci6010003

Gandhi, D., Joshi, H., Hartman, L., & Hassani, S. (2025). *Approaches to Responsible Governance of GENAI in organizations*. arXiv.org. https://www.arxiv.org/abs/2504.17044

Goodfellow, I. J., Pouget-Abadie, J., Mirza, M., Xu, B., Warde-Farley, D., Ozair, S., Courville, A., & Bengio, Y. (2014). Generative adversarial networks. *arXiv (Cornell University)*. https://doi.org//arxiv.1406.2661DOI: 10.48550

Gulrajani, I., Ahmed, F., Arjovsky, M., Dumoulin, V., & Courville, A. (2017). Improved training of wasserstein GANs. *NIPS'17: Proceedings of the 31st International Conference on Neural Information Processing Systems, 30*, 5769–5779.

Gupta, P., Ding, B., Guan, C., & Ding, D. (2024). Generative AI: A systematic review using topic modelling techniques. *Data and Information Management*, *8*(2), 100066. DOI: 10.1016/j.dim.2024.100066

Gwon, H. J., Yoo, Y., & Lee, J. Y. (2025). Improving Generative Ai Reliability: A Qualitative Study of Hallucination in Large Language Models. *SSRN*. https://doi .org/DOI: 10.2139/ssrn.5118420

He, R., Cao, J., & Tan, T. (2025). Generative Artificial Intelligence: A historical perspective. *National Science Review, 12*(5). Advance online publication. DOI: 10.1093/nsr/nwaf050 PMID: 40191253

Higgins, I., Matthey, L., Pal, A., Burgess, C., Glorot, X., Botvinick, M., Mohamed, S., & Lerchner, A. (2017). beta-VAE: Learning Basic Visual Concepts with a Constrained Variational Framework. *International Conference on Learning Representations*. https://dblp.uni-trier.de/db/conf/iclr/iclr2017.html#HigginsMPBGBML17

Hillary, V. E., Gopalsamy, R. G., Da Mota Santana, L. A., De Jesus, P. C., De Souza, J. B., Silva, D. M. R. R., Moura, P. H. M., Santos, R. S., Barreto, M. D. S., Borges, L. P., & Silva, E. E. D. (2024). The impact of generative artificial intelligence (AI) on the development of personalized pharmaceuticals and the future of precision medicine. *PubMed, 23*, 1459–1462. https://doi.org/DOI: 10.17179/excli2024-7915

Janssen, M. (2025). Responsible governance of generative AI: Conceptualizing GenAI as complex adaptive systems. *Policy and Society*. Advance online publication. DOI: 10.1093/polsoc/puae040

Joshi, S. (2025). Comprehensive Review of AI Hallucinations: Impacts and Mitigation Strategies for Financial and Business Applications. *International Journal of Computer Applications Technology and Research, 14*(6), 38–50. DOI: 10.7753/IJCATR1406.1003

Kanbach, D. K., Heiduk, L., Blueher, G., Schreiter, M., & Lahmann, A. (2023). The GenAI is out of the bottle: Generative artificial intelligence from a business model innovation perspective. *Review of Managerial Science, 18*(4), 1189–1220. DOI: 10.1007/s11846-023-00696-z

Kingma, D. P., & Welling, M. (2013). Auto-Encoding variational Bayes. *arXiv (Cornell University)*. https://doi.org//arxiv.1312.6114DOI: 10.48550

Kumar, S., & Sharma, Ms. K., & IARJSET. (2025). Text Generation with the help of natural language processing: A Review. In *International Advanced Research Journal in Science, Engineering and Technology, 12*(1), 273–274. https://doi.org/DOI: 10.17148/IARJSET.2025.12131

Li, W., Fan, L., Wang, Z., Ma, C., & Cui, X. (2020). Tackling mode collapse in multi-generator GANs with orthogonal vectors. *Pattern Recognition, 110*, 107646. DOI: 10.1016/j.patcog.2020.107646

Lim, D. (2025). Governing Generative AI. SSRN *Electronic Journal*. https://doi.org/DOI: 10.2139/ssrn.5167491

Lin, X., & Losavio, M. (2025). A Comprehensive Survey on Bias and Fairness in Generative AI: Legal, Ethical, and Technical Responses. *SSRN*. https://doi.org/DOI: 10.2139/ssrn.5164147

Marchesi, R., Micheletti, N., Kuo, N. I., Barbieri, S., Jurman, G., & Osmani, V. (2025). Generative AI mitigates representation bias and improves model fairness through synthetic health data. *PLoS Computational Biology, 21*(5), e1013080. DOI: 10.1371/journal.pcbi.1013080 PMID: 40388536

Matulionyte, R., & Lee, J. (2022). Copyright in AI-generated works: Lessons from recent developments in patent law. *SCRIPTed a Journal of Law Technology & Society*, *19*(1), 5–35. DOI: 10.2966/scrip.190122.5

Michel-Villarreal, R., Vilalta-Perdomo, E., Salinas-Navarro, D. E., Thierry-Aguilera, R., & Gerardou, F. S. (2023). Challenges and opportunities of Generative AI for higher Education as explained by ChatGPT. *Education Sciences*, *13*(9), 856. DOI: 10.3390/educsci13090856

Mishra, A., Majumder, A., Kommineni, D., Joseph, C. A., Chowdhury, T., & Anumula, S. K. (2025). Role of Generative Artificial intelligence in Personalized Medicine: A Systematic review. *Cureus*. Advance online publication. DOI: 10.7759/cureus.82310 PMID: 40376348

Nees, J. V., & Waltman, L. (2019). *VOSViewer Manual.* https://www.vosviewer.com/documentation/Manual_VOSviewer_1.6.11.pdf

Palaniappan, N. N. (2025). Demystifying generative ai and transformer architectures. *International journal of advanced research in engineering & technology, 16*(2), 15–28. https://doi.org/DOI: 10.34218/ijaret_16_02_002

Paul, D., Sanap, G., Shenoy, S., Kalyane, D., Kalia, K., & Tekade, R. K. (2020). Artificial intelligence in drug discovery and development. *Drug Discovery Today*, *26*(1), 80–93. DOI: 10.1016/j.drudis.2020.10.010 PMID: 33099022

Remolina, N. (2023). Generative AI in Finance: Risks and potential solutions. SSRN *Electronic Journal*. https://doi.org/DOI: 10.2139/ssrn.4628235

Sadiq, Z., & Aqib, M. (2023). Advancing Trustworthy explainable artificial intelligence: Principles, goals, and strategies. *OAlib*, *10*(11), 1–14. DOI: 10.4236/oalib.1110870

Sengar, S. S., Hasan, A. B., Kumar, S., & Carroll, F. (2024). Generative Artificial Intelligence: A Systematic Review and Applications. *arXiv (Cornell University).* https://doi.org//arxiv.2405.11029DOI: 10.48550

Singh, A. (2025). Analysis of Using Generative AI for the Classifications in Pharmacology of Medical Sciences. *SSRN*. https://doi.org/DOI: 10.2139/ssrn.5171513

Singh, N. M. (2024). Generative Models Beyond GANS: Innovations in image and text synthesis. *Deleted Journal*, *28*(3s), 354–374. DOI: 10.52783/anvi.v28.3061

Sohl-Dickstein, J., Weiss, E. A., Maheswaranathan, N., & Ganguli, S. (2015). Deep Unsupervised Learning using Nonequilibrium Thermodynamics. *arXiv (Cornell University)*. https://doi.org//arxiv.1503.03585DOI: 10.48550

Sun, G., Xie, W., Niyato, D., Mei, F., Kang, J., Du, H., & Mao, S. (2024). Generative AI for Deep Reinforcement Learning: framework, analysis, and use cases. *arXiv (Cornell University)*. https://doi.org//arxiv.2405.20568DOI: 10.48550

Taeihagh, A. (2025). Governance of Generative AI. *Policy and Society*. Advance online publication. DOI: 10.1093/polsoc/puaf001

Tang, G., Müller, M., Rios, A., & Sennrich, R. (2018). Why Self-Attention? A targeted evaluation of neural machine translation architectures. *Proceedings of the 2021 Conference on Empirical Methods in Natural Language Processing*. https://doi.org/DOI: 10.18653/v1/d18-1458

Tembhekar, P., Devan, M., & Jeyaraman, J. (2023). Role of GenAI in Automated Code Generation within DevOps Practices: Explore how Generative AI. *Journal of Knowledge Learning and Science Technology ISSN 2959-6386 (Online), 2*(2), 500–512. https://doi.org/DOI: 10.60087/jklst.vol2.n2.p512

The Lens. (2025). *Search results for "Generative AI"*. Retrieved June 18, 2025, from https://www.lens.org/lens/search/scholar/list?q=Generative%20AI

Thirunagalingam, A. (2025). Generative AI Ethics: A comprehensive safety and regulation framework. SSRN *Electronic Journal*. https://doi.org/DOI: 10.2139/ssrn.5047540

Vebritha, S. (2024). Redefining Ownership and Originality in the age of AI: A Legal and Ethical review. *Sinergi International Journal of Law*, *2*(4), 312–324. DOI: 10.61194/law.v2i4.726

Wahid, A., Yahya, M., Breslin, J. G., & Intizar, M. A. (2023). Self-Attention Transformer-Based architecture for remaining useful life estimation of complex machines. *Procedia Computer Science*, *217*, 456–464. DOI: 10.1016/j.procs.2022.12.241

Wyczik, J., & Wieczerzak, R. (2024). Rethinking Copyright: The art of ownership in AI outputs. *Eastern European Journal of Transnational Relations*, *8*(1), 39–52. DOI: 10.15290/eejtr.2024.08.01.04

Yang, J., Zhao, Y., & Jia, Z. (2025). Conditional Generative Adversarial Network based on Self-Attention Mechanism and VAE Algorithm and its applications. *TS. Traitement du Signal*, *42*(1), 423–431. DOI: 10.18280/ts.420136

Zhou, E., & Lee, D. (2024). Generative artificial intelligence, human creativity, and art. *PNAS Nexus*, *3*(3). Advance online publication. DOI: 10.1093/pnasnexus/pgae052 PMID: 38444602

ADDITIONAL READINGS

Generative, A. I. current trends and applications. (2024). In *Studies in computational intelligence*. https://doi.org/DOI: 10.1007/978-981-97-8460-8

Intelligence, G. A. (AI) approaches for industrial applications. (2025). In *Information systems engineering and management*. https://doi.org/DOI: 10.1007/978-3-031-76710-4

Leslie, D., & Rossi, F. (2023). ACM TechBrief: Generative Artificial Intelligence. In *ACM eBooks*. https://doi.org/DOI: 10.1145/3626110

Liu, J., Ma, X., Wang, L., & Pei, L. (2024). How Can Generative Artificial Intelligence Techniques Facilitate Intelligent Research into Ancient Books? *Journal on Computing and Cultural Heritage*. https://doi.org/DOI: 10.1145/3690391

The pioneering applications of generative AI. (2024). In *Advances in computational intelligence and robotics book series*. https://doi.org/DOI: 10.4018/979-8-3693-3278-8

KEY TERMS AND DEFINITIONS

Algorithmic Bias: The existence of an unfair and single-sided bias in AI-driven systems that can be manifested as the use of biased structural data and systems or by an algorithm on which that discrimination is exercised.

Data Privacy: Data privacy refers to safeguarding personal information against the unauthorized use or access, especially when it comes to an AI system using sensitive data.

Diffusion Models: A type of generative models which specify both a forward process to add noise to data and a reverse process to remove it, enabling the high-dimensional data-generative models.

Ethical Governance: The structures and guidelines that govern the ethical advancement and evolvement of AI technologies that are able to cater to society and the wider good.

Generative Artificial Intelligence (GAI): A type of AI that is able to create new material autonomously and which statistically matches the training data it is exposed to.

Generative Adversarial Networks (GANs): A family of machine learning models that involves competing neural networks (a generator and a discrimination network) adversarial with the goal of generating real data.

Interdisciplinary Collaboration: The mutual effort of the experts in different fields to solve the problem of complex challenges due to GAI, combining various points of view and experience.

Variational Autoencoders (VAEs): VAEs are a generative model that learns encodings of the input data into a continuous latent space, and then decode it back, such that input can be reconstructed, with optimization over a variational lower bound.

Chapter 3
Generative AI as an Accelerator for Data Engineering

N. Rajkumar
https://orcid.org/0000-0001-7857-9452
Alliance School of Advanced Computing, Alliance University, India

C. Viji
https://orcid.org/0000-0002-2759-8896
Alliance School of Advanced Computing, Alliance University, India

Balusamy Nachiappan
https://orcid.org/0009-0006-0951-8078
Prologis, USA

A. Mohanraj
Sri Eshwar College of Engineering, India

Judeson Antony Kovilpillai
Amity University, India

Oswalt Manoj S.
https://orcid.org/0000-0001-8251-2920
Alliance School of Advance Computing, Alliance University, India

ABSTRACT

The exponential growth of data in the digital era has heightened the importance of efficient data engineering practices. Traditional approaches to data ingestion, cleaning, transformation, and governance often require significant manual intervention, domain expertise, and development time, leading to bottlenecks in analytics and decision-making. By leveraging natural language prompts, contextual learning, and synthetic data generation capabilities, GenAI can facilitate code generation for data pipelines, improve data quality, enhance metadata documentation, and support intelligent decision-making in real-time environments. This chapter explores the integration of Generative AI into data engineering workflows, providing a comprehensive review of relevant technologies, conceptual frameworks, industrial

DOI: 10.4018/979-8-3373-5616-7.ch003

applications, and challenges. Several case studies highlight the tangible benefits of this synergy, including improved productivity, reduced operational costs, and higher data accuracy.

INTRODUCTION

In these days's virtual monetary device, records has emerged as a strategic asset, frequently defined because the "new oil." but, in comparison to crude oil, raw information in itself holds limited fee; it must go through a chain of strategies collectively with ingestion, cleansing, transformation, enrichment, and governance earlier than it can be converted into actionable insights. Those procedures together define the challenge of data engineering, which paperwork the backbone of modern-day analytics, commercial enterprise intelligence, and artificial intelligence structures. Over the last decades, data engineering has advanced appreciably. In the early 2000s, Extract-Transform-Load (ETL) methods dominated, usually going for walks in batch mode on relational databases. The upward push of huge data within the 2010s, supported with the aid of allotted computing frameworks like hadoop and spark, ushered in new paradigms which consist of data lakes, schema-on-examine, and actual-time streaming. Extra these days, cloud-native architectures and the concept of the information mesh have in addition decentralized and democratized information engineering responsibilities throughout organizations (duan et al., 2024; nguyen & hoang, 2024).

In spite of these technological shifts, a fundamental assignment persists making ready first-rate, integrated, and reliable information stays labour-in depth. Studies via gartner (2023) highlights that information scientists nevertheless spend an average of 60–eighty% of their challenge time on data instruction in place of analysis or modelling. This bottleneck not simplest delays insight generation however also restricts the scalability of data-driven projects.

Despite the fact that automation tools together with apache nifi, talend, and dbt have alleviated a number of the load, traditional information engineering workflows nonetheless face sizable obstacles. The art work often needs excessive guide overhead, requiring engineers to write down ETL scripts, control schema adjustments, and keep documentation. The tool environment is complex, forcing practitioners to navigate exceptional systems for ingestion, transformation, excellent tests, and storage. Talent shortages in addition compound the hassle, as data engineering calls for proficiency in a couple of programming languages, database structures, and cloud offerings—abilties which may be increasingly scarce. Scalability additionally stays a hurdle, particularly with rapidly developing data volumes and the rise of streamingIOTrecords that necessitates near actual-time processing. Furthermore, documentation and metadata control regularly attain inadequate attention due to time constraints, developing governance and compliance dangers. These barriers highlight the want for extra sensible and adaptive automation approaches.

Generative artificial intelligence (GenAI or GenAI) gives a transformative opportunity. GenAI fashions are capable of growing new, genuine content—whether text, pics, audio, or code—primarily based on patterns discovered from tremendous datasets. Not like conventional rule-based totally ai, which executes predefined tasks, GenAI can produce novel outputs conditioned on individual input activates. The upward thrust of GenAI has been fueled thru breakthroughs including transformer architectures like gpt and bert, large-scale pretraining on huge textual content and code corpora, and first-class-tuning techniques that adapt models to unique domains, which consist of data engineering. While first of all celebrated for modern programs which encompass artwork and storytelling, generative AI's functionality to generate code—examined with the aid of gear like github copilot, openai codex, and meta's code llama—makes it specifically suitable for automating repetitive programming obligations in records pipelines(wang et al., 2024).

The relevance of GenAI to information engineering is a long way-engaging in. It can automate code generation for square queries, spark scripts, or ETL pipelines from herbal language turns on. It could infer schemas and format database fashions based on new records codecs. It is able to recommend or even execute data cleaning and transformation steps, generate synthetic datasets for checking out or model training at the same time as keeping privacy, produce technical and enterprise documentation routinely, and summarize logs or find out anomalies in actual time. In those ways, GenAI acts every as an accelerator and as an assistant, easing the operational and cognitive load on human engineers.

However, while automation has long been a goal in information engineering, most existing solutions are rule-pushed and absence the adaptability to deal with unexpected records patterns. GenAI offers a greater bendy, studying-based possibility, however its use in information engineering is still in its early degrees. An lousy lot of the modern literature and enterprise speak makes a speciality of its applications in software program development, customer support, or progressive industries, with little systematic exploration of its capability to enhance up records engineering. Without deeper have a have a look at, companies hazard each overestimating its abilities or failing to capitalize on its blessings.

The aim of this chapter is to find out the intersection of GenAI and records engineering, mapping the era's abilities to every degree of the records lifecycle. It objectives to discover the advantages and boundaries of integrating GenAI into engineering workflows, present actual-world case research that show off measurable gains in productivity and accuracy, address the risks and ethical problems of ai-powered pipelines, and advocate techniques for future studies and implementation.

Through doing so, it lays the foundation for data how GenAI can emerge as a real accelerator for cutting-edge records engineering practices..

HOW GENAI WORKS IN DATA ENGINEERING

GenAI in data engineering operates at the principle of studying from present datasets to generate new, contextually applicable records, code, or alterations that mimic and decorate the patterns located within the proper sources. Now not like conventional deterministic tactics that rely on predefined regulations, generative fashions hire deep learning architectures—including Generative Adversarial Networks (GANs), Variational Autoencoders (VAEs), Transformer-based Large Language Models (LLMs), and diffusion models—to recognize complex statistical distributions and semantic relationships in data(chen et al., 2023). In exercise, because of this GenAI does no longer simply memorize inputs; it builds probabilistic fashions of the underlying patterns, permitting it to offer simply new outputs which might be statistically normal with real-global data while additionally adapting to specific domain necessities(goyal et al., 2024). This foundational capability allows data engineers to apply GenAI now not most effective for artificial data introduction however moreover for intelligent data differences, schema mapping, anomaly detection, and automatic code generation(almazrouei et al., 2023; mittal & bhatia, 2023).

The operational workflow of GenAI in information engineering usually begins with records ingestion and schooling. Relevant datasets are accumulated from multiple resources—dependent databases, unstructured textual content files, logs, images, orIOTsensor streams—and are pre-processed to remove noise, normalize formats, and make sure compatibility with the selectedAIversion. For the duration of the training phase, the version learns the statistical homes, relationships, and latent capabilities of the dataset(brown et al., 2023). For example, a model designed to easy and remodel sales data can also moreover observe seasonal buy patterns, foreign exchange codecs, and how lacking entries correlate with different variables. The more complete and representative the training data, the extra correct and area-relevant the model's generative talents end up (Rajkumar et al., 2026a, 2026b).

As soon as skilled, the GenAI enters the inference section, wherein it is accomplished to stay or batch records engineering workflows. In this phase, the version takes activates, policies, or contextual inputs and produces outputs that serve specific engineering functions. For example, it is able to generate sq. Queries from herbal language activates, map mismatched database schemas through spotting column semantics, or fill missing values in datasets using contextually knowledgeable predictions. The adaptability of GenAI lies in its capacity to cope with ambiguous or incomplete commands—leveraging its located context to produce accurate, relevant, and regularly progressive answers without rigid programming constraints.

Figure 1. High-level workflow of GenAI in data engineering pipelines

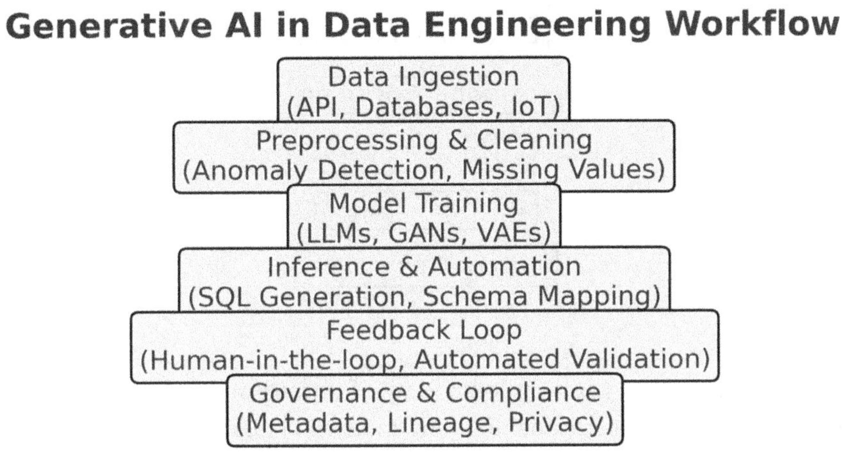

Figure 1 depicts the overarching degrees in a generative ai–ai-stronger data engineering lifecycle, highlighting in which AI abilties growth traditional techniques. The workflow starts offevolved with information ingestion, where uncooked data is gathered from diverse assets together with API, databases, and IOT gadgets. GenAI intervenes at this degree with the useful resource of automating schema inference, generating api connectors, and harmonizing disparate codecs. The preprocessing and cleaning stage follows, throughout which AI fashions discover anomalies, fill lacking values, and normalize inconsistent codecs without counting on fixed regulations. Inside the version schooling segment, architectures including Large Language Models (LLMs), Generative Adversarial Networks (GANs), and Variational Autoencoders (VAEs) study place-particular styles from ancient datasets. Inside the route of inference and automation, the model applies these observed out patterns to generate sq. Queries, transformation scripts, or perhaps whole ETL workflows. A comments loop ensures non-stop improvement via human validation and automated mistakes detection, making the device adaptive to evolving information patterns. Subsequently, governance and compliance layers make sure that ai-driven outputs align with metadata requirements, data lineage necessities, and regulatory mandates, remaining the loop for a sustainable, scalable records pipeline (luo et al., 2023).

Figure 2. Simplified transformer-based LLM architecture for data engineering tasks.

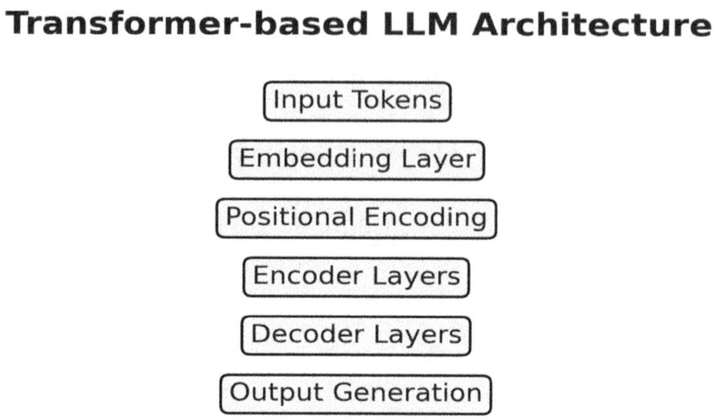

This diagram offers a high-diploma view of a transformer-primarily based totally structure, that is foundational to many modern GenAI systems in information engineering. Enter tokens—including words from a herbal language query or area names from a dataset—are transformed into vector embeddings via an embedding layer. Positional encoding is brought to the ones embeddings to hold series order, that is essential for context understanding. The encoder layers manner those enriched embeddings the usage of self-attention mechanisms to seize complex dependencies between tokens. In parallel, decoder layers obtain encoded representations and generate contextually relevant outputs together with sq. Queries, python scripts, or schema mappings. The output technology element ensures that responses are coherent, syntactically accurate, and optimized for the challenge at hand. This structure's capability to generalize during duties makes it notably effective for automating a massive variety of records engineering operations, from pipeline code generation to clever data transformation suggestions

Figure 4 gives the feedback loop mechanism in GenAI pipelines. The loop lets in models to examine from mistakes, include human remarks, and enhance through the years. This guarantees adaptability to evolving datasets and enterprise necessities.

Figure 3. Feedback loop and continuous learning process in GenAI-enhanced pipelines.

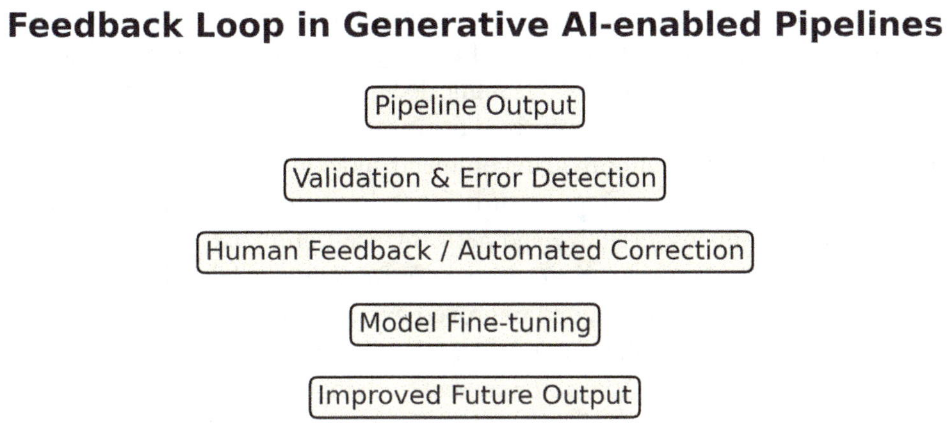

The remarks loop proven on this diagram is vital for maintaining the accuracy, adaptability, and robustness of ai-pushed records engineering workflows. The system begins with pipeline output, in which the GenAI gadget produces adjustments, scripts, or enriched datasets. Validation and errors detection mechanisms—each automated or manual—study the ones outputs for correctness and compliance with organizational necessities. If discrepancies are determined, human comments or computerized corrections are carried out. This corrective records is then fed lower back into the model exceptional-tuning manner, allowing theAIto alter its internal parameters. Through the years, this non-prevent refinement consequences in improved destiny outputs, with the machine studying from beyond mistakes to keep away from repeating them. Such an iterative technique not handiest increases accuracy but also complements recall and transparency, as stakeholders can have a look at tangible overall performance improvements over successive iterations(andonian et al., 2023).

Figure 4. Integration of GenAI capabilities in a traditional ETL/ELT pipeline.

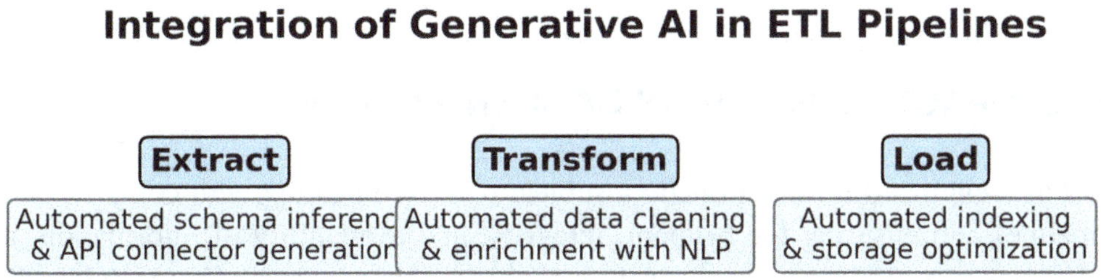

This diagram demonstrates the points of integration for GenAI within a conventional ETL (Extract, Transform, Load) or ELT (Extract, Load, Transform) pipeline. During the Extract phase, GenAI automates schema inference and generates API connectors to integrate heterogeneous data sources more quickly and accurately. In the Transform phase, AI-driven Natural Language Processing (NLP) and pattern recognition facilitate automated data cleaning, deduplication, and enrichment, adding contextually relevant metadata or derived attributes. In the Load phase, theAIsystem analyzes workload patterns to recommend indexing strategies, partitioning schemes, and compression settings, ensuring that storage in data warehouses, lakes, or lakehouses is both cost-effective and performance-optimized. By embeddingA-Icapabilities at each stage, organizations benefit from reduced development times, minimized manual intervention, and improved overall pipeline reliability.

A great differentiator in the manner GenAI works in information engineering is its remarks loop mechanism. Via reinforcement studying or non-stop best-tuning, the version improves with every interplay by way of way of incorporating corrections and remarks from engineers or automated validation structures. That is especially critical in dynamic environments in which datasets evolve over time, schemas change, and new styles emerge. For example, if a schema mapping model incorrectly fits "orderid" to "clientid" in an integration pipeline, the comments provided will recalibrate the model's knowledge, reducing the threat of similar mistakes inside the future.

GenAI additionally operates synergistically with metadata and governance structures. By way of way of information and generating metadata descriptions, it could suggest tagging conventions, lineage documentation, and compliance annotations automatically. This integration guarantees that generated outputs are not most effective functionally correct but moreover aligned with organizational requirements, regulatory necessities, and operational first rate practices.

In the end, the internal workings of GenAI in information engineering constitute a shift from rigid automation closer to smart, adaptive orchestration. The fashions do not simply execute instructions; they interpret context, are looking forward to best pathways, and create new solutions that mix statistical accuracy with operational relevance. This adaptability permits corporations to optimize information workflows, accelerate development cycles, and maintain excessive data tremendous even in complicated, large-scale, and continuously evolving records ecosystems.

THE IMPACT OF GENAI ON DATA ENGINEERING

Facts engineering, traditionally a subject rooted in dealing with complex data pipelines and ensuring the brilliant, integrity, and availability of information, is gift manner a profound transformation with the emergence of GenAI (GenAI).

Generative ai, powered thru big-scale fashions, complements automation, streamlining techniques, and empowering engineers to shift from recurring obligations to strategic choice-making.

Automation in Data Pipeline Advent

GenAI has emerged as a powerful ally in automating numerous components of statistical engineering, particularly in the introduction and renovation of ETL (Extract, Redesign, and Load) pipelines.

Use Case: computerized ETL Pipeline generation at a monetary organization

A large economic services enterprise leverages GenAI gadget like github copilot to unexpectedly generate ETL pipelines for on boarding new clients. Historically, those involved weeks of manual coding, but with AIhelp, pipeline introduction may be computerized by feeding metadata and data transformation hints into the AItool. The AI generates preliminary scripts, which engineers refine as wished.

Effect:

Decreased improvement time from weeks to days.

Records engineers can reputation on optimizing workflows in place of manual coding.

Stepped forward with high-quality information and Anomaly Detection

Records are paramount for any data pipeline, and GenAI plays a pivotal function in making sure that incoming data is accurate and loose from anomalies.

Use Case: Real-Time Anomaly Detection forIOTinformation in manufacturing

A manufacturing company techniques real-time data from loads ofIOTsensors. GenAI models are hired to reveal the information continuously, figuring out anomalies together with uncommon sensor readings or data corruption. TheAInot handiest flags anomalies however moreover predicts accurate values, permitting the corporation to keep immoderate information exquisite for the duration of its production systems.

Effect:

Stepped forward truth accuracy via way of detecting and resolving anomalies in actual time.

Automated data corrections that shop from disruptions in production processes.

Stronger records Integration and Interoperability

Integrating data from multiple assets, every with precise formats and systems, is one of the key disturbing conditions data engineers faces. GenAI assists in simplifying this tool.

Use Case: move-Platform data Integration at a Healthcare company

A healthcare organization integrates affected individual information across multiple structures — ehrs, lab effects, and wearable devices. GenAI automatically maps unique fact schemas and ensures interoperability between structures. Moreover, AI permits natural language querying of databases, permitting non-technical employees to retrieve data without writing square queries.

Effect:

Progressed data integration within the direction of structures.

Advanced accessibility of data thru natural language queries.

Optimizing the Data Structure and Garage

Data engineers have to continuously optimize data architectures to ensure stability, price, and overall performance. GenAI enables this via manner of studying statistical utilization styles and suggesting improvements.

Use Case: Price-Optimized Cloud information garage for an E-trade Platform

An e-exchange platform uses AI to optimize information garage strategies throughout a huge-scale cloud infrastructure. GenAI models take a look at information benefit right of get admission to to styles, and endorse partitioning techniques to reduce garage prices through transferring no longer often accessed information to less expensive, slower storage, at the same time as maintaining regularly accessed records results easily available.

Impact:

Value savings via optimized storage control.

Progressed question typical performance by using neatly partitioning immoderate-call for datasets.

Statistics, Safety, and Privacy Improvements

GenAI can be used to at ease sensitive information and make certain privacy compliance, especially in industries dealing with rather regulated records, which consist of finance and healthcare.

Use Case: artificial data technology for GDPR Compliance in Finance

A worldwide financial organization needs to test tool mastering fashions without exposing actual customer information, in compliance with gdpr. GenAI is used to create synthetic datasets that mirror the characteristics of real global records, permitting the financial group to carry out conduct exams and improvement even as maintaining compliance with information privacy regulations.

Impact:

More potent data privateness the usage of ai-generated artificial records in non-production environments.

Regulatory compliance without sacrificing the superb of development and trying out efforts.

AI-Assisted Monitoring and Upkeep

Tracking and keeping data pipelines can be a useful useful resource intensity project; but, GenAI offers predictive talents that automate hundreds of this artwork.

Use case: predictive renovation for information pipelines in a telecom agency

A telecom business enterprise uses AI-driven models to display and count on disasters in its ETL pipelines. Through using the analysing ancient pipeline everyday performance, the AI predicts at the identical time as problems like data loading disasters are probably to stand up. It can even practice computerized fixes, which embody rerouting web site visitors or adjusting assignment configurations, lowering downtime, and minimizing guide intervention.

Effect:

Decreased operational downtime and quicker healing from pipeline screw ups.

Fewer manual interventions, enhancing operational performance.

The Shift toward AI-Driven Information Engineering

The position of data engineers is shifting as GenAI automates many habitual duties. Records engineers at the moment are required to popularity more on strategic selection-making, optimization, and governance.

Use case: AI-higher records governance at an global store

A global store uses GenAI to automate elements of its data governance software program. The AI identifies sensitive records, recommends elegance and cataloguing techniques, and guarantees compliance with inner data dealing with guidelines. It additionally tracks how data are used across exceptional organizations, supporting the business enterprise in keeping updated governance practices.

Impact:

Streamlined data governance with decreased guide oversight.

Engineers can be aware of strategic options regarding information shape and coverage enforcement.

GenAI is swiftly reshaping the panorama of information engineering, automating traditionally manual obligations, improving records exceptional, and optimizing infrastructure. Through automating ETL pipelines, improving data integration, and providing ai-driven answers for anomaly detection, privateness, and governance, engineers are empowered to transport beyond the technical factors and make contributions extra strategically to their businesses.

The real international use times highlighted proper here show the tangible advantages that GenAI brings to the table, revolutionizing how data engineers carry out, and taking off new possibilities for innovation and performance in the data-pushed global.

As AI keeps to comply, data engineers who embody this period will discover themselves on the main edge of contemporary data architectures, capable of strain significant alternate and industrial organisation effects with the assistance in their ai-powered tool.

Key Applications of GenAI in Data Engineering

GenAI is revolutionizing the sector of data engineering via introducing clever, adaptive, and context-aware automation that surpasses the regulations of traditional, rule-based totally structures. In desire to counting on pre-defined excellent judgment, generative models—powered with the aid of advanced neural architectures collectively with transformers, Generative Adversarial Networks (GANs), Variational Autoencoders (VAEs), and diffusion models—can have a look at complex patterns from historic datasets, infer context, and generate completely new, top notch data or code tailor-made to particular wishes. These capabilities span the entire data engineering lifecycle, from data ingestion and transformation to integration, governance, and first-class tracking, enabling businesses to advantage greater overall performance, decreased charges, and progressed records-pushed preference-making (Nachiappan et al., 2026).

One of the maximum outstanding applications is synthetic records era, which addresses the challenge of information shortage and privacy in sensitive domains which incorporates healthcare, finance, and protection. Generative models can reflect the statistical distributions of actual datasets without exposing real records, for this reason permitting compliant records sharing and experimentation. For instance, in healthcare, synthetic patient information may be created to teach predictive fashions without compromising personal privacy, whilst in finance, simulated fraud eventualities can assist boom more sturdy fraud detection algorithms, overcoming the imbalance inherent in real-global records. Carefully tied to that is the usage of GenAI in automated data cleaning and pre-processing, a challenge that traditionally consumes most people of a information engineer's time. By way of know-how the semantic and statistical context of datasets, GenAI can fill missing values, detect anomalies, harmonize inconsistent codecs, and even recommend corrections with minimum human intervention. This no longer most effective speeds up coaching but additionally ensures higher tiers of accuracy and consistency (ghosh & sanyal, 2023).

Each different transformative utility lies in schema mapping and information integration, which is probably critical in companies handling heterogeneous structures and varied records codecs. Traditionally exertions-significant, this system can now be automated the usage of GenAI fashions able to information column semantics and supplying accurate mappings without specific commands. For instance, the version can robotically understand that "cust_id" in one system corresponds to "customer identifier" in every other, even generating the crucial transformation code in square or python. Similarly, GenAI supports data enrichment by means of deriving valuable context from unstructured assets including documents, logs, audio, or pix. As an example, AI can extract sentiment from client opinions and append it to established sales records, or observe satellite imagery to perceive production hobby for reinforcing actual assets datasets.

Pipeline documentation and automation additionally gain substantially from generative AI's abilities. The technology can routinely generate exact pipeline documentation, create code annotations, tune historical changes, or maybe produce visible data float diagrams in actual time as pipelines evolve. Beyond documentation, GenAI can generate boilerplate ETL scripts, produce automated unit exams for data validation, and endorse overall performance optimizations with the aid of analysing execution logs. This level of automation guarantees that pipelines live nicely-documented and maintainable, even at some point of personnel transitions. Moreover, GenAI complements data brilliant tracking with the aid of analysing baseline operational behaviours, detecting anomalies which include data go with the flow or schema modifications, predicting destiny screw ups, and suggesting preventive measures. As an instance, a machine would probably stumble on that a dataset is lacking entries from a particular geographic region and proactively flag the problem for overview.

Some different noteworthy development is natural language question technology, which permits non-technical clients to get entry to and explore data without writing square or programming scripts. By way of manner of translating easy language queries into optimized database commands, GenAI democratizes information get right of access to, fostering a way of life in which choice-makers the least bit degrees can without delay have interaction with data. This ability, mixed with the aforementioned applications, demonstrates that GenAI isn't limited to automating isolated responsibilities—it basically reshapes the data engineering manner via integrating semantic reputation, predictive intelligence, and modern synthesis at every diploma. From ingestion and garage to transformation, enrichment, governance, and assessment, GenAI empowers companies to liberate deeper insights, decorate operational performance, and stress innovation in their data ecosystems.

Integrating GenAI into the Data Engineering Lifecycle

The integration of GenAI into the data engineering lifecycle represents a transformative jump in how groups manage, approach, and leverage data. Historically, information engineering includes a series of steps—data ingestion, cleansing, transformation, storage, and governance—every requiring giant guide strive, area understanding, and iterative development cycles. GenAI disrupts this paradigm with the aid of manner of introducing automation, clever choice-making, and creativity at every degree. Via embedding ai-driven capabilities into the pipeline, records engineering shifts from a rigid, procedure-pushed situation to an adaptive, self-improving environment.

Inside the data ingestion section, GenAI assists in automating schema mapping, api integration, and connector generation. In vicinity of manually coding ETL (extract, redesign, load) pipelines for disparate data assets, AI fashions can interpret metadata, infer schema relationships, and car-generate ingestion scripts in more than one programming languages. This appreciably reduces improvement time at the same time as minimizing human mistakes in integration logic.

All through information cleansing and pre-processing, GenAI brings superior anomaly detection and automatic restore capabilities. It could select out outliers, missing values, and inconsistent codecs, then suggest or practice corrections based totally on observed out styles from historic datasets. Not like rule-based totally systems, Ai-driven pre-processing constantly adapts to evolving records traits, making pipelines more resilient to adjustments in source systems. Artificial data era additionally performs a role here—permitting AI to fill data gaps without compromising privacy or introducing statistical distortions.

Figure 5. Layered Human–AI Collaboration Architecture

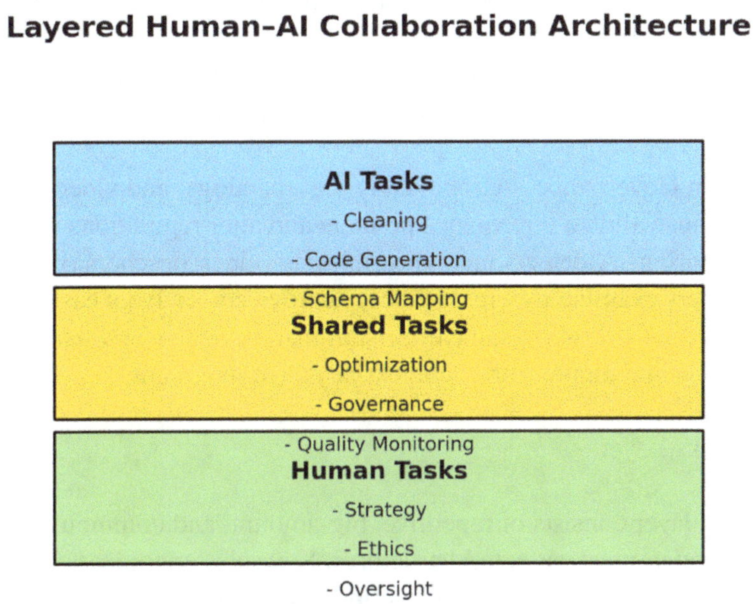

Figure5 illustrates a primarily based framework that defines how human knowledge and GenAI abilities have interaction in the data engineering lifecycle. This version organizes obligations into 3 tremendous but interconnected layers, emphasizing the complementary nature of human strategic oversight and ai-driven operational performance.

1. Human Tasks Layer

This pinnacle layer represents the excessive-level activities that depend frequently on human judgment, ethical reasoning, and vicinity knowledge. Key functions include:

Strategic Choice-Making – figuring out organizational priorities, selecting information engineering goals, and aligningAIpackages with industrial company desires.

Moral Oversight – ensuring ai-driven techniques take a look at fairness, transparency, and regulatory requirements.

Operational Supervision – monitoringAIoutputs for contextual relevance, accuracy, and capability unintentional outcomes.

2. Shared Tasks Layer

The middle layer reflects regions in which human information andAIautomation work collaboratively. These duties advantage from every human intuition and AI's pace, precision, and scalability:

Optimization –AIindicates standard performance improvements in ETL strategies, at the same time as people take a look at change-offs among price, time, and compliance.

Information Governance –AIrobotically tags, catalogs, and video display units datasets; humans validate governance pointers and alter regulations while desired.

Best Monitoring –AIdetects anomalies, missing values, or schema modifications; human engineers examine root reasons and approve corrective measures.

This shared control fosters adaptive decision-making, in whichAIhandles massive-scale processing and humans offer context-sensitive judgment.

3.AI Tasks Layer

The lowest layer consists of repetitive, big-amount, and common sense-pushed sports delegated in most cases toAIstructures. Key roles encompass:

Computerized data cleansing – detecting and repairing inconsistencies, standardizing codecs, and imputing missing values.

Code generation – generating ETL scripts, square queries, or transformation common feel primarily based on herbal language commands.

Schema mapping – automatically aligning heterogeneous information assets by inferring semantic relationships among fields.

Those duties leverage AI's ability to system complex data patterns without fatigue or oversight delays.

Inside the information transformation and enrichment stage, GenAI fashions can convert raw, unstructured information into dependent, analytics-ready formats with minimal manual intervention. Natural Language Processing (NLP) strategies permit AI to interpret files, logs, and pictures, then generate standardized tabular data. Furthermore, AI can enhance datasets via synthesizing extra contextual attributes, together with generating product descriptions from SKU data or inferring missing geographic classifications based on region styles.

With regards to data garage and optimization, GenAI can analyse utilization patterns to recommend optimum partitioning techniques, indexing techniques, and compression strategies. This ensures that storage answers—whether in data warehouses, lakes, or lake houses—are rate-efficient and standard performance-optimized. Ai-pushed garage control structures may additionally even simulate question workloads to proactively restructure garage layouts for expected demands.

Inside the governance and compliance layer, GenAI allows automated tagging, lineage tracking, and coverage enforcement. Ai-powered metadata enrichment permits maintain accurate data catalogues, whilst computerized compliance tests make sure that datasets adhere to applicable regulatory requirements. This reduces the burden on governance businesses, letting them cognizance on oversight and strategic desire-making in choice to normal audits.

One of the maximum impactful contributions of GenAI is final the feedback loop in information engineering. Via constantly tracking pipeline overall performance, information super, and transformation accuracy, AI models can endorse optimizations or autonomously modify configurations. Through the years, this consequences in self-healing pipelines that evolve with the organization's needs (li et al., 2023).

In the long run, integrating GenAI into the data engineering lifecycle is not approximately replacing human knowledge, however about augmenting it (hao et al., 2023). The human role transitions towards strategic supervision, ethical oversight, and organization alignment, whilst AI handles repetitive, excessive-quantity, and logic-extensive tasks. This collaboration among human intelligence and gadget technology accelerates delivery timelines, improves data awesome, and empowers companies to derive fee from records at unparalleled speed and scale.

Risks and Ethical Considerations

Whilst GenAI gives outstanding ability for accelerating data engineering, its adoption moreover introduces vast risks and moral annoying conditions that businesses ought to deal with proactively. One of the maximum pressing worries is records privateness and safety. GenAI structures regularly require great portions of training records, which may encompass sensitive private or proprietary records. If improperly handled, this may cause privacy breaches or unauthorized information exposure. As an instance, producing synthetic data without right anonymization strategies might inadvertently re-become aware of people. Data engineers ought to therefore enforce rigorous data governance frameworks, encryption, and privacy-preserving strategies including differential privateness to make sure compliance with tips like gdpr and ccpa.

Some other primary threat consists of bias and equity. Given that GenAI fashions examine patterns from cutting-edge datasets, they're able to inherit and even boom biases present inside the supply records. This may result in discriminatory outputs in computerized choice-making pipelines, especially in industries like finance, healthcare, or recruitment. Moral AI practices require continuous bias audits, transparent dataset documentation, and the incorporation of fairness constraints into the model training approach. Without the ones safeguards, data-driven merchandise threat perpetuating systemic inequalities.

Hallucinations and incorrect records additionally pose a mission. Generative fashions are vulnerable to generating outputs which are factually incorrect or fabricated, a phenomenon often called "hallucination." in data engineering workflows, such inaccuracies can propagate through pipelines, contaminating downstream analytics and desire-making. Incorporating verification layers, human-in-the-loop validation, and automatic fact-checking mechanisms can help mitigate this danger (dwivedi et al., 2023).

From an operational perspective, version interpretability and obligation are important moral concerns. Complex GenAI fashions—along with huge language fashions—are frequently black bins, making it tough to trace how unique outputs are generated. This opacity complicates errors diagnosis, regulatory compliance, and client receive as real with. To deal with this, explainable AI (xai) strategies, version documentation, and audit trails have to be embedded into the information engineering architecture (gupta & pathak, 2023).

The environmental effect of massive-scale GenAI schooling is each different difficulty. Schooling foundation fashions consumes big computational assets, important to excessive carbon emissions. Businesses deploying GenAI for data engineering want to weigh the benefits of these generation in opposition to their ecological footprint, exploring optimizations along with version distillation, transfer mastering, and electricity-inexperienced hardware.

Ultimately, intellectual property and felony dangers cannot be ignored. GenAI outputs also can infringe on copyrighted substances, specifically if fashions are knowledgeable on datasets scraped from the internet without right licensing. This increases questions about ownership of ai-generated code, records differences, or reports interior a data engineering context. Jail frameworks for ai-generated content material are however evolving, necessitating warning and the usage of legally vetted datasets.

In precis, while GenAI can redesign data engineering with unprecedented overall performance and innovation, it additionally brings forth complicated ethical, operational, and jail demanding situations. Addressing those requires a multi-layered strategy concerning technical safeguards, regulatory compliance, continuous monitoring, and a subculture of accountable A Iadoption. Groups that stability innovation with moral integrity will be quality placed to harness the entire potential of GenAI while minimizing harm.

FUTURE DIRECTIONS AND EMERGING TRENDS IN GENAI FOR DATA ENGINEERING

GenAI (GenAI) is no longer constrained to creative or language-based totally programs; it is rapidly growing as a transformative pressure within the area of data engineering. As institutions face awesome boom in the amount, pace, and sort of records, conventional guide and rule-primarily based approaches to data processing conflict to maintain tempo. GenAI introduces a paradigm shift with the aid of enabling unbiased decision-making, context-conscious data processing, and real-time optimization of data workflows. These skills are not certainly incremental enhancements however sign a fundamental rethinking of approaches information engineering will perform within the coming decade.

One of the maximum promising trends is the upward thrust of self-optimizing data pipelines. Within the conventional method, optimizing ETL (extract, remodel, load) jobs requires steady human tracking and manual intervention to become aware of bottlenecks or inefficiencies. GenAI modifications this dynamic via allowing pipelines which could locate universal overall performance troubles, perceive root motives, and autonomously rewrite queries, regulate configurations, or reallocate computing resources. For instance, in a monetary institution's fraud detection workflow, an AI device may want to notice that a query is scanning billions of rows unnecessarily and robotically rewrite it to apply a filtered index, decreasing execution time from minutes to seconds. These self-recovery structures promise decreased downtime, progressed throughput, and reduce operational fees.

Another growing trend is multimodal data processing, which lets in AI to seamlessly integrate textual content, numerical data, pictures, video, and even audio within a unified analytic framework. This capability is essential in present day environments wherein selection-making often relies on combining records from a couple of modalities. A clever metropolis project, as an example, might integrate stay visitors digital feeds, weather forecasts, and public shipping schedules right into a single desire-making gadget. GenAI now not most effective helps this integration but also can infer bypass-modal relationships that might in any other case be invisible to conventional analytics (sun et al., 2023).

GenAI is also redefining the concept of synthetic data generation, especially for uncommon-event modelling and touchy domain names. Many industries—healthcare being a high example—face the dual task of desiring practical datasets for AI education while additionally ensuring records privacy. GenAI can produce artificial datasets that carefully mimic the statistical styles of real data without revealing any actual non-public data. A healthcare studies organization reading uncommon cardiac anomalies have to generate synthetic ECG waveforms for version schooling without breaching affected man or woman confidentiality. This method addresses both the scarcity of rare-event records and the stringent necessities of data protection policies alongside GDPR and HIPAA.

A further shift is happening in context-aware data governance. Traditional governance frameworks exercise static, one-duration-fits-all suggestions to all data, irrespective of context. In evaluation, GenAI permits dynamic governance mechanisms that modify suggestions in actual time based totally mostly on geographical region, user characteristic, or meant purpose of data use. For instance, an analyst in europe getting access to a global dataset should routinely get hold of masked non-public data from the us to comply with gdpr, on the identical time as although being capable of view aggregated records. This adaptability reduces compliance risks on the identical time as retaining operational performance.

The future of AI in information engineering will also be usual with the resource of a information-centric technique to AI development. As opposed to focusing absolutely on growing version complexity, hobby will shift in the direction of improving the exceptional, labelling accuracy, and metadata completeness of the records itself. GenAI can assist by way of detecting mislabelled entries, generating lacking metadata, and suggesting focused data augmentation techniques. In a retail analytics situation, for instance, GenAI could discover that positive product snap shots are incorrectly tagged, thereby enhancing recommendation machine performance without necessitating a entire retraining of the model.

Irrespective of those advancements, the mixing of GenAI into data engineering gives outstanding demanding situations. Moral concerns stand up from the possibility of biased or deceptive artificial data. Transparency troubles may additionally grow to be ai-optimized pipelines emerge as “black bins” that even professional engineers cannot fully offer an explanation for. Statistics sovereignty conflicts might also need to get up whilst AI systems method pass-border data without adhering to nearby rules, and opposed threats ought to exploit synthetic information generation to create risky or fraudulent datasets (raj & sharma, 2023).

Looking ahead, severa studies instructions will form the sphere. Federated generative pipelines, which method and generate information regionally to comply with data residency legal guidelines, are probable to benefit traction. Explainable GenAI structures may be crucial to growing ai-pushed pipeline optimizations apparent and auditable. Adaptive information contracts, which allow schemas and regulations to adapt dynamically among data manufacturers and customers, will increase flexibility (kim & choi, 2023). Moreover, the combination of GenAI into actual-time streaming systems collectively with apache KAFKA and FLINK will allow information enrichment and transformation in-flight.

Over the subsequent decade, adoption will probable take a look at a clear trajectory. In the quick term (one to 3 years), industries will attention on ETL optimization, synthetic information generation for compliance-heavy sectors, and early implementations of context-aware governance. The mid-term (four to 6 years) will see massive adoption of multimodal pipelines, the upward thrust of explainable generative systems, and the proliferation of federated AI pipelines. By manner of the long term (seven to ten years), we might also witness sincerely independent information ecosystems able to self-healing, self-governing, and dynamically complying with global rules even as orchestrating complex multimodal analytics in actual time.

In stop, GenAI is poised to essentially redefine data engineering. It will transition the sector from static, human-based strategies to dynamic, self-optimizing, and clever structures. Whilst the ability blessings are vast—starting from efficiency profits to regulatory compliance—the journey would require robust governance, transparency, and global cooperation to ensure the ones technologies serve each industrial organization dreams and societal pursuits. The future of information engineering may be one in which GenAI acts now not just as a device, but as an energetic, self enough accomplice within the advent, transformation, and governance of data.

CONCLUSION AND FUTURE RESEARCH OPPORTUNITIES

The rapid convergence of generative synthetic intelligence (GenAI) and data engineering has created a transformative inflection aspect for modern-day data-pushed organizations. During this book, we've got explored how GenAI isn't simply an enhancement to existing workflows but a structural catalyst able to redefining the very foundations of data series, transformation, integration, governance, and usage. The realization that emerges is clear: data engineering, as soon as intently reliant on static regulations and human intervention, is evolving right into a dynamic, sensible surroundings where automation, adaptability, and creativity function in tandem.

The sensible implications of this variation are profound. Organizations can now envision self-restoration pipelines that optimize themselves in actual time, multimodal frameworks that combine numerous records sources effortlessly, and synthetic data engines that conquer privacy and shortage obstacles without compromising ethical requirements. GenAI enables those skills thru mastering from ancient records styles, predicting destiny dreams, and offering modern-day answers that human engineers may not count on. In doing so, it hurries up the rate at which companies can reply to marketplace needs, regulatory changes, and technological disruptions.

But, the adventure closer to complete GenAI integration is neither linear nor free from barriers. The demanding conditions stated in in advance chapters—bias in synthetic datasets, opacity in AI selection-making, dangers of adverse manipulation, and the complexity of aligning international regulatory compliance—remain massive hurdles. Those problems aren't insurmountable however call for planned strategies that combine technological safeguards, ethical frameworks, and strong governance. Groups should adopt a mind-set that balances innovation with duty, making sure that GenAI programs are obvious, explainable, and aligned with societal values.

From a studies perspective, the sphere is ripe with possibilities that boom past cutting-edge-day abilities. One promising avenue is explainable GenAI for data engineering—growing models that can articulate the motive behind information changes and pipeline optimizations in human-readable phrases. Some different is federated generative pipelines, in which AI systems function in decentralized environments to comply with local records sovereignty felony pointers while nonetheless taking gain of shared intelligence(kaur et al., 2023). Researchers may moreover consciousness on adaptive compliance engines that use GenAI to dynamically interpret and have a look at changing criminal requirements in real time, lowering the operational burden on compliance teams (bommasani et al., 2023).

Furthermore, the aggregate of real-time GenAI into event-pushed architectures consisting of apache KAFKA or AWS kinesis gives unexplored capacity for instant data enrichment and anomaly detection. In parallel, there's developing hobby in energy-inexperienced generative models that restriction computational fees and environmental impact—a vital interest as information engineering workloads preserve to scale. Move-disciplinary research that blends machine mastering, allotted systems, prison research, and human-computer interaction may be instrumental in tackling the ones multifaceted annoying conditions.

The destiny landscape of GenAI in records engineering is possibly to be described with the aid of a remarks loop amongst practice and theory. As organisations installation and refine GenAI-driven answers, they may generate novel requirements, scenarios, and datasets that, in flip, will inform educational studies. This symbiotic dating will accelerate the tempo of innovation on the identical time as making sure that rising answers are grounded in sensible realities. Crucially, success will rely upon fostering collaborations amongst academia, corporation, and regulatory our bodies to co-create requirements, benchmarks, and moral guidelines.

In summary, the convergence of GenAI and information engineering marks a paradigm shift in the direction of wise, self-adaptive, and ethically conscious data ecosystems. At the identical time because the transformative potential is large, knowledge it's going to require a deliberate, research-knowledgeable method that addresses each technological possibilities and societal obligations. The subsequent decade will decide whether or not GenAI turns into a sustainable foundation for data engineering or a fleeting trend overshadowed via ethical and governance disasters. The studies community, enterprise leaders, and policymakers share an equal stake in shaping this destiny, making sure that GenAI serves no longer only as an accelerator of technical development however also as a steward of agree with, equity, and innovation inside the records economic device.

REFERENCES

Almazrouei, E., Al-Ali, A., AlShamsi, A., & al Dhaheri, A. Falcon LLM: The new state of the art in open large language models. arXiv preprint arXiv:230601116. 2023

Andonian, A., Tseng, E., Zhang, K., & Isola, P. (2023). Robust data pipelines for machine learning with generative AI. *IEEE Transactions on Artificial Intelligence*, *4*(5), 1200–1213.

Bommasani, R., Hudson, D. A., & Adeli, E. (2023). others. On the opportunities and risks of foundation models. *Journal of Artificial Intelligence Research*, *76*, 1–97.

Brown, T. B., Mann, B., & Ryder, N. others. Language models are few-shot learners. In: Advances in Neural Information Processing Systems. 2023. p. 1877–901.

Chen, M., Tworek, J., & Jun, H. (2023). others. Evaluating large language models trained on code. *ACM Transactions on Software Engineering and Methodology*, *32*(3), 1–43.

Duan, Y., Chen, X., & Houthooft, R. (2024). others. GenAI for automated data engineering in cloud environments. *IEEE Cloud Computing*, *11*(2), 56–67.

Dwivedi, Y. K., Hughes, L., & Baabdullah, A. M. (2023). others. Artificial Intelligence (AI): Multidisciplinary perspectives on emerging challenges, opportunities, and agenda for research, practice, and policy. *International Journal of Information Management*, *69*, 102642.

Ghosh, A., & Sanyal, S. (2023). Synthetic data generation using generative adversarial networks for privacy-preserving analytics. *Expert Systems with Applications*, *225*, 120072.

Goyal, N., Kumar, R., & Kherwa, P. (2024). Role of large language models in accelerating ETL processes. *Journal of Big Data*, *11*(1), 50.

Gupta, A., & Pathak, P. (2023). Explainable GenAI for trustworthy data pipelines. *ACM Computing Surveys*, *55*(12), 1–34.

Hao, M. C., Dayal, U., & Hsu, M. (2023). others. AI-augmented data engineering: Concepts, architectures, and applications. *Proceedings of the VLDB Endowment International Conference on Very Large Data Bases*, *16*(12), 3765–3778.

Kaur, P., Singh, S., & Ahuja, S. (2023). Federated learning and GenAI for privacy-preserving data analytics. *Future Generation Computer Systems*, *145*, 415–427.

Kim, H., & Choi, J. (2023). Enhancing data integration through generative AI-based schema matching. *Information Sciences*, *625*, 448–461.

Li, X., Chen, J., & Zhang, Y. (2023). Autonomous data pipelines using large language models. *IEEE Transactions on Knowledge and Data Engineering*, *35*(8), 7994–8007.

Luo, Y., Wang, L., & Li, J. (2023). Adaptive governance in AI-driven data engineering systems. *Decision Support Systems*, *169*, 113859.

Mittal, S., & Bhatia, R. (2023). Leveraging diffusion models for synthetic data creation in high-dimensional datasets. *Pattern Recognition Letters*, *172*, 61–69.

Nachiappan, B., Rajkumar, N., Radha, V., Kalpana, C., Viji, C., Nagarajan, G., Mohanraj, A. (2026). Fusion of Generative AI and Blockchain: Conceptual Framework. In: Fusion of Multimodal Generative AI and Blockchain Technology in Digital Media. IGI Global Scientific Publishing. p. 57-86.

Nguyen, T., & Hoang, D. (2024). A human-in-the-loop framework for GenAI in ETL optimization. *Information Systems*, *122*, 102200.

Raj, R., & Sharma, P. (2023). AIethics in generative data engineering: Bias, fairness, and transparency. *AI and Ethics*, *3*(2), 255–272.

Rajkumar, N., Viji, C., Nachiappan, B., Mohanraj, A., Nagarajan, G., Ravi, J., Prabhu, S.B. (2026a). Generative AI in Virtual Media Image, Video, and Animation Generation. In: Fusion of Multimodal Generative AI and Blockchain Technology in Digital Media. IGI Global Scientific Publishing. p. 209-230.

Rajkumar N., Viji C., Nachiappan B., Nagarajan G., Mohanraj A., Kovilpillai, J.A., Prabhu, S.B. (2026b). Generative AI in Text and Language Processing for Digital Media. In: Generative AI Applications and Intelligent Systems: From Chatbots to Cybersecurity. IGI Global Scientific Publishing. p. 1-26.

Sun, Z., Wu, L., & Yang, X. (2023). Multimodal data engineering using transformer-based generative models. *Knowledge-Based Systems*, *278*, 110997.

Wang, Y., Zhou, F., & Li, K. (2024). Real-time anomaly detection in data pipelines using generative AI. *IEEE Internet of Things Journal*, *11*(4), 6772–6784.

Chapter 4
Generative Adversarial Networks in Feature Engineering:
An Unsupervised Approach

Rohini Vijay Tarade
https://orcid.org/0009-0002-4682-0250
Ajeenkya D.Y. Patil University, India

Sneha Ashish Shirke
Ajeenkya D.Y. Patil University, India

Pooja Dehankar
Ajeenkya D.Y. Patil School of Engineering, India

Susanta Das
https://orcid.org/0000-0002-9314-3988
Ajeenkya D.Y. Patil University, India

ABSTRACT

The process of collecting & choosing features from unprocessed data is made much easier in ML because of the breakthrough work of GANs. GANs are ideal for unsupervised feature engineering as they are composed of a generator & discriminator that participate in adversarial training. This allows the discovery of hidden patterns without the need for predetermined labels. GANs improve datasets & strengthen models by boosting diversity & decreasing overfitting. They help to reduce dimensionality, which reduces computational expenses & simplifies model complexity. GANs increase model accuracy in many domains (computer vision, NLP, healthcare, etc). However, some obstacles are there (challenging training,

DOI: 10.4018/979-8-3373-5616-7.ch004

problems with synthetic data quality, expensive computing, & moral dilemmas). It is imperative to make advancements in training procedures, integrate them with other ML paradigms & establish ethical norms for the usage of synthetic data. This chapter aims to review GANs in unsupervised feature engineering, examining their theoretical underpinnings, real-world applications, & prospects.

INTRODUCTION

Generative Adversarial Networks (GANs) have transformed the labour-intensive process of feature extraction from raw data, known as feature engineering in machine learning. GANs, first presented by Ian Goodfellow in 2014, uncover latent patterns without labels through adversarial training with a generator and discriminator. This chapter examines how GANs enhance unsupervised feature engineering, particularly in situations when obtaining labelled data is expensive or challenging (Spyridon & Boutalis, 2018).

The process of turning raw data into features that work with machine learning models is called feature engineering. To put it another way, it's the process of identifying, removing, and modifying the most pertinent features from the accessible data to create machine learning models that are more precise and effective (Zheng & Casari, 2018).

In order to convert unstructured data into useful inputs for machine learning models, feature engineering is essential, as seen in Figure 1.

Figure 1. Feature engineering

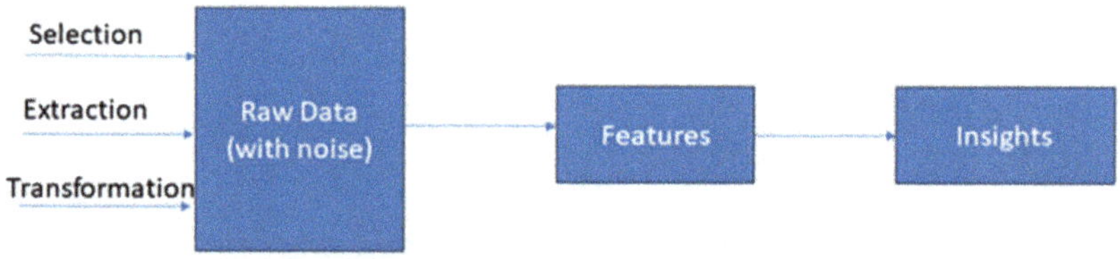

Synthetic data can be created which mimics basic patterns to change current features through scaling and normalization, change current and impute missing values and find new features. GANs also aid in dimensionality reduction, which lowers computing expenses and simplifies model complexity (Lu et al., 2023).

GANs are used in computer vision to produce synthetic images to improve model resilience and training datasets. They create synthetic images in medical imaging to enhance diagnostic models. GANs improve text corpora for NLP, resulting in better translation, sentiment analysis, and text generation. GANs are used in financial modelling to help predictive models by simulating market scenarios and producing synthetic data for stress testing. Through the enhancement of clinical databases, GANs in healthcare produce synthetic patient records that improve models for disease prognosis and treatment effectiveness (Radford et al., 2015).

In feature engineering, GANs have a number of obstacles despite their potential. Because GANs are adversarial, training them is challenging and requires careful hyperparameter tuning for steady convergence. Synthetic data quality is important since poor data can cause the model to perform less well. GAN training takes a lot of time and money in terms of computation. Furthermore, the development and use of synthetic data raises ethical and privacy issues. Strict ethical standards are required to guarantee responsible decision-making, stop data misuse, and protect privacy (Figueira & Vaz, 2022).

These problems need to be fixed if GANs are to be utilised extensively in feature engineering. Potential paths of inquiry include advances in training techniques, such as more robust and scalable GAN architectures that can improve reliability and performance. Integrating GANs with other machine learning paradigms, including semi-supervised learning or reinforcement learning, may increase their effectiveness in a range of applications. Establishing moral standards and best practices for the proper use of synthetic data is essential to minimising risks and ensuring the ethical deployment of GANs (Salimans et al., 2016).

Some of the applications of Generative Adversarial Networks are shown in following Figure 2.

Figure 2. Applications of Generative Adversarial Networks

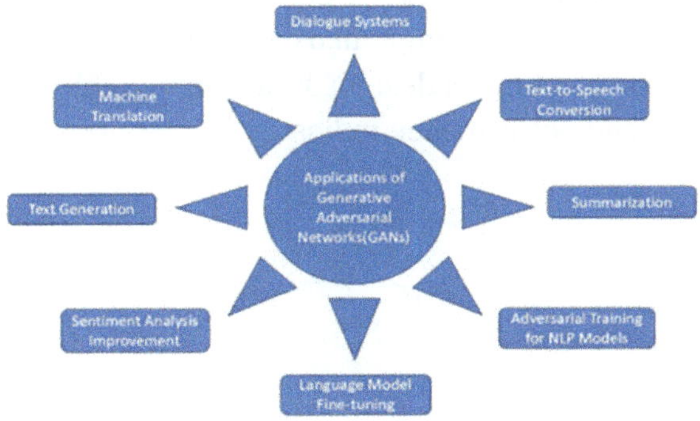

GANs can be applied to unsupervised feature engineering in ways beyond traditional applications. For instance, in the field of autonomous systems, GANs can generate synthetic sensor data to improve and fortify the robustness of self-driving automobiles. In environmental monitoring, GANs can generate synthetic climate data to enhance studies on climate change and weather forecasting predictive models. Robotics, security, and entertainment are just a few of the many fields where GANs' remarkable ability to simulate complex distributions and generate reliable data is evident. Through GANs, industries that create movies, video games and virtual reality could produce scenes and characters that look very realistic (Lu et al., 2022).

Further achievements in GANS will probably make them essential for the modern machine learning field. Automating feature engineering using GANs makes it possible to build more advanced models that accurately and efficiently deal with tough issues. Thanks to being unsupervised, GANs are greatly useful when data is plentiful but properly labelled data is scarce and hard to obtain. By Generative Adversarial Networks (GANs) offer academics and professionals an inventive method to perform data analysis and make models, inspiring creativity in many industries (Zheng & Casari, 2018).

With the use of GANs in robotics to provide synthetic data that replicates various environments and scenarios, robots can learn and adapt without requiring a great deal of real-world testing. This can significantly reduce the time and cost associated with developing and deploying robotic systems. In the security industry, GANs can generate synthetic data for cybersecurity system testing and training, helping to identify vulnerabilities and bolster defences against cyberattacks. (Lu et al., 2022).

The objective of this chapter is to present a thorough analysis of GANs' function in unsupervised feature engineering, emphasising their theoretical underpinnings, real-world uses, and future potential. It will also give more knowledge of how GANs may automate and improve feature engineering, promoting creativity and excellence in machine learning, by examining comprehensive examples and case studies. This chapter aims to add to the expanding body of knowledge on GANs and their use in feature engineering by offering a comprehensive and perceptive.

A comparison of different GAN designs is shown in Table 1 according to their salient characteristics and performance indicators.

Table 1. Comparison of various GAN Architectures

GAN Variant	Key Feature	Primary Use Case	Strengths	Challenges
Vanilla GAN	Simple GAN architecture featuring a discriminator and a generator	General generative modelling (e.g., generating simple images)	Basic architecture, laying the groundwork for more GAN variations	Prone to mode collapse and unsteady training
Cycle GAN	Introduces cycle consistency loss for translation across unpaired images.	Image-to-image translation (e.g., photo to painting)	Versatile for cross-domain operations and capable of operating without paired data	May result in artefacts during intricate changes.
DCGAN (Deep Convolutional GAN)	Convolutional layers are used in the discriminator and generator.	Image generation (especially for low-resolution images)	High-quality images are produced with greater stability than Vanilla GAN.	Requires more data, prone to mode collapse
Big GAN	Uses more data and a significantly bigger model to produce high-resolution images.	large-scale image creation (ImageNet, for example)	produces large-scale, high-resolution, photorealistic photographs	Needs a lot of processing power and big datasets.
WGAN (Wasserstein GAN)	Employs a critic rather than a discriminator and the Wasserstein distance.	Increased training stability and generative modelling	less prone to mode collapse and more stable than Vanilla GAN	Need gradient penalty (WGAN-GP) or weight clipping for stability.
Style GAN & Style GAN2	Employs an innovative technique to manage visual styles at various granularities.	High-quality, photorealistic image generation (especially faces)	Modern image quality and improved command over created characteristics	Computationally costly, requiring substantial resources

1. SYNTHETIC DATA

Artificially generated data that is intended to mimic the statistical characteristics and organisational structure of real-world data is referred to as synthetic data. It is made without utilising actual occurrences by simulating real-world settings utilising a variety of algorithms and methodologies. Data testing and validation, privacy protection, machine learning, and other related industries are using more and more of this kind of data. Because synthetic data removes the need to access sensitive real-world data directly, it is beneficial for protecting individual privacy (Bellovin & Miller, 2019). Emam et al. (2020) assert that this method not only facilitates compliance with data protection rules such as GDPR and HIPAA, but it also allows organisations to communicate data more freely without jeopardising privacy.

Furthermore, artificial data is frequently employed to supplement datasets in machine learning applications, particularly in situations when obtaining real data is difficult or costly. Large, varied training datasets can be produced with it, which can enhance model performance (Emam & Mosquera, 2021). Synthetic data is used in the healthcare industry to improve clinical datasets for research, protecting patient privacy while yet offering valuable information for analysis (Chen et al., 2021). Additionally, artificial intelligence is used to test and validate systems and algorithms across a range of domains, guaranteeing reliable performance in a variety of scenarios (Quinlan et al., 2018). All things considered, synthetic data is essential to contemporary data science and artificial intelligence since it offers a workable and moral response to privacy and data scarcity issues. Table 2 lists some techniques for creating synthetic data.

Table 2. Synthetic data generation methods

Sr. No.	Reference	Methods Used
1	(Ciro et al., 2022)	Variational autoencoder framework, Graph neural networks
2	(Sakib et al., 2022)	Decision-tree based methods, Various choices of imputation parameters
3	(Krishna et al., 2023)	CT-VAE approach using Combinatorial Testing and Variational Autoencoder, VAE to learn the distribution of real-world data and encode it in a latent space
4	(Akahori et al., 2020)	Acquiring reference time length, sampling time interval, frequency fluctuation rate, Calculating rotation angle, synthesizing values, generating synthetic wave data pieces
5	(Yazeed et al., 2022)	Synthetic data generation using 3D rendering software (Blender and Unity), Validation of models with a subset of real labelled images
6	(Sergey et al., 2022)	Use of real and synthetic data for training neural network models, Development of an intelligent information system and software for synthetic image generation
7	(Kevin et al., 2022)	UniformGAN with a novel uniform loss function, Modified DCGAN architecture with SeLU activation functions
8	(Dom, 2021)	Synthetic embedding-based data generation (SEDG), Comparison with deep generative models and traditional sampling methods
9	(Kaushik, 2023)	Genetic search algorithm for synthetic data generation, Under sampling, oversampling, and SMOTE techniques were proposed earlier
10	(Natsuki, 2020)	Orthogonal transformation (linear method), Sandglass-type neural networks (nonlinear method)

continued on following page

Table 2. Continued

Sr. No.	Reference	Methods Used
11	(Sanket et al., 2021)	Generative Adversarial Networks (GANs), Probabilistic model with copula theory and normalising flows
12	(Hyunwoo et al., 2023)	Synthpop, Variational Autoencoder, Generative Adversarial Network used for data generation, Evaluated exposure risk and utility metrics for comparison.
13	(Truong & Goodsitt, 2020)	Categorize consumer data based on characteristics, Generate synthetic dataset using data model and machine-learning system
14	(Adam, 2021)	Sinusoidal components for shafts, blades, gearboxes, Decaying pulses for rolling-element bearings, jitter modeling under load
15	(Jaaskelainen et al. 2021)	Data synthesis model generated and trained using downhole sensor data and input variable data for an electric frac pump, Well AI system uses generated synthetic data value, sensor data, and respective electric frac pump control values.

To improve the quality of data generation, adversarial training uses a dynamic feedback loop between the discriminator and generator, as seen in Figure 3.

Figure 3. Diagram to depict process of adversarial training

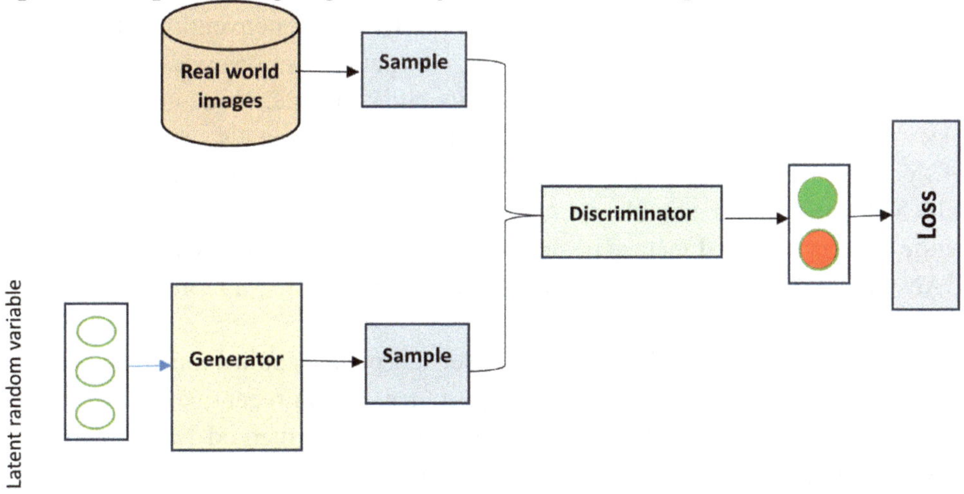

2. RELATED WORK

According to Suryawati et al. (2021), conventional methods in deep learning-based object categorization mostly depend on supervised learning, which requires large amounts of training data. The need to reduce reliance on data has sparked interest in unsupervised learning techniques. A viable substitute is provided by unsupervised deep learning, which allows features to be automatically extracted from data. Such techniques include autoencoders and Generative Adversarial Networks (GANs), albeit random initialization of GANs might lead to unpredictable feature learning. An Encoder-Deep Convolutional Generative Adversarial Network (EGAN) hybrid architecture is presented to tackle this problem. To stabilise feature learning, EGAN incorporates an encoder onto the generator of the GAN. Two Deep Convolutional Neural Networks (DCNNs), AlexNet and DenseNet, use the features from EGAN for classification tasks. Tests on three datasets, including the MNIST dataset, show that EGAN performs better in feature learning than both GANs and conventional autoencoders, yielding better classification results. The study also finds that adding layers to an encoder does not always improve performance and could even make it worse. The results emphasise the necessity of choosing the best epoch for layered training and the unpredictability in GAN learning outcomes caused by random noise inputs. In order to improve the effectiveness of the suggested approach, future study will examine the resilience of EGAN in more detail as well as encoder variations, data preprocessing, and data augmentation strategies.

Zhang et al. (2018), stated that as hyperspectral imaging (HSI) data is high-dimensional, feature extraction (FE) is crucial. However, conventional techniques frequently fail to capture complex spectral and spatial relationships.

Test results demonstrate Training stability and convergence are improved by replacing the Jensen-Shannon divergence with the Wasserstein distance. The efficacy of this method is confirmed by experimental findings on three real HSI datasets, which demonstrate a notable decrease in the requirement for labelled samples while preserving good feature quality. Subsequent investigations seek to enhance GAN architectures and automate network design even more for more extensive HSI applications.

According to Wei et al. (2020), in remote sensing picture applications, unsupervised representation learning has grown in importance, and in recent years, Generative Adversarial Networks (GANs) have become a well-known method. Numerous GAN-based techniques are popular, but their practical use is hampered by inadequate data augmentation. In response, this work presents Multi-Layer Feature Fusion Wasserstein GANs (MF-WGANs), an improved unsupervised representation learning model created to enhance the extraction of feature information from unlabelled remote sensing photos for scene categorization. A multi-feature fusion layer is incorporated into the proposed model after the discriminator in order to efficiently gather high-level and mid-level feature information. Furthermore, the model combines the loss from this fusion layer with WGAN-GP in an effort to generate 256×256 pixel resolution remote sensing images that are more stable and of superior quality. A Multi-Layer

Perceptron (MLP) classifier is used to classify the extracted features. It is tested on several datasets, such as UC Merced Land-Use, AID, and NWPU-RESISC45. According to experimental results, MF-WGANs provide better data augmentation and classification performance than current unsupervised representation learning models such MARTA GANs. The architecture of the model additionally uses max pooling operations to create a multi-feature layer from the last three layers of the discriminator, and it incorporates a gradient penalty term to optimise the loss function of GANs. This multi-feature layer feeds input to the generator, improving its capacity to generate realistic samples, in addition to providing essential feature information for categorization. As a result, MF-WGANs outperform other techniques in terms of data augmentation and classification performance while requiring fewer parameters and less pre-training time.

Dai et al. (2020), have told that due to a lack of aberrant samples, traditional AI algorithms encounter difficulties in machinery prognostics and health management (PHM) in manufacturing. This paper presents a hybrid generative adversarial network (GAN) model that combines autoencoders (AE) with conventional GANs to enable unsupervised feature learning. The data distribution of normal samples is well-represented by the model in both latent areas and signal spectrum. Operationally, there are three steps involved: using dissimilarity in the latent space as a discriminative feature, testing the GAN on samples with unknown health problems, and training it on normal data. Its effectiveness in fault propagation characterization and anomaly identification outperforms traditional methods, as demonstrated by experimental validation on three machines. Interestingly, the technique, which was trained just on typical samples, shows adaptability to different mechanical parts. Its only dependence on frequency-domain data, however, might make fault evolution descriptions more constrained. Subsequent investigations will incorporate time-domain data and expand the applicability of the technology to increasingly complex systems, maybe on real-world platforms such as PLCs or microcontrollers.

Xu et al. (2023), in their work has stated that unsupervised learning has made great progress recently, especially since Generative Adversarial Networks (GANs) have become a prominent paradigm. Their paper explores the complex workings of GANs and reveals that they can linearly separable encode semantics in feature maps. Building on this realisation, the researchers suggest KLiSH, a cutting-edge clustering technique created to take use of the natural linear separability of GAN features. By means of comprehensive testing on a wide range of datasets containing different objects, such as vehicles, portraits, and animals, KLiSH exhibits its ability to extract granular semantics. This innovation makes it possible to sample images along with their segmentation masks, which in turn makes it easier to create paired image-segmentation datasets. Two important downstream applications—unsupervised semantic segmentation and semantic-conditional picture synthesis—are made possible by these synthesised datasets, which are made viable by KLiSH and don't require human annotations. KLiSH improves our knowledge of GANs and suggests that they may be used for more than just representation learning in the real world of artificial intelligence by outperforming conventional clustering techniques.

According to Bengio et al. (2014), data representation has a significant impact on the performance of machine learning algorithms because different representations can expose or variably entangle the underlying explanatory elements of variation in the data. Although the design of these representations has typically been influenced by domain expertise, the discipline is increasingly turning to learning-based approaches to improve the effectiveness of AI systems. It is this change that has prompted the creation of complex representation-learning algorithms. With an emphasis on probabilistic models, manifold learning, and deep learning techniques, recent work emphasises notable advances in unsupervised feature learning and deep learning. These developments raise a number of long-term research problems concerning the objectives of learning efficient representations, the procedures involved in calculating these representations (inference), and the geometric connections among density estimation, manifold learning, and representation learning.

Nargesian et al. (2017) stated that feature engineering modifies a dataset's feature space to improve predictive modelling. Conventional automated approaches are computationally costly; they grow datasets with all available characteristics and then pick them, or they explore altered feature spaces. For classification challenges, a unique technique known as Learning Feature Engineering (LFE) has been created to address this. Rather than requiring a thorough examination of the model or the addition of features, LFE leverages its knowledge of previous feature engineering experiences to suggest practical modifications for new datasets.

LFE predicts modifications that will enhance classification performance by using neural networks that have been trained on a variety of datasets. The method presents the Quantile Sketch Array (QSA), a feature representation that condenses variable-sized features into a fixed-size array while maintaining important qualities. Based on empirical findings, LFE performs better than conventional techniques on 89% of studied datasets and has far lower computational costs.In the future, LFE will be improved by including exploration-based techniques, introducing more transformations, and creating an iterative version. Recurrent neural networks (RNNs) will also be used to manage different dataset sizes and inter-feature interactions, which will improve transformation recommendations even further.

Yu et al. (2017) discussed variations in clothes, carrying conditions, and view angle can provide problems to the detection of gait. To address these, generative adversarial networks (GANs)-based GaitGAN generates invariant gait photos (i.e., side-view images without bags and with typical attire) without requiring prior knowledge of these differences. Two discriminators are used by GaitGAN: one to guarantee visual realism and another to maintain identify information. Evidence from testing proves that GaitGAN is successful, as it is the first technique of its kind to perform so well. GaitGAN overcomes differences in a person's viewpoint, clothing and what they are holding with the help of its derivative, PixelDTGAN. It can modify gait images and keep high performance which was confirmed while using the CASIA-B database, making it useful for video surveillance. After that, I will continue working on using bigger databases, advanced networks and looking for new methods to extract features.

Kamalov et al. (2022), discussed in their research that crucial area of study in data science and machine learning is feature selection. In this research, a set of artificial datasets intended to serve as standards for assessing feature selection methods is presented. These datasets, which are based on actual electronics scenarios, provide fine-grained control over data parameters and guarantee a thorough evaluation of feature selection techniques. A single dataset was utilised to test multiple widely-used methods, demonstrating their usefulness. The datasets are on GitHub for public use, which promotes benchmarking standardization. The primary advantage of synthetic datasets is the established relevance of the features and the programmable data parameters that allow for in-depth analysis. These datasets are available for use by researchers, with associated code permitting parameter tweaks; initially, it is advised to utilise the default settings for consistency. Future additions could improve the breadth and usefulness of the benchmark collection by include synthetic datasets from other domains, such as gene data used in medical research and regression problems using continuous features.

Bulmer et al. (2022) in their study discussed that the constraints of real-world data are drawing attention from statisticians and educators in the use of synthetic data, even with the ubiquity of "big data." It can be difficult to find real-world datasets that satisfy educational requirements. If synthetic data is realistic, supports learning objectives, and is sufficiently rich to enable thorough learning, it presents a competitive substitute. In order to guarantee relevance, realism, and depth, this study presents criteria for creating synthetic datasets. These rules are essential for categorising already-existing data as well as creating new synthetic data to satisfy educational requirements. These factors are prioritised differently by different stakeholders, including the industry, students, and instructors. The industry frequently seeks graduates who can solve a wide range of challenges and values richness. Because they want to deal with issues that arise in the real world, students might emphasise realism. Relevance is usually given top priority by instructors, who make sure that graduates have the abilities listed in their learning objectives. Furthermore, accessibility is an important factor that needs to be weighed against richness, realism, and relevance. In conclusion, synthetic data can be customised to serve a variety of statistical education objectives, as long as it complies with the established principles, even though no single dataset can satisfy everyone's expectations.

Kokosi and Harron (2022), stated that medical research could benefit from synthetic data while depending less on personal data. Although synthetic data approaches have been around for more than 30 years, Theodora Kokosi and Katie Harron explained that their use in medical and health research is still limited due to a number of problems. Whether synthetic data can ever completely replace genuine data for decision-making is a big question. Although the dangers of disclosure are reduced by synthetic datasets, ensuring privacy becomes more difficult when unique observations resulting from rare diseases or outliers are included. It is difficult to estimate high-dimensional distributions accurately without reproducing individual data. Furthermore, more investigation is required to assess the cost-effectiveness of creating synthetic data and determine whether the advantages outweigh the time and effort needed to create data that are appropriate for the intended use.

Van Breugel et al. (2023), discussed that in the machine learning (ML) field, generative models are being used more and more to generate synthetic data since they can provide customised datasets. But synthetic data is frequently flawed, which can lead to mistakes in jobs that come after. This work explores the effects of the generative process on machine learning tasks and finds that treating synthetic data as real-world data results in models that perform poorly when applied to real-world data. The Deep Generative Ensemble (DGE) framework is suggested as a solution to issue. Motivated by Deep Ensembles, DGE seeks to improve model training, evaluation, and uncertainty quantification by approximating the posterior distribution of generative process model parameters. When it comes to minority classes and low-density data regions where generative uncertainty is highest, DGE performs noticeably better than the naive technique

3. WHAT ARE SOME POTENTIAL FUTURE WORKS IN THE FIELD OF GAN RESEARCH?

Some potential future works in the field of Generative Adversarial Network (GAN) research include addressing the limitations of GAN architecture, such as the development of high-quality generative models. This involves breakthroughs in theoretical aspects to tackle issues like difficulties in training, non-union, and model breakdown. Additionally, future improvements may involve incorporating new theories and research outcomes in machine learning models, such as attention mechanisms for capturing global features and policy gradient procedures in reinforcement learning to overcome weaknesses in dealing with discrete variables. Furthermore, advancements in GAN research may focus on stabilizing the training and generation of large, high-quality images, as well as exploring the incorporation of GANs in different conditions to increase the scope of their application. Overall, future works in GAN research aim to address existing challenges and expand the capabilities and applications of GANs in various domains (Lim et al., 2024).

In the research article "Unsupervised Generative Adversarial Network with Background Enhancement and Irredundant Pooling for Hyperspectral Anomaly Detection," the authors propose a novel model, BEGAIP, for hyperspectral anomaly detection (HAD). The study addresses the limitations of existing generative adversarial network (GAN)-based methods by introducing background spatial feature enhancement and irredundant pooling to improve the background generation ability and address the disturbance caused by redundant information in hyperspectral images (HSI). The proposed model combines spatial and spectral features to enhance the detection of anomalies in HSI. The study compares BEGAIP with several classical algorithms and demonstrates its superior performance in detecting anomalies in various HSI datasets, as evidenced by the higher area under the curve (AUC) values (Li et al., 2022).

In the document "Generative Adversarial Networks (GANs): Challenges, Solutions, and Future Directions," Divya Saxena and Jiannong Cao from The Hong Kong Polytechnic University present a comprehensive survey of the advancements in GANs design and optimization solutions proposed to handle GANs challenges. The authors identify major challenges in GANs training, including mode collapse, non-convergence, and instability, and propose a new taxonomy to structure solutions by key research issues.

4. WHAT ARE THE CHALLENGES IN PERSON RE-IDENTIFICATION AND HOW ARE GANS BEING USED TO ADDRESS THEM?

The challenges in person re-identification include various human poses, domain differences, and occlusions, which make it a complex task. To address these challenges, Generative Adversarial Networks (GANs) have been utilized in several ways. One approach involves using GANs to handle the issue of occlusion and low resolution of pedestrian attributes. For instance, Fabbri et al. proposed a model that uses deep generative models (DCGAN) to reconstruct and super-resolve images, addressing the problem of occlusion and low resolution. Additionally, Fulgeri et al. integrated neural network architectures, U-nets and GANs, to de-occlude people shapes, optimizing a loss function to generate images without occlusion, similar at the pixel level to a completely visible people shape, and conserving similar visual attributes of the original one. Overall, GANs have been employed to address challenges in person re-identification by handling issues such as occlusion, low resolution, and pose variation, demonstrating their effectiveness in improving the performance of re-identification models (Saxena & Cao, 2020).

5. CASE STUDY

The research addresses the challenges of automated myocardium segmentation in late gadolinium enhancement cardiac magnetic resonance (LGE CMR) images and offers a comprehensive analysis of the proposed framework's performance, comparing it with state-of-the-art segmentation methods. The study focuses on the significance of LGE CMR in diagnosing cardiac diseases, particularly in identifying and characterizing scar tissue within the heart muscle, and emphasizes the need for automated CMR interpretation to improve patient outcomes. The proposed framework incorporates self-supervised attention generative models and aims to address the intensity heterogeneity, complex enhancement patterns, and overlapping intensity ranges in LGE CMR images. It leverages novel segmentation architecture and transformer-based approaches to improve the accuracy and reliability of cardiac quantification, particularly in scar tissue segmentation.

The research conducts experiment on four different LGE datasets, namely, MYOSAIQ, MS-CMRSeg 2019, MyoPS, and EMIDEC, and presents an in-depth comparative analysis of the proposed framework's performance with and without style transfer, as well as state-of-the-art models. The results indicate that the proposed framework with style transfer demonstrates superior performance in terms of overall Dice and Hausdorff distances compared to state-of-the-art models across the different datasets.

The study's findings demonstrate the potential of the proposed framework, particularly with style transfer, in addressing the challenges of automated myocardium segmentation and improving the accuracy and efficiency of diagnosing and managing heart conditions in clinical practice (Abdul Qayyum & Steven A Niederer, 2024).

Finally, it gives innovative way to scar tissue segmentation in LGE CMR images, and giving comprehensive study of the work compared to state-of-the-art model.

6. ETHICAL FRAMEWORKS

Table 3 and Table 4 show the ethical frameworks and ethical violations, respectively.

Table 3. Ethical Frameworks

Section	Category	Description / Principle	Application / Example	Reference(s)
6.1 Typical Ethical Structures	6.1.1 Deontology	Focus on rules, duties, or obligations, regardless of outcomes.	Ensures actions align with legal or moral standards.	Zheng & Casari (2018); Saxena & Cao (2020)
	6.1.2 Utilitarianism	Maximize overall happiness or minimize harm for the greatest number.	Guides optimal decisions using cost-benefit analysis.	Bellovin & Miller (2019); Sakib et al. (2022)
	6.1.3 Virtue Ethics	Focuses on character and virtues of the decision-maker, not just actions or results.	Encourages moral traits like integrity, courage, and compassion.	Kevin et al. (2022); El Emam & Mosquera (2021)
	6.1.4 Care Ethics	Emphasizes empathy, care, and interpersonal relationships in decision-making.	Highly relevant in healthcare and social work.	Wu, Stouffs, & Biljecki (2022); Lu et al. (2023)
	6.1.5 Social Contract Theory	Decisions should align with community agreements that promote harmony and cooperation.	Applied in governance and social welfare contexts.	Kokosi & Harron (2022); Lin et al. (2017)

Table 4. Ethical Violations

6.2 Actual Instances of Misuse	**6.2.1 Cambridge Analytica (2018)**	**Unauthorized harvesting of Facebook user data for political purposes.**	**Violated informed consent; breach of deontological ethics.**	**Radford et al. (2015); Bellovin & Miller (2019)**
	6.2.2 Volkswagen Emissions (2015)	Installed defeat devices to falsify emissions test results.	Prioritized profit over environmental welfare; failed utilitarian principles.	Sakib et al. (2022); Saxena & Cao (2020)
	6.2.3 AI Bias in Hiring	Discriminatory AI decisions in recruitment against certain groups.	Contradicts virtue ethics; lacks fairness and inclusiveness.	Kevin et al. (2022); El Emam & Mosquera (2021)
6.3 Strategies for Mitigation	6.3.1 Transparent Policies	Clearly communicate ethical standards and decision-making processes.	Example: Tech firms publishing clear privacy policies.	Zheng & Casari (2018); Lin et al. (2017)
	6.3.2 Regular Audits & Accountability	Establish oversight committees and conduct periodic reviews.	Example: Independent audits to ensure algorithmic fairness.	Bellovin & Miller (2019); Radford et al. (2015)

continued on following page

Table 4. Continued

6.2 Actual Instances of Misuse	**6.2.1 Cambridge Analytica (2018)**	**Unauthorized harvesting of Facebook user data for political purposes.**	**Violated informed consent; breach of deontological ethics.**	**Radford et al. (2015); Bellovin & Miller (2019)**
	6.3.3 Ethics Education & Training	Train staff and stakeholders in ethical principles and practices.	Example: Mandatory ethics modules in universities and companies.	Saxena & Cao (2020); El Emam & Mosquera (2021)
	6.3.4 Inclusive Decision-Making	Engage diverse stakeholders to reflect multiple perspectives.	Example: Community consultations in urban planning.	Kokosi & Harron (2022); Wu, Stouffs, & Biljecki (2022)
	6.3.5 Whistleblower Protection	Encourage ethical reporting by protecting informants.	Example: Legal protection for employees reporting misconduct.	Sakib et al. (2022); Kevin et al. (2022)
	6.3.6 Proactive Risk Assessment	Identify and address ethical risks before deployment.	Example: Pre-launch ethical evaluations of new technologies.	Lu et al. (2023); Zheng & Casari (2018)

CONCLUSION

A thorough overview of Generative Adversarial Networks (GANs) and their use in unsupervised feature engineering has been given in this chapter. After studying the main theories and their uses, we have highlighted how advanced GANs are expected to simplify obtaining features and boosting performance of machine learning models. The ability of GANs to make artificial data, find patterns and lessen overfitting matters for computer vision as well as healthcare. Although there are some encouraging achievements, a number of problems remain to be handled. Examples are how complicated it is to teach GANs, the quality of generated data and moral problems. For this the field can only get better if the problems are handled with greater the creation of training protocols, their integration with other machine learning approaches and the development of moral standards. In the future, researchers ought to focus on making GAN structures better and studying new apps, methods and strategies to guarantee that the data produced is reliable. We can open up new avenues for creativity in a variety of fields by improving our knowledge of and use for GANs.

In conclusion, GANs are an important advancement in machine learning that provide strong instruments for unsupervised feature engineering. The significance of continuous research and cooperation in maximising the potential of GANs for technological advancement and bettering real-world outcomes is emphasised in this chapter.

REFERENCES

Chen, R. J., Lu, M. Y., Chen, T. Y., Williamson, D. F. K., & Mahmood, F. (2021). Synthetic data in machine learning for medicine and healthcare. *Nature Biomedical Engineering*, *5*(6), 493–497. DOI: 10.1038/s41551-021-00751-8 PMID: 34131324

Dai, J., Wang, J., Huang, W., Shi, J., & Zhu, Z. (2020). Machinery health monitoring based on unsupervised feature learning via generative adversarial networks. *IEEE/ASME Transactions on Mechatronics*, *25*(5), 2252–2263. DOI: 10.1109/tmech.2020.3012179

Figueira, A., & Vaz, B. (2022). Survey on synthetic data generation, evaluation methods and GANs. *Mathematics*, *10*(15), 2733. DOI: 10.3390/math10152733

Kamalov, F., Sulieman, H., & Cherukuri, A. K. (2022). Synthetic data for feature selection. *arXiv (Cornell University)*. https://doi.org//arxiv.2211.03035DOI: 10.48550

Kokosi, T., & Harron, K. (2022). Synthetic data in medical research. *BMJ Medicine*, *1*(1), e000167. DOI: 10.1136/bmjmed-2022-000167 PMID: 36936569

Li, Z., Shi, S., Wang, L., Xu, M., & Li, L. (2022). Unsupervised Generative Adversarial Network with Background Enhancement and Irredundant Pooling for Hyperspectral Anomaly Detection. *Remote Sensing*, *14*(5), 1265. DOI: 10.3390/rs14051265

Lim, W., Yong, K. S. C., Lau, B. T., & Tan, C. C. L. (2024). Future of generative adversarial networks (GAN) for anomaly detection in network security: A review. *Computers & Security*, *139*, 103733. DOI: 10.1016/j.cose.2024.103733

Lin, D., Fu, K., Wang, Y., Xu, G., & Sun, X. (2017). MARTA GANS: Unsupervised Representation Learning for Remote Sensing Image Classification. *IEEE Geoscience and Remote Sensing Letters*, *14*(11), 2092–2096. DOI: 10.1109/lgrs.2017.2752750

Lu, Y., Wang, H., & Wei, W. (2023). Machine Learning for Synthetic Data Generation: A review. *arXiv (Cornell University)*. https://doi.org//arxiv.2302.04062DOI: 10.48550

Nargesian, F., Samulowitz, H., Khurana, U., Khalil, E. B., & Turaga, D. (2017). Learning feature engineering for classification. *IJCAI (United States)*, •••, 2529–2535. DOI: 10.24963/ijcai.2017/352

Qayyum, A., Razzak, I., Mazher, M., Lu, X., & Niederer, S. A. (2024). Unsupervised unpaired multiple fusion adaptation aided with self-attention generative adversarial network for scar tissues segmentation framework. *Information Fusion*, *106*, 102226. DOI: 10.1016/j.inffus.2024.102226

Radford, A., Metz, L., & Chintala, S. (2015). Unsupervised Representation Learning with Deep Convolutional Generative Adversarial Networks. *arXiv (Cornell University)*. https://doi.org//arxiv.1511.06434DOI: 10.48550

Salimans, T., Goodfellow, I., Zaremba, W., Cheung, V., Radford, A., & Chen, X. (2016). Improved techniques for training GANs. *arXiv (Cornell University)*. https://doi.org//arxiv.1606.03498DOI: 10.48550

Saxena, D., & Cao, J. (2020). Generative Adversarial Networks (GANS Survey): Challenges, solutions, and future Directions. *arXiv (Cornell University)*. https://doi.org//arxiv.2005.00065DOI: 10.48550

Spyridon, P., & Boutalis, Y. S. (2018). Generative adversarial networks for unsupervised fault detection. *2022 European Control Conference (ECC)*. https://doi.org/DOI: 10.23919/ecc.2018.8550560

Suryawati, E., Pardede, H. F., Zilvan, V., Ramdan, A., Krisnandi, D., Heryana, A., Yuwana, R. S., Kusumo, R. B. S., Arisal, A., & Supianto, A. A. (2021). Unsupervised feature learning-based encoder and adversarial networks. *Journal of Big Data*, *8*(1). Advance online publication. DOI: 10.1186/s40537-021-00508-9

Wei, Y., Luo, X., Hu, L., Peng, Y., & Feng, J. (2020). An improved unsupervised representation learning generative adversarial network for remote sensing image scene classification. *Remote Sensing Letters*, *11*(6), 598–607. DOI: 10.1080/2150704x.2020.1746854

Wu, A. N., Stouffs, R., & Biljecki, F. (2022). Generative Adversarial Networks in the built environment: A comprehensive review of the application of GANs across data types and scales. *Building and Environment*, *223*, 109477. DOI: 10.1016/j.buildenv.2022.109477

Yu, S., Chen, H., Reyes, E. B. G., & Poh, N. (2017). GAITGAN: Invariant GAIT feature extraction using generative adversarial networks. *IEEE*, 532–539. https://doi.org/DOI: 10.1109/cvprw.2017.80

Zhang, M., Gong, M., Mao, Y., Li, J., & Wu, Y. (2018). Unsupervised feature extraction in hyperspectral images based on Wasserstein Generative adversarial network. *IEEE Transactions on Geoscience and Remote Sensing*, *57*(5), 2669–2688. DOI: 10.1109/tgrs.2018.2876123

Zheng, A., & Casari, A. (2018). Feature engineering for machine learning: Principles and techniques for data scientists. *OREILLY April 2018, First Edition*. https://www.oreilly.com/catalog/errata.csp?isbn=9781491953242

ADDITIONAL READING

Booth, A., Reed, A. B., Ponzo, S., Yassaee, A., Aral, M., Plans, D., Labrique, A., & Mohan, D. (2021). Population risk factors for severe disease and mortality in COVID-19: A global systematic review and meta-analysis. *PLoS One*, *16*(3), e0247461. DOI: 10.1371/journal.pone.0247461 PMID: 33661992

Goodfellow, I. J., Pouget-Abadie, J., Mirza, M., Xu, B., Warde-Farley, D., Ozair, S., Courville, A., & Bengio, Y. (2014). Generative adversarial networks. *arXiv (Cornell University)*. https://doi.org//arxiv.1406.2661DOI: 10.48550

Kuhn, M., & Johnson, K. (2019). Feature engineering and selection. In *Chapman and Hall/CRC eBooks*. https://doi.org/DOI: 10.1201/9781315108230

Lewis, M. C., & Lacher, L. (2016). Introduction to Programming and Problem-Solving using Scala. In *Chapman and Hall/CRC eBooks*. https://doi.org/DOI: 10.1201/9781315382609

Patki, N., Wedge, R., & Veeramachaneni, K. (2016). The synthetic data vault. *IEEE*, 399–410. https://doi.org/DOI: 10.1109/dsaa.2016.49

KEY TERMS AND DEFINITIONS

Convolutional Neural Network (CNN): It is a type of artificial neural network used primarily for image recognition and processing.

Encoder-Deep Convolutional Generative Adversarial Network (EGAN): It is is a generative adversarial network architecture. It uses a couple of guidelines, in particular: Replacing any pooling layers with strided convolutions (discriminator) and fractional-strided convolutions (generator).

GAN (Generative Adversarial Networks): A generative adversarial network (GAN) is a machine learning (ML) model in which two neural networks compete with each other by using deep learning methods to become more accurate in their predictions.

General Data Protection Regulation (GDPR): Across the world, the EU general data protection regulation (GDPR) offers the most advanced privacy and security protection. The regulation updated the laws set in place by the 1995 data protection directive.

Hyperspectral Imaging (HSI): It is an emerging imaging modality for medical applications, especially in disease diagnosis and image-guided surgery.

Learning Feature Engineering (LFE): LFE is based on learning the effectiveness of applying a transformation (e.g., arithmetic or aggregate operators) on numerical features, from past feature engineering experiences.

Multi-layer perceptron (MLP): It is a supplement of feed forward neural network. It consists of three types of layers—the input layer, output layer and hidden layer

NLP (Natural Language Processing): It is a subfield of computer science and artificial intelligence (AI) that uses machine learning to enable computers to understand and communicate with human language. **Feature Engineering –** Raw data is transformed into features which are suitable for machine learning models. This process is called as Feature engineering. **Synthetic Data Generation -** Synthetic data generation is the process of creating artificial data that mimics the features, structures, and statistical attributes of production data, while maintaining compliance with data privacy regulations. **Data Augmentation –** In data augmentation New data can be generated from existing data which can be basically used to train new machine learning (ML) models.

Reinforcement Learning (RL): By using this machine learning (ML) technique a software can be trained that trains software which make decisions to achieve the most optimal results.

Recurrent Neural Network (RNN): It is a deep learning model that is trained to process and convert a sequential data input into a specific sequential data output.

The Health Insurance Portability and Accountability Act of 1996 (HIPAA): It is Public Law 104-191, was enacted on August 21, 1996. Sections 261 through 264 of HIPAA require the Secretary of HHS to publicize standards for the electronic exchange, privacy and security of health information.

Two Deep Convolutional Neural Networks (DCNNs): Within Deep Learning, a Convolutional Neural Network or CNN is a type of artificial neural network, which is widely used for image/object recognition and classification.

Chapter 5
GENALYTICS: A Deep Dive Into Real-Time Insights via Generative AI

Monika Dandotiya
https://orcid.org/0000-0002-5501-4210
Poornima University, Jaipur, India

Nikhil Kumar Goyal
https://orcid.org/0009-0007-4532-8033
Poornima University, Jaipur, India

Priyanka Yadav
Swami Keshvanand Institute of Technology, Management, and Gramothan, Jaipur, India

Kriti Sankhla
Poornima University, Jaipur, India

Monika Kumari
https://orcid.org/0000-0002-8468-3552
Poornima University, Jaipur, India

ABSTRACT

With today being an age of hyper-connected systems and real time decision-making, it is no wonder that real time analytics have emerged as the key to organizations looking to draw actionable intelligence out of constantly changing data streams. Lastly, the chapter talks about the issues of implementation, ethical concerns, and legal issues involved with real-time generative systems. Future directions are explained, such as the changes towards federated learning, autonomous analytics, and quantum-assisted generative AI. The chapter will also be a conceptual guide

DOI: 10.4018/979-8-3373-5616-7.ch005

and practical road map to the researcher, practitioners and industry professionals, whether the landscape of intelligent real-time analytics is playing out according to the initial expectations or not.

1. INTRODUCTION

1.1 Background and Motivation

Data in the current hyper connected world has been created in volumes and speeds that have never been witnessed before. Whether they are on social networks or sensor networks in industrial systems, there is no stopping the streams of data that was, is and will always be huge in volume, and usually complex in nature. Analytical techniques that rely on a specific batch-based approach are insufficient when the decisions are required in the real-time environment. This has brought to fore real-time analytics, which is a vital feature to companies that seek to identify patterns, respond to incidents and get insights in real-time. Real-time processing and analysis of data streams is becoming an industry within an industry, whether it be outsourcing financial fraud detection or predictive maintenance (Aggarwal, 2013).

Artificial intelligence has advanced greatly along with this data explosion and especially in the ability to generatively model. Generative AI, which is based on deep learning innovations, has acquired the ability to create new content, find solutions to possible future events, optimize partially complete datasets, and improve poor-quality datasets. GANs or transformers are only a few of the models that have transformed the creative sector but are also taking hold as solutions to more analytical tasks where the results rely on the quality of data, the ability to augment that data, and generate synthesized insight needed to support solutions.

Generative AI and real-time analytics pose an intriguing future of creating intelligent dynamic systems that can respond to emerging events and at the same time produce realistic senses or forecasts. This is the point of contention, and this chapter explains how generative models can be introduced to supplement real-time decision making, make systems more resilient, and introduce high-value applications across several industries (Goodfellow et al., 2014).

1.2 Evolution of Real-Time Analytics

Real-time analytics is a descendent of old decision support systems and online transaction processing applications. Early incarnations of real-time analytics meant reporting close to real-time data within dashboards used in operations. The definition however has expanded enormously with the introduction of big data ecosystem and stream processing architectures. In the present time, real-time analytics includes the possibility to analyze, respond and process data that comes, sometimes even in seconds.

Technology that has brought such an evolution includes distributed computing, in-memory processing, and data streaming systems, including Apache Kafka, Apache Flink, and Spark Streaming. These processes offer the ability to process large applications of streaming data with the computational foundation that allows developers and analysts to create responsive systems that extend well beyond basic pattern monitoring and alerts. Real-time analytics at the edge has also become important: in an area where latency matters and bandwidth restriction does not allow centralized processing (Kingma & Welling, 2014).

Although these technological leaps have overridden the determinism to great extents in the use of analytical intelligence on real-time streams that are deterministic or rule-based to a large degree. Static statistical models and simple machine learning algorithms are frequently limited in the desirable flexibility and the generation potential in a very dynamic setting. This gap leaves the possibility to apply generative AI to the real-time analytics systems to solidify the frontier of reactive to predictive and even prescriptive analytics.

Real-time analytics has come a very long way since its initial days in the decision support systems and online transaction processing. Started as just near-real-time dashboards allowing to see insights of the operations, currently, real-time analytics has evolved into a mature, dynamic field that can analyze, respond, and process streaming data in a matter of seconds. Increment is greatly powered by advances in technology like distributed computing, in-memory processing, and sophisticated data streaming engines, such as Apache Kafka, Apache Flink and Spark Streaming. These technologies have permitted it to work with data flow with huge sizes of incoming data and minimal latency to produce reactive and smart systems. One of these changes is the emergence of edge analytics, in which data is processed near to where it was collected in order to circumvent bandwidth issues and latency, rendering real-time analytics decisive in Internet of Things (IoT) as well as mission-critical applications.

Although these innovations have benefited biotechnology, traditional types of analytical models that mostly emphasize on rule based or static statistical analysis find it difficult to remain relevant in the relatively dynamic environment. They have low levels of flexibility which limit on how to come up with knowledge in the situations where trends change rapidly. As a solution to this shortcoming, the insertion of generative AI in real-time analytics systems is currently proving to be a significant addition. Analytics systems can go beyond the reactive models and become predictive and even prescriptive by exploiting the context-awareness and adaptability of generative models to make the next generation of smart decision-making frameworks that can anticipate and act on what will happen before it does happen.

1.3 The Rise of Generative AI in Data Processing

Generative AI has brought a lot of momentum over the last several years because it produces new data instances which look similar to the existing datasets. First made known in applications in image synthesis, text generation, and artwork, its usefulness has increased into more technical and analytical fields. Generative models are fundamentally based upon the notion that we can learn the underlying distribution of our data, and can subsequently utilize this knowledge to generate a reasonable new example. That makes them priceless in simulation, generation of scenarios, data extension, as well as the imputation of missing data (Vaswani et al., 2017).

Trends in the increased accessibility of massive computing resources and high-quality datasets have increased the speed at which generative models are trained and deployed. Transformers like GPT and diffusion based models have been deployed multiple industries and reached new records in those areas, demonstrating versatility and scale. More to the point, generative AI is not limited to offline or even static data anymore- now it is being configured to work in dynamic and streaming data where time and versatility are the utmost concerns.

The introduction of a generative AI into a real-time analytics would introduce new opportunities, including producing predictive information in the situation of partial information, improving the interpretability of anomaly detection, or simulation of a possible state in order to facilitate proactive decision-making. As companies find themselves with smarter methods to address the imminent data velocity and complexity, generative AI is presenting itself in the analytics sphere as a game changer (Goyal et al., 2025).

2. REAL-TIME ANALYTICS

2.1 Characteristics of Real-Time Analytics

Real-time analytics is the process of inspecting data soon after the data set is gathered to give instant perception and responses. In contrast to typical analytics, which may require retrospective review of pre-existing data, real-time analytics is done on live data feeds (typically with a goal of identifying events, detecting trends, or responding in milliseconds to seconds). This type of analytics can be fundamentally important where timeliness is of the essence, like with algorithmic trading, emergency response systems, or even on intrusion detection in the sphere of cybersecurity.

The most important features of real time analytics are low latency, constant stream of new data and requirement of incremental calculation. These systems are required to pick streaming data, work on it with the minimum of latency, and provide the results or visualization on the spot. Therefore, the real-time analytics architecture demands very optimised data processing pipeline with the ability to scale effectively with the inflow of the data into the architecture as well as the consistency and the accuracy of the data processing.

In order to do this in real-time analytics systems are based on in-memory computing, distributed computing, and complex event processing (CEP) technologies. These elements help the system to prevent the bottlenecks and keep the throughput up. But when full or clean data processing has to be done, often on the need to impose some form of control over incomplete or noisy data streams which are in real time, the problem of maintaining accuracy and generating quality data output seems to linger, and this is where generative AI can be of great help (Zaharia et al., 2010).

2.2 Real-Time vs Batch Processing: A Comparative View

In batch processing, the data are gathered over a time period and stored and processed at some points in time. Such a table is effective when handling massive data like aggregation and the pooling of historical data but not responsive enough when time sensitivity is an aggravating factor in decision-making. Real-time processing is, on the other hand, optimized toward low-latency computation, and thus can provide immediate insights which can be used to correct currently processing events or raise alarms.

Although the batch processing can be applicable to business intelligence and reporting processes, a real-time analytics is vital where there is steady flow of data and requirement of immediate reaction. As an example, the fraud detection systems with end-of-day reports cannot help stop financial loss, but the ones that work in real time are capable of stopping suspicious transactions on the go (Kreps et al., 2011).

Technically, both batch and real-time systems have a greater deal of difference in terms of architecture, storage and computation model. Real-time systems should support volatile data, must do out of order processes, and has tough latency requirements. This requires even more sophisticated processing plans and the introduction of generative AI can assist such plans by filling in the gaps of missing data, estimating subsequent events, and adapting in real-time without re-learning anew as in figure 1.

Figure 1. Real-Time Application Development from Technical Perspective

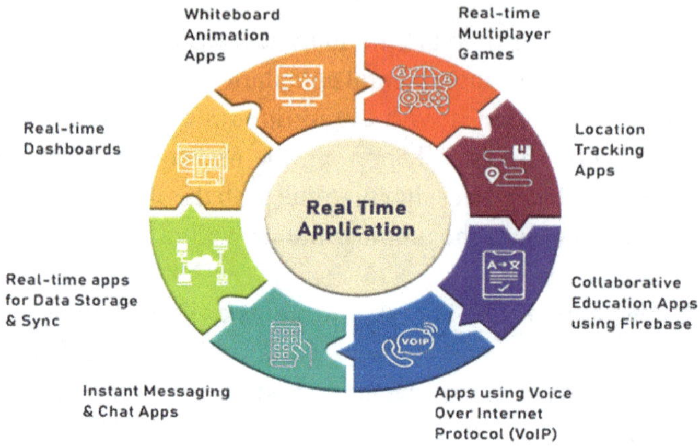

2.3 Data Stream Processing Architectures (Lambda, Kappa, Delta)

The real-time analytics systems today are created on the basis of scalable systems capable of processing and absorbing never-ending streams of data. One of the simplest and the most popular models is the Lambda architecture with its low level, the batch layer (where all the large volume computations are performed), and the high level, the speed layer (where all the real-time processes are calculated). It is quite efficient in delivering accuracy and latency balance, but has been criticized with duplication of its code and complexity in managing two pipelines (Carbone et al., 2015).

The reason behind that is that there was proposed the Kappa architecture that was designed so that instead of having two pipelines of streams to process, both real-time and non-real-time, there is only a single stream processing pipeline. Kappa is not based on a batch layer, but it is entirely stream-oriented, which results in its being more agile and simpler to operate, particularly when immediacy is more important than completeness in an application. It may however falter when it comes to fault tolerance and reprocessing of data in complex situations (Dwork & Roth, 2014).

The newer Delta constellation of architectures tries to solve both with a single source of truth by merging both batch and streaming data by using transactional storage systems like Delta Lake. This will enable time-travelling skills and increased consistency with the possibility of almost real-time performance. Every architecture will face trade-offs, but this is a decision based on the use case and the analytical work to be done

3. EXPLORING GENERATIVE AI: ARCHITECTURES, TECHNIQUES, AND APPLICATIONS

Generative Artificial Intelligence (Generative AI) is a subdiscipline of AI related to training new texts, images, audio, video, code or synthetics, learning on the basis of old data patterns and structures. Generative models differ to traditional AI systems, which are based on a classification or prediction result of input data, in that they are intended to generate results that are novel and authentic. Generative AI has experienced a boom as deep learning and computation powerfulness improve across many sectors including healthcare, education, entertainment, and cybersecurity (Shokri & Shmatikov, 2015).

3.1 Generative Models

Generative models Generalized machine learning algorithms Generative models are machine learning algorithms which can generate new instances of the data, based on learning the structure underlying a set of data. One of the most notable ones is called Generative Adversarial Networks (GANs); this model is comprised of a generator and discriminator operating antagonistically. The generator seeks to generate real-looking data whereas the discriminator, on its part, endeavours to differentiate between real and synthetic data. The two elements enhance with time and this leads to very realistic synthetic results (Goyal, 2025a).

Another important direction is the Variational Autoencoders (VAEs): they also use probabilistic modeling to apply stimulated code to data but decode it into elementary simulations. VAEs perform less well visually that GANs, but are easier to train and can be more useful in representation learning and interpolation of data. More recent innovation are diffusion models which operate by modelling the progressive denoising of data as a random process and have attained state-of-the-art results on image and video generation tasks.

Transformers, that were originally developed to natural language processing, have demonstrated impressive scaling abilities in generative tasks. Such models as GPT and BERT variants may produce coherent text, code and even learn zero-shot. These architectures are currently being translated toward multi-modal generative operations, and therefore form the core of real-time AI applications that must be able to produce different forms of content at real time and contextual degrees and scopes (Chalapathy & Chawla, 2019a).

3.2 Strengths and Limitations

Generative models have quite a number of benefits to recommend them as part of real time analytics. They may be used to generate plausible samples of synthetic data that might resemble the statistical characteristics of the corresponding original data, to enlarge training data sets, to model low-probability occurrences, or to interpolate missing data. In addition, generative models are applicable in prediction, scenario analysis as well as anomaly detection all of these are a critical part of real-time applications.

Yet, there are also significant challenges of generative models. Emblematic of GANs, in general, are the infamously hard-to-train nature of these models including instability and mode collapse. VAEs also tend to generate blurs where GANs shine, and often have a challenge when actual data is of high dimensionality. Transformers, despite their power, are computationally intensive and demand large amounts of memory and inference time that can cause a problem in the latency-sensitive setting (Sutton & Barto, 2018).

The second drawback is the possibility to present wrong or false data, in case models are not properly calibrated. This may cause erroneous decision in real-time systems when generative outputs are blindly trusted. Therefore, to achieve integration of generative models in real-time pipelines, tight validation, interpretability, and safety protocols must be implemented to satisfy reliability and ethical ownership.

Figure 2. Flow-based Deep Generative Models

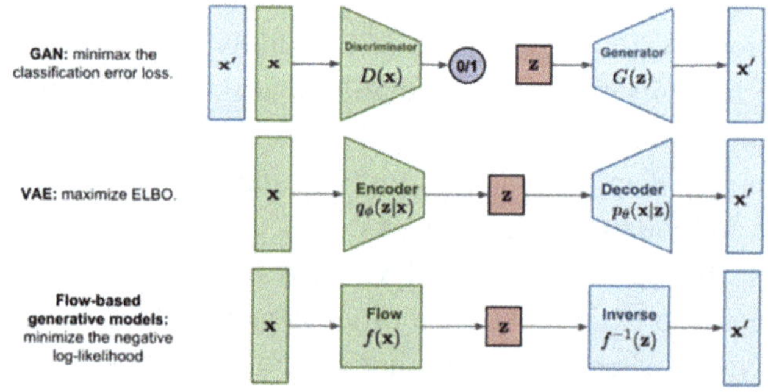

Figure 2 below shows a comparative overview of three widespread architectures of generative models in deep learning; Generative Adversarial Networks (GANs), Variational Autoencoders (VAEs), and Flow-based generative models networks. The process of data transformation and reconstruction in changing architecture is presented in each row.

3.3 Real-Time Capabilities of Generative Architectures

In the past, generative models are trained and in a batch fashion, but modern research has allowed them to be adapted to streaming environments. Generative AI has been applied in the real time context due to lightweight architectures, incremental learning strategies, and deployment frameworks that are compatible with streaming. Online learning, continual learning, edge inference are among the techniques that are opening a path to low-latency generative computation (Li, He, & Wu, 2020).

Generative models provide an opportunity to generate or forecast data paths, and thus, they are suitable when combined with real-time decision systems. But this needs to be formulated with keen engineering practices so as to make the generative procedure quite effective, adaptable, and in coherence with the timing of the information flows being passed through (Silver et al., 2017).

4. INTERSECTION OF REAL-TIME ANALYTICS AND GENERATIVE AI

Real-time analytics is the analysis of data in real-time of when it is being created and allows the immediate analysis and decisions to be made about the data. Generative AI, conversely, is aimed at generating novel content based on learned data patterns, such as GANs, VAEs, Transformers. The meeting point of the two fields is also facilitating smarter, responsive, and strong systems in any industry.

4.1 Synthetic Data Generation for Streaming Pipelines

Possibly, the most promising use of generative AI in real-time analytics is on-demand generation of synthetic data. In most cases, real-time data streams can experience one or more problems like missing values, jittery sampling rates or data sparsity. Generative models, particularly GANs or VAEs, can facilitate filling these gaps by creating credible data points depending on the patterns that were observed in past and current data. This allows systems to have continuity and coherence in its streaming pipelines despite poor or unfinished original data inputs (Goyal et al., 2025a).

In fraud detection systems, as an example, it is hard to model proper models since some of the transactions are generally rare (such as fraudulent transactions). Real-time generative model can be used to provide realistic but fictional examples of fraudulent activities that can enhance the training of classifiers in a manner, which does not affect privacy. In a similar way, in sensor networks with the loss of connectivity or corrupted data, generative models will provide plausible sensor readings that will allow continuous decision-making.

This skill to amplify or fake real time data feeds equips systems toward becoming more resilient and lessvvendable to change or disturbance in the data flow. It can also aid in the continual training on machine learning models being supplied with balanced and diversified data inputs particularly in situations that idealize or minority give inference classes that require augmentation (Deng & Yu, 2014).

4.2 Predictive Insights and Anomaly Detection in Real Time

Generative AI provides a breakthrough benefit to the predictive analytics of the present. Generative models in contrast to the traditional models can simulate the probable future of a system, and this allows preemptive decisions to be made. These models are able to predict future scenarios in various conditions since they learn the implicit form of the data thus being able to estimate the likelihood of different outcomes, which is paramount in ever-changing contexts like supply chain, energy grids, or traffic control.

In detecting anomalies, generative models provide potent models of learning and discovering what will be considered within the norm of the data. Any deviation to this normalcy can be pointed out as a probable norm. Of specific interest is the effectiveness of Autoencoders and VAEs in this respect; data fed into these systems may be reconstructed, and any error in this reconstruction may be used as the anomaly signal during the real-time process. The method has become popular in information security mechanisms such as intrusion detection systems and monitoring the health of systems (Abadi et al., 2016).

4.3 Reinforcement Learning for Real-Time Adaptation

Although not conventionally considered a part of generative AI, reinforcement learning (RL) may be seen as a particular generative mechanism (particularly when applied to decision sequence generation in dynamic settings). RL agents are able to learn to make the best actions via trial-and-error in real-time analytics, interacting with streaming data. Generative models may also enable efficient RL by exploring the environment to simulate to generate future states or to create training episodes to enable the learning process to be more data-efficient and robust.

An example is in automated trading systems where a RL agent can be trained on buying or selling assets in real time market information. The use of a generative model in order to generate market situations will ensure that the agent trains on a wide variety of conditions which makes it more resilient and generalizable. In a different scenario, generative simulation of vehicle movement can be used to train

RL-based control policies in smart traffic systems whose aim will be to reduce congestions (Goyal et al., 2025b).

When generative modeling is combined with reinforcement learning in real-time systems, the adaptive agents are used to not only respond to the existing data but also foresee and prepare against the expected events. This mixed-model provides a smarter real-time analytics platform and the potential to allow full autonomous systems, which continually evolve to fit data perfectly with time.

5. ARCHITECTURAL FRAMEWORKS FOR REAL-TIME GENERATIVE SYSTEMS

5.1 Core Components of a Real-Time Generative AI System

A real-time generative AI architecture is a collective ensemble of multiple components chained together to consume, process, analyze, and outputs data with a minimum latency. The data ingestion layer supports ingestion of streaming data originating in many sources, including IoT devices, web apps or transactional systems and makes it the simplest layer of the stack. This layer usually makes use of tools such as Apache Kafka, MQTT, or stream APIs over clouds to manage the data of high throughput (Howard et al., 2017).

Ingested data is then run through a preprocessing engine to clean, normalize and encode the received streams to a format amenable to analysis. At this step, the feature extraction, temporal alignment, and missing values processing is done in order to have compatibility with the generative model pipeline.

The output layer represents or forwards the output to other downstream applications. This would involve utilization of automated alerting systems, dashboards or APIs that activate control in case of a critical environment such as in medical or an industrial automation setting. Other components should restrict latencies they work by and should be able to scale across the distributed computing environments to deal with real deployments situations successfully.

Figure 3. Flow-based Deep Generative Models

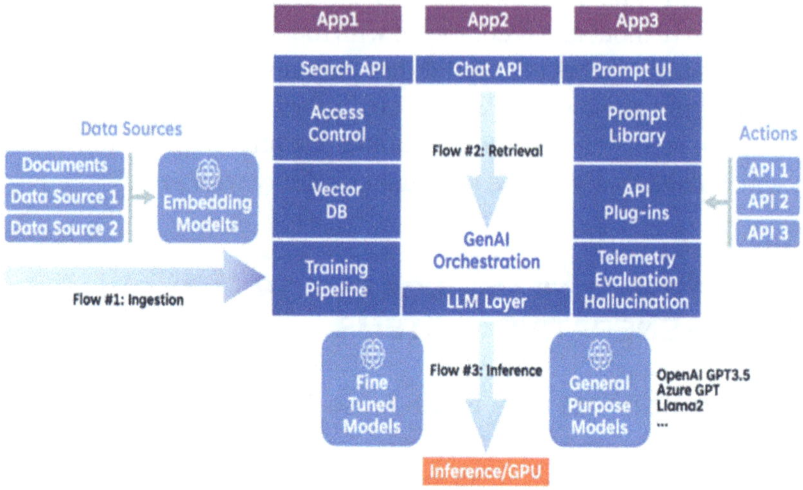

The picture 3 denotes a conceptual layout of a Generative AI (GenAI) framework that connects information entrance, gathering, organization, and inference mechanisms in numerous applications by means of Large Language Models (LLMs).

5.2 Data Ingestion and Preprocessing in Real Time

The speed and reliability of data ingestion in a real-time becomes heavily relevant in the efficiency of the analytics pipeline. Apache Kafka, Flink, or Amazon Kinesis streaming systems are the classical example of these tools that can be used to stream data continuously and push it to different consumer services. These systems have high availability, fault tolerance, and scalable partitioning that are essential in the applications at the industrial level (Pascanu, Mikolov, & Bengio, 2013).

Nonetheless, ingestion is not a simple data-gathering process because it should deal with unstructured formats, sampling rates, and sudden data quality drops. To control such challenges, real-time preprocessing is required. Such methods as stream windowing, sliding windows, events-time processing, allow organizing data by time to gain context-sensitive feature engineering.

In many cases, data compression, deduplication and data anonymization can be added at this stage, particularly with privacy-sensitive applications. A generative model can also be used in preprocessing to impute missing entries or even synthesize other features so that analytics pipeline continues to perform well despite poor quality of the raw data (Xu, Wang, Chen, & Li, 2015).

5.3 Integration with Tools: Kafka, Spark Streaming, Flink

To adopt real-time generative AI, there should be effortless compatibility with the large data tools and systems that permit extended stream processing. Apache Kafka is a resilient infrastructure in the communication of messages or messages broker, where information can be passed efficiently by the producer to the consumer. Persistence and replication features offered by Kafka enable it to be resilient so that no data can be lost during transit.

This ecosystem is expanded with Apache Flink and Spark Streaming to allow micro-batch or stream-based continuous computation over data. These products give developers the ability to execute complex event processing logic, work with machine learning models and to scale the deployment of analytical functions. One can develop their own inference pipelines using the MLlib library in Spark Streaming and the CEP library in Flink to incorporate generative models as prediction and synthesis.

Generative AI models have to be serialised and used as scalable inference services. These models can either be low-latency streaming query response using containers, serverless functions, or GPU-accelerated environments. This close integration of the generative models to technology such as Kafka and Flink capability to provide timely inputs to the models as well as to deliver actionable output within a millisecond, not only makes the integration successful, but highly efficient as well (Li, Kadav, Durdanovic, Samet, & Graf, 2017).

5.4 Edge, Cloud, and Hybrid Deployment Models

Deployment strategy of real-time generative system is critical in making this system responsive and efficient. Edge deployment implies the deployment of the models as near to data as possible, e.g., in vehicles or sensors or mobile phones. This configuration makes latency smaller and less prone to the use of central machines, which is critical when dealing with such applications as self-driving navigation or factory automation systems.

However, cloud deployment is characterized by huge scalability, central control, and resource-intensive manifestation like GPUs or TPUs. It is appropriate when an application needs a high computation requirement and can be slightly Latency tolerant, like a business intelligence system on an enterprise level or a huge-scale recommendation system (Kairouz et al., 2021).

6. APPLICATIONS ACROSS DOMAINS

6.1 Smart Manufacturing and Predictive Maintenance

Generative AI with real-time analytics is transforming equipment and production optimization in modern manufacturing environments by supporting managers in handling the process. Predictive maintenance involves the use of sensor information to predict component failures in advance resulting in downtime elimination and increased productivity. Generative models may allow simulating potential scenarios of failure, synthesizing failure data to train the model, and even the remaining useful life of equipment.

Factories containing IoT-sensors generate a high-frequent data, which is incomplete or noisy. In this case generative models will be indispensable when imputing and enhancing datasets so that more representative and lower-noise data can be input into the predictive systems. Such systems are able to pre-plan maintenance and the logistics of spares by constantly creating possible degradation patterns (Goyal et al., 2025c).

Furthermore, generative AI has the capacity to simulate the actions of a complicated machine or system in various conditions of operation. This is in support of digital twin technologies, where virtual version of a material artefact is updated real time based on both observers and produced data. The results of such possibilities are better informed decision making and increased resilience in operations.

6.2 Finance: Fraud Detection and Market Simulation

Financial sector is one of the first to implement real-time analytics, particularly in such domains as fraud detection and high frequency trading. Generative AI augments the above systems by generating realistic synthetic transactions with fraudulent patterns, therefore increasing the performance of the detection models. This is especially useful when the environment is adversarial and the malicious behavior develops unpredictably and thus, rapidly.

Generative models can be applied to market simulation and generate future market scenarios based on real-time signal. Those simulations facilitate stress testing, the crafting of algorithmic trading strategies, and risk management. Generative AI offers a more subtler and non-linear view of how a market behaves as compared to traditional stochastic models (Cohen, Afshar, Tapson, & van Schaik, 2017).

When deployed into real-time pipelines, these models enable financial institutions to move quicker than the market, capture anomalies as they occur and predict trend in assets more accurately. Streaming data and generative modeling leads to an agiler and more informed financial ecosystem that is supported by the continuous feedback loop.

6.3 E-commerce and Personalized Recommendations

Personalization is the backbone of e-commerce platforms, and real time-based analytics utilising generative AI is changing the way they provide recommendations to users. Generative models on the basis of analysis of live user interactions are able to synthesize profiles of users, generate suggestions, anticipate preferences and make suggestions on real time basis. This has made the user interaction stronger and conversion rates rise.

Further, generative models can predict the behavior of customers in order to pre-test new marketing activities or interface issues to ensure they have the desired effect before implementing them to a wider audience. The A/B testing non-stop and backed by the cohorts of simulated users will help innovate quicker and make more customers satisfied with the final product (Cho et al., 2014).

Timely and contextual product recommendations are also possible due to the fact that such variable changes in user behavior could easily be addressed by the system. Generative AI enables it to do so by keeping up the user embeddings and maintaining the content features, such that recommendations can keep up with the trends over time without the need to constantly update the recommendation system.

7. IMPLEMENTATION CHALLENGES AND TECHNICAL CONSIDERATIONS

7.1 Real-Time Constraints and Latency Bottlenecks

The application of generative AI to the real-time analytics setting opens up a new set of strict requirements-latency-to-which many of the traditional AI models have not been optimized. Generative models (and deep neural networks in particular transformers and diffusion models) are frequently computation-intensive and may take a long time to produce their output. Small delays are temporary, but in real-time applications, delays of even a few milliseconds can destroy system responsiveness and hence lost opportunities or failure of applications, including fraud detection, autonomous, or emergency response.

Much change is needed to optimize such models to low-latency scenarios, such as pruning, quantization, and knowledge distillation. These methods both shrink model and inference time considerably without negatively impacting much on performance. Further, running models on accelerators such as GPUs, TPUs, and even FPGAs can assist in staying below latency limits and this becomes complex in terms of deployment and requires more resources and hence cost.

The other underlying problem is the coordination of the data ingestion, model prediction and delivery in a system with several parallel tasks in a pipeline. Stream processing platforms should plan the calls of models such that it does not freeze the whole pipeline. Buffering, asynchronous processing and the management of state becomes very important in order to guarantee constant throughput without compromising data integrity.

Moreover the end-to-end performance is affected by factors at the system level e.g. network latency, serialization time of data and load balancing. Real time systems require a steady performance reconfiguration and active resource management in order to sustain quality of service. This can especially be very tricky in situations that have unpredictable data load as any instances of sudden spikes may overload the most optimized systems unless adequate scaling mechanism are put in place (Rahi et al., 2023).

7.2 Scalability and Model Optimization

The most important technicalities in the implementation of the generative AI systems in real-time environment refer to scalability. As streaming data volume increases systems not only have to process increased data but they are also required to sustain performance without being compromised. Generative models suffer particularly because their requirements (both memory and computational) are high, and thus do not result in a linear scale, and may need to incorporate complex distributed systems to achieve efficient scale.

Model modularization Splitting a complex generative model into smaller, independent model modules that can be run in parallel or served separately is one of the strategies to increase scalability. In the instance of a video stream synthesis application, there may be modules to deal with different aspects of the scene (such as object motion, background rendering, anomaly scoring). This scaling not only provides a means of parallelization, but also enables the scaling of large-load modules in a distributed fashion, both increasing fault tolerance and performance (Dandotiya et al., 2023).

It is also usual to scale horizontally using containerization and orchestration systems such as Kubernetes. The model inference services can be scaled dynamically by enabling easy replications of the containers. But copying those stateful generative models that presuppose time dependencies add on overload. State synchronization is more than non-trivial which demands niche engineering solutions like use of persistent storage layers or shared memory caches.

Scalability is also assisted by model optimization methods, which require fewer areas of large models to be trained freshly concerning each use case thus enabling scalability. These methods enable more domain-customized models to borrow knowledge of general-purpose generative models, which can be more efficient without compromising accuracy. Nonetheless, speed-accuracy-complexity trade-offs are to be maintained properly.

7.3 Handling Data Drift and Concept Drift

Under real-time conditions, the distributions of data may vary fast with the changes of season, or altering user behaviour, or with some external disturbances. This is a process referred to as data drift or concept drift and this is a serious problem to the reliability and accuracies of generative models. Otherwise left to the mercy of drift, a low level of work outputs and misclassifications as well as possible security loopholes in important programs such as threat detection and financial forecasting might emerge (Li, Zhao, & Wang, 2019).

Generative models are also susceptible to drift since it makes use of the distribution of input data. In case of the change in the distribution of data, the models trained in the past may no longer correspond to the current reality of synthetic data, so the obtained will be misleading or false. As an example, a historical model based customer transactions can be unable to detect fraudulent schemes that will occur through a new payment mechanism or a new route of transaction.

Real-time detection of drift Real-time detection of drift follows statistical properties of the arriving data and compares it to past baselines. Estimation of drift may be aided by use of techniques like KullbackLeibler divergence, population stability index and moving window validation. After the drift has been noticed, appropriate adaptive strategies need to be preempted online, one of them might be learning online, or incremental training, or even retraining of the data models with newly labeled data (Devlin, Chang, Lee, & Toutanova, 2019).

Hybrid systems are becoming common as a mitigation to concept drift, as a combination of a static, pre-trained model and many adaptive components, constantly training on new data. Ensemble learning is another kind of approach, where several models which learn about various time windows will be weighted on the fly, based on their level of performance. These tactics support the relevancy and reliability of models so real-time generative analytics would be trustworthy and valid in the long run.

7.4 Infrastructure, Cost, and Maintenance

The use of generative AI models under real-time conditions is expensive in terms of facilities and overheads. These incorporate calculational capacity to start inferences, stores and transmission of data and the human effort that way that goes into checking and repairing. Generative modeling can be extremely expensive in many cases, as while employing large-scale models, and in particular, in latency-sensitive cases, this may prove to be non viable to most organizations unless customised deployment methods are implemented.

Cloud computing is flexible and scalable for infrastructure purposes, and it might prove expensive in cases of high-frequency data and real-time inference opportunities. In others, edge computing is cheaper through diminishing the transmission of data and allowing inference locally. But edge devices are also resource-limited, and might be unable to host large generative models using specialized hardware or model compression techniques.

Operational maintenance does not simply mean maintaining the models alive but also being performant and on course with the business objectives. It involves frequent retraining, validation of abnormalities in the quality of output, version management, rollback mechanisms, and meeting current standards spelled by regulators. To minimize overhead and automatize the model life process, organizations are forced to invest in MLOps pipelines (Chalapathy & Chawla, 2019b).

Also, the user needs model observability and explainability tools to evaluate the behavior enacted by generative systems. Failures, decision audit, or output verification become hard to diagnose when there are no adequate instrumentation and logging. Quite often, these tools assist in identifying the degradation of performance well in advance and concluding that the generative system is reliable within mission-critical tasks.

8. LEGAL AND DATA GOVERNANCE CONCERNS

8.1 Privacy Implications of Generating Data in Real Time

Real-time analytics with the help of generative AI creates novel aspects of data privacy issues. In case of generating synthetic data to reflect actual persons, transactions, or activities there is a suspicion that sensitive information can be stolen or re-identified. For example, a generative model trained using anonymized data may replicate patterns that are identifiable in training data even when these patterns are not predictive of the training data (i.e., generated by a subset of the training data) when the training process does not have the appropriate differential privacy primitives.

The risk is increased in cases of real-time applications since data is to be continually processed, and decisions can be taken in real time without any possibility of checking by humans. In the cases where privacy is strictly controlled, like a business in the industry of health care or financial sector, any kind of breach including a synthetic one can lead to legal penalties and loss of reputation. Generative models thus need to be inbuilt with a precautionary measure that would not allow the redevelopment of personally identifiable information (Rajpurkar et al., 2017).

Such concerns can be alleviated by privacy-preserving methods like federated learning, differential privacy and secure multiparty computation. When using these techniques training data never leaves its source or is obscured enough during processing. Nevertheless, to incorporate these techniques into the real-time pipelines, prominent architectural changes and performance optimization needs to be conducted.

In the end, the model uses need to find a balance in utility and privacy in organizations. These include carrying out privacy impact assessment, being transparent concerning the use of data and leaving decisions regarding data to the users. There should be strict regulatory rules like General Data Protection Regulation (GDPR) and the Health Insurance Portability and Accountability Act (HIPAA) to be followed especially in the aspects of real-time personal data.

8.2 Bias and Fairness in Real-Time AI Decisions

The problems of bias in AI systems are well described and generative models are not an exception. In situations where biased generative results are utilized in real-time decision-making, previous disparities can remain unchanged, and even the factor of increase. As an example, such supervised learning models can be applied in hiring platforms or financial scoring systems, where a biased generating model could favor one group of people and exclude another on a regular basis, which is discriminatory.

Real-time systems are prone to bias more so due to the absence of human intervention into the decision loop. Predictions provided by a generative model might be taken with blind faith when being a part of a pipeline, causing unintentional harm. In addition, negative feedback loops may make the situation even worse, biased decisions will support the data used to update the model in future, reproducing the bias or discrimination.

To work out fairness in generative models, special metrics like demographic parity, equalized odds, and disparate impact are needed. These metrics should be recalculated on an ongoing basis so that the model performance could be tracked on various subgroups. Also, training data sets are to be selected with representation in mind and models are subject to bias reduction methods such as reweighting, adversarial debiasing or counterfactual generation.

To some extent, the issue of promoting fairness in real-time generative analytics is a technical issue, but also societal and ethical. Such systems ought to be designed and examined by stakeholders of different backgrounds. Reporting model decisions and appropriate ethical review boards clearly can assist in imposing accountability and citizen trust.

8.3 Compliance with Data Protection Regulations (GDPR, HIPAA)

The laws concerning data protection are a legal requirement in the deployment of generative AI in real-time set-ups. EU data protection regulation like the GDPR or the HIPAA in the United States, enacts strict regulations on how personal data must be processed and shared, collected, and stored. In order to evade punishment, generative models, particularly those that give synthetic counterparts of confidential information, should function within the confines of such laws.

In the case of GDPR, people, for instance, are entitled to information about the use of their personal data, access to the same, and deletion. In case of a generative modeling resulting in an inadvertent recreation or inference of identifiable data, then this can be counted as a breach of data rights. Organizations should make record of how a model is trained, data minimization, and a robust access control mechanism.

HIPAA, the law set to regulate the application of health data in the United States, mandates that an application of patient data, both in analytics and machine learning application, must be secured by encryption and de-identification. Real time systems have to be bestowed with protection mechanisms that ensure protection of PHI (Protected Health Information) in such a way that it cannot ever be revealed, not even model outputs or logs (Tran, Ranganath, & Blei, 2016).

The challenges of meeting such compliance standards require support of a complex between legal scholars, data engineers, and AI practitioners. Frequent auditing, sound documentation and integrity in data stewardship is necessary. The development of generative AI provides new possibilities and should be implemented carefully regarding the laws and the rights of individuals.

8.4 Responsible Use and AI Explainability

As real-time systems gradually become more multifaceted to introduce generative AI, the problem of explainability and responsible usage becomes more salient. In most high-stakes applications (examples: medical diagnosis, self-driving cars, or emergencies), first users and regulators need to know why a certain decision or prediction was reached. This is made particularly difficult by generative models that are frequently discussed as being black boxes.

Explainable generative AI entails identifying the mechanism by which input data, model architecture and internal parameters are used to formulate or be used in the generated output. Models like saliency maps, SHAP (SHapley Additive exPlanations) and LIME (Local Interpretable Model-agnostic Explanations) can provide some view into model behavior. These tools are however more likely applied to classification models and might have to be adjusted to be applied to generative outputs.

Responsible AI guidelines prioritise transparency, accountability and human-in-the-loop decision making. In real-time applications, it implies to design systems which do not merely produce the content or predictions but also pass the certainty level, assumptions and context of these results. To give an example, a medical AI system must not only provide a proposed diagnosis, but also indicate which features have mainly contributed to a certain diagnosis.

Integrating explanations in real-time generative systems will facilitate effective trust and usability. It also clarifies that users may also demand and make exception to automated decisions where need be. All in all, technical measures, ethical controls, and user empowerment are one and the same elements of mindful treatment of generative AI, especially in high-stress circumstances where integrated safety precautions such as human lives or societal consequences are put in danger.

9. FUTURE TRENDS AND RESEARCH OPPORTUNITIES

9.1 Federated Generative Learning for Real-Time Use

Federated learning, roughly defined as a method of collaborative model training that does not involve centralization of data, will play a central role in deciding the future of real-time generative AI. This is of particular interest when dealing with privacy-sensitive application (such as mobile health monitoring, smart cities, or personalized recommendation systems), where the users create data within geographically dispersed and privately controlled settings.

Federated generative learning allows real-time AI systems to adapt to new edge device information in real-time without any raw user data ever being generated. Rather, models are trained locally and do not communicate except with a central server the gradients/model updates, which privacy-preserves the data. Such a configuration permits real-time customization of generative models, as in the case of a localized traffic forecast or personal health hazard assessment.

Nevertheless, challenges of federated learning in generative setting are emerging, such as communication overhead, device heterogeneity, and resistance to noisy or adversarial partners. The fact that generative models even tend to converge in a convergent system of distributed nodes is also open research, especially when each device running the generative models can have an arbitrary view of the data-distribution (Radford, Narasimhan, Salimans, & Sutskever, 2018).

With improvements in the infrastructure and protocols, the federated generative AI may empower exceptionally personalized, privacy-sensitive real-time analytics in a way that respects the autonomy of users. This has been a paradigmatic change in thinking on model-training and deployment-modes- now it is about user centric (decentralised) intelligence that is constantly learning.

9.2 Self-Healing and Autonomous Analytical Systems

Self-healing systems Self-healing systems are already one of the most exciting future directions in generative AI in real-time: analytic platforms that can monitor and respond to internal errors or performance deterioration and heal without human involvement. These systems draw on biological resilience, and seek to enhance up-time, span of maintenance, and ongoing service in high availability systems such as those in network operations, industrial control systems, and mobile autonomous cars.

Generative AI has two functions in such systems. First, it will be able to be applied in simulating various future states of the system, predictively detecting faults before they occur, and mitigating those that will appeared. Using streaming data to generate likely fault conditions or degradation patterns, the system is able to frame contingency measures or bypass processing pipelines prior to a real-time failure. Second, it is possible to recover corrupted or lost streams of data in real time by use of generative models and as such analysis may continue uninterrupted even when the environment is unfavorable.

The use of meta-learning capabilities is another advantage of autonomous systems: the generative model learns on its part to learn. As an example of anomaly detection model that might work, a model that detects rare events might self-tune its parameters using feedback. The described adaptive intelligence model enables real-time analytics technologies to become more sensitive, accurate, and robust with continued use.

Nevertheless, creating self-healing analytics systems is also quite a research issue. Such systems need to be able to recognize signs of very slight degradation, prevent misdetection of degradation, and need to trade performance and energy / computational cost. Furthermore, in autonomous contexts, explainability dealing with self-repair mechanisms is of much more crucial importance and arguably needs to be auditable by design. The concept of incorporation of generative AI in self-healing systems can be exceptionally valuable in the development of resilient and 24 hours of analytical systems.

9.3 Integration with Quantum and Neuromorphic Computing

The future of realtime analytics with generative AI is the next integration with the emerging paradigm of hardware, which includes quantum computers and neuromorphic processor paradigms. The purpose of the technologies is to circumvent the computing constraints of classical von Neumann architectures, notably to those tasks dealing with high-dimensional data, intricate patterns generation, or ultra-low latency.

Generative models and quantum computing are a good match: quantum computing is by design directed at executing probabilistic and superposed states. In quantum generative algorithms, quantum versions of GANs such as Quantum GANs (QGANs) and Variational Quantum Circuits (VQCs) have demonstrated early potential of being efficient to simulate hard-to-simulate distributions. In real-time analytics this may dramatically transform fields such as cybersecurity or market forecasting, where the dynamically changing probability distribution may be highly complicated, and one needs to act instantly (Goyal, 2025b).

Neuromorphic computing alternatively replicates the parallel and event-based structure of the human brain. The use of spikes (instead of continuous signals) is common in chips such as the Loihi produced by Intel or the TrueNorth produced by IBM to enable ultra-low-power, real-time inference on edge devices. By combining with weight-efficient generative models, use of neuromorphic systems can support entirely autonomous sensors, not just detection devices but full data generators, like in real time environmental sensors, or in prosthetic feedback.

Nevertheless, neither quantum nor neuromorphic computing is at a stage of practical applicability, maturity of tools, and, accordingly, compatibility with popular AI-based frameworks. The research should create hybrid architectures in which it is possible to run parts of the computation in different backends (classical, quantum, or neuromorphic) depending on the workload, and in which generative models can run on generative models. As these technologies evolve, there is a strong likelihood that they will release never before seen real-time generative potential that reinvents the magnitude and pace of smart analysis.

9.4 Open Challenges and Emerging Solutions

Even though there is a huge opportunity in the integration of real-time analytics and generative AI, there are still numerous unaddressed challenges on the technical, operational, and ethical fronts. The verification of models is one of the most essential problems that need to be addressed, and it can be described as the guarantee that the generative outputs are spotless, pertinent, and safe, when they are used to make high-stakes judgments. When deployed in real-time environments, it is commonly not possible to perform post-processing, nor use human verification, so model verification in this case should be dynamic and independent.

The last issue that has not been resolved is lifelong learning without disastrous forgetting. Generative models adapted to streaming scenarios should be flexible to embrace new patterns of data whereas having the past knowledge. Ways to do it are being researched, including elastic weight consolidation, rehearsal strategies, as well as online meta-learning, yet there is still no single universal technique universally applicable to any problem. There is the issue of maintenance of stability and flexibility.

Moreover, optimization of the available resources is hindering the scalability of real-time generative AI. Fluctuating demand is a problem on many real-world deployments and the overhead of allocating resources to a deployment often results in over-provisioning (wasting cost) or under-provisioning (when resulting latency occurs). New approaches are dynamic model switching, in which a generative model is deployed in different versions across resource tiers and the model to use is selected dynamically depending upon the current load or context.

Finally, there has been the need to integrate disciplines. Generative analytics systems in various fields of endeavor when realized in real time interact with systems engineering, human-computer interaction, legal policy, and behavioral sciences. The joint work of these branches is what will be needed to create really good and ethical systems. This is because any more powerful technological convergence that has taken place will require research into the transparent interfaces, co-designed decision workflows and models of adaptive governance to achieve its full potential.

CONCLUSION

Real-time analytics with the help of generative AI is taking shape to be an excellent paradigm shift in the manner in which organizations receive streams of data and how they process, interpret, and perform actions based on the data. Marrying the performance and timeliness of real-time data processing with the imaginative and forecasting power of generative models opens up new opportunities in a wide array of fields, including smart manufacturing and finance as well as healthcare and e-commerce. This integration enables the systems not only to respond immediately to the incoming data but have the ability to predict the future states, model scenarios, and close the gaps in partial data, improving both the accuracy of the decisions and the resilience of operations.

But the use of generative AI in real-time systems is associated with significant technical and ethical dilemmas. Challenges such as latency, scalability, model drift and the cost of infrastructure involve developing new architectural frameworks and constant optimization. At the same time, issues relating to privacy, fairness and transparency, and the compliance with the law should be taken care of in advance to make its use responsible. With the advancement of the sophistication of generative models and the increasing pressure on real-time requirements the necessity to integrate explainability and governance mechanisms is going to be essential in gaining trust and acceptance.

As the future unfolds, new developments like federated learning, quantum and neuromorphic computing and self-healing systems promise to improve the potential of real-time generative analytics and make it accessible to many. However, the innovations present new complexities that would require multidisciplinary work and long-term research. With these challenges, the area has the potential to change not only the ways of analyzing data but the way smart systems help humans develop judgment in the more complex and changing and dynamic environment.

REFERENCES

Abadi, M., Barham, P., Chen, J., Chen, Z., Davis, A., Dean, J., & Zheng, X. (2016). TensorFlow: A system for large-scale machine learning. *12th USENIX Symposium on Operating Systems Design and Implementation (OSDI)*, 265-283. https://doi.org/DOI: 10.5555/3026877.3026899

Aggarwal, C. C. (2013). *Data streams: Models and algorithms.* Springer., DOI: 10.1007/978-3-642-36481-6

Carbone, P., Katsifodimos, A., Ewen, S., Markl, V., Haridi, S., & Tzoumas, K. (2015). Apache Flink: Stream and batch processing in a single engine. *A Quarterly Bulletin of the Computer Society of the IEEE Technical Committee on Data Engineering, 38*(4), 28–38. DOI: 10.1109/BigData.2015.7368627

Chalapathy, R., & Chawla, S. (2019). Deep learning for anomaly detection: A survey. *arXiv preprint arXiv:1901.03407.* https://doi.org//arXiv.1901.03407DOI: 10.48550

Chalapathy, R., & Chawla, S. (2019). Deep learning for anomaly detection: A survey. *arXiv preprint arXiv:1901.03407.* https://doi.org//arXiv.1901.03407DOI: 10.48550

Cho, K., van Merrienboer, B., Gulcehre, C., Bahdanau, D., Bougares, F., Schwenk, H., & Bengio, Y. (2014). Learning phrase representations using RNN encoder-decoder for statistical machine translation. *EMNLP*, 1724-1734. https://doi.org/DOI: 10.3115/v1/D14-1179

Cohen, G., Afshar, S., Tapson, J., & van Schaik, A. (2017). EMNIST: Extending MNIST to handwritten letters. *2017 International Joint Conference on Neural Networks (IJCNN)*, 2921-2926. https://doi.org/DOI: 10.1109/IJCNN.2017.7966217

Dandotiya, M., Rahi, P., & Khunteta, A. A. Anushya, and Sayed Sayeed Ahmad. 2023. SAFE: A Secure Authenticated & Integrated Framework for E-learning. In Proceedings of the 4th International Conference on Information Management & Machine Intelligence (ICIMMI '22). Association for Computing Machinery, New York, NY, USA, Article 89, 1–9. https://doi.org/DOI: 10.1145/3590837.3590926

Deng, L., & Yu, D. (2014). Deep learning: Methods and applications. *Foundations and Trends® in Signal Processing, 7*(3–4), 197-387. https://doi.org/DOI: 10.1561/2000000039

Devlin, J., Chang, M.-W., Lee, K., & Toutanova, K. (2019). BERT: Pre-training of deep bidirectional transformers for language understanding. *NAACL-HLT*, 4171-4186. https://doi.org/DOI: 10.18653/v1/N19-1423

Dwork, C., & Roth, A. (2014). The algorithmic foundations of differential privacy. *Foundations and Trends® in Theoretical Computer Science, 9*(3–4), 211-407. https://doi.org/DOI: 10.1561/0400000042

Goodfellow, I., Pouget-Abadie, J., Mirza, M., Xu, B., Warde-Farley, D., Ozair, S., & Bengio, Y. (2014). Generative adversarial nets. *Advances in Neural Information Processing Systems, 27*, 2672–2680. DOI: 10.5555/2969033.2969125

Goyal, N. K. (2025). Weaponizing Misinformation and Cyberattacks on Supply Chains. In Bukhari, S., & Zafar, I. (Eds.), *Mass Media and Impact of Fake News on Supply Chains* (pp. 177–210). IGI Global Scientific Publishing., DOI: 10.4018/979-8-3373-2175-2.ch007

Goyal, N. K. (2025). Security and Privacy in IoT, Fog, and Blockchain Networks. In Sathio, A., Rind, M., Awan, S., & Junejo, A. (Eds.), *Energy-Efficient Deep Learning Approaches in IoT, Fog, and Green Blockchain Revolution* (pp. 371–398). IGI Global Scientific Publishing., DOI: 10.4018/979-8-3373-0300-0.ch015

Goyal, N. K., Dandotiya, M., Kumari, M., Kaloria, S., & Anushya, A. (2025). AI-Powered Haptic Devices for Patient Rehabilitation. In Mamodiya, U., Kalam, A., Bossoufi, B., Awad, M., & Somwanshi, D. (Eds.), *Integrating AI With Haptic Systems for Smarter Healthcare Solutions* (pp. 143–170). IGI Global Scientific Publishing., DOI: 10.4018/979-8-3373-2307-7.ch007

Goyal, N. K., Dandotiya, M., Kumari, M., Sheikh, M. F., & Sharma, S. (2025). Emerging Job Roles in the Tourism Sector Leveraging Artificial Intelligence. In Silic, M., Luthia, M., Ahmad, F., & Chakraborty, P. (Eds.), *Empowering Sustainable Performance and Competitive Advantage in Tourism* (pp. 89–126). IGI Global Scientific Publishing., DOI: 10.4018/979-8-3373-4546-8.ch004

Goyal, N. K., Dandotiya, M., Qurashi, J. A., Kumari, M., & Sharma, S. (2025). AI-Driven Predictive Analytics for Disease Management. In Ouaissa, M., Ouaissa, M., Imad, M., Qurashi, J., & Farooq, M. (Eds.), *Utilizing AI of Medical Things for Healthcare Security and Sustainability* (pp. 231–276). IGI Global Scientific Publishing., DOI: 10.4018/979-8-3373-0690-2.ch008

Goyal, N. K., Kumari, M., Kushwah, V., Dandotiya, M., & Vijay, A. (2025). Evaluating blockchain security: Trade-offs in consensus mechanisms. *IET Conference Proceedings*, 2024(38), 80–88. https://doi.org/DOI: 10.1049/icp.2025.0775

Howard, A. G., Zhu, M., Chen, B., Kalenichenko, D., Wang, W., Weyand, T., . . . Adam, H. (2017). MobileNets: Efficient convolutional neural networks for mobile vision applications. *arXiv preprint arXiv:1704.04861*. https://doi.org//arXiv.1704.04861DOI: 10.48550

Kairouz, P., McMahan, H. B., Avent, B., Bellet, A., Bennis, M., Bhagoji, A. N., ... & Zhao, S. (2021). Advances and open problems in federated learning. *Foundations and Trends® in Machine Learning, 14*(1–2), 1-210. https://doi.org/DOI: 10.1561/2200000073

Kingma, D. P., & Welling, M. (2014). Auto-encoding variational Bayes. *International Conference on Learning Representations (ICLR)*. https://doi.org/DOI: 10.48550/arXiv.1312.6114

Kreps, J., Narkhede, N., & Rao, J. (2011). Kafka: A distributed messaging system for log processing. *Proceedings of the NetDB*, 1-7. https://doi.org/DOI: 10.1145/2070911.2070916

Li, H., Kadav, A., Durdanovic, I., Samet, H., & Graf, H. P. (2017). Pruning filters for efficient convnets. *International Conference on Learning Representations*. https://doi.org/DOI: 10.48550/arXiv.1608.08710

Li, Q., He, B., & Wu, D. (2020). Federated learning: Challenges, methods, and future directions. *IEEE Signal Processing Magazine*, *37*(3), 50–60. DOI: 10.1109/MSP.2020.2975749

Li, X., Zhao, Z., & Wang, H. (2019). A survey on federated learning systems: Vision, hype and reality for data privacy and protection. *arXiv preprint arXiv:1907.09693*. https://doi.org//arXiv.1907.09693DOI: 10.48550

Pascanu, R., Mikolov, T., & Bengio, Y. (2013). On the difficulty of training recurrent neural networks. *International Conference on Machine Learning*, 1310-1318. https://doi.org/DOI: 10.5555/3042817.3043083

Radford, A., Narasimhan, K., Salimans, T., & Sutskever, I. (2018). Improving language understanding by generative pre-training. *OpenAI*. https://doi.org//arXiv.1801.06146DOI: 10.48550

Rahi, P., (2023). Edge-Cognitive Computing for Improvising the Healthcare 5.0. In *Contemporary Applications of Data Fusion for Advanced Healthcare Informatics, edited by G.S. Karthick and Sathishkumar Karupusamy* (pp. 369–391). IGI Global Scientific Publishing., DOI: 10.4018/978-1-6684-8913-0.ch016

Rajpurkar, P., Irvin, J., Zhu, K., Yang, B., Mehta, H., Duan, T., . . . Ng, A. Y. (2017). CheXNet: Radiologist-level pneumonia detection on chest X-rays with deep learning. *arXiv preprint arXiv:1711.05225*. https://doi.org//arXiv.1711.05225DOI: 10.48550

Shokri, R., & Shmatikov, V. (2015). Privacy-preserving deep learning. *Proceedings of the 22nd ACM SIGSAC Conference on Computer and Communications Security*, 1310-1321. https://doi.org/DOI: 10.1145/2810103.2813687

Silver, D., Schrittwieser, J., Simonyan, K., Antonoglou, I., Huang, A., Guez, A., & Hassabis, D. (2017). Mastering the game of Go without human knowledge. *Nature, 550*(7676), 354–359. DOI: 10.1038/nature24270 PMID: 29052630

Sutton, R. S., & Barto, A. G. (2018). *Reinforcement learning: An introduction* (2nd ed.). MIT Press., DOI: 10.1109/TNN.1998.712192

Tran, D., Ranganath, R., & Blei, D. (2016). Variational Gaussian process. *International Conference on Learning Representations*. https://doi.org/DOI: 10.48550/arXiv.1511.06499

Vaswani, A., Shazeer, N., Parmar, N., Uszkoreit, J., Jones, L., Gomez, A. N., & Polosukhin, I. (2017). Attention is all you need. *Advances in Neural Information Processing Systems, 30*, 5998–6008. DOI: 10.5555/3295222.3295349

Xu, B., Wang, N., Chen, T., & Li, M. (2015). Empirical evaluation of rectified activations in convolutional network. *arXiv preprint arXiv:1505.00853*. https://doi.org//arXiv.1505.00853DOI: 10.48550

Zaharia, M., Chowdhury, M., Franklin, M. J., Shenker, S., & Stoica, I. (2010). Spark: Cluster computing with working sets. *Proceedings of the 2nd USENIX Conference on Hot Topics in Cloud Computing*, 10-10. https://doi.org/DOI: 10.5555/1863103.1863113

Chapter 6

AI-Integrated Data Governance Frameworks for Real-Time, Scalable, and Ethical Data Architectures

Rituraj Jain
https://orcid.org/0000-0002-5532-1245
Marwadi University, India

Adalbert Musengamana
Marwadi University, India

ABSTRACT

In the context of modern big data environments, this chapter explores how data governance reshapes the portrayal and management of data—an essential factor in maintaining data quality, security, and compliance. This underlines the fact that data has not only become a record-keeping asset, but also a strategic driver of insights and decisions. Against the volume, velocity, variety, and veracity challenges that characterize big data, this chapter surveys flexible, integrated, adaptive governance frameworks based on a core reflection of elements of compliance, real-time access, data stewardship, and security. It analyzes practical issues, such as no architecture, no visibility of the data, and no sponsorship, and develops solutions for automation, balancing accessibility with security, and promoting data literacy. Firms, such as Airbnb, Uber, and GE Aviation, provide tangible examples of good governance. Finally, the chapter discusses future trends, such as AI, NLP, and hybrid cloud innovations, that would create sustainable data-driven ecosystems.

DOI: 10.4018/979-8-3373-5616-7.ch006

1. INTRODUCTION

1.1 Significance of Data Governance in Big Data Ecosystems

In today's data-driven landscape, organizations increasingly rely on data-derived insights to enhance speed, innovation, and competitiveness. This reliance has grown with the integration of artificial intelligence (AI), which transforms data into a strategic asset for real-time analytics, predictive modeling, and intelligent automation. However, without robust data governance, AI-generated insights may become unreliable or non-compliant. Effective data governance ensures data integrity, consistency, and adherence to legal and ethical standards, safeguarding against risks such as data breaches, regulatory penalties, and poor decision-making (Fattah, 2024; Prakash, 2024; Sadiq et al., 2022).

Governance plays a critical role in fostering trust and accountability across big data ecosystems. It enables organizations to adapt to shifting market or regulatory demands without undermining stakeholder confidence (Chukwurah et al., 2024; Nwobodo et al., 2024; Dam et al., 2023). As organizations manage vast volumes of information from customer interactions, market trends, and operations, governance provides a structured framework ensuring security, reliability, and accessibility. Moreover, AI's success in extracting meaningful insights depends on the quality of underlying data. Governance frameworks help mitigate inaccuracies, biases, and compliance risks by establishing clear policies and standards. Especially in high-stakes sectors like healthcare and finance, data governance can define the boundary between success and failure (Antwi et al., 2024).

Data governance is now one of the most crucial planes in contemporary business and is driven by paper-driven data. As a result of the growth in the number of organizations that rely on huge volumes of information, data governance has become an essential issue to derive meaning or insight from the data and be innovative. The history of research in this area of study has shown how data science has evolved over the years, where data was once an outcome of operations processes to a value adding strategic resource out of which wise decisions can be made.

Notably, the idea of data governance has been developed owing to the increased complexity of data ecosystems. The earlier methods were a type of data integrity and standardization exercise that was largely operation-limited. When big data appears in the form of the '4Vs' or volume, velocity, variety, and veracity, the conventional ways of governance become ineffective, and it has become an oxymoron to mention governance of big data.

Most of this information is due to the enormous amount of information that can be generated from customer interaction, operations, and market trends, and according to researchers, the current methods of storage and processing have become ineffective. As the speed of data creation and the processing power needed grow exponentially, there has been a necessity for real-time analytics creation to further complicate the governance task. To cope with the complexity of data types, it has covered structured databases, unstructured text and multimedia, and increasingly flexible tools of analysis and governance. Finally, the veracity of data has now been the determining factor with regard to the need for high-level authentication and validation mechanisms of data used to check the quality and trust of data.

However, many studies have claimed that there is a need for a more flexible and adaptable governance model in response to these pressures. These new strategies could be used in the sense that they take up the best technologies available, artificial intelligence, and machine learning to automate the data classification factor, track data lineages, and enhance security policies (Samara et al., 2024; Olubusola et al., 2024). Moreover, researchers have pointed to the need to align data governance with business goals because efficient governance is more about reducing risks and, at the same time, deriving as much value as possible from data assets (Singh & Khan, 2024; Prabaharan et al., 2025).

Although the field is still dynamic, the present study aims to develop a governance framework to reach a compromise between data openly and data security, to be responsive in very fast-evolving regulatory environments, and to instill a data culture across companies.

Although much of the literature regarding data governance has flourished, there exist some key gaps to fill when dealing with the challenges that brim up in big data ecosystems. In many cases, conventional governance systems cannot be applied to dynamic data phenomena where the workload is dynamic, structured data is scarce, or the datasets increase with time. The majority of existing practices are not able to keep up with this speed of creating and processing data, that is, in a real-time scenario. Moreover, current structures are more likely to fail to deal with the broad range of types of data that are available within contemporary ecosystems.

Moreover, no studies have been conducted on the integration of artificial intelligence (AI) and machine learning (ML) in data governance activities. Such a gap is critical because of the increased role of AI in analyzing and creating decisions on big datasets in most industries.

The gap this study attempts to address is related to the lack of data governance frameworks for big data and AI-driven contexts. Specifically, our contributions are as follows:

1. Adaptive and scalable governance regimes that will do well as technology evolves, cropping up as requirements on the relevant and effective governance regimes change dramatically with the rapidity of the data landscapes.

2. AI-powered tools are integrated with tools for automating data classification, monitoring, and security used in the governing process, thereby making it efficient and accurate.
3. Investigating possible strategies for data governance in AI communities emphasizes the need to obtain a good balance between data accessibility and security, which is one of the major challenges of modern data governance.
4. Investigations into the place of data governance and trust building regarding the use of AI systems in an individual and given context.

1.2 Big Data Characteristics and Challenges

The complexity of present-day data governance consists of certain features of big data, such as the so-called 4Vs: volume, velocity, variety, and veracity. The rate at which new information is produced in the form of new data is referred to as velocity, which means that information is processed in real time; in this case, organizations are forced to maintain this velocity by adopting technologies that are capable of real-time processing. Variety deals with the heterogeneous character of data-structured databases, files of unstructured text, images, and audio, and requires super-tool analysis materials to extensively analyze the data. Veracity refers to how trusted the data are. Partial or incomplete data would misrepresent AI models, resulting in less desirable outcomes or even harmful outcomes. Old governance approaches, which were designed with more fixed, organized datasets, became ineffective in these complicated matters. This outlines the discrepancy in the conventional governance system and the significance of formulating a dynamic and flexible governance system that facilitates the instant application of scientific innovations associated with AI and machine learning. It is possible to automate data classification using modern and advanced technology, improve data lineage monitoring, and improve security (Bengio et al., 2024).

As big data is gathered within a blink of an eye and it covers correspondence via email and on a social platform to the work of IoT sensors and transaction history, data storage and processing processes will probably be left far behind. This immense dataset will challenge the effort of data governance, and uniformity and governance will thus be difficult to impose on the datasets (Pajooh et al., 2021). Another issue is the sheer speed at which the data are generated and need to be processed. Nevertheless, the structure of governance might be speeded up to reflect the same velocity of the rapidly cascading data only if there are options for real-time analytics of decision-making. The application of automation tools is required to enforce governance without business disruption (Janssen et al. 2020).

The types of data that are available, structured, semi-structured, and unstructured raise different requirements in terms of governance standards. For instance, while structured data housed in databases can easily be governed using traditional protocols for most parts, the entire universe of unstructured data housed in emails, videos, and social media poses complexity to classification, security, and quality checks (Shen et al., 2024). This refers to the uncertainty regarding the authenticity and credibility of the data. Poor data veracity will result in inaccurate analyses and incorrect decisions. Data governance policies must provide processes for authenticating and validating information to ensure rational decision making (Aroyo et al., 2021). Figure 1 below visually summarizes the "4Vs" of Big Data—Volume, Velocity, Variety, and Veracity—each representing a core challenge in managing and governing large-scale data ecosystems. These dimensions necessitate adaptive governance strategies, particularly in AI-driven environments.

Figure 1. 4 Vs of Big Data Explained

Traditional governance strategies for less complex data fail to achieve the standards required by big data. Typically, they cannot offer scalability or flexibility to fast-moving data ecosystems. For example, traditional approaches can become reliant on manual oversight and static policies that quickly become archaic as new sources of information keep flooding; such a strategy has weaknesses, and the structures of governance need to change and adapt to future applications of the technology, such as AI and machine learning.

2. LITERATURE REVIEW: EXISTING DATA GOVERNANCE FRAMEWORKS

2.1 Historical Approaches to Data Governance

Structured and static datasets, including those found in traditional databases, have historically been used to support data governance frameworks. Early models concentrated on controlled systems such as data integrity, standardization, and access management. Policies tend to be very simple and are usually supported by manual control and low-technology management. However, as organizations expanded, so did the complexity of data systems. Distributed databases, cloud storage, and real-time data streams have revealed several handicaps in these traditional approaches (Abu-Salih et al., 2021). New issues began to appear as the scaling of such frameworks supported the massive expansion of big data. The heterogeneity, high velocity, and volume of data emanating from the modern source of governance related to an enterprise have been difficult to handle using traditional governance. This had given space to inefficiencies, bottlenecks in decision-making processes, and an increase in the likelihood of non-compliance to newly added regulations. To this effect, the governing structures must be rebooted and repurposed to be adaptive and end-to-end in nature to harness new technologies that can equal big data in speed and scale.

Conventional methods of data governance exist when the size and type of data are not near that present today. In essence, these methods have focused on centralized control under which data have been managed using strict hierarchies where many manual activities have been carried out. Governance structures are a series of checks and approvals that ensure integrity, adherence, and access to data. Although these strategies perfectly served structured data in relational databases, they quickly became inadequate once institutions started to capture impressive volumes of unstructured and semi-structured data that originated in a vast variety of digital sources (Zhao et al., 2021). Data silo is a historical method in which various departments have data repositories at their disposal. Even with this kind of approach, individual departments were in a position to have control over their information based on their desires, which caused inefficiency, duplication, and inconsistency at the organizational level. Siloed data governance was also a deterrent to cross-departmental cooperation in the collection of all-round observations based on composite datasets. Big data technology is not easy to scale in legacy governance models. The needs of frameworks have changed not only in the amount of data required, but also in the speed and data types required with the availability of sources such as IoT devices, real-time social feeds, and cloud services that can provide a large amount (Janssen et al., 2020).

2.2 Characteristics of an Effective Governance Framework

An effective data governance framework for big data should be flexible, integrated, and adaptable. This means that the policy must be enabled to tackle the changes in data in very rapid sequences without compromising the quality and security of data. Flexibility also supports changing policies with the emergence of different types of data and when organizational needs change. Integration ensures that governance practices are well-connected to operational workflows and analytic processes. It allows data governance not only as a separate set of rules but also as part of the data lifecycle.

These requirements include compliance and real-time data access. An appropriate framework must be made up of automatic checks for compliance and permit access to data in real time without derogating security or privacy. This balanced approach ensures that an organization can stay nimble and responsive to its internal analytics needs and external regulatory mandates. The integration of these characteristics into a governance structure allows an organization to maintain its integrity and usability while spawning innovation and trust (Baijens et al., 2021). An effective data governance framework for modern big-data ecosystems would be flexible, integrated, and proactive. Thus, frameworks must be agile enough to permit organizations to pivot and update protocols as these data sources and regulations do. Flexibility: This makes governance always relevant and efficient; it helps instead of hindering business objectives. Integrated: Another salient feature of a proper governance framework is that it integrates other organizational processes. Data governance should not be an isolated initiative, but rather a part of the organization's data strategy. This may involve directly integrating governance tools into data pipelines for continuous validation, classification, or monitoring compliance. For example, integration with data lineage tools helps map the flow of data from its source to its end use, making tracking changes possible, ensuring consistency, and maintaining trust over the associated data assets (Aldoseri et al., 2023).

Adaptability also involves making use of real-time data access and management solutions. The traditional batch processing of data is similar to real-time decision-making. The finance, healthcare, and e-commerce sectors increasingly require real-time decision-making. Effective governance frameworks consist of automated systems that monitor and enforce policies without human intervention and help firms to stay compliant while responding quickly to new opportunities or threats. Modern governance frameworks with increased strictness in regulations on data privacy, such as GDPR and CCPA, focus on compliance. Good frameworks ensure that at all stages of a data lifecycle, its collection, storage, processing, and eventual deletion, the ability to demonstrate compliance is ensured. A compliance-centric approach not only prevents illegal risks, but also gives customers trust that the data are managed responsibly and ethically (Goldsteen et al., 2019).

3. THE TRANSFORMATIVE ROLE OF DATA IN ORGANIZATIONS

3.1 Evolution of Data's Role

What was always considered to be a byproduct of any operational process, data were relegated to record-keeping and retrospective analysis over the last two decades. Today, data has become one of the prime strategic assets that fuels informed decision-making, thanks to the latest analytics and data integration technologies that allow it to be used not only to understand past performance but also to forecast what may happen in the future. Currently, data are used not only to analyze past performance but also to project new trends and opportunities (Ramzi et al., 2021). This change reflects a broad range of industries. In retail business, for example, data analytics is the means by which businesses gain knowledge about customers and, in turn, adjust many levels of inventory and the factors that affect customer choices. Patient data in the health sector are often the first indication of early or developing diseases, speed-up, and focus intervention. Businesses have become competitive and proactive in such an environment by treating data as an active and valuable asset (Dash et al., 2019).

The role of information in organizations has changed dramatically over the past few centuries. Initially, data was mostly used to support record keeping, where the information is stored in ledgers, spreadsheets, and simple databases. Normally, updates are done manually, and access is limited to certain teams, which also reduces its utility. Technology changed what used to be just a passive record of past transactions to become an asset influencing business decisions, indicating future trends and optimizing operations. Such a change came as a result of the emergence of data analytics tools capable of processing information in large quantities to yield meaningful insights. Companies discovered that data could not only be used to describe the past but also miraculously predict future outcomes and produce the correct courses of action. (Wu et al., 2019)

This was seen in firms like Amazon, which through customer data paved the way for more personalized shopping experiences, and in Netflix with viewing data where content development strategies were informed. Companies have turned data from a source that did very little to become an active business success enabler when it is governed in a manner that makes all data everywhere in the organization accurate, accessible, and secure.

3.2 Strategic Importance in AI-Driven Business Intelligence

Data governance is key to unlocking the promise of AI-driven business intelligence. As AI systems rely on vast amounts of high-quality data, an AI model can amplify the benefits of governed data by providing deeper actionable insights. Well-governed data fosters improved certainty regarding the accuracy and reliability of AI models; thus, data governance delivers smarter strategies and more effective decision-making. For example, if data in the financial services sector are well governed, AI algorithms can better anticipate the patterns of movement of the market, perfect the management of risks, and render the deal to customers as personalized as possible (Antwi et al., 2024). Figure 2 illustrates the contrasting outcomes of well-governed and poorly governed data in AI-driven decision making. While high-quality governed data lead to accurate insights and effective strategies, poor governance results in biased outputs and erroneous decisions, undermining the trustworthiness of business intelligence systems.

Figure 2. Big Data AI Driven Business Intelligence

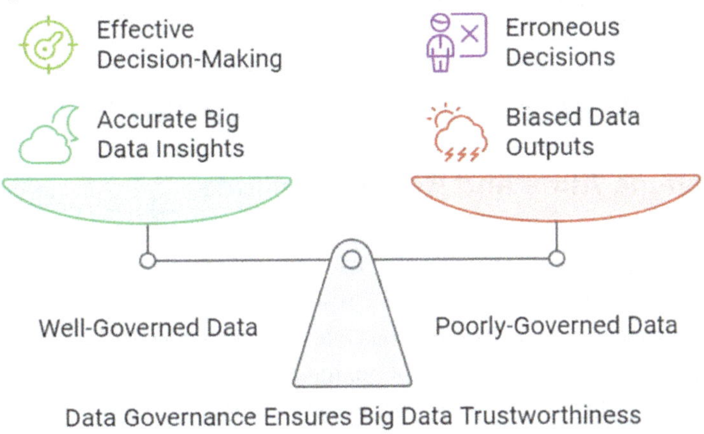

Second, governance frameworks enhanced by AI can automatically monitor and manage data quality. Organizations can achieve high standards for data integrity with minimal human intervention using techniques such as anomaly detection and machine-learning-based validation. Seamless integration using such methods ensures compliance with regulations and builds the ability of the organization to innovate at speed. Business organizations are thus enabled to turn their data into drivers of sustainable growth and resilience through the strategic use of AI. AI has multiplied the value of data by opening up complex business intelligence applications. Gated data are the backbone of AI systems, and they rely on data to train, learn, and sharpen their models. A good governance structure is very important in AI, as it helps ensure that the data used do not introduce bias into the AI system, increases wrong outputs, and damages the trustworthiness of business intelligence initiatives (Díaz-Rodríguez et al., 2023). AI integration with business intelligence enables organizations to integrate automated data analysis, hidden patterns, and real-time decision making regarding accuracy. For instance, predictive models of the supply chain may determine fluctuations in demand by using feeds for real-time data that enable companies to change their strategy and minimize waste as they maximize resources. The better the data, the worse the model. Poorly governed data, whether incomplete, outdated, or even inaccurate, might lead to faulty predictions and strategic missteps.

Proper data governance means that inputs into an AI application are clean, relevant, and timely. It provides a means by which practices and data are deployed with ethical considerations to ensure that the data-driven AI process is in compliance with laws and social norms. Alignment builds trust in AI-powered systems and enforces a culture of responsible data use. The stronger and more inclusive the data governance, the better an organization can use AI for strategic gains, feeding innovation, and sustainable growth (Urquhart et al., 2022).

4. CORE COMPONENTS OF DATA GOVERNANCE

4.1 Programme Aims and Responsibilities

A robust data governance program has strong definitions for its purpose and responsibility areas. They constitute the foundational elements of ownership and stewardship, so that every piece of data has responsible parties managing its lifecycle. In general, data ownership is the role of business leaders or departments responsible for the value and utility of data. Stewardship is conducted on a day-to-day basis to ensure that the data remain precise, available, and safe. The sound governance standards supporting these roles provide a consistent foundation for guiding decisions and operational protocols.

Roles must be well established; otherwise, data governance is likely to become siloed or fragmented, resulting in gaps in the implementation of policies, and data reliability will suffer. Governance programs that work effectively empower teams by educating them on their responsibilities and equipping them with tools to enforce such roles and create a culture to manage data proactively and strategically (Said et al., 2022). The mission and role definition in a data governance program properly direct the focus towards successful operations. A well-planned program starts with the determination of ownership and stewardship roles, which describe who is responsible for the data element. A data owner is typically an executive or department head responsible for strategic decisions regarding data assets to the corporation. Their role is to create policies and ensure that data administration meets all other objectives of the organization. Data stewards are also responsible for ensuring that governance policies are effectively implemented at a day-to-day level. They are responsible for the quality of the data, coordinate different compliance activities, and address any issues raised by the data.

Determining these roles prevents ambiguity in the data management practice. Sharing governance responsibilities among teams and individuals also prevents overburdening any team or individual. Dedicated stewardship by different business units leads to accountability and cooperation in fostering consistent application of governance policies across the organization (Nazari-Aref et al., 2021). Clearly, clear governance standards cannot be overemphasized. Standards indicate how the data are collected, stored, processed, and archived. These standards should be communicated throughout the organization to ensure that everyone in the company follows the same standards and practices for managing their data. For example, clear guidelines on classifications of data help to determine which data should be classified as sensitive and which ones are not sensitive to avoid breaches and non-compliance. Figure 3 illustrates the three foundational components of an effective data governance framework: data lineage, cataloging and classification, and data-worthiness techniques. These elements ensure transparency, facilitate proper usage, and maintain the accuracy and reliability of organizational data.

Figure 3. Core Components of Data Governance

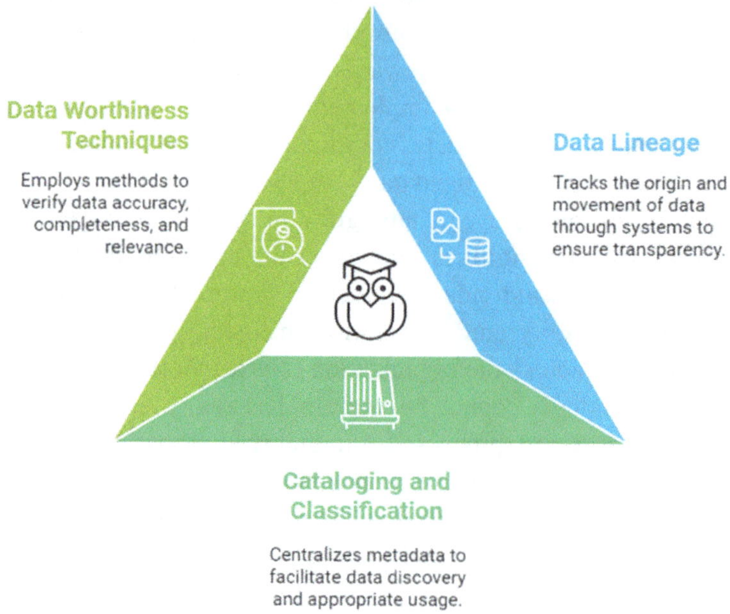

4.2 Practical Procedures

The key procedures forming the backbone of any data governance framework are data lineage, cataloging, and classification. The data lineage provides a line of origin and a path for transformation through various systems. This is important to maintain transparency and trust. Proper cataloging helps organizations maintain an organized inventory of their data assets, facilitating easy location and proper usage by stakeholders. Furthermore, classification refers to marking the data based on the sensitivity and importance level so that proper control measures over security and compliance can be applied (Aldoseri et al., 2023). Data trustworthiness techniques involve data auditing on a schedule, automated quality checks, and metadata to improve data management. The advanced technologies used in machine-learning algorithms can automate parts of the process, thus enabling the detection of anomalies or inconsistencies that human oversight might miss. It is a collection of practical procedures that implies data reliability and is meant to assure organizations that there is a high level of trust in their data and reduce the associated risks with bad practices related to handling data.

Therefore, good data governance is a practical and well-documented procedure that guides the management, protection, and utilization of data. Among the key procedures in the management of data is the concept of data lineage; that is, the origin and movement of data at various junctures of its flow through different systems. Data lineage is a key enabler of transparency in data production and enables organizations to quickly spot a consistent error or fault in data production and resolve it. Transparency is essential for establishing the accuracy of data because it supports better decision making (Renggli et al., 2021).

Catalogs and classifications are important for data governance. Data catalogs are centralized repositories that deliver comprehensive metadata for every organization's data assets, including the source, structure, and usage history. Maintaining the latest cataloging of data may thus prove useful in making the discovery of data more feasible and locating data with much ease to enable employees to apply it appropriately when required.

Techniques for determining whether the data are worthy include verification of accuracy, completeness, and pertinence using methods that 'prove' the data. Data profiling, though a non-daily tool, can be used to evaluate the quality of a dataset regarding patterns, outliers, and other types of relationships. Automation tools can therefore run such analyses frequently enough, signaling questionable anomalies or potential quality issues. The next technique is the use of validation rules at the time of data entry, so that inaccuracies do not creep in from the very beginning (Nieto et al., 2021). To build confidence in the validity of the data, an organization requires solid backing and disaster recovery practices. Backups protect against unexpected loss of data due to system failure or cyber-attack. Regularly scheduled backups kept in safe locations enhance one's ability to quickly restore data in the most expedient manner possible, with minimal disruption to business operations.

The fact is that the implementation of these core procedures will bring organizations closer to building trust in the reliability of their data assets through the impressive enhancement of their data governance framework.

5. PRACTICAL CHALLENGES IN BIG DATA GOVERNANCE

5.1 Key Problem Areas

Large fragments of big data governance do exist with some significant challenges, beginning with inconsistent architectures. These organizations have developed their systems over time and, therefore, have fragmented data systems across the organizational domain, resulting in patchworks of legacy technologies and modern platforms. There will be consistency in governance policies that can be an issue, and equally problematic is the consistency of quality data across the organization. The lack of a unified architecture adds complexity to integrating data sources and further complicates the development of a coherent governance framework. The other major barriers are data invisibility and poor sponsorship. Data visibility involves knowing what data exists, where it resides, and how it is being used. Organizations struggle to maintain an inventory that is transparent to their data assets in difficult, fast-moving data environments. Another similar barrier is inadequate sponsorship by senior leaders. It is unlikely that such programs will be linked to the overall organizational strategy, funded appropriately, or invested in without support from champions among executives who champion data governance initiatives. This means that there are challenges for data governance initiatives, such as lack of resources and poor execution, making it ineffective at providing benefits (Wong et al., 2020).

Big-data environments are often associated with inconsistent architectures that impede effective data governance. These are a consequence of the disparate systems and platforms that organizations have implemented over time through mergers and acquisitions or through gradual upgrades to newer technologies. Such broken topography brings quite a few challenges to using uniform governance policies for data. The data might reside in legacy on-premises systems, public cloud offerings, or third-party applications, all with their governance capabilities and limitations. It is challenging to enforce the uniformity of governance standards in such disparate environments. Most of the time, this leads to siloed environments where data are less than optimally integrated and often inaccessible to key stakeholders (Koivisto & Taipalus, 2023). Lack of visibility of the data is another major challenge that hampers the ability of an organization to manage its data assets effectively. Organizations are not conversant with the breadth and depth of their data without proper visibility. This calls for inefficiencies in their operations as well as possible breaches in data compliance. A governance program with a lack of strategic alignment and authority will most definitely be caused by a lack of sponsorship in governance by senior leadership. This requires strong leadership sponsorship to push the benefits of data governance, ensure proper resource allocation, and create a value message as part of the business strategy. Unless this sponsorship exists, the initiative is likely to collapse, with governance perceived as an add-on rather than a core enabler in doing business.

Table 1. Big Data Challenges

No.	Challenge
1	Lack of big data governance frameworks.
2	Shortage of the required skilled people on big data.
3	Big data security and privacy.
4	Lack of required tools to generate insight from the data in timely manner.

continued on following page

Table 1. Continued

No.	Challenge
5	Organisations resistance to use data in goal setting and decision-making.
6	Insufficient knowledge on big data by the business managers.
7	Digitisation of the businesses remain a challenge to most of the organisations.
8	Complexity of the data collected and stored (e.g. unstructured data).

5.2 Addressing Organizational Challenges

To this end, organizations need to align data governance strategies with overall business goals to ensure that governance is not perceived as a standalone function, but rather as an integral part of the realization of company objectives. Leadership plays a critical role in this regard. The executives will make data governance undeniable to all, and will ensure that appropriate resources are secured in order to have a true governance program. The other tools for data cataloging and metadata management to improve data visibility in an organization are described above. This enables stakeholders to create data assets; hence, they are easily visible and manageable. Embedding governance practices in the culture and aligning them with appropriate operational objectives builds the capability of companies to effectively meet the challenges of the day and the challenges that will be in the future regarding data management. Such challenges require a multifaceted approach toward solving them. In particular, the alignment of governance frameworks with business objectives is required. The issue here begins with how the strategic importance of data governance is communicated so that the benefits of business growth, compliance, and risk management become apparent. When governance aligns with business goals, it is no longer an administrative burden but rather one of the main pillars of corporate strategy (Jiménez et al., 2019). This implies that improved data visibility depends largely on the application of data cataloging and metadata management tools. These tools create an absolute, comprehensive inventory of an organization's data assets, thus enhancing both its discoverability and traceability. For instance, through data catalogs, organizations can map relationships between different datasets; understand their usage, origin, and ownership; and thereby enjoy a level of visibility that fosters effective data governance to accommodate compliance audits and risk assessments by clear data lineage. There must also be a culture for valuing data stewardship. Educating employees on responsibility for data quality and security is required for this purpose. Organizational culture can be built by offering regular workshops, training programs, and awareness campaigns. Educating teams about best practices and the importance of data governance can encourage this community to feel responsible as all, not just a few dedicated ones (Hyun et al., 2020).

6. BEST PRACTICES FOR EFFECTIVE DATA GOVERNANCE

As shown in Figure 4, effective data governance is grounded in a multidimensional approach that integrates people, processes, and technology.

- Automation and Modernization refer to the application of advanced tools and technologiessuch as machine learning and AIto streamline governance activities. Automating tasks such as data validation, anomaly detection, and policy enforcement reduces human error and allows organizations to operate at the scale and speed of modern data systems. Recent work has emphasized the importance of scalable infrastructures that can support AI-powered automation and real-time data handling at scale (Li, 2025). Such intelligent automation of data processes represents a shift toward AI-integrated governance architectures (Achanta, 2025).
- Accessibility and Security underscore the importance of making data readily available to those who need it, while maintaining strict protection to prevent misuse. Striking this balance ensures that data remain both strategic assets and resources.
- Data Literacy emphasizes human elements in governance. When individuals across an organization are educated on how to interpret, question, and ethically apply data, they become active participants in maintaining high standards of data quality and compliance.

By embedding these practices within organizational culture, institutions are better positioned to realize the full value of their data assets while ensuring alignment with regulatory and ethical standards.

Figure 4. Best Practices for Effective Data Governance.

6.1 Automation and Modernization

Automation and modernization, through the integration of AI, have transformed data governance in various ways. AI can take the process forward by automating repetitive procedures such as classification, compliance checks, and quality assessment, which require significant manual effort. These technologies enable organizations to maintain high-quality data integrity while reducing the time and effort required to go into governance. For example, AI tools classify data based on predefined rules, or even learn to classify new types of data using machine learning algorithms. This dynamic capability allows organizations to adapt to changes in data sources and types without requiring significant interference by hand. Anomaly detection is one of the primary areas in which AI impacts the modernization process. By using machine learning algorithms, data streams can be monitored in real time for changes in patterns that may reflect irregularities, errors, breaches, or compliance issues; thus, organizations can act in a timely manner to mitigate the risks before they are allowed to blow out of proportion. Predictive analytics using AI-based predictive analytics can predict future governance-related issues by using historical data patterns to alert the organization ahead of time, so that it can prepare itself and make adequate adjustments in strategy to counter the challenges beforehand (Medaglia et al., 2021). Automation also allows for the periodic updating of data governance documentation, often put by the side because it is cumbersome to create and maintain. Generating and automatically updating governance policies through tools means keeping the documents current and reflective of operational realities;

the process becomes more transparent, and all stakeholders better understand the data practices and procedures.

Data governance significantly depends on AI and automation; it can automate many governance tasks, such as data classifications, quality checks, and monitoring of compliance, thus enabling the processing of big datasets with minimal human intervention, thereby ensuring lower error rates and improving efficiency in the process. For instance, AI algorithms can be applied to identify real-time anomalies in data. This would immediately raise red flags in areas related to the data and consequently ensure that problems with the data are promptly identified and corrected. Automation of Data Governance modernizes data governance not only by making the processes faster but also by making it scalable and growth dependent on the landscape of data (Wong et al., 2020; McGregor & Hostetler, 2023).

6.2 Balancing Accessibility and Security

One perennial challenge facing data governance is the mutual role of accessibility and security. Open access to data can spur innovation and enable employees to make data-driven decisions. However, if not balanced with adequate controls, this openness leads to potential security vulnerabilities and noncompliance with privacy regulations. Data governance must find a balance in which the data are accessible where needed but inaccessible from unauthorized access. This can be achieved through role-based access controls, in which permissions are tailored based on the roles of users and the sensitivity of the data. Organizations also use advanced encryption and anonymization techniques to protect data usability. A governance structure would therefore need to be established so that data are leveraged efficiently and safeguards against misuse and compliance with legal requirements (Anwar et al., 2021). One of these issues will be access-security balance, as organizations attempt to construct data-driven ecosystems. Open access to data forms an important trigger for innovation and a platform to ensure that employees know what they are doing; however, this must be balanced with a much more robust security that ensures this does not occur and that they are compliant with any and all regulatory requirements relative to data protection. Role-based access controls (RBAC), of course, are one of the underpinning elements of this balance that allow organizations to assign specific permissions to roles based on the responsibility of the user or his role, along with the sensitivity of the data involved.

Organizations must also implement masking and anonymization techniques. The masked and anonymized sensitive data allows sensitive data access without compromising individual privacy or regulatory requirements. These techniques modify the data to obscure the PII while maintaining the utility of the dataset for analysis purposes. Layered security combines the use of encryption, multifactor authentication, and activity monitoring to protect data that are not overly limiting access (Protivash et al., 2024).

Accessibility and security entail constant trade-offs. This translates to regularly reviewing access permissions and security protocols to ensure that these evolve with the fluidity of business needs and regulatory needs. In the case of organizations becoming remote and hybrid, data governance policies must be articulated in a manner that allows them to consider specific security matters pertaining to the access of data across locations and devices.

6.3 Building Data Literacy

A good data governance strategy goes beyond technology and processes, as well as a culture in which stakeholders understand and value data. These people in the organization should be able to interpret and use data appropriately, from frontline workers to senior leaders. Empowering stakeholders with the skills to read, work with, and communicate data supports quality decision-making and builds even firmer adherence to governance protocols. Organizations can gain data literacy via targeted training programs, workshops, and continuous education initiatives. Encouraging collaboration between data experts and non-expert teams helps bridge gaps and fosters a culture of shared responsibility for the quality and governance of data. When stakeholders are well-versed in data principles, they contribute to maintaining data integrity and maximizing value from governed data for strategic purposes (Aldoseri et al., 2023).

Empowerment begins by establishing a strong base for data literacy in the organization. Data literacy refers to the ability to read, understand, create, and communicate data. The quality and consistency of data-driven decision-making significantly improves when stakeholders at every level—whether data scientists, business analysts, or even non-technical staff—are at least baselined in knowing how to work with data.

Data literacy can be encouraged in organizations through standardized employee training programmes that focus on roles within the company. Such training should include main topics, such as interpretation from data dashboards, knowing the sources of data, and ensuring that data are ethical. As events are simulated, employees have increased trust in what they know as they apply it in interactive workshops or scenario-based training (Marti & Smith, 2023). From a practical point of view, as teams share the development of data competencies, a sense of interdependence improves collaboration. One perspective is that of the internal consultant, which can be a data steward offering expertise to help teams work through complexity and share best practices to promote governance policies. In due course, this close collaboration aids in strengthening the collective capability of the organization to use data responsibly and effectively. Promoting cross-departmental projects that encourage practical use of data in varied contexts helps support the imperative of data literacy, underlining the value it adds. Employees will be much more engaged and proactive about maintaining governance standards when they see the effects that data can have on outcomes.

7. CASE STUDIES: REAL-WORLD APPLICATIONS

7.1 Airbnb and Uber

Examples of data-governance-based customer-centric innovations are provided by two large tech companies, Airbnb and Uber. The latter relies on big, dynamic streams of data that generate personally relevant experiences and optimize their offerings for users. For instance, the security and responsible use of host and guest data ensures the improvement of recommendation flows and smoothens booking processes. Their governance framework includes data encryption, clear data ownership policies, and compliance checks, which foster trust among users and enhance platform reliability. Uber uses data governance for complex datasets linked to the real-time GPS tracking of riders, the usual practices preferred by riders, and payment handling. Governance protocols protect users' data and keep Uber compliant with global regulations because Uber operates in various jurisdictions with different laws regarding data privacy. The proactive approach that Uber employs regarding data governance allows it to innovate by using data without compromising user security or violating local regulations (Kollnig et al., 2021). As an example, the scalable data ecosystem of My Uber has already ingested tens of terabytes of new data each day into a Hadoop data lake of 100+ petabytes that is run on over 10000 vCores and has over 100000 batch jobs running daily. They have one of the largest Presto queries, Spark jobs, and Hive query executions with nearly 100,000, 10,000, and 20,000, respectively, towards the end of the day. These figures vividly depict the sheer magnitude at which contemporary organizations have to manage information (Reza, 2018).

7.2 GE Aviation

The case of GE Aviation is interesting, from which one can learn to make operational efficiency tenable through data governance. In fact, the aviation business generates enormous volumes of data, from engine performance metrics to maintenance records. GE Aviation focused on ensuring that these datasets, which are highly critical to predictive maintenance and operational planning, would remain consistent and accurately representative. GE Aviation improves process safety, maintains optimum schedules, and avoids downtime through efficient stewardship of data and automated quality checks. The governance framework often integrates intimately with the processes related to the analytics of companies' data in the pursuit of monitoring and making real-time decisions. This has led to reduced costs and efficiency because insights from data can be better used in resourcing and managing fleets. (Wirges & Neyer, 2022; Thomas et al., 2020). These benefits are echoed in GE Vernova's broader ecosystem. For instance, its SmartSignal platform currently monitors over 7,000 critical assets worldwide, supporting predictive maintenance, which has saved more than $1.6 billion USD. GE's use of AI/ML-powered Digital Twins, including 3D contextual models for asset inspections and Process Digital Twins for optimizing manufacturing, demonstrates the scalable impact of real-time, data-governed decision-making. In practice, these models have led to reductions in product waste by up to 75%, improved throughput by up to 20%, and increased operational efficiency across complex systems, reinforcing the value of strong data governance integrated with predictive analytics (GE Vernova, 2024)

7.3 CSE Insurance

CSE Insurance represents the importance of data governance based on compliance in the financial sector. For any insurance company, data include customer details, policy documents, and claims information, all of which need to be carefully protected and strictly adhere to financial regulatory compliance. The multi-faceted data governance model, CSE Insurance, has various aspects, many of which encompass data classification, encryption, and perfectly safe protocols in accessing the data.

This is also true in the compliance tracking area, where AI is applied by the firm in automatically flagging potential breaches or anomalies in data handling. This means there will be proactive practice: CSE Insurance adheres to requirements set by regulatory bodies but ensures confidence among its clients in showing commitment to data privacy and security (Cartagena et al., 2020; Thapa & Camtepe, 2020).

8. FUTURE TRENDS IN DATA GOVERNANCE

8.1 Emerging Technologies and AI Integration

Going forward, it will link data governance to emerging technologies and AI itself will be a prime area of focus. Applications to NLP-classify and tag unstructured data automatically; better anomaly detection through data quality monitoring ensures that machine learning algorithms perform. To an extent, hybrid cloud environments dictate how data governance plays out as organizations store and process data in different infrastructures, with robust protocols maintaining background operations.

AI's integration of AI into data governance frameworks will allow organizations to transition from reactive to proactive data management. It can predict data quality issues in advance and, hence, take proactive measures. Such a shift will not only make governance processes easier but also inculcate governance in the dynamics of changing organizations (McCullough, 2024; Jiménez et al., 2019).

8.2 Shaping a Data-Driven Culture

It is only upon instilling data governance as an organizational culture that it will be effective. Future trends will point to the emergence of a data-driven mindset where workers at every level will understand that they are valuable assets in the maintenance of data standards. Thus, the culture will ensure sustained innovations based on a trusted base of AI-driven insights and strategic decisions developed based on governed data. Companies will then invest in placing those investments in continuous education, reproducing data literacy programs that can equip teams with confidence in the use and management of data. There will be a drive toward building a culture in which data governance is not perceived as an impediment, but rather as creativity, agility, and responsibly innovative (Ghodoosi et al., 2023).

9. IMPLEMENTATION DETAILS AND REAL-WORLD APPLICABILITY OF AI-INTEGRATED DATA GOVERNANCE FRAMEWORKS

Translating AI-integrated data governance frameworks into practical, scalable solutions requires a careful fusion of theoretical models and engineering implementation. The Digital Twin architectural framework offers a structured path for operationalizing governance needs across varied infrastructures—on-premise, cloud, or hybrid—facilitating functions such as compliance auditing, data lineage tracking, and real-time monitoring (Fett et al., 2024). The Multiphase Optimization Strategy (MOST), initially developed for behavioral interventions, reinforces the importance of modular design, iterative development, and adaptability—qualities critical to evolving governance structures (Szeszulski & Guastaferro, 2024). Technologically, platforms like Apache Spark and CUDA-enabled GPUs support real-time data processing, model training, and anomaly detection in dynamic environments (Myllis et al., 2025). A successful implementation strategy must prioritize modularity, scalability, and ethical principles such as privacy, fairness, and transparency. Furthermore, involving stakeholders through participatory design and continuous feedback ensures the framework remains resilient, context-aware, and capable of delivering sustainable value in complex data ecosystems.

10. CONCLUSION

For starters, it represents data governance as what transforms the big ecosystem into an assurance of data quality, security, and compliance towards unlocking the hidden value of data for strategic use. A few case studies include achievements toward customer-centric innovation, business efficiency, and compliance at Airbnb, Uber, GE Aviation, and CSE Insurance. The future of data governance will thus be significantly influenced by emerging technologies, such as AI, NLP, and hybrid cloud environments, while being steeped in the culture of developing a data-driven culture. Today, this means balancing innovation with robust governance at the heart of what any enterprise must do to deal with the changing context for AI-driven decision-making. Balanced governance in pursuit of technological advancement will enable firms to build resilient data practices that support growth, decrease risk, and uphold trust in the digital era.

Future research should focus on developing real-time, domain-specific data governance solutions enhanced by explainable AI (XAI), which promotes transparency, accountability, and trust in automated decision-making. XAI is especially vital in ethically sensitive sectors like healthcare, finance, and government. Comparative cross-sectoral studies are needed to explore governance differences across domains—such as data privacy in healthcare versus compliance in finance—to inform tailored policy development. Additionally, longitudinal studies examining the long-term impact of AI-based governance on regulation, risk management, and stakeholder trust will offer valuable insights for building ethical, resilient, and sustainable data ecosystems across various industries.

REFERENCES

Abu-Salih, B., Wongthongtham, P., Zhu, D., Chan, K. Y., & Rudra, A. (2021). Introduction to Big Data Technology. https://arxiv.org/pdf/2104.08062v1.pdf

Achanta, P. R. D. (2025). Transformative Effect: Rise of Intelligent Data Management in Integration with AI. *Transactions on Engineering and Computing Sciences, 13*(1), 116–123. DOI: 10.14738/tecs.131.18275

Aldoseri, A., Al-Khalifa, K., & Hamouda, A. M. S. (2023). Re-Thinking Data Strategy and Integration for Artificial Intelligence: Concepts, Opportunities, and Challenges. In A. Aldoseri, K. Al-Khalifa, & A. M. S. Hamouda, Applied Sciences (Vol. 13, Issue 12, p. 7082). Multidisciplinary Digital Publishing Institute. https://doi.org/DOI: 10.3390/app13127082

Antwi, B. O., Adelakun, B. O., & Eziefule, A. O. (2024). Transforming Financial Reporting with AI: Enhancing Accuracy and Timeliness. In B. O. Antwi, B. O. Adelakun, & A. O. Eziefule, International Journal of Advanced Economics (Vol. 6, Issue 6, p. 205). Fair East Publishers. https://doi.org/DOI: 10.51594/ijae.v6i6.1229

Anwar, M. J., Gill, A. Q., Hussain, F. K., & Imran, M. (2021). Secure big data ecosystem architecture: challenges and solutions. In M. J. Anwar, A. Q. Gill, F. K. Hussain, & M. Imran, EURASIP Journal on Wireless Communications and Networking (Vol. 2021, Issue 1). Springer Nature. https://doi.org/DOI: 10.1186/s13638-021-01996-2

Aroyo, L., Lease, M., Paritosh, P., & Schaekermann, M. (2021). Data Excellence for AI: Why Should You Care. In L. Aroyo, M. Lease, P. Paritosh, & M. Schaekermann, arXiv (Cornell University). Cornell University. https://doi.org/DOI: 10.48550/arXiv.2111

Baijens, J., Huygh, T., & Helms, R. (2021). Establishing and theorising data analytics governance: a descriptive framework and a VSM-based view. In J. Baijens, T. Huygh, & R. Helms, Journal of Business Analytics (Vol. 5, Issue 1, p. 101). Taylor & Francis. https://doi.org/DOI: 10.1080/2573234x.2021.1955021

Bengio, Y., Hinton, G. E., Yao, A. C.-C., Song, D., Abbeel, P., Darrell, T., Harari, Y. N., Zhang, Y.-Q., Lan, X., Shalev-Shwartz, S., Hadfield, G. K., Clune, J., Maharaj, T., Hutter, F., Baydin, A. G., McIlraith, S. A., Gao, Q., Acharya, A., Krueger, D., . . . Mindermann, S. (2024). Managing extreme AI risks amid rapid progress. In Y. Bengio, G. E. Hinton, A. C.-C. Yao, D. Song, P. Abbeel, T. Darrell, Y. N. Harari, Y.-Q. Zhang, X. Lan, S. Shalev-Shwartz, G. K. Hadfield, J. Clune, T. Maharaj, F. Hutter, A. G. Baydin, S. A. McIlraith, Q. Gao, A. Acharya, D. Krueger, … S. Mindermann, Science (Vol. 384, Issue 6698, p. 842). American Association for the Advancement of Science. https://doi.org/DOI: 10.1126/science.adn0117

Cartagena, S., Gosrani, V., Grewal, J. S., & Pikinska, J. (2020). Silent cyber assessment framework. In S. Cartagena, V. Gosrani, J. S. Grewal, & J. Pikinska, British Actuarial Journal (Vol. 25). Cambridge University Press. https://doi.org/DOI: 10.1017/s1357321720000021

Chukwurah, N., Adebayo, V., Eyieyien, O., & Ige, A. (2024). Frameworks for effective data governance: Best practices, challenges, and implementation strategies across industries. *Computer Science & IT Research Journal*, *5*(7), 1666–1679. DOI: 10.51594/csitrj.v5i7.1351

Dam, T., Krimbacher, A., & Neumaier, S. (2023). Policy Patterns for Usage Control in Data Spaces. In T. Dam, A. Krimbacher, & S. Neumaier, arXiv (Cornell University). Cornell University. https://doi.org//arxiv.2309.11289DOI: 10.48550

Dash, S., Shakyawar, S. K., Sharma, L., & Kaushik, S. (2019). Big data in healthcare: management, analysis and future prospects. In S. Dash, S. K. Shakyawar, L. Sharma, & S. Kaushik, Journal Of Big Data (Vol. 6, Issue 1). Springer Science+Business Media. https://doi.org/DOI: 10.1186/s40537-019-0217-0

Díaz-Rodríguez, N., Ser, J. D., Coeckelbergh, M., de Prado, M. L., Herrera-Viedma, E., & Herrera, F. (2023). Connecting the dots in trustworthy Artificial Intelligence: From AI principles, ethics, and key requirements to responsible AI systems and regulation. In N. Díaz-Rodríguez, J. D. Ser, M. Coeckelbergh, M. L. de Prado, E. Herrera-Viedma, & F. Herrera, Information Fusion (Vol. 99, p. 101896). Elsevier BV. https://doi.org/DOI: 10.1016/j.inffus.2023.101896

Fattah, I. A. (2024). Decision making performance of business analytics capabilities: The role of big data literacy and analytics competency. *Business Process Management Journal*, *30*(6), 2096–2126. DOI: 10.1108/bpmj-11-2023-0894

Fett, M., Kraft, M., Wartzack, S., Goetz, S., Wilking, F., & Kirchner, E. (2024). Medium-Level Architectures for Digital Twins: Bridging Conceptual Reference Architectures to Practical Implementation in Cloud, Edge and Cloud–Edge Deployments. *Electronics (Basel)*, *13*(7), 1373. DOI: 10.3390/electronics13071373

Ghodoosi, B., Torrisi-Steele, G., West, T., & Li, Q. (2023). An Exploration of the Definition of Data Literacy in the Academic and Public Domains. In B. Ghodoosi, G. Torrisi-Steele, T. West, & Q. Li, International Journal of Adult Education and Technology (Vol. 14, Issue 1, p. 1). IGI Global. https://doi.org/DOI: 10.4018/ijaet.325218

Goldsteen, A., Douek, T., Cohen, Y., Gokhman, I., Keren-Ackerman, O., Katsovich, G., Weintraub, G., & Ben-Ari, D. (2019). Forgotten @ Scale: A Practical Solution for Implementing the Right To Be Forgotten in Large-Scale Systems. In A. Goldsteen, T. Douek, Y. Cohen, I. Gokhman, O. Keren-Ackerman, G. Katsovich, G. Weintraub, & D. Ben-Ari, arXiv (Cornell University). Cornell University. https://doi.org/DOI: 10.48550/arXiv.1910

Hyun, Y., Kamioka, T., & Hosoya, R. (2020). Improving Agility Using Big Data Analytics: The Role of Democratization Culture. In Y. Hyun, T. Kamioka, & R. Hosoya, Pacific Asia journal of the Association for Information Systems (Vol. 12, p. 34). Association for Information Systems. https://doi.org/DOI: 10.17705/1thci.12202

Janssen, M., Brous, P., Estévez, E., Barbosa, L. S., & Janowski, T. (2020). Data governance: Organizing data for trustworthy Artificial Intelligence. In M. Janssen, P. Brous, E. Estévez, L. S. Barbosa, & T. Janowski, Government Information Quarterly (Vol. 37, Issue 3, p. 101493). Elsevier BV. https://doi.org/DOI: 10.1016/j.giq.2020.101493

Jiménez, L., Polo, J., & Duarte, N. (2019). Overview of Data Governance in Business Contexts. In L. Jiménez, J. Polo, & N. Duarte, IOP Conference Series Materials Science and Engineering (Vol. 519, Issue 1, p. 12023). IOP Publishing. https://doi.org/DOI: 10.1088/1757-899x/519/1/012023

Koivisto, K., & Taipalus, T. (2023). Pitfalls in Effective Knowledge Management: Insights from an International Information Technology Organization. In K. Koivisto & T. Taipalus, arXiv (Cornell University). Cornell University. https://doi.org/DOI: 10.48550/arXiv.2304

Kollnig, K., Binns, R., Kleek, M. V., Lyngs, U., Zhao, J., Tinsman, C., & Shadbolt, N. (2021). Before and after GDPR: tracking in mobile apps. In K. Kollnig, R. Binns, M. V. Kleek, U. Lyngs, J. Zhao, C. Tinsman, & N. Shadbolt, Internet Policy Review (Vol. 10, Issue 4). Alexander von Humboldt Institute for Internet and Society. https://doi.org/DOI: 10.14763/2021.4.1611

Li, A. (2025). AI-Driven Big Data Analytics: Scalable Architectures and Real-Time Processing. *European Journal of AI. Computer Information*, *1*(1), 33–41. DOI: 10.71222/pw8kw891

Marti, D., & Smith, M. (2023). Motivating Data Science Students to Participate and Learn. In D. Marti & M. Smith, Harvard Data Science Review (Vol. 5, Issue 1). The MIT Press. https://doi.org/DOI: 10.1162/99608f92.d3b2eadd

McCullough, A. (2024). Defining a new perspective: Enterprise Information Governance. In A. McCullough, arXiv (Cornell University). Cornell University. https://doi.org//arxiv.2409.14388DOI: 10.48550

McGregor, S., & Hostetler, J. (2023). Data-Centric Governance. In S. McGregor & J. Hostetler, arXiv (Cornell University). Cornell University. https://doi.org/DOI: 10.48550/arXiv.2302

Medaglia, R., Gil-García, J. R., & Pardo, T. A. (2021). Artificial Intelligence in Government: Taking Stock and Moving Forward. In R. Medaglia, J. R. Gil-García, & T. A. Pardo, Social Science Computer Review (Vol. 41, Issue 1, p. 123). SAGE Publishing. https://doi.org/DOI: 10.1177/08944393211034087

Myllis, G., Vrana, V. G., Tsimpiris, A., & Aggelopoulos, S. (2025). High-Performance Computing and Parallel Algorithms for Urban Water Demand Forecasting. *Algorithms*, *18*(4), 182. DOI: 10.3390/a18040182

Nazari-Aref, G., Farokh-Seresht, B., Ahmadi, G. A., & Eslami, S. (2021). Designing a Good Corporate Governance Model in the Context of Ethics and Rationality. In G. Nazari-Aref, B. Farokh-Seresht, G. A. Ahmadi, & S. Eslami, International Journal of Ethics & Society (Vol. 3, Issue 1, p. 41). https://doi.org/DOI: 10.52547/ijethics.3.1.41

Nieto, F. J., Aguilera, U., & López-de-Ipiña, D. (2021). Analyzing Particularities of Sensor Datasets for Supporting Data Understanding and Preparation. In F. J. Nieto, U. Aguilera, & D. López-de-Ipiña, Sensors (Vol. 21, Issue 18, p. 6063). Multidisciplinary Digital Publishing Institute. https://doi.org/DOI: 10.3390/s21186063

Nwobodo, L., Adegbola, A., & Nwaimo, C. (2024). Enhancing cybersecurity protocols in the era of big data and advanced analytics. *GSC Advanced Research and Reviews*, *19*(3), 203–214. DOI: 10.30574/gscarr.2024.19.3.0211

Olubusola, O., Ajayi-Nifise, A., Falaiye, T., Mhlongo, N., & Daraojimba, D. (2024). Machine learning in financial forecasting: A U.S. review: Exploring the advancements, challenges, and implications of AI-driven predictions in financial markets. *World Journal of Advanced Research and Reviews*, *21*(2), 1969–1984. DOI: 10.30574/wjarr.2024.21.2.0444

Pajooh, H. H., Rashid, M. A., Alam, F., & Demidenko, S. (2021). IoT Big Data provenance scheme using blockchain on Hadoop ecosystem. In H. H. Pajooh, M. A. Rashid, F. Alam, & S. Demidenko, Journal Of Big Data (Vol. 8, Issue 1). Springer Science+Business Media. https://doi.org/DOI: 10.1186/s40537-021-00505-y

Prabaharan, G., Chithrakumar, T., Vidhya, S. M., Balakrishnan, M. B., & Sika, K. (2025). AI-Driven Computational Frameworks: Advancing Edge Intelligence and Smart Systems. *International Journal of Computational and Experimental Science and Engineering*, *11*(1). Advance online publication. DOI: 10.22399/ijcesen.1165

Prakash, D. (2024). Data-Driven Management: The Impact of Big Data Analytics on Organizational Performance. *International Journal for Global Academic & Scientific Research*, *3*(2), 12–23. DOI: 10.55938/ijgasr.v3i2.74

Protivash, P., Durrell, J., Kifer, D., Ding, Z., & Zhang, D. (2024). Reconstruction Attacks on Aggressive Relaxations of Differential Privacy. In P. Protivash, J. Durrell, D. Kifer, Z. Ding, & D. Zhang, Journal of Privacy and Confidentiality (Vol. 14, Issue 3). https://doi.org/DOI: 10.29012/jpc.871

Ramzi, B., Alsuliman, A., & Elrayah, M. (2021). The Reasons that Affect the Implementation of HR Analytics among HR Professionals. In *B. Ramzi* (p. 29). A. Alsuliman, & M. Elrayah, Canadian Journal of Business and Information Studies., DOI: 10.34104/cjbis.021.029037

Renggli, C., Rimanic, L., Gürel, N. M., Karlaš, B., Wu, W., & Zhang, C. (2021). A Data Quality-Driven View of MLOps. In C. Renggli, L. Rimanic, N. M. Gürel, B. Karlaš, W. Wu, & C. Zhang, arXiv (Cornell University). Cornell University. https://doi.org//arxiv.2102.07750DOI: 10.48550

Reza, R. (2018), Uber's Big Data Platform: 100+ Petabytes with Minute Latency. Uber Blog. https://www.uber.com/en-IN/blog/uber-big-data-platform/

Sadiq, S., Aryani, A., Demartini, G., Hua, W., Indulska, M., Burton-Jones, A., Khosravi, H., Benavides-Prado, D., Sellis, T., Someh, I., Vaithianathan, R., Wang, S., & Zhou, X. (2022). Information Resilience: the nexus of responsible and agile approaches to information use. In S. Sadiq, A. Aryani, G. Demartini, W. Hua, M. Indulska, A. Burton-Jones, H. Khosravi, D. Benavides-Prado, T. Sellis, I. Someh, R. Vaithianathan, S. Wang, & X. Zhou, The VLDB Journal (Vol. 31, Issue 5, p. 1059). Springer Science+Business Media. https://doi.org/DOI: 10.1007/s00778-021-00720-2

Said, J., & Alam, Md. M., & Khalid, M. A. (2022). Relationship between good governance and integrity system: Empirical study on the public sector of Malaysia. https://doi.org/DOI: 10.31235/osf.io/hdcf7

Samara, H. H., Qudah, H. A., Abualhijad, S., Alqudah, M. Z., Mohsin, H. J., Al Rahamneh, S., & Bani Hani, L. Y. (2024). Artificial intelligence and machine learning in corporate governance: A bibliometric analysis. *Human Systems Management*, •••, 1–27. DOI: 10.3233/hsm-240114

Shen, X., Brown, H., Tao, J., Strobel, M., Tong, Y., Narayan, A., Soh, H., & Doshi-Velez, F. (2024). Directions of Technical Innovation for Regulatable AI Systems. In X. Shen, H. Brown, J. Tao, M. Strobel, Y. Tong, A. Narayan, H. Soh, & F. Doshi-Velez, Communications of the ACM. Association for Computing Machinery. https://doi.org/DOI: 10.1145/3653670

Singh, M., & Khan, S. (2024). Advances in Autonomous Robotics: Integrating AI and Machine Learning for Enhanced Automation and Control in Industrial Applications. *International Journal for Multidimensional Research Perspectives*, *2*(4), 74–90. DOI: 10.61877/ijmrp.v2i4.135

Szeszulski, J., & Guastaferro, K. (2024). Optimization of implementation strategies using the Multiphase Optimization STratgey (MOST) framework: Practical guidance using the factorial design. *Translational Behavioral Medicine*, *14*(9), 505–513. DOI: 10.1093/tbm/ibae035 PMID: 38906703

Thapa, C., & Camtepe, S. (2020). Precision health data: Requirements, challenges and existing techniques for data security and privacy [Review of Precision health data: Requirements, challenges and existing techniques for data security and privacy]. Computers in Biology and Medicine, 129, 104130. Elsevier BV. https://doi.org/DOI: 10.1016/j.compbiomed.2020.104130

Thomas, S. A., Dubey, A., Viassolo, D., & Zanette, M. (2020). Digital Fleet Management: A Scalable Cloud Framework based on Data-driven Prediction Models. In S. A. Thomas, A. Dubey, D. Viassolo, & M. Zanette, Annual Conference of the PHM Society (Vol. 12, Issue 1, p. 8). https://doi.org/DOI: 10.36001/phmconf.2020.v12i1.1273

Urquhart, L., McGarry, G., & Crabtree, A. (2022). Legal Provocations for HCI in the Design and Development of Trustworthy Autonomous Systems. https://doi.org/DOI: 10.1145/3546155.3546690

Vernova, G. E. (2024). *Digital Twin Technology | GE Vernova*. Gevernova.com. https://www.gevernova.com/software/innovation/digital-twin-technology

Wirges, F., & Neyer, A. (2022). Towards a process-oriented understanding of HR analytics: implementation and application. In F. Wirges & A. Neyer, Review of Managerial Science (Vol. 17, Issue 6, p. 2077). Springer Science+Business Media. https://doi.org/DOI: 10.1007/s11846-022-00574-0

Wong, D. H.-T., Maarop, N., & Samy, G. N. (2020). Data Governance and Data Stewardship: A Success Procedure (By D. H.-T. Wong, N. Maarop, & G. N. Samy; Vol. 202, p. 54). https://doi.org/DOI: 10.1109/icimu49871.2020.9243574

Wu, L., Hitt, L. M., & Lou, B. (2019). Data Analytics, Innovation, and Firm Productivity. In L. Wu, L. M. Hitt, & B. Lou, Management Science (Vol. 66, Issue 5, p. 2017). Institute for Operations Research and the Management Sciences. https://doi.org/DOI: 10.1287/mnsc.2018.3281

Zhao, S., Peng, Q., Mou, X., Wang, Y., & Han, T. (2021). An artificial intelligence-based real-time monitoring framework for time series. In S. Zhao, Q. Peng, X. Mou, Y. Wang, & T. Han, Journal of Intelligent & Fuzzy Systems (Vol. 40, Issue 6, p. 10401). IOS Press. https://doi.org/DOI: 10.3233/jifs-200366

Chapter 7
Autonomous Data Orchestration With Generative AI:
Redefining Pipelines for Intelligent Analytics

Muhammad Usman Tariq
https://orcid.org/0000-0002-7605-3040
Abu Dhabi University, UAE & University College Cork, Ireland

ABSTRACT

Orchestration of autonomous data using generated AI transforms traditional analytics pipelines by introducing intelligent automation, context-related decision-making, and adaptive data workflows. This ambitious paradigm leverages the capabilities of large-scale models and basic AI systems to dynamically manage the absorption, transformation, integration, and delivery of data, eliminating the need for constant human supervision. Generated AI enables the system to interpret metadata, understand the data's intent, and optimize the pipeline itself based on power metrics or actual time analysis requirements. In contrast to the traditional static architecture, autonomous orchestration introduces continuous learning, enabling the pipeline to evolve further and adapt to changing business requirements and data ecosystems. Enhance agility, eliminate operational bottlenecks, and enhance accessibility for advanced analytics. This shift redefines the role of data engineers, focusing on governance, monitoring, and strategic design while minimizing manual intervention in pipeline operations.

DOI: 10.4018/979-8-3373-5616-7.ch007

INTRODUCTION

The development of data pipelines over the past 20 years has been characterized by a significant transformation of manual code capabilities into intelligent and autonomous systems. In the early stages of data technology, pipelines were created manually using scripting languages and batch-oriented ETL processes (extract, transformation, load). These pipelines were stiff, fragile, and required deep technical knowledge. As data volume, speed, and diversity increased, the limitations of manual engineering became clearer, and orchestration frameworks such as Apache Airflow and Luigi were developed, improving dependency management, planning, and monitoring. However, even these systems remained largely dependent and relied on human intervention (Kurnia et al., 2025). The rise of cloud computing ecosystems, real-time analytics, and API control has given us more complex and necessary pipelines, which are more adaptive, scalable, and resilient. This demand for flexibility has laid the foundation for integrating artificial intelligence into data orchestration. Generation AI introduces new layers of cognitive skills in the orchestration stack, enabling the system to interpret data, generate transformation logic, automate the creation of metadata, and even interact with users in natural language.

Pipelines are no longer limited to specified logic. Now, you can develop dynamically in response to changes in data schemes, business goals, or system anomalies. It represents a fundamental change in the creation and behavior of a data system. Generated AI can analyze the structure and content of data, identify relevant processing steps, generate code, and explain decisions in a manner that aligns with the business context. It fills the gap between data engineering and domain expertise, enabling non-technical users to launch and manage complex workflows with simple input requests (Khokhlov, 2025). This democratization of orchestration encourages greater cooperation, accelerates time, and makes analysis more responsive, adapting to the organization's needs. It examines how traditional pipeline concepts, such as orchestration, planning, transformation, surveillance, and governance, are reinterpreted through the lens of AI. This chapter provides an overview of the fundamental components of intelligent pipeline design, including recording, transformation, observability, and feedback loops. Secondly, the unique functions that the generative model brings to these components include Dynamic schema inference, metadata enrichment, and prompt-based pipeline production. In subsequent sections, we explore architectural patterns, critical tools and platforms, evaluation metrics for AI-controlled orchestration, and key aspects of security, privacy, and governance. This chapter also explores emerging trends, including the self-parenting pipeline and agent-based engineering, offering insights into the ethical and operational implications of fully autonomous systems. Ultimately, this chapter aims to provide readers with a fundamental redesign in a new era of intelligent analytics infrastructure, as well as improving data orchestration. Figure 1 provides a summary of the historical progression of data pipelines over the past two decades, culminating in the integration of generative AI and autonomous orchestration.

Figure 1. Evolution of Data Pipelines: From Manual ETL to Autonomous Generative Orchestration

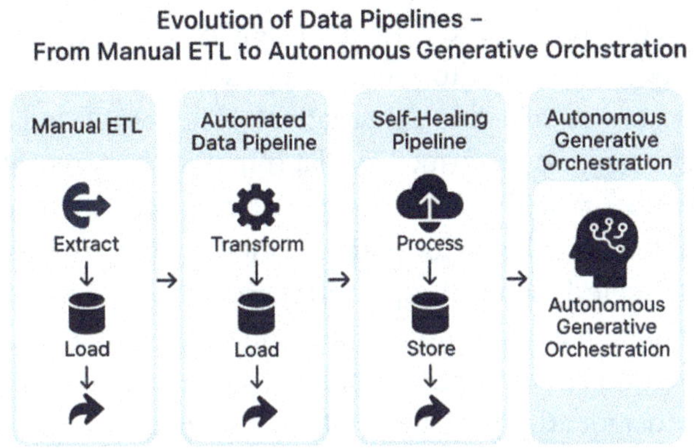

FOUNDATIONS OF AUTONOMOUS DATA PIPELINES

The basis of an autonomous data pipeline lies in the convergence of traditional data development principles with advanced artificial intelligence and machine learning technology, particularly in the integration of large language models (LLMs) and generative models. In the past, data pipelines have been built on core concepts such as orchestration, planning, data lines, and observability. These foundations enabled the structured movement and transformation of data. However, they were primarily manual, fragile, and challenging to adapt in real-time. With the advent of intelligent orchestration agents and generative AI, the data technology landscape is rapidly changing today from static and procedural systems to dynamic, contextual, conscious, and self-exhaustive infrastructure. This shift is more than just an evolution of technology; it is a profound transformation (Khokhlov, 2025). Defines data processes, rules, and methods used to support modern enterprise decisions. In its most basic form, the orchestration system ensures that data flows in the correct order, dependencies are satisfied, and errors are recognized and processed. Tools like Apache Airstrow, Luigi, and Dagster have long dominated this room, offering engineers a declarative way to define workflows as directed acyclic graphs (DAGs). These systems are characterized by planning and dependency management. However, they require extensive manual configuration and offer limited adaptability, particularly when the data environment or business requirements suddenly change.

Traditional orchestration models expose sophisticated decision-making and stability assumptions that are no longer applicable in a more complex, multi-cloud, real-time data ecosystem. It is based on fixed intervals (every hour, daily), event control triggers (such as file updates or API changes), or conditional logic (such as job completion). While planning remains an essential part of the orchestration process, strict implementation in legacy systems often leads to inefficiency (Khokhlov, 2025). For example, if you want to process new data and calculate resources, the pipeline can run on a fixed schedule. Alternatively, if external signals are delayed or unpredictable, they cannot be performed. As data pipelines become more autonomous, planning evolves into a more intelligent and critical process, where workflows can respond to system state, user behavior, and even model versions. Intelligent planning enables pipelines to scale dynamically, prioritize urgent tasks, and pause or reconsider processes based on anomalies or limitations. This line is essential for debugging, governance, testing, and compliance. It helps teams understand the dependencies between data records, identify the origins of anomalies, and assess the downstream impact of changes. In traditional systems, descent is often maintained quickly by outdated manual documents or embedded metadata (Tariq, 2025).

In contrast, autonomous pipelines allow for automatic generation and maintenance of parent-child relationships. These pipelines can create dynamic phylogenetic diagrams with machine-readable metadata and integrated observation tools developed with systems and enriched with semantic annotations. If a generative model is involved, the line is extended to the model itself. The logic used to generate input requests, training data, and transformations must be attributed to ensure transparency and reproducibility. Includes a collection of metrics, logging, alarms, and perception. Observability enables engineers to identify data quality issues, jobs, and latency peaks before they are implemented in downstream systems, allowing for proactive resolution. In traditional environments, observability tools often work independently of orchestration platforms, requiring manual integration and configuration. However, autonomous pipelines natively include observability on any component, so real-time telemetry guides orchestral decisions. For example, suppose the conversion step exceeds the Service Level Agreement (SLA) or consistently produces a missing value. In that case, the system can automatically apply logic, escalate the issue to a human operator, or convert it to a fallback model. This feedback-controlled architecture is of great importance for maintaining trust and operational excellence in autonomous systems. These agents act as autonomous units that can make actual decisions about performing tasks, recovering from errors, and implementing optimizations. They rely on contextual awareness, historical knowledge, and predictive analytics to coordinate workflows in a way that addresses business priorities and operational limitations. Intelligent agents monitor both the technical conditions of the pipeline and its business semantics, enabling adaptive behavior (Musiol, 2024). For example, an agent can prioritize financial reporting orders at the end of the quarter if it encounters an unexpected input pattern. This level of responsiveness is not possible with static planning or hard-coded logic. Natural Language and Conversation - Through the AI interface, users can create, modify, or query pipelines without writing complex code. Agents can implement business intent in executable logic, document documents, and surface recommendations for optimization or error resolution. Over time, these agents learn from user feedback, improve their accuracy, and become valuable co-pilots in the data development process. This shift not only increases productivity but also democratizes access to data infrastructure, allowing a wider range of stakeholders to participate in pipeline development and maintenance. These models serve as cognitive functions in autonomous systems, enabling context, decision-making, and content production. In the orchestration layer, LLMS workflows can plan and adapt to high targets or varying input conditions. For example, you can determine which data sources to prioritize during a failure or how to clean up data if dependencies fail. In the conversion layer, LLMS codes, card schemes, or business rules may be generated from examples or descriptions. It allows pipelines to be developed quickly without the need for hand-coded updates for source system changes or business logic changes.

In the Metadata and Observatory layers, generative models enrich the data with context-related tags, generating explanations for users in a human-readable format that includes pipeline behavior, as well as anomalies and errors. For example, if the data quality check fails, the system can create a natural language report. Furthermore, LLMS acts as an interface layer, lists pipeline tools from text, and allows users to define workflows via input requests (Khokhlov, 2025). Business analysts can say, "Extract customer orders from the last 30 days, group them by product category, and load them into the marketing dashboard." The system automatically generates the entire pipeline, including planning, transformation, and output logic. Pipelines are not static cables but dynamic systems that feel, think, and act. They understand their context, learn from those around them, and continuously improve. They can interpret user intent, adapt their actions in real-time, and document their actions for testing and compliance purposes. This autonomy drives innovation as well as operational efficiency, allowing organizations to focus on experimentation, insights, and value creation rather than infrastructure maintenance. Convergence of orchestration, scheduling, data lineage, and observations between intelligent agents and the capabilities of generative models. These systems are transformed from deterministic workflows into adaptive learning units that work with humans and continuously optimize themselves. Embed LLM into core components and use real-time feedback to allow businesses to achieve new levels of mobility, transparency, and intelligence with data manipulation. This development serves not only as a data pipeline tool for moving data but also lays the foundation for future strategic insights, automation, and innovation.

GENERATIVE AI CAPABILITIES IN DATA ORCHESTRATION

Generative AI revolutionizes the data orchestration landscape by introducing new layers of intelligence beyond static workflows, rigid configurations, and manually coded logic. Traditionally, data orchestration systems rely on human engineers to define and maintain the schemes, transformations, and sequences of data pipelines. These systems are robust but naturally fragile, time-consuming, and dynamic, with uneven scaling environments. Generated AIS in the data orchestration process, particularly large-scale speech model (LLM) injection (adaptive, autonomous, and context-related skills to significantly reduce technical costs and extend the era. Production and optimization of pipelines tailored to the context and expansion of pipeline interfaces from text using data engineer input requests. In traditional systems, schema inference often relies on rule-based analysis or manual input. However, the ability to close structures becomes essential, especially as data volume and diversity grow on modern architectures, APIs, protocols, semi-structured files, and SaaS platforms from third-party providers (Abel et al., 2025). Generated AI models can derive the best scheme by analyzing raw data records, such as nested JSON, XML, and even unstructured text, and identifying patterns, key-value relationships, data types, and implicit hierarchies. These models not only recognize structural information, but also, for example, a model can conclude that a field named "cust_id" in a data record corresponds to another "customer_identifier," even if the conventions' format and naming are different. It enables intelligent schemes, the generation of transformation logic, and the standardization of data without requiring human intervention (Tariq, 2025).

By understanding both the source and target schemes, LLM can generate the transformation logic needed to combine different data records, process missing values, standardize formats, and enrich the data records using derived attributes. If a company user can create instructions such as "transforming all timestamps to ISO 8601 and normalizing product names, the model can create corresponding code (such as SQL, Pyspark, and DBT models) and integrate them into the pipeline. These transformations are context-related and often have national knowledge in adapting the operational model. They propose assignments to coordinate data across the clinical system. This dynamic capability reduces the complexity of data shifts, particularly in environments where schemes must adapt quickly to changes. Metadata information about data, such as origin, quality, classification, frequency of use, ownership, etc., is essential for governance, discovery, and conformance (Khokhlov, 2025). Generative AI Capabilities Across the Data Orchestration Lifecycle are illustrated in

Figure 2. Generative AI Capabilities Across the Data Orchestration Lifecycle

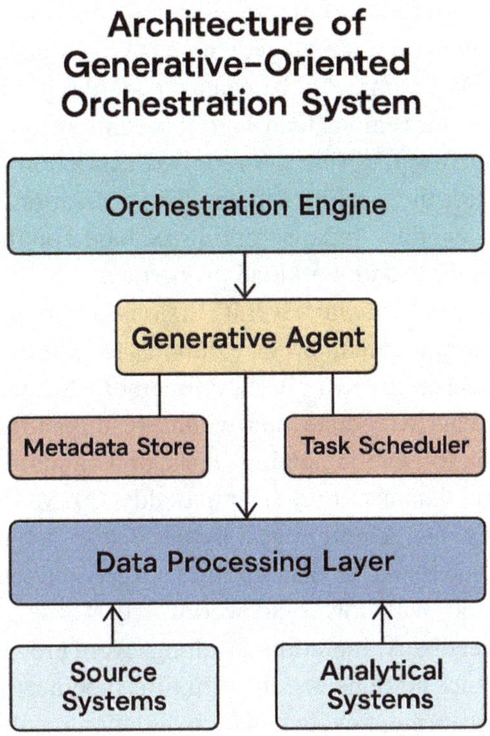

However, the manual production and maintenance of metadata are often overlooked due to their labor-intensive nature. Generation AI allows orchestration systems to create comprehensive metadata artifacts on running flights. When retrieving a new data record, the system describes its structure, proposes a day based on the content, uses language and pattern recognition to identify PII or sensitive fields, and classifies the data record according to the subject area or domain. It not only improves the usability of the data catalog and line tools but also enables the automatic use of governance engines, security guidelines, access controls, and compliance rules. For example, suppose a data record contains columns "click_timestamp" and "page_url." In that case, the generative model can characterize the "Web Activity Protocol" and link it to a broader ontology of customer loyalty. This semantic tagging enables AI control detection tools to be recommended for the relevant dataset, facilitating the most automatic relationships that a particular analysis or users may not consider. Additionally, enriched metadata can provide context during anomaly detection, thereby improving data observability. B. and sign that a sudden drop in transactions is due to a well-known API failure or scheme change in the upstream system. The structure of a pipeline traditionally requires a deeper understanding of the source system, transformation requirements, orchestration logic, and the technical syntax of the platform used. Generated AI greatly abstracts this complexity by explaining the intent of a system in natural language, which is then translated into a workflow that can be executed. For example, a data analyst could say: Create daily pipelines that aggregate sales to the region, load large amounts of output, and the system creates DAGs (e.g., airflow), define the required extraction steps, generate SQL transformations, and test the starting scheme for verification. These pipelines are not only dynamically generated but also optimized based on the execution context, historical performance data, and workload properties.

Generation models can evaluate several versions of the pipeline and even recommend or perform improvements. For example, to improve performance, it is recommended to switch or suggest a column memory format from line-based to columnar memory formats to mediate intermediate results and reduce the computing load. It also allows you to generate claims, tests, and validation reviews to ensure pipeline robustness and data accuracy (Narapareddy, 2025). Furthermore, generation optimization takes into account not only performance but also the automatic enforcement of guidelines, such as data minimization and retention restrictions, by adapting governance and workflow logic accordingly. These systems continuously learn from execution feedback, including teachings from previous errors, user connections, and performance bottlenecks, and refine the pipeline for future generations. It leads to a clever improvement cycle in which direction pipelines develop, both in terms of technical efficiency and business relevance (Chickermane, 2025).

ARCHITECTURE OF GENERATIVE-ORIENTED ORCHESTRATION SYSTEMS

The architecture of generation-oriented orchestration systems is a critical development from traditional ETL and data pipeline models. These next-generation systems are designed not only for automation but also for intelligence, adaptability, and self-improvement. They seamlessly integrate large language models (LLMs) and generate AI at multiple levels, enabling context-aware decisions, dynamic transformations, and human interaction with data systems. An architecture typically consists of several linked core components, particularly recording, transformation, monitoring, and feedback loops (Sendas & Rajale, 2025). These are improved through generation capabilities to ensure flexibility and response to data, business requirements, and operational conditions. You are responsible for capturing data from various structured, semi-structured, and unstructured sources, including APIs, databases, file systems, data lakes, news feeds, and real-time data streams. In a generation-oriented system, recording is not a static process determined solely by connectors and schemes. Instead, generative models can support scheme inference, anomaly detection, and metadata enrichment in the data on board.

Generation-oriented systems use LLMS to dynamically create, modify, and optimize these transformations based on intent or perceived conditions. For example, an analyst can explain natural language transformation goals, such as the following: Furthermore, generative models can eliminate misleading schemes between data sources, automatically normalize categorical variables, and propose new features for downstream ML models based on trends identified in historical data. These models are built into the transformation engine and serve as both peer clarification and automatic corrections, enabling pipelines to develop smoothly in response to business needs and data complexity. Instead of collecting passive metrics such as workplace, latency, and data quality reviews, generative models interpret protocols and metrics to provide an analysis of root causes and prescribed actions. For example, suppose the pipeline fails due to a change in the source system's schema. In that case, the monitoring component can call the generation agent to verify the schema configuration, update the conversion script, and propose a practical analysis of the downstream assets. These systems can also generate user-oriented warning messages or status reports in natural language. That is, the health of the system is equally accessible to both technical and non-technical stakeholders. Over time, surveillance systems equipped with generative AI will learn from previous incidents to predict potential pipeline errors, provide preventive measures, and shift the orchestration of reactive maintenance to a more stable state. Feedback is collected from multiple sources, including user interaction, model output, data quality metrics, and operating protocols. This feedback is continuously analyzed by an embedded model identifying the region for optimization (Benala & Dehuri, 2025). Figure 2 illustrates the multi-layer architecture of an intelligent, generative-AI-powered orchestration system, showing how components interact in real-time with embedded LLMs and feedback loops.

Figure 3. Architecture of Generative-Oriented Orchestration System

Pipeline Stage	Traditional Approach	Generative AI Enhancement
Schema Inference	Manual or rule-based schema detection	Automated dynamic schema detection via LLMs (e.g. JSON/XML parsing
Transform-tion Logic	Hand-coded SQL/ PySpark/DBT scripts	Prompt-to-code generation in natural language
Metadata Generation	Manually tagged or missing metadata	Automated enrichment with contextual, semantic tags
Workflow Automation	Static DAGs and predefined triggers	Adaptive, prompt-based pipeline generation and auto-adjustment

The orchestration tier can outsource generative models, incorporating workflow planning and adaptation based on dynamic conditions, such as SLA changes, data information patterns, or business priorities. It can also address context-conscious task planning, resource allocation, and failover strategies. In the transformation layer, the generative model facilitates the creation, validation, and optimization of data processing logic (Khokhlov, 2025). They support the structure of scalable data flows that adapt to shift schemes or analytical needs under development without the need for a complete renovation. At the analytic level, the generative model interacts with business users, converts natural language queries into executable code, generates dashboards, and provides contextual stories about trends and anomalies. This layered embedding enables orchestration systems to be not only autonomous but also accessible, explainable, and provide in-depth access to technical and business workflows.

However, a cloud-native approach can promptly address concerns about data residency, supplier closures, and compliance with local data protection regulations. It is where the hybrid implementation pattern takes effect. The hybrid architecture enables businesses to store sensitive data and perform critical processing while utilizing generated orchestration components hosted on-site or in a private cloud, simultaneously in the public cloud. In this model, orchestration logic can be performed from a cloud-based tax level. However, data recording, modification, and storage occur in a secure, localized environment. The principles of secure APIs, encrypted communication protocols, and zero loyalty ensure that the generated components can only access the required metadata or models without directly exposing them. The hybrid model is beneficial for large healthcare companies, as well as the financial and government sectors, where regulatory obligations limit the movement of data beyond controlled limits (Kanka, 2024; Tariq, 2025).

CASE STUDIES OF INDUSTRY APPLICATIONS

Actual applications of generative AI in the orchestration of autonomous data are beginning to redesign the industry by introducing adaptive intelligence at the core of data manipulation. As for sectors such as retail, healthcare, and finance, it not only improves performance but also facilitates the creation, maintenance, and direction of pipeline production, maintenance, and control. These case studies demonstrate how the integration of large-scale language modeling (LLM) and AI operational orchestration has transformed outcomes in domains with specific requirements for accuracy, compliance, and real-time response (Coimbatore Ramalingam, 2025). The traditional ETL process for forecasting demand requires analysts to manually integrate point data, sales data, delivery data records, advertising data, and data records from third-party providers and load them into the forecasting model. With the advent of generator AI, these ETL pipelines are dynamically generated and continuously optimized. Retailers are currently using LLMS to automatically generate and update data transformations based on real-time changes and sales events. For example, suppose a new product is introduced or a PhD is launched. In that case, the pipeline will automatically adapt the functions of the associated attributes, reconstructions, and predictive models to meet the new requirements.

Furthermore, the natural language interface enables category managers to inquire about sales forecasts by requesting simple language applications, thereby reducing reliance on data teams and accelerating decision-making cycles. The result is an agile prognostic process that responds more quickly to market signals, thereby improving inventory optimization and customer satisfaction. Organizations that wish to utilize patient data for research or operational efficiency are often hindered by regulatory hurdles, particularly when it involves actual health data (Joshi, 2025). The innovative application of AI is in orchestrating pipelines for generating synthetic health data. These pipelines are designed to simulate realistic yet anonymized health files that can be safely used for model training, testing, and release without compromising patient confidentiality. Genetic models, such as those in geese (a generally controversial network) and LLMs trained with structured health data, are coordinated with safe and conscious workflows. For example, suppose synthetic data records are generated to replicate the course of a disease. In that case, the orchestration system ensures that data transformation logic respects predefined rules regarding demographic balance, clinical realism, and ethical use. The orchestration platform utilizes the generated documentation tool to create detailed test passes, enabling regulators or internal reviewers to track the derivation and verification of synthetic data. This level of safe orchestration, enabled by AI, opens up new avenues for innovation in healthcare while maintaining trust and accountability. Financial institutions process large amounts of transaction data, where the early detection of fraud is crucial. Relatedly, traditional batch pipelines are too slow, and even static real-time pipelines struggle to keep up with ambitious scams. Integrated into an orchestration system, LLMS continuously generates, tests, and provides identification rules that evolve in response to behavioral changes. For example, suppose it is possible to identify an increase in peer-to-peer broadcasts that contain round numbers for a particular area. In that case, the orchestration engine, led by the generation AI, can modify the fraud recognition logic to mark similar samples in the future. These adaptation pipelines also include synthetic feedback loops, and investigator decisions are used to improve controlled production and reduce false-positive results. LLMS can automatically create incident reports that summarise suspicious activities and provide context-related knowledge to risk analysts (Sapkota et al., 2025).

SECURITY, PRIVACY, AND GOVERNANCE CONSIDERATIONS

As the autonomous data orchestration systems of modern analytical infrastructure acquire meaning, the integration of security, privacy, and governance principles is not only a technical necessity but also a fundamental requirement. The increased dependence on orchestration associated with AI leads to new complexities and risks, especially when these systems, which rely on static and regular pipelines, transition to dynamic, self-promoting workflows that involve some degree of agency. Traditional governance models, which rely on manual enforcement, regular audits, and static controls, are no longer sufficient. Instead, organizations should adopt AI-controlled governance strategies that integrate continuous, adaptive, scalable data protection and compliance directly into their orchestration logic. It illustrates the transition from governance to governance as a code, serving as a form of supervision. The intelligent agents of the data infrastructure itself enforce it. Instead of relying on humanly written validation scripts or role-based access control models, AI rules can dynamically interpret and enforce data lifecycle guidelines (O'Connor, 2024; Tariq, 2025).

Traditional data protection approaches, such as access control and encryption systems, should be complemented by orchestration-level protection measures that monitor how data is used and transformed. Methods such as differential privacy, federated learning, homomorphic encryption, and other techniques are increasingly integrated into orchestration platforms to enable data protection calculations (Chaccour et al., 2024). Autonomous pipelines operating with generative AI can directly incorporate different data protection algorithms into the conversion step, allowing noise parameters to be adapted based on data sensitivity and analysis purposes. Federated Learning enables distributed model training across multiple data silos, allowing raw data to remain within the source environment. In such cases, orchestration layers coordinate model updates, ensure communication protocols, and only certified agents participate in the training process while simultaneously maintaining audibility and repeatability (Morabito & Jang, 2025). These data protection patterns are significant for global companies that need to comply with a patchwork of data protection laws across various jurisdictions, such as the European GDPR, US HIPAA, and China's PIPLA. As pipelines become more autonomous and complex, all data movements, transformations, and decisions are recorded, explained, and then guaranteed to be challenged beyond the scope of traditional protocol tools.

Generated AI, when integrated into the orchestration layer, can produce rich, natural language documents that explain the measures taken, why they were taken, and the associated political contexts. For example, suppose a pipeline changes its processing of user data in response to a change in the consent status of a region. In that case, the system can generate compliance notes. With the consent payment on April 12, 2025, the region A user data has been anonymized in accordance with Article 25 of the GDPR. The transformation logic has been adjusted to exclude personal identifiers from the report dataset. This level of narrative documentation significantly improves the economy and reduces manual effort. It is usually related to preparation for a regulatory inspection or internal assessment. These trails are automatically updated and stamped promptly, providing regulators, auditors, and internal stakeholders with a transparent view of how data is being handled over time. These test functions must not be post-effect add-ons but rather an important part of the orchestration system itself, embedded in every node of the workflow. Combined with an immutable protocol infrastructure such as blockchain, the resulting testing pathway offers a high degree of integrity and verifiability, as it is only at Upper Lake. It not only supports compliance protection but also creates organizational resilience by allowing faster response and analysis of route actions in the event of violations or failures (Ismail et al., 2025). Orchestration engines that can create transformation logic, initiate API calls, and modify permissions based on AI-driven insights must be monitored in strict sandboxes. AI-generated decisions, particularly those that affect the movement of external data or privileged access, should be evaluated against a predefined security baseline. It requires a guideline framework as code under conditions that allow AI agents to act autonomously and require human consent. Duration management, such as motion monitoring, anomaly recognition, and security warnings generated by AI, can identify potentially malicious measurements.

EVALUATION METRICS FOR AUTONOMOUS PIPELINES

As the orchestration of autonomous data becomes an important part of modern analytical infrastructure, evaluating effectiveness requires a fundamental rethinking of traditional metrics. While legacy data pipelines are often evaluated based on throughput, latency, and error rates, autonomous pipelines introduce new dimensions of intelligence, adaptability, and decision-making that operational metrics cannot adequately capture. Evaluation of this new paradigm should include not only performance and reliability but also the quality of explanation, adaptability, and human-AI collaboration. These emerging systems operate like less deterministic machines, incorporating cognitively active ingredients that are effective in complex, developed environments. Therefore, a multidimensional frame of valuation metrics is required to assess the overall value and risk of an autonomous orchestration system.

Performance is scaled in relation to autonomous pipelines, encompassing not only speed and resource efficiency but also other key aspects. The effectiveness of AI control decisions, including the accuracy of the generated transformation logic and the relevance of the model control workflow, must also be documented (Khokhlov, 2025). For example, suppose an LLM-based agent generates a conversion script to clean product data. In that case, performance should be measured more than if you manually wrote whether the resulting data is clean, better structured, and more useful. It means integrating domestically specific quality metrics such as integrity, uniqueness, consistency, and domestic relevance, especially when AI systems implement semantic conclusions. Autonomous pipelines operate with limited or non-human surveillance. It means that schemes, lazy data sources, conceptual drifts, or infrastructure errors must be resistant to. A reliable autonomous orchestration system should be able to recognize anomalies, redirect jobs, and return to ensure default settings in case of prediction failure. Therefore, new reliability metrics include error recovery time, false negative rates in recognition of abnormalities, accuracy of pipeline self-healing, and volatile indexes. These metrics not only quantify whether the system works but also contribute to whether it recovers gracefully and maintains operational integrity under stress. In contrast to static ETL scripts, which can be manually checked, AI-generated conversion or routing decisions are often opaque. Explanation benchmarks should measure how a system can clearly and accurately communicate its arguments, decision criteria, and data lines to human stakeholders. For example, suppose an autonomous agent is connected to several data records. In that case, you need to justify why you chose a particular key or filter, especially if these decisions affect downstream business intelligence or machine learning models. Human interpretability assessments, transparency audits, or structured reviews, such as form values for model-driven components and DAG-level line declarations for orchestration workflows, can quantify descriptions. These benchmarks are important not only for debugging but also for fostering user trust and ensuring compliance with regulatory requirements. In contrast to traditional pipelines that are regularly and manually tested, autonomous systems learn to adapt to the requirements of a continuous evaluation mechanism (Kaal, 2025). Feedback loops allow human users or downstream systems to evaluate the outcome of actions generated by AI. Successful accuracy or predictive release of generated data allocation. These reviews are then returned to the orchestration model to optimize the behavior. Metrics such as annual feedback word time, improved accuracy per iteration, and sensitivity of drift detection quantify how effectively system feedback flows and improves performance over time. By generating controlled data records with known properties, edge cases, and anomalies, teams can guide the system in various scenarios that are not yet represented in production data. It allows tension testing of pipeline logic, model rain, and anomaly recognition systems.

The most important metrics include test coverage of data patterns, false positive and false negative rates in the detection of abnormalities, and execution stability under synthetic stress. Additionally, synthetic data can simulate future data scenarios such as sudden changes, new user behavior types, and geographical extensions. It evaluates how generalized orchestration logic is to new contexts. It is essential for pipelines that support customer-oriented systems where reliability directly affects user experience and trust. These are systems in which both human experts and autonomous agents participate in the design, execution, and adaptation of data workflows. Assessing the effectiveness of such cooperation requires metrics that assess the balance, quality, and outcome of everyday activities. For example, orchestration systems can track how often decisions generated by AI-supported pipelines override user input (Joshi, 2025). Metrics such as intervention rates (human interventions), reduced assessments (whether human trust in AI decisions corresponds to accuracy), and co-creation index (when agents and people characterize workflows) provide insight into the symbiosis between human components. A high override rate can indicate a lack of trust in AI skills, inadequate explanations, or inconsistencies in business logic. Conversely, excessive automation with little human involvement in the system can send signals to the system, which can lead to blind spots and ethical risks. The aim is to achieve an optimal balance in which the system autonomously handles well-understood tasks and takes over daily tasks effectively. A mixed-initiative assessment not only supports performance tracking but also contributes to systemic government, ensuring that the orchestration process is transparent, fair, and responsible. Apart from immediate performance, these metrics have long-term strategic value. As autonomous orchestration systems become the fundamental infrastructure, businesses must continually adapt their development to focus on business goals, regulatory requirements, and technological changes. Evaluation frameworks should be developed into live systems that can be implemented in real-time, similar to the orchestration system being measured (Shethiya, 2024). It should be seamlessly integrated into observability platforms, governance dashboards, and incident response tools. Furthermore, industry-wide benchmarks and joint evaluation protocols can promote standardization, comparability, and reliability of a broader ecosystem, as well as benchmarks for model accuracy and software reliability today.

TOOLS, FRAMEWORKS, AND PLATFORMS

As the architecture of data-controlled systems becomes increasingly complex and intelligent, tools, frameworks, and platforms need to be developed to create and manage autonomous orchestration. At the heart of this transformation is the confluence of three significant trends: the rise of open-source orchestration tools, the rapid integration of large-scale language models (LLMs) in execution pipelines, and the development of configurable future stacks, a combination of vector databases, and the creation of fast engineering and flexible workflow motors. Together, these innovations form the backbone of next-generation analytics platforms, enabling more dynamic, scalable, and intelligent data systems. Initially developed for Airbnb, Apache Airflow is a comprehensive workflow orchestration tool known for its flexibility and modularity. It allows engineers to define task-directed acyclic graphs (DAGs), show dependencies, and plan in a declarative, Python-based format. Airflow was initially developed to manage data pipelines. However, it was later expanded to include various plugins, operators, and sensors that integrate it with cloud services, APIs, and data warehouses. Its scalability makes it a core component of many corporate data stacks, especially when combined with modern observation tools and container infrastructure. It is specifically designed for machine learning (ML) application cases. It supports the full lifecycle of model training and hyperparameter tuning, tailored to deliver and monitor models in a containerized, scalable environment. Kubeflow Pipelines allows users to define complex ML workflows with reusable components. It facilitates reproducibility and experimentation at scale. In contrast to the airflow that is generally nearby, Kubeflow is closely integrated into the data science process, offering benefits such as distributed training, GPU planning, and native support for TensorFlow. It makes it ideal for organizations using AI in scaled production environments, especially when real-time inference and resource-intensive training are involved. It provides chaining input requests, manages contexts, and offers abstraction and integration for connecting LLMs with external tools and databases (Liu et al., 2025). Langchain makes it easy to create LLM drives that can invoke documents, make API calls, and maintain memory through interactions. When LLMS switches from an experimental chatbot to a core infrastructure component, Langchain plays a central role in enabling organized thinking about dynamic and unstructured data. Developers can configure complex workflows where voice models act as autonomous agents, transfer tasks, evaluate options, and generate executable code as part of a broader orchestration framework. Traditionally, data workflows were procedural and deterministic, based on precisely defined inputs, outputs, and rules.

Using LLMS for the orchestration layer enables the workflow to be adaptive and generative. For example, instead of creating static transformation logic, developers can instruct LLM to normalize new data sources or generate the code needed to assign different schemas. These instructions can be dynamically injected in this term, allowing pipelines to adapt to changes in the data environment. It is particularly powerful in applications such as real-time personalization, where orchestral engines dynamically interpret, generate properties, and insert them into models that adapt to all interactions. With these improvements, the LLM not only processes the data but also converts it into an orchestral agent that manages the pipeline itself. For example, LLM can monitor job success numbers, recognize abnormal delays, suggest code optimizations, and also rewrite DAGs based on shift priorities. It increases orchestration from mere planning to intelligent adjustments. It generates AI that plays an active role in maintaining the health and alignment of the pipeline. As LLMS grows, it will likely standardize integration into orchestration systems, similar to SQL queries and API calls, and thus act as a leading citizen of the enterprise data ecosystem. These stacks consistently combine the performance of Vector databases, fast engineering, and workflow engines with modular architectures that support real-time, contextual, and adaptive analytics (Coimbatore Ramalingam, 2025). Vector databases, such as Pinecone, Weaviate, and Chroma, are designed to store high-dimensional embeddings generated by LLMS or other AI models. These embeddings enable systems to perform similarity search, semantic access, and context-related recommendations with significantly higher accuracy and speed compared to traditional keyword-based approaches. By integrating Vectord databases into an orchestration pipeline, applications such as semantic search over protocols, dynamic user profiles, and document rankings can be run as part of an automated workflow. It includes design, testing, and versioning of natural language requirements that guide the behavior of LLM. In the context of orchestration, fast engineering determines model interactions, ensuring they are safe and align with business goals. For example, the prompt may instruct you to standardize this dataset according to the ISO 8601 date format and generate SQL code to join the customer and transaction tables using the best available foreign keys. The workflow allows the various components of the stack to be controlled and interoperable with LLM in an explanatory way. Unlike traditional schedulers, these modern engines offer strong observability, dynamic execution graphs, and native support for asynchronous tasks and retries.

Merging these components will generate a configurable and resilient orchestration platform that is not only intelligent but also robust. Future stacks include a vector ship database of contextual memory, a long-chain-based agent layer for decision-making, a prompt repository with governance controls, and a Dougster engine for coordinating execution through a cloud-native environment. Such stacks can continuously learn from feedback, adapt to new requirements, and maintain a high level of reliability even under rapidly changing data conditions. It also supports modularity, allowing businesses to exchange new models, databases, or tools without requiring modifications to the entire infrastructure (Jiang et al., 2025). Open-source projects such as Airflow, Kubeflow, and Langchain provide the basic skills for orchestrating stacked jobs, ML workflows, and LLM applications. Improved LLM integration enables the pipeline to be more intelligent, autonomous, and adaptable to change (Khokhlov, 2025). After all, future stacks, fast engineering, and workflow engines, combined with Vector databases, provide the prerequisites for fully adaptive, real-time, and human-oriented analytical systems. As businesses embrace these technologies, the orchestration layer is no longer a passive scheduler; instead, the intelligent, generative brain of the data infrastructure can be discussed in an unprecedented way to adapt and collaborate with human users.

FUTURE TRENDS AND RESEARCH DIRECTIONS

The future of data orchestration is poised to go far beyond everyday product automation, especially if you are skilled in generating AI. Three ambitious trends—the ethical implications of self-healing pipelines and generative observability, agents as genes within corporate data environments, and fully autonomous decision orchestration—fundamentally redefine how data infrastructure is designed, managed, and controlled. These developments not only provide opportunities to expand intelligence and resistance throughout the data lifecycle but also ask important questions about the responsibility, monitoring, and trust of AI control systems (Lakkarasu, 2024). Traditional data pipelines often rely on static dependencies, brittle schemes, and manually coded logic. It makes it susceptible to minor obstacles, such as changes in column names, shifts in upstream API formats, or issues with the incubation period for distributed jobs. Generation AI enables pipelines to recognize anomalies in real-time by learning the basic behavioral patterns of the ingestion, conversion, and delivery stages. If deviations, such as sudden drops or non-matching line counts of data volumes, can initiate a self-healing mechanism through automatic schema adjustments and rollbacks, rerouting dynamic tasks, or providing case back logic. For example, pipelines that process product data from multiple providers autonomously identify corrupt input files, enabling the synthesis of new transformation scripts to clean and reevaluate the data and notify stakeholders without requiring human intervention (Xu et al., 2025). While traditional observation tools focus on collecting metrics, protocols, and traces for retrospective analysis, they introduce the generative observability of proactive AI-controlled narrative explanations of pipeline health and behavior. Instead of being mandated to engineers in the dashboard panel or protocol, the generative model can summarise the basic causes, predict cascade errors, and recommend preventive interventions in natural language. For example, an AI agent can create a data platform that contains messages, such as a sales analytics pipeline, in the CRM source column of the CRM source. The change is likely due to a recent update to Salesforce's export API. Furthermore, these systems can further simulate future failure scenarios under developed data conditions and propose redesigns at the architectural level to reduce brittleness. It creates a paradigm in which observability exists, where active and generated employees are involved in maintaining the ecosystem for reliable analysis rather than merely relying on passive monitoring.

Operating with basic models and multimodal discussion functions, these AI agents can perform a wide range of data technology tasks. Create new data source workflows for transformations, optimize performance queries, generate documentation, and manage CI/CD pipelines for data code. In contrast to human engineers who need domain expertise, historical background, and time to write and test code, these agents can teach about natural language or business goals. For example, you can request a marketing lead. "When you create a dashboard showing the migration rates to the region over the past six months, agents will create related tables, engineering capabilities, ETL jobs, SQL queries, and publishing output on the BI platform. As these agents are enhanced and improved through organizational feedback, a sustainable role will be assigned to you to train digital employees on providing corporate assistance. Companies need to implement robust governance systems that incorporate human oversight, automated testing, and oversight of explanatory mechanisms to ensure that data products derived from AI-generated data meet organizational standards. There is also a growing need for meta-agents or orchestration controllers that manage a fleet of professional AI agents for recording, transformation, quality assurance, or line pursuit, ensuring the consistency of the pipeline and target orientation (Gudipudi, 2025). If the generator AI system gains the ability to move and prepare data, autonomy questions and institutional concerns are at the forefront when making decisions about which data should be prioritized, how to interpret it, and which actions will be triggered in response. Retailers can work with orchestration systems that decide to autonomously reduce marketing editions for a particular region based on predicted demand analysis. In financial services, similar systems can decide to freeze transactions based on pattern recognition algorithms that indicate potential fraud. While these actions are often technically justified and even advantageous, the lack of human review in a high-maneuver context can lead to opacity, unintended consequences, and, ultimately, a loss of trust. It includes clear boundaries that allow autonomous systems to act independently, require human consent, and specify how exceptions are treated. Additionally, a robust data generation mechanism is required to ensure that autonomous decisions are attributable to data lines, model assumptions, and orchestration logic. Furthermore, organizations need to develop new forms of governance that take into account the emerging institutions of AI systems, which some scientists refer to as "algorithm management."

Moreover, ethical orchestration is not only about preventing harm but also about enabling positive outcomes, particularly in sectors like healthcare, education, and climate response. In these domains, generative orchestration can significantly enhance the speed and precision of interventions, such as routing medical supplies during a pandemic, optimizing energy consumption in real-time, or tailoring educational content to learners' evolving needs (Sinha, 2025). However, the benefits must be distributed equitably, and the systems must be designed with inclusive values in mind to avoid reinforcing systemic biases. For example, suppose a healthcare data pipeline prioritizes treatments based on historical utilization patterns. In that case, it may inadvertently deprioritize communities with a history of limited access to care. Ethical orchestration frameworks must, therefore, incorporate fairness-aware algorithms, diverse training data, and participatory feedback loops to ensure that systems serve all users justly.

In conclusion, the future of autonomous data orchestration with generative AI holds immense promise and equally significant responsibility. The self-healing pipeline and generative observability enable a resilient, intelligent infrastructure that adapts to obstacles in real-time (Khokhlov, 2025). Autonomous agents redefine a company's data workflow as speed, scalability, and accessibility increase. However, these advancements raise concerns about ethical questions related to autonomy, agency, and accountability. Building an orchestration system that is not only intelligent but also transparent, fair, and aligned with human values is a critical challenge and opportunity for the next era of data innovation. Through joint governance, responsible AI design, and interdisciplinary commitment, organizations can ensure that orchestration layers become not only technical enablers but also strategic forces for making ethical, integrative, and practical decisions.

CONCLUSION

Generative AI-driven data orchestration is poised to recast the very foundations of modern analytics; therefore, any meaningful conclusion must grapple with the scale of systemic change already underway and the still more dynamic transformation to come (Peddinti et al., 2024). Where yesterday's data pipelines resembled carefully engineered aqueducts —rigid, linear, and heavily supervised —tomorrow's will look more like adaptive river networks that redirect themselves in real-time toward emergent opportunities. At the center of that evolution is generative AI: a class of models capable not only of deriving patterns from historical data but of synthesizing new structures, recommending optimizations, writing code, and even interpreting ambiguous business intent expressed in natural language. Its integration into the orchestration tier redefines the boundaries between constructing, managing, and utilizing analytics. Instead of brittle ETL scripts that frequently break when upstream schemas drift, organizations can now rely on self-documenting, self-healing workflows that automatically rewrite their transformation logic, reconcile anomalies by referencing domain taxonomies, or reroute jobs to alternative compute clusters when latency spikes. It radically reduces the friction that once slowed analytical cycles to a crawl and frees practitioners to concentrate on higher-order design questions, such as data policy, semantic modeling, and outcome alignment, instead of perpetual break-fix firefighting.

However, automation alone does not fully capture the importance of the change. Generative orchestration incorporates a feedback loop that helps bridge the gap between the pipeline's performance and the actual value it brings to the business. In the past, data teams gauged their success by tracking technical metrics such as the number of rows, load times, and success rates. While those metrics are still important, an autonomous system can go even further by monitoring downstream effects, such as conversion rates, churn reduction, and inventory accuracy, and then conducting experiments to improve those metrics. Did a revised customer segmentation model result in increased revenue? The orchestrator can identify the positive change, propose a possible cause, and plan additional data-gathering activities to strengthen its impact. If the uplift plateaus, it may indicate the need to prune low-signal features or gather new external datasets that the metadata parsing process has not previously analyzed. In essence, the pipeline becomes a dynamic engine that evolves together with the organization's strategic goals (Khokhlov, 2025). Governance, which was previously considered a hindrance to experimentation, becomes crucial in guiding this adaptive capacity. Policy constraints, such as data residency, model ethics, and privacy budgets, are expressed in a machine-readable format and directly incorporated into the reasoning of the orchestrator. The outcome is a positive cycle where compliance goals and innovation speed support and strengthen each other.

That convergence has profound implications for human functions. The roles of data engineers, stewards, and analysts are not vanishing; instead, their skills are being elevated to higher levels of abstraction. As generative models generate the basic code for ingesting new sources or routing Spark jobs, engineers establish guardrails by setting limits on cardinality, defining semantic agreements, and reviewing model-generated pull requests before they are merged into production (Molinari & Ciravegna, 2025). Analysts, liberated from the grind of SQL wrangling, can converse with the orchestrator in rich 'data stories,' asking it to surface edge cases that might bias an attribution model or to simulate how a change in procurement lead time would ripple through the cost of goods sold. While the data product managers gather for cross-functional design reviews, generative agents present pipeline performance narratives using financial or marketing language. The cultural change is just as significant as the technical one: instead of data as a service and analytics as a final result, organizations become data product ecosystems where continuous learning is a responsibility for everyone.

However, considering generative orchestration as a cure-all solution would be overly optimistic. Autonomy amplifies both benefits and dangers. One limitation of the system is that it can only perform certain transformations or make inferences based on the training data, which may contain biases from the past. Suppose marketing pipelines automatically expand a personalization model using unverified social data. In that case, they may unintentionally perpetuate stereotypes or breach privacy regulations specific to certain regions. Consequently, ethics and bias monitoring should be regarded as essential orchestration artifacts, managed and tracked with the same level of care as other critical components, such as definitions or container images. Paradoxically, transparency becomes more challenging when explainability is most crucial (Khokhlov, 2025). When a lengthy 40-step process is simplified to 'ask the model to create a comprehensive customer profile,' the responsibility for understanding the reasoning behind the results shifts from the procedural code to the complex decision-making within the hidden layers of the network. Progressive disclosure techniques, such as auto-generated data lineage graphs, transformation narratives, and counterexample units, can be helpful; however, they necessitate careful planning and collaboration among researchers specializing in machine learning, user experience specialists, and compliance teams.

The scalability of the system is a third conflict. Generative models can accelerate pipeline authoring, but at a petabyte scale, they also introduce new classes of compute-heavy workloads: natural language–driven SQL generation, semantic similarity joins, and on-the-fly feature synthesis. The orchestration layer needs to include schedulers that consider the cost of an AI-enhanced transformation and evaluate its incremental value compared to the resources it requires. It is where reinforcement learning or multi-objective optimization becomes invaluable, continuously balancing freshness, cost, carbon impact, and quality targets. Cloud vendors already expose programmatic cost signals, and GPU time can be negotiated in a spot-market style (Molinari & Ciravegna, 2025). The orchestrator's intelligence now includes economic reasoning, enabling the selection between model compression, retrieval-augmented generation, or deferred execution windows based on a forecast of resource prices and SLA tolerance. As a result, financial responsibility is built into the pipeline's design rather than being added as an afterthought.

Compatibility raises another set of considerations. No business operates in a uniform tooling stack. Warehouses, lakes, real-time streams, and edge devices need to connect and communicate with each other. Generative orchestration flourishes when its semantic layer can seamlessly connect with diverse schemas and runtime environments; however, this capability hinges on the availability of open standards, such as OpenAPI specifications for data services, universal data catalogs, and metadata compliant with differential privacy. Vendor ecosystems that prioritize composability and transparent APIs will surpass walled gardens because the orchestrator's strength lies in bridging silos, not reinforcing them. Organizations must make strategic decisions about which proprietary optimizations to accept and which open interfaces to require to ensure the long-term viability of their autonomous pipelines. Those decisions mirror previous discussions in service-oriented architecture but with greater significance: locking in at the orchestration level not only limits technical flexibility but also eliminates the crucial learning loops that distinguish data-driven strategies.

Unsurprisingly, security becomes a primary obstacle. An orchestrator skilled in writing transformation code can, theoretically, be deceived into stealing sensitive information or tampering with downstream models with carefully crafted payloads. Adversarial prompts, data drift attacks, and supply-chain vulnerabilities intersect in unique and unexpected ways (Oluwaferanmi, 2025). Defense-in-depth necessitates embedding policy-as-code that restricts the generative layer, isolating code generation, and implementing continuous runtime anomaly detection to identify deviations from established safe patterns. Additionally, security operations teams need to familiarize themselves with interrogating generative policies, much like they analyze Terraform plans or Kubernetes manifests. Ironically, the very features that increase the risk of cyber threats also provide new ways to defend against them. The orchestrator can automatically scan its code, compare changes to a secure version, or change service credentials when it detects unusual behavior.

In this landscape of both potential and risk, the most lasting effect of AI-driven data orchestration may be its ability to reshape how organizations think and operate. Reducing the time delay between asking a question and finding an answer brings decision-making timelines more in line with real-world occurrences, such as supply disruptions, changes in public opinion, or geopolitical events (Samaras et al., 2024; Oluwaferanmi, 2025).

REFERENCES

Abel, M., Ahmad, I., Casado, C. A., Berner, R., Bettinelli, M., Björk, K. M., . . . Zourmand, A. (2025). *Large Language Models in the 6G-Enabled Computing Continuum: a White Paper* (Doctoral dissertation, University of Oulu).

Benala, T. R., & Dehuri, S. (2025). Transforming Software Development: From Traditional Methods to Generative Artificial Intelligence. In *Boosting Software Development Using Machine Learning* (pp. 1–13). Springer.

Chaccour, C., Karapantelakis, A., Murphy, T., & Dohler, M. (2024). Telecom's artificial general intelligence (agi) vision: Beyond the genai frontier. *IEEE Network*.

Chickermane, H. (2025). How Machine Learning and Generative AI Are Enabling the Autonomous Supply Chain. In *Supply Chain Transformation Through Generative AI and Machine Learning* (pp. 1–28). IGI Global Scientific Publishing.

Coimbatore Ramalingam, B. (2025). Efficient Implementation of AI Agents in Enterprise Application Integration (EAI) and Electronic Data Interchange (EDI). *International Journal of Scientific Research in Computer Science. Engineering and Information Technology*, *11*(2), 10–32628.

Gudipudi, S. (2025). Redefining Business Intelligence Infrastructure: Core Skills for the AI-Driven Era. *Journal of Computer Science and Technology Studies*, *7*(6), 717–724.

Ismail, K. R., Brata, Z. A., Nelistiani, G. A., Heo, S., Kim, H., & Kim, H. (2025). Toward Robust Security Orchestration and Automated Response in Security Operations Centers with a Hyper-Automation Approach Using Agentic Artificial Intelligence. *Information (Basel)*, *16*(5), 365.

Jiang, F., Pan, C., Dong, L., Wang, K., Dobre, O. A., & Debbah, M. (2025). From Large AI Models to Agentic AI: A Tutorial on Future Intelligent Communications. *arXiv preprint arXiv:2505.22311*.

Joshi, S. (2025). A Review of Generative AI and DevOps Pipelines: CI/CD, Agentic Automation, MLOps Integration, and Large Language Models. *CD, Agentic Automation, MLOps Integration, and Large Language Models (June 01, 2025)*.

Joshi, S. (2025). Comprehensive Review of Artificial General Intelligence AGI, Agentic AI and GenAI: Current Trends and Future Directions.

Joshi, S. (2025). Review of data pipelines and streaming for generative AI integration: Challenges, solutions, and future directions. *Solutions, and Future Directions (March 03, 2025).*

Kaal, W. A. (2025). Artificial Intelligence: The Final Frontier. *U of St. Thomas (Minnesota) Legal Studies Research Paper*, (25-04).

Kanka, V. (2024). *Scaling Big Data: Leveraging LLMs for Enterprise Success.* Libertatem Media Private Limited.

Khokhlov, Y. (2025). Advancing operational efficiency in software companies through generative AI. *The American Journal of Engineering and Technology*, *7*(01), 11–18.

Kurnia, R., Brata, Z. A., Nelistiani, G. A., Heo, S., Kim, H., & Kim, H. (2025). Toward Robust Security Orchestration and Automated Response in Security Operations Centers with a Hyper-Automation Approach Using Agentic Artificial Intelligence. *Information (2078-2489), 16*(5).

Lakkarasu, P. (2024). From Model to Value: Engineering End-to-End AI Systems with Scalable Data Infrastructure and Continuous ML Delivery. *European Journal of Analytics and Artificial Intelligence (EJAAI) p-ISSN 3050-9556 en e-ISSN 3050-9564, 2*(1).

Liu, Y. J., Du, H., Xu, X., Zhang, R., Feng, G., Cao, B., ... & Tafazolli, R. (2025). A Survey of Integrating Generative Artificial Intelligence and 6G Mobile Services: Architectures, Solutions, Technologies and Outlooks. *IEEE Transactions on Cognitive Communications and Networking*.

Molinari, G., & Ciravegna, F. (2025). Towards Pervasive Distributed Agentic Generative AI—A State of The Art. *arXiv preprint arXiv:2506.13324*.

Morabito, R., & Jang, S. (2025). Smaller, Smarter, Closer: The Edge of Collaborative Generative AI. *IEEE Internet Computing*.

Musiol, M. (2024). *Generative AI: Navigating the course to the artificial general intelligence future*. John Wiley & Sons.

Narapareddy, V. S. R. (2025). Generative AI and Foundation Models. *Universal Library of Innovative Research and Studies, 2*(2).

O'Connor, A. J. (2024). *Organizing for Generative AI and the Productivity Revolution: Reshaping Organizational Roles in the Age of Artificial Intelligence*. Springer Nature.

Oluwaferanmi, J. K. A. (2025). Automating ETL Pipelines Using Artificial Intelligence: Transforming Legacy Data Integration Systems into Intelligent Data Workflows.

Peddinti, S. R., Katragadda, S. R., & Tanikonda, A. (2024). Deep Learning for Autonomous Data Quality Enhancement: A Paradigm Shift in Machine Learning Pipelines. *Available at SSRN* 5251229.

Samaras, G., Mertiri, M., Xezonaki, M. E., Theodorou, V., Chartsias, P. K., & Bozios, T. (2024, June). Democratizing Predictive Analytics with Generative Artificial Intelligence towards AI-Native Networks. In *2024 IEEE Symposium on Computers and Communications (ISCC)* (pp. 1–6). IEEE.

Sapkota, R., Roumeliotis, K. I., & Karkee, M. (2025). AI agents vs. agentic ai: A conceptual taxonomy, applications and challenge. *arXiv preprint arXiv:2505.10468.*

Sendas, N., & Rajale, D. (2025). Future Trends in MLOps. In *The Definitive Guide to Machine Learning Operations in AWS: Machine Learning Scalability and Optimization with AWS* (pp. 371–423). Apress.

Shethiya, A. S. (2024). Engineering with Intelligence: How Generative AI and LLMs Are Shaping the Next Era of Software Systems. *Spectrum of Research, 4*(1).

Sinha, R. K. (2025). Generative Migration Architectures: Accelerating Cloud-Native Data Integration Through AI Orchestration. *Journal of Computer Science and Technology Studies, 7*(5), 709–718.

Tariq, M. U. (2025). Integrating Advanced Technologies for Multi-Stakeholder Collaboration: Driving Sustainability in Supply Chains Through Industry 4.0. In Frichi, Y., & Jawab, F. (Eds.), *Multi-Stakeholder Collaboration for Sustainable Supply Chain* (pp. 313–334). IGI Global Scientific Publishing., DOI: 10.4018/979-8-3693-8925-6.ch014

Tariq, M. U. (2025). Harnessing Collective Power-Multi-Stakeholder Synergies for Sustainable Supply Chain Transformation. In Frichi, Y., & Jawab, F. (Eds.), *Multi-Stakeholder Collaboration for Sustainable Supply Chain* (pp. 245–264). IGI Global Scientific Publishing., DOI: 10.4018/979-8-3693-8925-6.ch011

Tariq, M. U. (2025). Empowering Women Entrepreneurs: Innovative Crowdfunding and Alternative Financing Models for Sustainable Business Growth. In Katper, N. (Ed.), *Crowdfunding and Alternative Financing Models for Women Entrepreneurs* (pp. 1–34). IGI Global Scientific Publishing., DOI: 10.4018/979-8-3693-9193-8.ch001

Tariq, M. U. (2025). AI-Powered Cybersecurity: Defending Green IT Systems With Intelligent Solutions. In Gupta, B., Pramod, D., & Moslehpour, M. (Eds.), *Sustainable Information Security in the Age of AI and Green Computing* (pp. 141–156). IGI Global Scientific Publishing., DOI: 10.4018/979-8-3693-8034-5.ch007

Tariq, M. U. (2025). Unveiling Consumer Insights: The Power of Qualitative Research in Market Analysis. In Segura, L., Vasconcelos, A., & Slomski, V. (Eds.), *Exploring Qualitative Research in Business: Approaches, Strategies, And Methods* (pp. 127–154). IGI Global Scientific Publishing., DOI: 10.4018/979-8-3693-7698-0.ch005

Xu, H., Sun, Y., Tupayachi, J., Omitaomu, O., Zlatanov, S., & Li, X. (2025). Towards the Autonomous Optimization of Urban Logistics: Training Generative AI with Scientific Tools via Agentic Digital Twins and Model Context Protocol. *arXiv preprint arXiv:2506.13068.*

KEY TERMS AND DEFINITIONS

Autonomous Pipelines: Self-managing data procedures without manual input
Data Orchestration: Synchronizing data flow across multiple systems
Generative AI: AI that creates data or content unconventionally

Chapter 8

A New Approach for Federated, Shared, and Collaborative Learning via a SAN Storage Network

Saad Mahmoudi
https://orcid.org/0009-0007-3873-7197
Computer Science Research Laboratory, Ibn Tofail University, Kenitra, Morocco

Mohamed Amnai
Computer Science Research Laboratory, Ibn Tofail University, Kenitra, Morocco

Tarik Elmouden
https://orcid.org/0000-0002-6963-6686
Computer Science Research Laboratory, Ibn Tofail University, Kenitra, Morocco

ABSTRACT

The exponential emergence of IoT devices in a smart city generates significant data traffic on the network. This traffic can be affected by changes in the values exchanged between IoT devices and the aggregation server, which further guarantees the lack of parameter integrity, leading to unreliable learning. For this reason, we propose a new approach to protecting the private and confidential data of IoT devices required for federated learning of an AI model. Our approach aims to improve accuracy of learning model predictive values based on Fiber Channel technology, which adjusts

DOI: 10.4018/979-8-3373-5616-7.ch008

the sharing and storage of learning parameters over the network, ensuring a reliable connection between IoT devices and storage arrays. This technology accelerates the AI model training phase while reducing latency.

1 INTRODUCTION

Given that the IoT network is overwhelmed by data from many IoT devices, the importance of security is considered a critical key in the process of creating a learning model. Learning time is also essential for the reliability and affinity of AI models. In this context, we have designed an architecture that aims to secure, improve the accuracy rate of the model, as well as reduce the learning time which depends on the case, it can be very long, taking the example of the distribution and collection of categorically different data, which generates a problem of data heterogeneity. Our architecture allows in the first place to achieve shared, distributed, and collaborative learning between the different connected objects. The architecture aims to preserve the confidentiality of IoT data centrally on a high performance storage network by using network data transmission technologies such as Fiber Channel over IP and iSCSI commands encapsulated in Fiber Channel transfer protocol to ensure reliable and certifiable writing and reading of both learning parameters and data collected from a smart city ecosystem environment.

In this article, we analyzed different architectures with a sharp focus on the security of learning parameters, which are iteratively transmitted between IoT devices and the aggregation server so that the model is well-refined, adjusted, and reliable. The accuracy of the learning model depends on the distribution rate and the distribution of data among the different connected objects (Liu et al., 2020). For better convergence of local models, the IoT objects participating in the learning phase must have almost identical data classes. Then the training results will be sent to the cloud server for the aggregation process of the training parameters. For this reason, the distribution management of the training parameters in accordance with the situation of non-independent identical distribution (non-IID) is mandatory in the infrastructure of the ecosystem of a smart city (Zhao et al., 2018). To address all the previously identified challenges including data privacy, limited computational resources, secure communication, and efficient data storage, we propose the implementation of a federated learning model deployment architecture that is integrated with a Storage Area Network (SAN). This architecture leverages the high speed and secure capabilities of SAN to optimize both the storage and retrieval of training data and model parameters across the distributed network.

Key enabling technologies within this architecture include the Fiber Channel protocol, which facilitates high bandwidth, low latency data transmission within the

SAN. This ensures rapid access to and storage of large datasets and intermediate model parameters, which is critical for maintaining efficiency during the training cycle. Additionally, the use of IPSec (Internet Protocol Security) provides robust encryption and compression mechanisms for securing data as it is transported over the IoT network. IPSec helps to protect the confidentiality and integrity of information being exchanged between devices, while compression reduces the size of the data packets, thereby minimizing bandwidth consumption. We begin with an analysis of the different architectures for deploying federated learning, then we propose an architectural approach that provides solutions to frequent problems, notably security and data heterogeneity in the smart city environment.

1.1 Client-Server FL Architecture

In the client-server architecture, illustrated in Figure.1, also called centralized FL architecture, there is a central server that initializes the global model with initial training parameters and distributes it to different IoT devices for training on their local datasets. After local training, the trained model parameters of the client devices are collected by the server. The server then aggregates the parameters of different trained learning models by reconstructing a global model and broadcasting it to all IoT devices. On the other hand, in the conventional client-server architecture where the server hosts and trains a model on shared data sent by the set of IoT devices that are involved in the training phase, where the server operates only on data received locally from the clients, synchronously or asynchronously (Shanmugam et al., 2023).

The centralized FL architecture allows reduce the communication cost, not to overload the network bandwidth with data, as well as ensures the integrity and privacy of the data of each IoT object of the ecosystem (Shanmugam et al., 2023). This type of architecture introduces challenges that degrade the performance of AI model training, which primarily relies on regularly transmitting data to a central server to reconstruct a global model that is then distributed to IoT devices. These challenges mainly stem from data transmission over limited bandwidth. Real time data capture can lead to network congestion, either on the local network or within the intranet, depending on the VPN configurations at the sites hosting the IoT devices involved in the training phase.

Figure 1. Client-server FL architecture

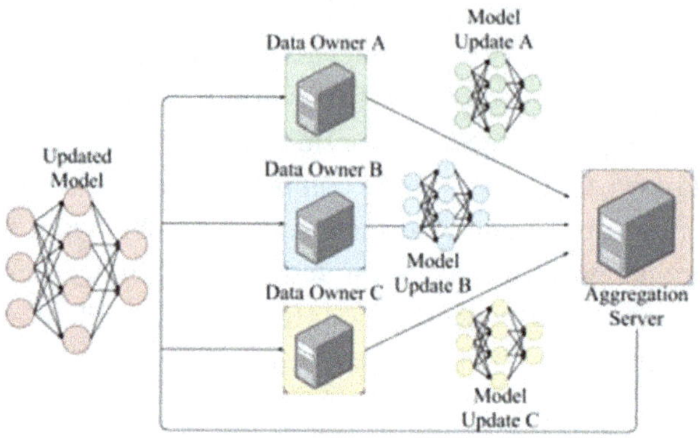

(Shanmugam et al., 2023)

1.2 Peer-to-Peer FL Architecture

In the peer-to-peer FL architecture, illustrated in Figure.2, the concept of a central server for model aggregations, as it appears in the client-server architecture, is absent. Each IoT device involved in the FL environment has its own model that makes it train according to its own data which allows it to ensure the security of its own information collected from its environment, once it finishes its training, it shares the obtained information with neighboring participants. This architecture provides enhanced security by enabling direct communication between participating clients, eliminating the need for a centralized third-party coordinator to manage or facilitate the exchange of information. By removing the central authority, the system reduces the risk of a single point of failure or compromise, making it more resilient to external attacks and data breaches. This peer-to-peer communication model strengthens privacy, as sensitive data and model parameters are not exposed to potentially vulnerable or untrusted central servers (Shanmugam et al., 2023). The architecture also allows for enhanced security and autonomy by avoiding third-party intermediaries, it also demands higher computational overhead, posing challenges for low power or lightweight IoT devices that may struggle to efficiently perform the required security operations

Figure 2. Peer-to-peer architecture

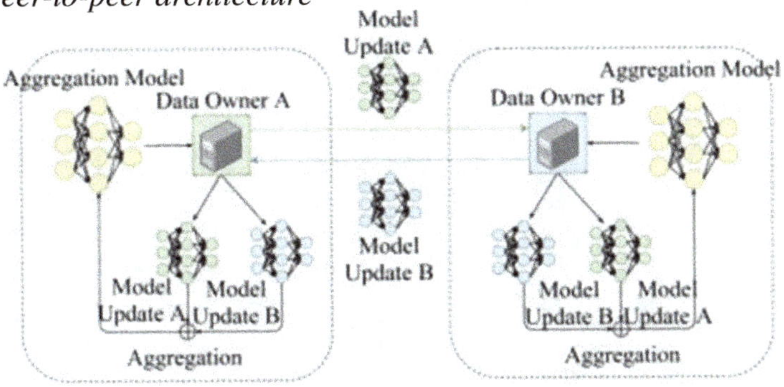

(Shanmugam et al., 2023)

1.3 FL-Based Architecture on 6G

In this architecture illustrated in Figure 3. In each communication cycle, fog server carefully selects a subset of devices to participate in this training cycle and will reject the rest of the registered devices. The fog server will send back via wired or wireless (6G radios) model parameters, to each selected smart device. Each participating device will then perform local training based on the initial training model parameters received. The updates will be sent from all selected devices to the fog server for aggregation (Shanmugam et al., 2023).

Once the fog server receives enough updates, it will send the aggregation result back to the participating devices. The devices will update their respective models with the results received. The above process will be repeated multiple times until the training cycle ends. The learned model as well as the knowledge related to the model can be transferred and used by other servers as well as by the cloud data center for the benefit of other services and users over a wider geographical area (Yang et al., 2019).

Figure 3. FL architecture based on 6G

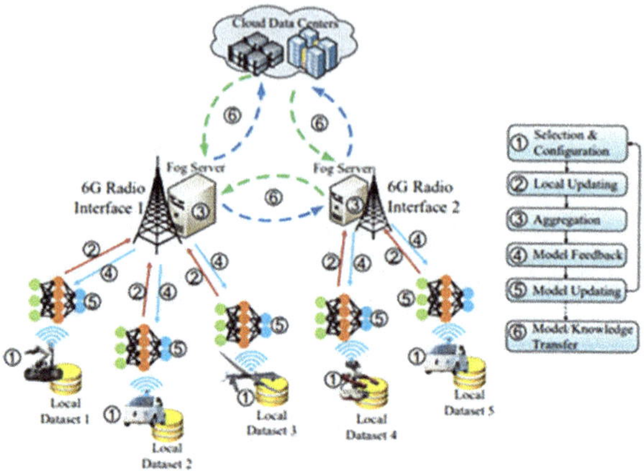

(Xiao et al., 2020)

Federated learning leverages several advanced services and potential benefits offered by emerging 6G technology, which are expected to significantly enhance the performance, scalability, and security of distributed learning systems. It takes advantage of some of the services and potential benefits, including:

1) Optimal network traffic management is achieved by techniques such as reducing the data size of each device side update or limiting the frequency of model updates sent to the central aggregator (Li et al., 2019a). These strategies play a crucial role in alleviating communication overhead, especially in large scale federated learning environments where frequent data exchange between numerous edge devices can cause significant network congestion. The integration of 6G technology further enhances this optimization by offering ultra-high bandwidth, ultra-low latency, and intelligent traffic routing capabilities. These features enable the network to handle distributed training processes more efficiently by ensuring that data packets and model updates are transmitted with minimal delay and reduced packet loss.
2) FL's heterogeneous data processing: the ability to collect datasets from different devices in terms of hardware, services, and even the type of data they process. FL supports model training applied across diverse IoT devices with non-identically distributed (non-IID) datasets (Bonawitz et al., 2019). This performance involves collecting data from a heterogeneous ecosystem comprising many devices that may differ not only in computational power and storage capacity but also in the nature and distribution of their local data, including variations in data quality, sampling rates, and contextual relevance. It addresses the challenge of hetero-

geneity, which is critical for building robust and generalized models capable of performing well across diverse user environments.

3) Data security in federated learning model training cycle: the parameters from the learning model training do not demonstrate the dataset on which the model performs its local training, this process allows the model to learn parameters without directly revealing the underlying dataset used for training on each device. This design inherently provides a layer of privacy, as the central server only receives aggregated model updates rather than accessing the sensitive data of devices IoT. For this reason, the security level of FL needs to be further improved by adopting more advanced encryption and security measures, such as secure aggregation on each fog server and differential privacy at the user level (Li et al., 2019b).

1.4 The SDN Architecture With(a) Centralized Model, and(b) Decentralized Model

In this section of the article, two architectures are presented, as illustrated in Figure 4, to carry out the training phase of a learning model. The first is to carry it out centrally by imitating the SDN operating process. Indeed, each node has a data plane, which will submit it to the controller so that it can train the model on the data. The controller selects the learning model from the knowledge plane hosted by the controller. Then, it trains its chosen model on the data set that is collected and stored in the SDN Controller server, as mentioned in Figure 4 (a). In the same context, if there are changes to the data plane, the node must regularly notify the SDN controller, which generates network traffic overload. This problem degrades the performance of the training phase of an AI model. Regarding decentralized learning, as illustrated in Figure 4 (b), each node stores its data in its data plane. The SDN controller selects the appropriate model from the knowledge plane, which then sends it to the nodes. These nodes train their data by applying different learning models based on LSTM (The long short term memory) and BILSTM (The bi-directional long short term memory) to the data. Once they complete their training phases, each of them sends their model to the SDN controller. This solution not only reduces network traffic overhead but also reduces latency and model processing time. The decentralized learning approach, like how SDN works, is a solution that aims to address the following problems: latency, bandwidth flooding due to data frequently sent to the SDN controller, storage memory saturation, and data security, since each node maintains its confidentiality. However, several challenges still hinder the effectiveness and quality of the learning model training process. These challenges include issues related to knowledge plane security, where the protection of global training knowledge and parameter exchange is not sufficiently robust. Additionally, the non-scalability of the architecture limits the system's ability to efficiently support a growing number of devices and training tasks. Another major concern is the centralized nature of the SDN (Software-Defined Networking) controller, which acts as a single point of failure posing a significant risk to the continuity and reliability of any ongoing model training phases. Lastly, the security of the data plane, which consists of IoT devices that often operate in untrusted or vulnerable environments, remains a critical issue, as compromised devices can negatively impact the integrity of the entire federated learning process (Chakraborty et al., 2024).

Figure 4. A SDN architecture with(a) centralized model, and(b) decentralized model

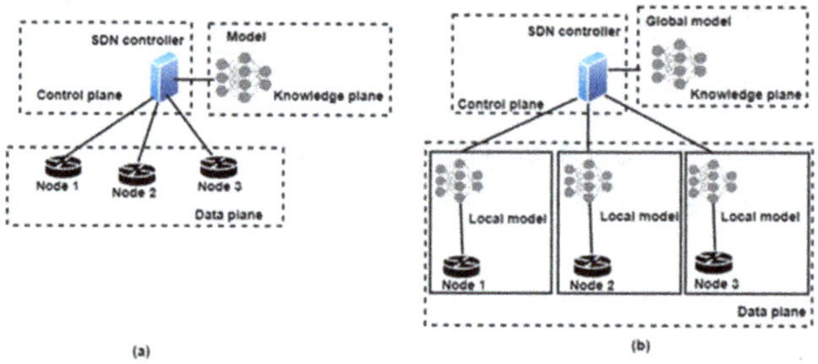

(Chakraborty et al., 2024).

2 MATERIALS AND METHODS

Despite the significant advancements that researchers are making in refining the process of training federated learning models particularly those deployed in distributed and robust architectures that emphasize fast processing and secure exchange of learning parameters. These challenges must be addressed to achieve satisfactory outcomes from the collaborative learning phase, which relies on the participation of a network of interconnected devices. These devices, often operating under constraints such as limited computational power, intermittent connectivity, and heterogeneous data distributions, can hinder the overall performance and convergence of the shared model. Moreover, ensuring privacy, maintaining model accuracy across diverse clients, and defending against potential adversarial attacks continue to be pressing concerns in real world federated learning deployments. However, to ensure the success and effectiveness of the shared learning process carried out by a group of interconnected IoT devices, several additional challenges must be carefully addressed. These challenges go beyond the basic setup of a federated learning system and have a significant impact on the quality, scalability, and reliability of the final model. Among the most critical issues are:

- The security of the parameters of local learning models
- The congestion of the IOT network
- The unavailability of the nodes that participate in the training of the federated learning model.

The availability of data is crucial during the model training phase, and any lack or unavailability of data can significantly hinder the performance and reliability of the learning process. In distributed environments like IoT networks, data may become unavailable due to device connectivity issues, storage limitations, power constraints, or privacy policies that restrict data access.

For all these reasons, we have chosen to design novel architecture aimed at enabling the deployment of learning models in a fully decentralized manner. This new architecture is specifically built upon the principles of a Storage Area Network (SAN) (Tate et al., 2018), which provides a high speed, dedicated network that interconnects and presents shared pools of storage resources to multiple devices. By leveraging the capabilities of a SAN, our proposed design seeks to overcome the limitations of traditional centralized systems enhancing scalability, improving fault tolerance, and ensuring more secure and efficient data access and sharing among distributed nodes involved in the training process. This approach allows for better handling of large datasets, robust coordination among devices, and more resilient learning model deployment in heterogeneous and dynamic environments such as IoT or edge networks, as depicted in Figure5. It aims to improve federated learning by combining both centralized and decentralized learning approaches for IoT devices.

Centralized learning refers to a machine learning approach in which the entire processing and training of the model are conducted on a centralized node, typically the IoT Gateway. In this setup, data collected from multiple IoT devices across the network is transmitted to the gateway, where it is aggregated and used to train the learning model in a centralized manner. By centralizing the model training on the IoT Gateway, this approach simplifies the architecture and makes it easier to manage the training process, monitor performance, and apply updates. However, it also comes with notable limitations, including increased network traffic, higher latency, and potential privacy concerns, since raw data must be transmitted from the edge devices to a central location. Furthermore, this architecture introduces a single point of failure, this means that if the IoT Gateway experiences downtime or becomes compromised, the entire learning process is disrupted.

Decentralized learning stores information sent by IoT devices on a distributed SAN. Storage. The latter is performed on storage arrays that use high performance RAID technology, combining HDD and SSD disks to ensure high-quality storage processing (Liu et al., 2024). This technology guarantees data redundancy on multiple hard drives to prevent data loss. It can also be deployed on different storage sites, by performing synchronous and real-time replication of data from one site to another, which ensures fault tolerance and high data availability.

The RAID technology used in storage arrays guarantees high performance of data storage and learning parameters in the SAN, because it allows data redundancy across all storage disks, which reduces the risk of data loss, which is considered a key factor for the model training phase. In the context of federated learning model training, the availability and accuracy of stored data and learning parameters are vital. During training, the model relies heavily on vast amounts of data and the ability to save intermediate results and parameters. Any data loss or corruption during this phase can lead to incorrect training outcomes or the need to restart the process, wasting time and computational resources. Therefore, RAID technology's ability to provide fault tolerance and maintain consistent data access enhances the performance and reliability of both the storage system and the overall model training process.

Figure 5. The deployment of federated learning within the centralized SAN storage network architecture

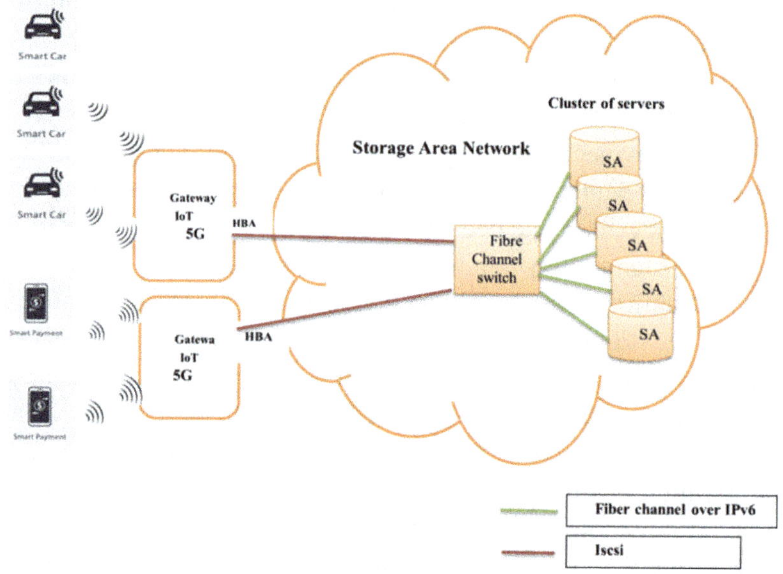

2.1 Components of the Proposed Architecture for FL Deployment

This architecture, as depicted in Figure5, consists of three layers:

- This layer is the foundational level of the architecture, responsible for connecting various physical devices and sensors. It includes connected objects, which refer to Internet of Things (IoT) devices such as sensors, actuators, smart appliances, and other embedded systems. These devices are typically lightweight, meaning they have minimal processing power and memory capacity. Due to their limited computing and storage resources, they rely on higher layers for data processing and long-term storage. The main role of this layer is to gather data from the physical environment and transmit it to the next layer in architecture.
- This intermediate layer acts as a bridge between the connected devices at the access layer and the storage infrastructure. It incorporates the IoT gateway, which serves as an intermediary device that aggregates data from multiple IoT devices. The gateway is enhanced with 5G technology (Ahmad et al., 2019), enabling fast, low-latency wireless communication. Additionally, this layer includes the IPsec security protocol, which ensures that data transmitted between IoT devices, and the internet is encrypted and protected from unauthorized access or tampering. By securely connecting IoT devices to the internet, this layer facilitates the rapid and reliable transmission of data to the storage array located within the storage network, ensuring data integrity and availability
- The topmost layer in this architecture is responsible for the efficient and secure storage of collected data. It utilizes a Storage Area Network (SAN), which is a specialized, high-speed network dedicated to data storage. SANs allow multiple servers and devices to access large volumes of data quickly and reliably. This layer emphasizes secure storage, implementing mechanisms to protect data from loss, corruption, or unauthorized access. Furthermore, it offers reduced latency compared to traditional fiber channel networks by leveraging advanced IPv6 technology (Gont & Chown, 2016), which provides improved addressing, routing, and security features. This results in faster access times and better performance when retrieving or managing stored data.

A SAN (Storage Area Network) is a storage network that enables extensive centralization of data on a virtualized storage space composed of multiple storage arrays. This virtualization ensures data protection and reliability, allowing data to be offloaded from IoT devices according to authorization restrictions approved by the server responsible for distributing the initial learning model to all IoT devices. Subsequently, learning parameters are shared among participants after they collaboratively train on datasets they have provided.

Fiber Channel over IPv6 (FC over IPv6) technology facilitates the intelligent and secure routing of data blocks exchanged among various IoT devices involved in the collaborative training of AI models (Jain et al., 2021). By combining the high-speed data transmission capabilities of Fiber Channel with the vast addressing space and advanced routing features of the IPv6 protocol, this approach enables efficient communication across a large-scale, distributed network of IoT devices.

This integration ensures that data transfer and sharing during the AI model training phase occur with minimal latency, high bandwidth, and improved reliability, which are critical for maintaining synchronization and performance in federated learning environments. The use of IPv6 also supports greater scalability, allowing a virtually unlimited number of IoT devices to participate in the training process without exhausting address space or encountering routing limitations (Jain et al., 2021).

Moreover, by optimizing the flow of data blocks and reducing network congestion, FC over IPv6 significantly mitigates the risks of network overload, which can otherwise slow down or interrupt the training process. As a result, this technology not only enhances the overall speed and efficiency of model training but also contributes to a more robust and scalable infrastructure for deploying AI-driven applications in real-time, resource constrained environments.

2.2 The Process of Running a Federated Learning Model via the Storage Network

Given the limited storage constraints and the local non scalability of hardware resources, specifically RAM and internal storage of IoT devices, an architecture was designed to address this problem through the high performance offered by SAN. Therefore, the operating process of architecture proposed in this article to meet storage needs, and the security of the learning model parameters is presented as follows:

- First, IoT devices initiate the process by transmitting their locally collected data to the Storage Area Network (SAN) through an interconnection device known as the IoT gateway. This gateway serves as a critical intermediary that bridges communication between the IoT devices and the storage infrastructure. It aggregates data from multiple devices and ensures that it is properly formatted and prepared for further processing or storage. The transmission is carried out using 5G technology, which offers high-speed, low latency, and reliable wireless communication. This technology is essential for supporting real-time data transfer in large scale IoT deployments. The use of 5G enables the seamless and efficient delivery of massive volumes of data from distributed IoT nodes to the SAN, even in environments with a high density of connected devices, thereby supporting faster data availability and responsiveness within the system.

- The IoT gateway plays a central role in coordinating the federated learning process by distributing the initial global learning model to all IoT devices participating in the training phase. This model serves as the baseline from which each device begins its local training using its own data. By broadcasting the global model to all participating nodes, the gateway ensures that every device starts from a synchronized and consistent version of the model.
- The IoT devices initiate the training phase by accessing and utilizing the distributed datasets stored on the Storage Area Network (SAN). This shared storage infrastructure allows each device to efficiently retrieve the relevant data needed for local model training while maintaining data organization, consistency, and scalability. During this phase, each IoT device independently trains a local version of the learning model based on the data it accesses from the SAN, without the need to transfer raw data outside the network, thereby preserving data locality and enhancing privacy.
- Once the local training phase is completed, each IoT device stores its learned model parameters or gradients back onto the SAN. This centralized storage of model updates facilitates the next stage of the federated learning process, where the stored parameters can be accessed and aggregated by a coordinating entity or distributed algorithm. By utilizing the SAN as a shared and high-performance storage layer, the architecture ensures reliable and efficient communication of model parameters among devices, while minimizing network overhead and potential data loss.
- At this stage of the federated learning process, the IoT devices attain a global view of the collective model parameters, which have been shared and aggregated from each participating device during the training phase. This means that each device, rather than working in isolation, now benefits from the collective intelligence of the entire network by incorporating the knowledge learned across all nodes. The aggregated global model, which is reconstructed through algorithms like FedAvg or FedProx, represents a combination of the local updates contributed by each device based on their unique data distributions.
- The IoT devices participate in the federated learning process by locally training models on their own data and then aggregating model parameters using well established algorithms such as FedAvg (McMahan et al., 2017) and FedProx (Li et al., 2020). These aggregation algorithms play a crucial role in reconstructing a consistent and accurate global model from the locally computed updates. FedAvg performs weighted averaging of the local model updates, while FedProx extends this by adding a proximal term to address issues arising from data heterogeneity and system variability across devices. Once the local updates are aggregated, the resulting global model is redistrib-

uted to the participating IoT devices for the next round of training. This entire process is iteratively repeated over several federated rounds, with the number of rounds predefined based on the initial configuration of the learning task, typically determined and communicated by the IoT gateway at the start of the process. Through these iterative updates, the model gradually improves its performance while preserving the privacy of the data stored on each individual device

This SAN based learning mechanism avoids the back-and-forth of learning parameters between the IoT devices and the device responsible for parameter aggregation, thus reducing bandwidth overhead from learning parameter traffic and ensuring their integrity on the network. Parameter and data integrity certify improved accuracy and data loss during the model training phase.

The deployment of a federated learning model within an architecture based on SAN (Storage Area Network) technology and 5G connectivity enables devices to align their local models more effectively with the overall learning objective. This alignment enhances generalization and performance across diverse and heterogeneous data environments. The high-speed, low-latency capabilities of 5G, combined with the centralized data access provided by the SAN, support efficient model synchronization and parameter sharing among distributed devices.

Moreover, this architecture strengthens the collaborative nature of federated learning, ensuring that the resulting global model is not biased toward the data of any single device. By synchronizing with the shared global model, IoT devices can either proceed with additional training rounds or deploy the model locally for inference tasks, achieving a higher degree of accuracy, robustness, and scalability in real world applications.

2.3 Scaling Federated Learning Perimeters Through SD-WAN Technology

The implementation of SD-WAN (Software-Defined Wide Area Network) technology (Troia et al., 2025) in the decentralized learning architecture as illustrated in Figure6 makes it possible to extend the learning perimeter to the scale of a smart city while maintaining the same advantages of setting up a storage area network (SAN) to ensure dynamic and intelligent sharing of the learning parameters of IoT devices. This technology allows for secure, distributed and extended storage. SD-WAN optimizes network traffic between several learning parameters by using different communication technologies (MPLS, 6G, high-speed internet) in parallel (Oladosu et al., 2021; Mine et al., 2020). This dynamic use of multichannel and communication services is used to better manage the traffic of learning parameters between different IoT devices even if they are in different storage networks. This architecture offers features enabling high quality model training, as follows:

- High availability of IoT device data: The data generated and produced by IoT devices are sent to storage servers, which are connected to storage arrays via an iSCSI, to protect and implement data replication and redundancy systems.
- High availability of training parameters: As soon as IoT devices train on the amount of data stored on the SAN, they share the parameters from the training phase with each other to move on to the aggregation phase, while each of them recreates a global AI model. This model must be stored on the storage space provided by the SAN.
- Collaborative training in IoT devices: it refers to a decentralized machine learning approach where multiple IoT devices work together to train a shared model without directly exchanging raw data. Instead of uploading sensitive or large datasets to a central server, each device performs local training on its own data and contributes to the global model by sharing only model updates or gradients.
- Centralization of data and training parameters on the wide area storage network: it refers to the strategy of consolidating both the datasets and the learned model parameters from multiple IoT devices onto a unified, high-performance storage infrastructure specifically, a Storage Area Network (SAN) extended across distributed environments. This centralization allows for efficient and secure access to training related resources, enabling IoT devices and coordinating systems to retrieve, update, and synchronize data and model parameters without relying on local storage or isolated systems.
- The replication of data and training parameters generated by IoT devices is achieved by leveraging the combined capabilities of RAID (Redundant Array of Independent Disks) and SAN (Storage Area Network) technologies. This integration provides a highly reliable and efficient storage solution that ensures data integrity and availability across the system.
- Scalability of IoT device storage systems: Given the constraints and limitations of storage resources deployed in IoT devices, SANs offer scalability and flexibility of storage pools to ensure highly qualified performance during the learning model training phase.
- Guaranteed recovery of training parameters after disasters: SANs are scalable in terms of the hardware resources that can be integrated into them, and in terms of software, which allows for the installation of backup and data restoration services in the event of a natural disaster or a system crash caused by a hacker during the AI model training phase.

Figure 6. The architecture of the functional extension of the shared learning perimeter on the scale of a smart city using SD-WAN technology

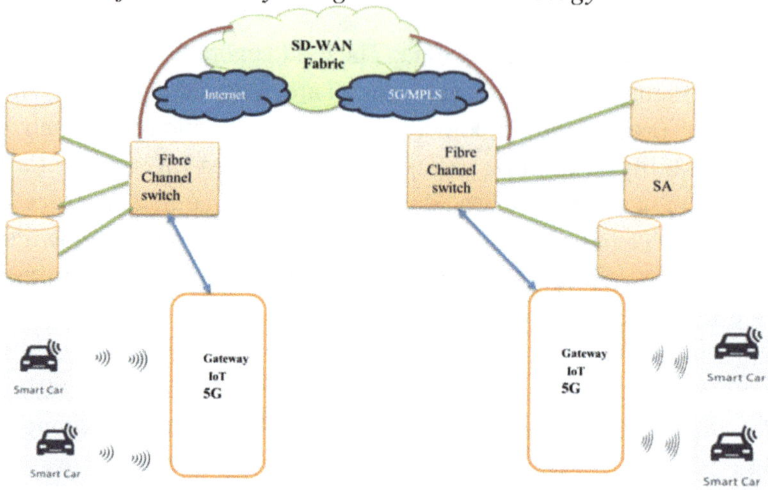

3 RESULTS AND DISCUSSIONS

All experiments are performed on a laptop equipped with an Intel® Core™ i5-8250U processor clocked at 1.60 GHz (8 processors) and an NVIDIA GeForce 1650 Ti 4 GB graphics card, using TensorFlow 2.4.0, cuda 11.0.3 and Keras 2.4.0. These technologies allow to first simulate a decentralized and virtualized infrastructure for the deployment of the Flower framework of federated learning within a SAN to ensure shared and collaborative learning among the various connected devices participating in the federated learning model training phase. Second, they serve to implement an approach to expanding the learning scope to the scale of a smart city using SD-WAN technology while linking the various SAN networks on which learning relies to improve and perform the model training phase to create a model that can be distributed across each IoT device.

Based on these experiments, virtually emulated on our laptop, in collaboration with several services offered by the cloud computing infrastructure, we obtain improvements to the learning model in terms of accuracy, losses, weight measurements, and even key features that contribute to the performance of the federated learning rate via the IoT network in an optimal manner, for example, in terms of network traffic optimization, data security to accelerate the training phase, and the implementation of a redundancy system that serves to backup and protect data and learning parameters.

Table 1 provides a comprehensive comparative study that evaluates the various federated learning architectures discussed throughout this article. The comparison focuses on the range of services each architecture offers, as well as the security protocols they implement to ensure data privacy and integrity during the learning process. Additionally, the table includes an analysis of two novel approaches proposed in this work, both of which leverage SAN (Storage Area Network) technology to enhance federated and shared learning frameworks. These SAN based approaches aim to improve data accessibility, scalability, and security, thereby addressing some of the limitations found in traditional federated learning systems. By juxtaposing these architectures and approaches, Table 1 offers valuable insights into their relative strengths and weaknesses, helping to guide future developments in secure and efficient distributed learning models.

Table 1. The characteristics and functions of different architectures for deploying federated learning.

	FL Architecture client/server	FL Peer to Peer Architecture	FL for 6G	The SDN architecture with(a) centralized model, and(b) decentralized model	The deployment of federated learning within the centralized SAN storage network architecture	The architecture of the functional extension of the shared learning perimeter on the scale of a smart city using SD-WAN technology
IoT network bandwidth optimization			*	*	*	*
IoT ecosystem network traffic optimization			*	*		*
The security of exchange parameters of the IoT ecosystem			*	*	*	*
The service for logging actions performed by devices in the IoT ecosystem				*		
Data heterogeneity			*	*	*	*
Heterogeneity of materials			*		*	*
The caching system						*
Intrusion Detection System for FL						
FL Backup						*
Single point of failure	*			*	*	

continued on following page

Table 1. Continued

	FL Architecture client/server	FL Peer to Peer Architecture	FL for 6G	The SDN architecture with(a) centralized model, and(b) decentralized model	The deployment of federated learning within the centralized SAN storage network architecture	The architecture of the functional extension of the shared learning perimeter on the scale of a smart city using SD-WAN technology
Data redundancy for FL		*			*	*
Protocol SSL			*		*	*
Low power consumption of IoT devices					*	*

As illustrated in Table 1, the SAN architecture supports powerful features that serve to centralize data from all IoT devices participating in the AI model training phase. Among these features, the data redundancy mechanism is cited, which allows for a disaster recovery system that recovers the learning ecosystem to its normal state after a disaster or digital incident. The SAN also contributes to reducing bandwidth loads, avoiding the problem that is obviously linked to the network congestion problem, which is the bottleneck. Regarding SDWAN technology that is implemented in SAN architecture for the deployment of federated learning model comes with features that guarantee not only the data but also the quality of service of interworking of learning parameters and data between different IoT devices. SDWAN restricts access to data that is stored in storage networks by building an intranet network between IoT devices that are geographically dispersed using communication technologies such as MPLS (Multiprotocol Label Switching) and also VPN (Virtual Private Network), which certifies secure and fast communication within the extended perimeter of federated learning. This technology avoids the problem of single point of failure, because the data is well maintained and replicated on different storage sites that each deploys a SAN network, this eradicates the problem of data loss that can occur during the training phase of the federated learning model.

Table 2 presents a comprehensive overview of the performance metrics obtained by deploying the federated learning model within the SAN (Storage Area Network) architecture. This evaluation focuses specifically on key security aspects such as the confidentiality and integrity of the learning parameters exchanged during the training process, ensuring that sensitive data remains protected against unauthorized access or tampering. Furthermore, the table highlights the improvements achieved by integrating SD-WAN (Software-Defined Wide Area Network) technology into this architecture. SD-WAN plays a crucial role in securely extending the learning perimeter, enabling a broader and more flexible connection of IoT devices across distributed networks. This integration not only enhances the robustness of data transmission but also optimizes network performance and scalability, thereby facilitating more efficient and secure federated learning operations within heterogeneous IoT environments.

Table 2. Performance statistics obtained from the federated learning model based on the Flower framework deployed in a distributed MQTT broker architecture.

	CRASH SYSTEM FOR IOT DEVICE	IOT DEVICE ENERGY DEPLETION	THE RISK OF SATURATION OF IOT DEVICE STORAGE MEMORY
THE INTEGRITY AND CONFIDENTIALITY RATE OF LEARNING PARAMETERS IN (%)	96%	96%	98%
THE LOSS RATE OF LEARNING PARAMETERS IN (%)	3%	5.4%	2.4%
TRAINING TIME	7min43s	7min42s	7min42s

According to the results presented in Table 2, it is evident that the federated learning (FL) model parameters are effectively maintained and secured, with a success rate ranging from 96% to 98%, even under conditions that would typically compromise the performance of FL training cycles. These results demonstrate the resilience and robustness of the proposed system, which is largely attributed to the deployment of learning models within a Storage Area Network (SAN) based architecture.

We also observe a significant reduction in the loss rate of parameters required for shared learning in the federated learning model. This improvement can be attributed to the advanced technologies integrated into the Storage Area Network (SAN) infrastructure. SANs typically utilize high-speed fiber channel protocols, which offer low-latency, high-throughput communication between storage systems and compute nodes. This ensures that large volumes of data, including AI model parameters, can be transferred efficiently and reliably across the network during the training process.

Additionally, the implementation of the IPsec (Internet Protocol Security) protocol within the SAN environment provides end-to-end encryption and authentication for data in transit. This not only protects the confidentiality and integrity of shared learning parameters against potential cyber threats but also ensures compliance with data security standards is an essential requirement in federated learning scenarios where data is distributed across multiple nodes.

Moreover, SANs are engineered with robust data redundancy mechanisms such as RAID (Redundant Array of Independent Disks), replication, and snapshotting. These features help maintain multiple copies of critical data and learning parameters, allowing for swift recovery in the event of failures. For example, if a system crash occurs or a group of IoT devices becomes unreachable due to power loss or network disconnection, the SAN can seamlessly restore the affected data without interrupting the ongoing AI model training. This fault tolerant architecture plays a vital role in maintaining the continuity, reliability, and accuracy of federated learning tasks across distributed environments.

As a result, even in challenging scenarios such as partial device dropout, intermittent connectivity, or data heterogeneity, the system manages to preserve the accuracy and security of the global model parameters to a remarkable degree. This highlights the effectiveness of integrating SAN technology into federated learning architectures, particularly in smart environments that demand scalability, robustness, and real-time responsiveness.

4 CONCLUSION AND FUTURE WORK

In this article, we propose a novel architecture for the deployment of federated learning models, which strategically leverages Storage Area Network (SAN) technology to centralize the storage of federated learning parameters. This centralized storage layer acts as a high performance, reliable repository where model updates such as gradients and weights, it can be efficiently shared among the participating IoT devices across the network. Our approach aims to address persistent challenges that continue to undermine the performance and reliability of federated learning in real world scenarios, particularly within the complex and dynamic environment of smart cities. In such ecosystems, data heterogeneity resulting from the diverse sources, formats, and distributions of data collected by various sensors and IoT devices poses a significant obstacle to model convergence and generalization

Given the constant revolution in access demands to the learning network by smart objects, some challenges remain, such as storage resource optimization, data security, and the bottleneck of devices participating in the shared training phase. Therefore, in future work, we will consider strengthening our architecture with technology that controls access to the learning perimeter through a process of verifying the identities of IoT devices.

REFERENCES

Ahmad, I., Shahabuddin, S., Kumar, T., Okwuibe, J., Gurtov, A., & Ylianttila, M. (2019). Security for 5G and beyond. *IEEE Communications Surveys and Tutorials*, *21*(4), 3682–3722.

Bonawitz, K., "Towards federated learning at scale: System design," arXiv preprint arXiv:1902.01046, Mar. 2019.

Gont, F., & Chown, T. (2016). Network reconnaissance in IPv6 networks (No. rfc7707).

Jain, N., Payal, A., & Jain, A. (2021). Performance analysis of routing protocols on IPv4 and IPv6 addressing networks. *Journal of Web Engineering*, *20*(5), 1389–1428.

Li, Q., "A survey on federated learning systems:vision, hype and reality for data privacy and protection," arXiv preprint arXiv:1907.09693, Dec. 2019.

Li, T., "Federated learning: Challenges, methods, and future directions," arXiv preprint arXiv:1908.07873, Aug. 2019.

T. Li, A. K. Sahu, M. Zaheer, M. Sanjabi, A. Talwalkar, V. Smith, Federated optimization in hetero geneous networks, Proceedings of Machine learning and systems 2 (2020) 429450.

Liu, J., Wang, T., Chen, X., Li, C., Shen, Z., & Zhang, Z. (2024). H2-RAID: Improving the reliability of SSD RAID with unified SSD and HDD hybrid architecture. *Microprocessors and Microsystems*, *105*, 104993.

Liuetal, Y. (2020). Federated learning for 6g communications: Challenges, methods, and future directions. *China Communications*.

McMahan, B., Moore, E., Ramage, D., & Hampson, S. (2017). B. A. y Arcas, Communication-e cient learning of deep networks from decentralized data. In *Arti cial intelligence and statistics* (p. 12731282). PMLR.

Mine, G., Hai, J., Jin, L., & Huiying, Z. (2020, August). A design of SD-WAN-oriented wide area network access. In *2020 International Conference on Computer Communication and Network Security (CCNS)* (pp. 174-177). IEEE.

Oladosu, S. A., Ike, C. C., Adepoju, P. A., Afolabi, A. I., Ige, A. B., & Amoo, O. O. (2021). The future of SD-WAN: A conceptual evolution from traditional WAN to autonomous, selfhealing network systems. *Magna Scientia Advanced Research and Reviews*, *3*(2), 95–107.

Shanmugam, L. (2023). *Ravish Tillu, Manish Tomar, Federated Learning Architecture: Design*. Implementation, and Challenges in Distributed AI Systems.

. (2024). Srija Chakraborty*, Ashok Kumar Turuk, Bibhudatta Sahoo, Federated Learning enabled software-defined optical network with intelligent control plane architecture. *Computers & Electrical Engineering*, *118*, 109329.

Tate, J., Beck, P., Ibarra, H. H., Kumaravel, S., & Miklas, L. (2018). *Introduction to storage area networks*. IBM Redbooks.

Troia, S., Borgianni, L., Sguotti, G., Giordano, S., & Maier, G. (2025). A Comprehensive Survey on Software-Defined Wide Area Network. *IEEE Communications Surveys and Tutorials*.

Xiao, Y., Shi, G., & Krunz, M. Towards Ubiquitous AI in 6G with Federated Learning arXiv:2004.13563v1 [eess.SP] 26 Apr 2020.

Q. Yang, Y. Liu, T. Chen, and Y. Tong, "Federated machine learning: Concept and applications," vol. 10, no. 2, pp. 1–19, Feb. 2019.

Zhao, Y., Li, M., & Lai, L. Naveen Suda, Damon Civin, Vikas Chandra, Federated learning with non-iid data, 2018, arXiv preprint arXiv:1806.00582.

Chapter 9
Generative AI for Fake News Detection in Data Architectures:
From Literature to Challenges and Future Directions

Bahaa Eddine Elbaghazaoui
https://orcid.org/0000-0002-3206-5162
National School of Applied Sciences, Sultan Moulay Slimane University, Beni Mellal, Morocco

Tarik el Moudden
https://orcid.org/0000-0002-6963-6686
Computer Science Research Laboratory, Faculty of Science, Ibn Tofail University, Kenitra, Morocco

Khalid Benabbes
https://orcid.org/0000-0001-9793-2581
ENS, Moulay Ismail University, Meknès, Morocco.

ABSTRACT

The proliferation of fake news threatens data integrity and public trust, challenging the foundations of modern data-driven systems. This chapter explores how Generative AI, particularly large language models (LLMs), can enhance fake news detection and support trustworthy data architectures. We review key techniques in misinformation detection and analyze the emerging role of GenAI in enabling automated content validation, explanation generation, and credibility assessment. The integration of these models into data pipelines introduces new opportunities but also raises concerns such as hallucinations, bias propagation, and ethical risks. We outline

DOI: 10.4018/979-8-3373-5616-7.ch009

the main challenges and propose future research directions to design autonomous, explainable, and resilient systems capable of mitigating misinformation in real time while upholding transparency and data governance principles.

1. INTRODUCTION

The rapid growth of digital content has significantly amplified the dissemination of information across a wide array of platforms, including social media networks, online news portals, blogs, and various communication channels. This digital acceleration has undeniably enhanced accessibility to information and contributed to the democratization of knowledge by enabling users from diverse backgrounds and locations to access content in real time. However, this same phenomenon has also given rise to an unprecedented surge in the spread of fake news. Fake news defined as false or misleading information that is deliberately presented as factual or credible poses a substantial challenge to societies worldwide. It undermines public trust in institutions, media, and authoritative sources, disrupts the public's ability to make informed decisions, and ultimately threatens the stability of democratic and social systems. As highlighted by Ifenthaler et al. (2021), the problem of misinformation is not merely a side effect of digital communication but a pressing concern that requires urgent attention from policymakers, researchers, and technology practitioners. Accordingly, detecting, classifying, and managing misinformation has become a critical issue, particularly for data-driven systems where the quality of input directly impacts the reliability of analytical outputs and policy recommendations.

In the context of modern data architectures and analytical ecosystems, fake news transcends being a simple media concern; it represents a deeper, more systemic issue related to the integrity and quality of data (Aïmeur et al., 2023). Today's organizations and platforms rely heavily on automated data ingestion pipelines, real-time stream processing, and machine learning algorithms to derive actionable insights from massive datasets. If the information fed into these systems is tainted by misinformation or lacks credibility, the entire chain of data-driven operations from analysis to visualization to decision-making can be severely compromised. Ensuring that only reliable and verified data enters these pipelines is therefore critical to maintaining the validity and trustworthiness of the resulting insights. The growing complexity and scale of data systems make manual validation infeasible, creating a pressing need for intelligent and scalable solutions to ensure data fidelity.

In this context, Generative Artificial Intelligence (Generative AI), and particularly the advancements in Large Language Models (LLMs), have introduced transformative possibilities (AlAli et al., 2024). These AI models are designed to not only process and generate natural language but also to understand semantic nuances, detect inconsistencies, and provide context-aware responses. Their ability to analyze linguistic patterns and extract latent meaning from unstructured text makes them powerful tools in the battle against fake news. By incorporating LLMs into data validation workflows, systems can go beyond simple keyword or rule-based filtering and move toward context-aware evaluation of content. These models can automatically flag suspicious narratives, provide explanatory reasoning for classifications, and assess the credibility of sources with high degrees of accuracy.

Furthermore, when deployed within larger data infrastructures, Generative AI enables a proactive and automated approach to misinformation detection and data integrity assurance. Instead of relying on post-hoc human moderation or reactive filtering, these systems can perform real-time analysis and classification of incoming news articles or social media posts. As illustrated in Figure 1, news content entering the system is immediately analyzed by LLMs that assess linguistic features, contextual relevance, and known patterns of disinformation. The output is a credibility score or binary classification (e.g., real vs. fake), which can then be directly embedded into downstream data pipelines. This facilitates automated decision-making about whether to propagate, review, or discard the content, thereby reinforcing the trustworthiness of data-centric applications and reducing the risk of misinformation influencing strategic outcomes.

Figure 1. Generative AI in Fake News Detection Pipelines

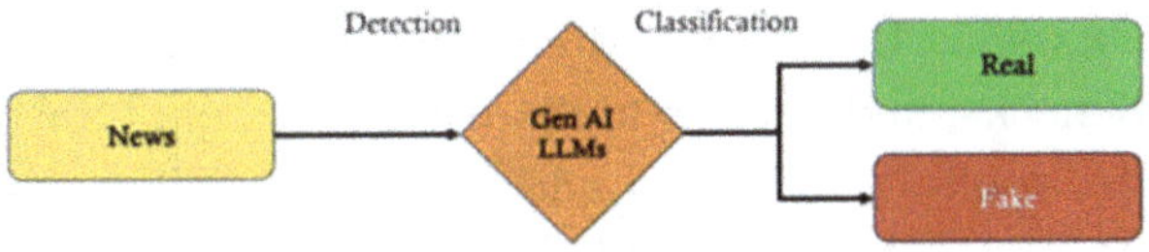

However, the integration of Generative AI into fake news detection systems is not without its share of complexities and limitations. Although these models offer promising capabilities in natural language understanding and generation, they also come with inherent risks and challenges that must be carefully managed. One of the most pressing issues is the phenomenon of *hallucination*, where models generate plausible-sounding but entirely fabricated or inaccurate information. This poses a significant risk in contexts where factual accuracy is critical, such as news verification, policy analysis, or legal reporting. Additionally, ethical concerns emerge regarding the use of AI to assess or censor public content, particularly when transparency and accountability are lacking in the decision-making process.

Bias propagation is another critical concern. Generative AI models are often trained on large-scale internet datasets that may contain implicit social, cultural, or political biases. If not properly mitigated, these biases can be reproduced or even amplified in the model's outputs, leading to unfair or discriminatory assessments of news content. Furthermore, there is an ongoing debate regarding the *explainability* and interpretability of LLM-based systems. In high-stakes domains like misinformation detection, stakeholders including journalists, policymakers, and end-users need to understand why a piece of content was flagged as fake or unreliable. Yet many current models operate as "black boxes," making it difficult to trace the reasoning behind their classifications or to justify their decisions in a meaningful, transparent manner.

Given these challenges, the deployment of Generative AI in fake news detection must be guided by rigorous design principles, robust evaluation mechanisms, and continuous oversight. Addressing these concerns is essential to ensure that such systems are not only effective but also fair, trustworthy, and aligned with ethical standards.

This chapter aims to explore the intersection of Generative AI and fake news detection within the broader and rapidly evolving field of data architecture. It seeks to provide a comprehensive review of the current state of the art in literature, highlighting key methodologies, tools, and applications that have emerged in recent years. Beyond simply describing technical approaches, the chapter also outlines important architectural considerations, such as data ingestion strategies, model integration workflows, feedback loops, and governance layers that support safe deployment in real-world systems. Moreover, it critically examines the limitations and blind spots of existing frameworks, including scalability challenges, real-time performance bottlenecks, and gaps in user trust and system transparency. Finally, it proposes forward-looking strategies and recommendations aimed at building resilient, adaptable, and ethically grounded data ecosystems capable of countering the increasingly sophisticated threat of misinformation in the digital age.

2. BACKGROUND AND LITERATURE REVIEW

Fake news has emerged as a prominent and pervasive phenomenon in the digital age, gaining widespread traction across social networks, news aggregation websites, online forums, and instant messaging platforms. With the exponential rise in user-generated content and the ease of information sharing, fake news can now reach vast audiences within minutes, often outpacing the dissemination of verified, factual information. Its ability to shape public opinion, manipulate electoral and political discourse, polarize communities, and erode trust in established institutions has transformed it from a fringe concern into a mainstream issue of global significance. Consequently, fake news has attracted intense scholarly interest, making it a focal point of research across a diverse range of academic disciplines, including computer science, communication and media studies, political science, and social psychology.

From a data science and information systems perspective, fake news presents a particularly complex challenge. It represents a dynamic, context-sensitive, and adversarial form of data pollution that not only distorts information ecosystems but also evolves rapidly in response to countermeasures. Detecting and mitigating fake news requires advanced analytical capabilities that can operate within real-time or near-real-time environments, particularly in systems that are responsible for delivering trusted content to users. As Shu et al. (2017) note, fake news is not static or easily classifiable it often mimics legitimate content in structure and tone, making detection all the more difficult without sophisticated computational models.

Early computational approaches to fake news detection focused primarily on *content-based methods*, which analyze the textual characteristics of articles to identify signs of deception or manipulation. These approaches relied heavily on the extraction of linguistic and stylistic features such as lexical diversity, word frequencies, use of sensational or emotionally charged language, sentiment polarity, readability scores, and syntactic patterns. Once these handcrafted features were extracted, traditional machine learning classifiers such as logistic regression, support vector machines (SVM), random forests, and decision trees were employed to perform binary classification tasks, distinguishing between real and fake news articles (Ruchansky et al., 2017). While these methods offered a useful starting point, they were limited in their ability to generalize across topics, domains, and evolving narrative tactics used by malicious actors.

To address these limitations, subsequent research expanded the scope of detection techniques by incorporating *context-based signals* alongside content features. These more advanced methods took into account how news spreads across social media platforms and who engages with it. For example, researchers began modeling *propagation dynamics*, such as retweet cascades, reply patterns, and temporal engagement trends, to capture how fake news travels through digital communities. They also analyzed *user behavior* including account credibility, posting history, and bot-like activity and *source reliability* by evaluating the historical trustworthiness of news outlets or individual content producers. By integrating these dimensions, context-aware models provided a more holistic understanding of fake news beyond the article text alone. Graph-based neural networks and diffusion models became increasingly popular in this line of work, enabling algorithms to learn from the structural and temporal aspects of information dissemination (Monti et al., 2019). These techniques not only improved accuracy but also offered insights into the mechanisms that enable fake news to go viral, thereby supporting the development of more robust and proactive defense strategies.

With the advancement of deep learning methodologies, particularly the emergence of sophisticated neural architectures such as convolutional neural networks (CNNs) and recurrent neural networks (RNNs), the field of fake news detection experienced a significant transformation. These deep learning models enabled a departure from traditional, manual feature engineering approaches by automatically learning hierarchical representations from raw text data. CNNs were especially effective in capturing local syntactic patterns, while RNNs, including their gated variants like LSTMs and GRUs, demonstrated strengths in modeling sequential dependencies and long-range contextual relationships within language. As a result, these models yielded improved performance and generalization, allowing systems to detect nuanced and subtle indicators of misinformation that traditional models often overlooked (Wang et al., 2018).

A major paradigm shift occurred with the introduction of transformer architectures, most notably the Bidirectional Encoder Representations from Transformers (BERT) model. BERT brought forth the capability of bidirectional context processing, meaning that the model could consider both left and right context simultaneously for any given token. This represented a considerable leap in natural language understanding tasks, allowing models to grasp more precise meanings, contextual dependencies, and semantic nuances. BERT and its derivatives quickly set new state-of-the-art results across multiple NLP benchmarks, including those for fake news detection (Devlin et al., 2019). Its pre-trained language representations, when fine-tuned on task-specific data, dramatically improved classification accuracy, especially in domains where context plays a critical role in interpreting textual intent.

Following BERT, a new generation of *Large Language Models (LLMs)* was introduced, further expanding the scope and power of deep learning in natural language processing. Models such as GPT (Generative Pre-trained Transformer), T5 (Text-to-Text Transfer Transformer), and BART (Bidirectional and Auto-Regressive Transformers) extended the capabilities of their predecessors by not only supporting discriminative tasks like classification, but also enabling generative functionalities including summarization, paraphrasing, translation, and explanation generation (Lewis et al., 2020; Raffel et al., 2020; Brown et al., 2020). These models are trained on massive corpora using self-supervised learning and can perform zero-shot or few-shot learning, making them particularly attractive for use in domains where labeled data may be scarce or rapidly evolving, such as misinformation detection.

Recent scholarly work has begun to explore novel applications of these generative models in the context of fake news beyond simple binary classification. For instance, researchers have investigated how these models can be used to compute *factual consistency scores* by comparing claims to external sources, to generate *natural language justifications* that explain why a news article might be deceptive or unreliable, and to detect *logical contradictions* within the body of a single article or between its headline and content (Zhou & Zafarani, 2020). These innovations represent a meaningful shift toward explainable and transparent AI systems. Instead of merely labeling content as fake, these systems are now able to articulate the reasoning behind their decisions, which is essential for gaining user trust and supporting human oversight in high-stakes applications.

However, despite these advances, the field continues to face several important challenges that must be addressed for broader and safer deployment. One major issue is the quality and relevance of available benchmark datasets. Many commonly used datasets are either outdated, limited to specific domains (e.g., politics or entertainment), or contain linguistic and regional biases that reduce their generalizability (Shu et al., 2020). This restricts the ability of models to adapt to emerging narratives or different cultural contexts. Additionally, the evaluation of generative models requires the development of new metrics that go beyond traditional accuracy or F1-score. Effective evaluation must consider not only the linguistic *fluency* of generated outputs but also their *factual correctness* and *interpretive trustworthiness*, which are harder to quantify with existing tools.

Furthermore, the dual-use nature of Generative AI introduces serious ethical concerns. The same models that can be used to detect and explain misinformation may also be exploited to generate convincing fake content at scale, thereby exacerbating the very problem they aim to solve. As highlighted by Solaiman et al. (2019), this dual-use dilemma necessitates careful governance, access controls, and responsible AI practices to prevent misuse and to ensure alignment with societal values.

In summary, this literature review establishes a foundational understanding of how the field of fake news detection has evolved from early content-based approaches to the integration of advanced deep learning and generative models. It underscores the transformative potential of Generative AI while acknowledging the limitations and responsibilities that accompany its use. This review serves as a prelude to further discussions on how these models can be effectively and ethically embedded within scalable, secure, and trustworthy data architectures designed to combat the multifaceted and evolving challenge of misinformation.

3. THE ROLE OF GENERATIVE AI IN FAKE NEWS DETECTION

Generative Artificial Intelligence (Generative AI), particularly through the use of large language models (LLMs), has introduced a transformative shift in how text is understood, synthesized, and validated. In the domain of fake news detection, Generative AI enables a new dimension of intelligence: beyond classifying or scoring content, it can explain, summarize, critique, and even suggest revisions tasks traditionally performed by human fact-checkers or expert reviewers (OpenAI, 2023; Ji et al., 2023).

Unlike traditional discriminative models that output a label (e.g., "fake" or "real"), generative models are designed to produce coherent and contextually grounded textual responses. This allows them to function not only as classifiers but also as content auditors. For instance, a model like GPT-4 can be prompted to explain why a claim appears unreliable, identify logical inconsistencies within an article, or generate more truthful and neutral alternatives to misleading headlines (Zhou & Zafarani, 2020; Kai et al., 2023).

One of the most impactful uses of generative models in fake news detection is explanation generation. Rather than assigning a simple probability score, the model can articulate the reasoning behind its decision highlighting factual inconsistencies, sensational language, or contradictions with known data. These capabilities contribute significantly to transparency, support human moderation, and improve user trust in AI-assisted systems. Moreover, they align with the growing demands for explainable AI (XAI) in high-stakes domains such as public health, finance, and politics (Doshi-Velez & Kim, 2017).

Figure 2 illustrates the operational flow of Generative AI in explainable fake news detection. The process begins with a news article submitted as input to the system. Rather than simply outputting a binary classification, the generative model performs multiple tasks in parallel. It evaluates the semantic content, cross-checks for factual consistency, and produces a set of human-readable outputs. These outputs include:

- The classification label (e.g., "Fake").
- Textual explanation that identifies the reasoning behind the decision (such as highlighting factual contradictions).
- A suggested correction based on verified knowledge.

This multifaceted output not only improves classification accuracy but also enhances interpretability, supporting human reviewers, improving transparency, and aligning the system with ethical AI principles. By embedding such capabilities into data validation pipelines, organizations can move beyond black-box AI toward accountable, explainable systems that foster greater trust in automated decision-making.

Figure 2. Generative AI for Explainable Fake News Detection

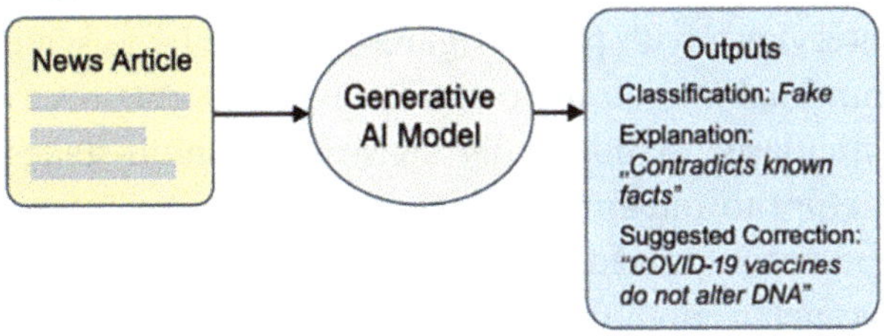

Generative AI also supports advanced capabilities such as *paraphrase detection* and *semantic consistency checking*, which are increasingly vital in identifying more subtle and sophisticated forms of misinformation. By leveraging the ability of Large Language Models (LLMs) to rephrase textual content and analyze linguistic variation, these systems can reformulate a given claim and then compare it to a database of verified facts or trusted sources. This enables the detection of distortions that may not involve outright falsehoods but rather rely on misleading tactics such as selective omission, exaggeration of details, or framing bias. For instance, an article might present accurate statistics but accompany them with misleading contextual framing that alters the reader's interpretation. LLMs can be trained or prompted to detect such discrepancies by analyzing the alignment between the original statement and its paraphrased, semantically equivalent form when juxtaposed against known information. This methodology is especially powerful in combatting misinformation that resides in a gray area content that is partially true yet still deceptive in its overall effect.

Another emerging and promising application of Generative AI in this context is the *automated generation of counter-narratives*. In this scenario, generative models are tasked with responding to potentially fake or harmful claims by producing informative rebuttals. These responses may include a succinct summary of verified data, an evidence-based correction, or a reference to authoritative sources such as scientific publications, fact-checking websites, or official reports. The generation of counter-narratives enables real-time mitigation of misinformation, particularly within fast-moving environments like social media platforms where the speed of information propagation can often outpace manual verification efforts. By equipping moderation systems or end-users with context-rich, AI-generated rebuttals, platforms can foster healthier discourse and prevent the unchecked spread of false or misleading content.

However, while these applications are promising, they also highlight the *dual-use nature* of generative models a critical concern that cannot be overlooked. The same technological foundations that support fake news detection and content verification can also be misappropriated for malicious purposes. Generative AI can be exploited to produce highly realistic yet entirely fabricated news articles, create synthetic interviews with public figures, or drive large-scale disinformation campaigns with minimal human intervention. This presents a serious ethical and security risk, particularly in politically sensitive or high-stakes environments. Therefore, any attempt to integrate Generative AI into misinformation detection workflows must be accompanied by robust *governance mechanisms*. These may include techniques such as digital watermarking of generated content, logging and traceability for auditability, and enforced human-in-the-loop systems to monitor outputs and intervene when necessary. Without such safeguards, the risk of misuse may outweigh the intended benefits.

Additionally, the *scalability* and *adaptability* of generative models contribute to their appeal for integration within modern, modular data architectures. These models can be encapsulated as microservices that operate within content validation pipelines, offering on-demand functionality such as claim verification, bias detection, and natural language explanations. They can also be used to *enrich metadata* associated with digital content, enabling downstream systems to make more informed decisions based on content credibility scores or linguistic markers of reliability. Furthermore, LLMs can be embedded directly into user-facing interfaces such as content dashboards, fact-checking tools, or moderation panels to provide end-users with intelligible explanations for why certain content has been flagged or downranked. However, such integration requires *careful orchestration* and thoughtful system design. Generative models are inherently *computationally expensive*, often requiring GPUs or specialized hardware, and their performance can vary depending on input quality, prompt structure, and surrounding context. Despite their fluency and coherence, the outputs of these models are not guaranteed to be factually accurate and should not be blindly trusted without appropriate post-verification and validation layers.

In conclusion, this section demonstrates that Generative AI serves not only as a mechanism for improving classification performance in fake news detection but also as a catalyst for the development of *intelligent, explainable, and partially autonomous* systems. These capabilities contribute to the creation of more robust and transparent information ecosystems, where automated tools can collaborate with human judgment to ensure content integrity. This discussion forms a conceptual bridge between the *technical capabilities* of generative models and their *architectural integration* into real-world data systems, a theme that will be examined in greater detail in the following section.

4. INTEGRATION IN DATA ARCHITECTURES

As data architectures evolve to support real-time analytics, autonomous processing, and scalable intelligence, the integration of fake news detection mechanisms becomes a critical design consideration. Ensuring the credibility of content within data pipelines goes beyond mere classification accuracy it requires a comprehensive architectural approach that embeds validation, interpretability, and governance directly into the system design (Hu et al., 2024). In this context, Generative AI offers a novel opportunity to enable both automated detection and semantic explanation within the data flow.

A modern data architecture typically comprises ingestion layers, processing engines, storage systems, metadata management tools, and consumption interfaces (Halevy et al., 2020). Fake news detection can be integrated across these components as part of a broader data validation and quality assurance subsystem. Generative AI enhances this process by introducing semantic reasoning, contextual interpretation, and natural language explanation capabilities features that go beyond traditional rule-based or statistical methods (Ji et al., 2023).

The pipeline begins at the ingestion layer, where unverified content from external sources such as news APIs, social media streams, or user-generated submissions enters the system. At this stage, basic preprocessing operations are applied, including language detection, normalization, and metadata extraction. These operations help ensure consistency across heterogeneous content formats and prepare the data for downstream analysis.

Subsequently, the preprocessed content is passed to a semantic embedding layer, where sentence encoders or large language models (LLMs) produce dense vector representations that capture both the syntactic structure and semantic meaning of the text (Reimers & Gurevych, 2019). These embeddings can be augmented with auxiliary features such as named entity recognition (NER), sentiment scores, or topic models to provide a richer feature space for classification or similarity comparison. When integrated with a hybrid detection framework, these representations empower both discriminative classifiers and generative models to operate effectively and transparently.

The core detection logic follows, where Generative AI plays a central role. A hybrid setup can be employed in which a discriminative model first flags content as potentially fake, and a generative model then provides an explanation or justification. For example, if a headline is classified as suspicious, a generative model might summarize the inconsistencies or highlight contradictions with verified facts. This two-step approach ensures that the system offers not only binary decisions but also human-readable insights.

Figure 3. Architecture of a Generative AI-Enhanced Fake News Detection Pipeline

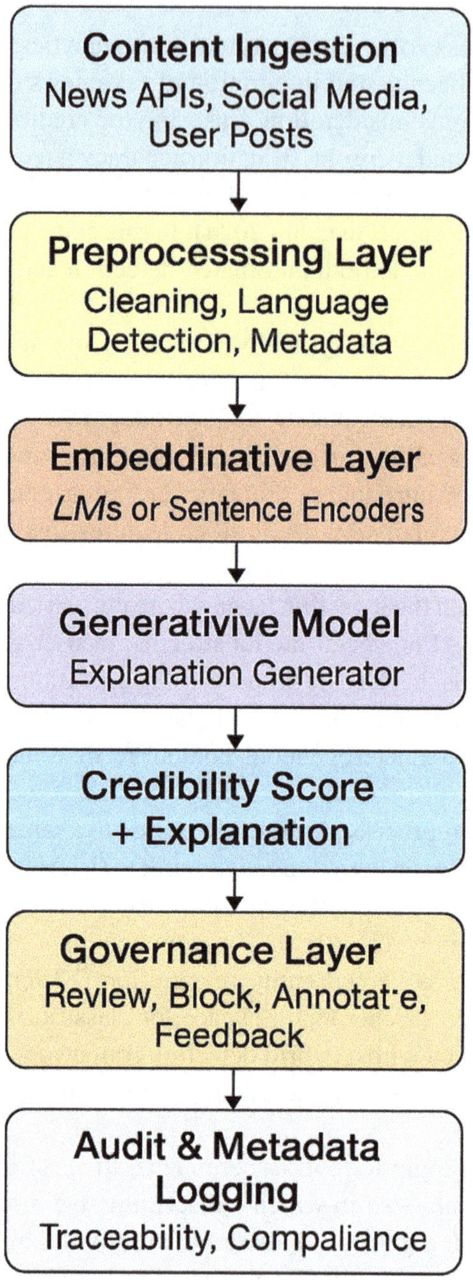

This diagram "Figure 3" illustrates the sequential integration of Generative AI within a modern data architecture designed for fake news detection. The process begins with the ingestion of content from various sources such as social media, news APIs, and user-generated posts. This raw content is then passed through a preprocessing layer, where it undergoes cleaning, language detection, and metadata extraction to ensure consistency and standardization. Next, semantic representations are generated through an embedding layer powered by language models or sentence encoders. At the heart of the pipeline, a generative model provides context-aware reasoning by producing explanations for flagged content, enhancing transparency and interpretability. These insights, combined with credibility scores, feed into a governance layer responsible for review, annotation, user feedback, and enforcement actions. Finally, audit and metadata logging ensures traceability and compliance, enabling organizations to monitor the integrity of the system over time. This layered architecture exemplifies how Generative AI can be embedded into data pipelines to enhance both detection performance and accountability.

Once a credibility score and corresponding explanation are generated by the system, this enriched information is passed to a *governance layer* a critical decision-making component within the overall architecture. Within this layer, various policies and workflows are applied to determine how the flagged content should be handled. Depending on the confidence level of the model and the context of the content, actions may include *automatically blocking* the content from being published, *escalating it to human moderators* for manual review, *tagging it with visual warnings* for end-user awareness, or *storing it along with annotations* for further downstream analysis. These decisions can be fine-tuned based on platform-specific risk tolerances, regulatory requirements, and the criticality of the information domain (e.g., public health, elections, or finance).

To support continual improvement and model accountability, *feedback mechanisms* can also be incorporated into the system. These allow human moderators, subject-matter experts, or even end-users to review system outputs and flag false positives or false negatives. This feedback is then fed back into the training loop or fine-tuning processes, enabling the models to learn from their mistakes and gradually improve classification accuracy and contextual sensitivity over time. This active learning paradigm ensures that the system does not remain static but evolves in response to real-world use and changing patterns in misinformation tactics.

The architecture is also designed to ensure *transparency and auditability*, two principles that are increasingly critical in sensitive domains and regulated industries. This is achieved through *comprehensive logging* and *metadata tagging* at every stage of the pipeline. Each module or service that interacts with a piece of content be it ingestion, preprocessing, classification, or explanation generates traceable metadata, including timestamps, versioned model identifiers, and decision logs. These artifacts can be used for *compliance audits*, *error tracing*, and *model interpretability assessments*, thereby supporting ethical oversight and regulatory alignment. In contexts such as government digital services, healthcare information systems, or educational portals, such traceability is not only a technical best practice but also a legal and ethical imperative to maintain public trust and institutional accountability.

From an infrastructure perspective, the modular nature of this system allows for flexible deployment. Each component whether it's the LLM inference engine, classification logic, feedback processor, or governance policy engine can be deployed as a *microservice* within a distributed architecture. Alternatively, the entire system can be orchestrated within a *data pipeline framework* using modern orchestration tools. Technologies such as *Apache Kafka* for real-time data streaming, *Apache Airflow* for workflow scheduling and dependency management, and *cloud-native LLM APIs* (e.g., OpenAI, Cohere, Hugging Face) for on-demand inference allow for scalable, robust, and maintainable implementations. However, it is important to *carefully manage trade-offs* related to *latency*, *operational cost*, and *data privacy* especially when invoking LLMs in production environments where responses must be generated in milliseconds and where sensitive user information is processed.

By *embedding Generative AI directly into the core layers of data architecture*, organizations can construct intelligent information pipelines that not only perform traditional functions like ingestion, transformation, and storage, but also *evaluate content credibility*, *generate human-readable justifications*, and *guide decision-making* based on policy and risk context. This architectural evolution shifts the role of the pipeline from a passive conduit for data flow into an *active guardian of information integrity*. In doing so, it helps institutions to more effectively manage the *societal, operational, and reputational risks* associated with fake news and other forms of digital misinformation, ultimately contributing to a more trustworthy and resilient information ecosystem.

5. CHALLENGES AND LIMITATIONS

While the integration of Generative AI into fake news detection systems offers promising capabilities, it also introduces a new set of technical, ethical, and operational challenges. These limitations must be carefully understood and addressed to ensure that such systems are trustworthy, explainable, and effective at scale. Figure 4 illustrates four of the most critical limitations that must be taken into account when designing such systems.

Figure 4. Challenges and Limitations of Using Generative AI in Fake News Detection

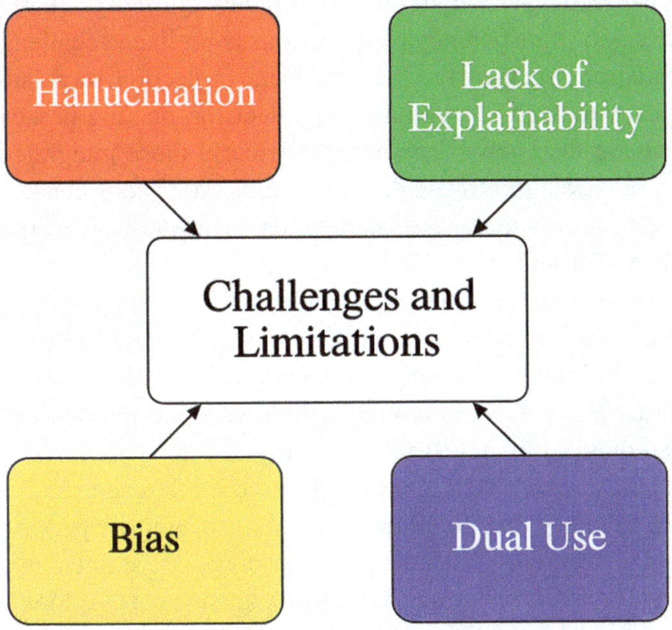

One of the most pressing and well-documented concerns associated with Large Language Models (LLMs) is the phenomenon known as hallucination. This refers to the model's tendency to generate content that is grammatically correct, syntactically fluent, and semantically plausible yet factually incorrect, unverifiable, or even entirely fabricated. In the context of fake news detection, such hallucinations pose a serious risk. A hallucinated explanation, misattributed citation, or incorrectly generated summary can mislead users instead of clarifying the truth, thereby undermining the reliability and credibility of the system. This is especially problematic in sensitive sectors such as healthcare, law, or public administration, where end-users including citizens, professionals, and policy-makers rely on information systems for guidance and decision support. Without robust mechanisms for fact-checking or cross-verification against trusted external sources, users may unknowingly accept incorrect outputs as accurate, potentially leading to misinformation propagation and compromised public trust (Farquhar et al., 2024).

Another critical limitation lies in the lack of explainability inherent to current LLMs. While Generative AI systems can produce human-readable justifications for their outputs, these explanations are often post-hoc and do not necessarily reflect the internal decision-making pathways of the model. In essence, modern LLMs operate as complex "black boxes" with billions of parameters and probabilistic representations that are difficult, if not impossible, to interpret meaningfully. This opacity complicates efforts to debug system errors, trace the origin of mistakes, or understand model behavior under different inputs. Moreover, in regulated environments, this lack of transparency poses serious compliance challenges with data protection regulations such as the General Data Protection Regulation (GDPR), which mandates explainability in automated decision-making processes. For applications involving fake news detection particularly those integrated into public sector services or media platforms this undermines user confidence and hampers the system's legitimacy in the eyes of stakeholders who demand accountability and traceability (Sina Mohseni et al., 2020).

Bias and fairness represent additional challenges that remain largely unresolved. LLMs are typically trained on massive and diverse corpora harvested from the internet, which while rich in linguistic variety often contain embedded social, political, or ideological biases. These biases are implicitly learned and encoded in the model's parameters, and they can manifest in subtle ways during generation. In fake news detection, such biases may skew the output based on language, cultural framing, region, or political viewpoint, potentially suppressing minority perspectives or amplifying dominant narratives. The consequences of this are serious: misinformation systems may inadvertently reinforce systemic inequalities or overlook controversial but valid viewpoints. This not only risks undermining the model's neutrality but also raises ethical concerns about the influence of algorithmic systems on democratic discourse and public opinion (Xiao Fang et al., 2024).

The problem is further compounded by the dual-use nature of Generative AI. While these models can be employed for detecting, summarizing, and countering fake news, they can just as easily be weaponized to generate convincing misinformation. Malicious actors can exploit LLMs to craft highly realistic fake news articles, synthetic expert commentary, or fabricated interviews that are stylistically indistinguishable from legitimate content. These outputs can include fabricated citations, deep linguistic coherence, and contextual fluency that help them evade traditional detection mechanisms. This creates an arms race between generation and detection, where the same underlying technology serves both offense and defense. As Su et al. (2023) highlight, this asymmetry presents a significant risk for public safety, information integrity, and democratic resilience especially during critical events such as elections, pandemics, or national crises.

Data scarcity and benchmarking limitations continue to hinder progress in this domain. Many of the publicly available datasets used for training and evaluating fake news detection models are either outdated, limited in scope, or domain-specific. They often fail to capture the complexity of evolving misinformation tactics or the linguistic and cultural diversity of global content ecosystems. Furthermore, traditional evaluation metrics such as accuracy, precision, recall, and F1-score are insufficient for assessing generative capabilities of models, particularly in terms of factual consistency, trustworthiness, and semantic faithfulness. This makes it difficult to conduct fair comparisons across systems and to measure improvements in a way that reflects real-world impact (Galli et al., 2022).

Scalability and resource constraints also present formidable barriers to deployment. Generative models with billions of parameters require substantial computational resources for inference typically involving specialized hardware such as GPUs or TPUs. This creates high operational costs and latency issues, particularly for applications that require real-time performance or low response times. For small and medium-sized organizations, or those operating in resource-constrained environments, deploying such models in production may be infeasible. Additionally, when models are deployed via external APIs, privacy concerns arise. User-generated or sensitive data must be sent to third-party services, which introduces risks related to data sovereignty, confidentiality, and compliance with data protection laws.

Lastly, there remain significant regulatory and ethical uncertainties surrounding the deployment of Generative AI in high-impact applications like fake news detection. Key questions include: Who is accountable when the model makes a mistake? What happens when a misclassification leads to reputational damage, political fallout, or public misinformation? How should systems respond to user complaints, appeals, or legal challenges? These questions demand clear ethical frameworks, auditable governance structures, and policy guidelines to ensure responsible and trustworthy AI adoption. As the societal impact of generative technologies grows, so too does the need for interdisciplinary collaboration among technologists, ethicists, legal scholars, and policymakers.

In summary, while Generative AI represents a transformative advancement in the detection and management of misinformation, its deployment is fraught with challenges that span technical, ethical, regulatory, and operational domains. To fully realize its potential in building reliable and fair information systems, these issues must be tackled through a coordinated combination of technological safeguards, transparent system design, and inclusive governance. The following section outlines future directions aimed at addressing these limitations and advancing the development of scalable, explainable, and ethically sound AI-powered data architectures.

6. FUTURE DIRECTIONS

The integration of Generative AI into fake news detection systems represents a paradigm shift in how data architectures can be designed to ensure trust, transparency, and resilience. While the challenges outlined in the previous section underscore the complexity of this endeavor, they also point to fertile areas for innovation and interdisciplinary research. Future progress will depend not only on technological advancements but also on ethical design principles, regulatory alignment, and robust evaluation frameworks. Figure 5 outlines four key directions shaping the future of Generative AI in fake news detection, including human-AI collaboration, fact-grounded generation, multimodal detection, and efficient architectures.

Figure 5. Future Directions in Generative AI for Fake News Detection

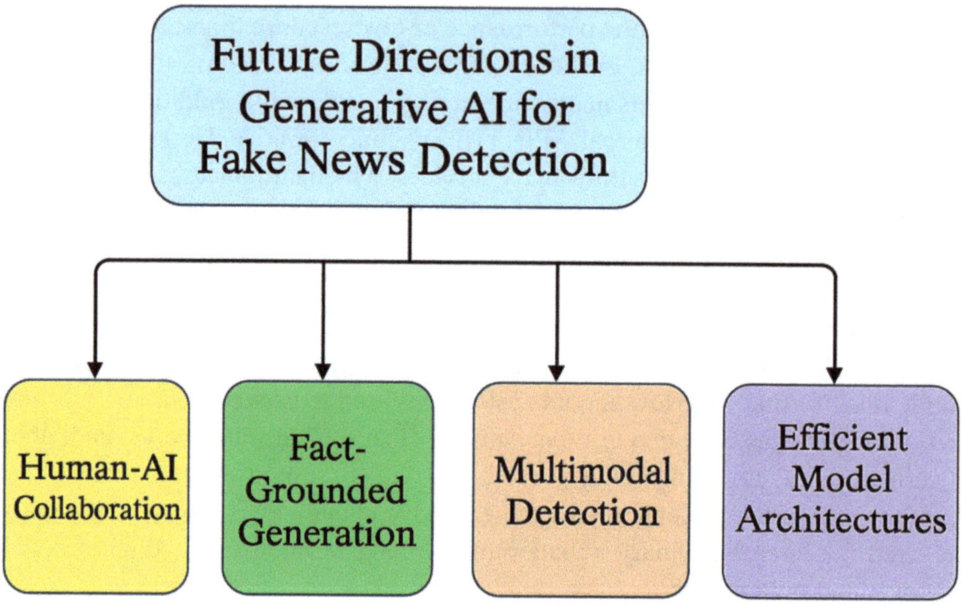

One promising direction is the development of **h**uman-in-the-loop systems that combine the strengths of AI with human judgment. Rather than replacing human fact-checkers, Generative AI can serve as an assistive tool, generating preliminary assessments, highlighting inconsistencies, and surfacing potential concerns for expert validation. Such hybrid systems are especially valuable in domains where the cost of false positives or negatives is high, and human oversight remains indispensable.

Another area of active exploration is the integration of Generative AI with structured knowledge sources such as knowledge graphs, verified databases, or domain-specific ontologies. By grounding the generative outputs in verifiable information, these models can improve factual consistency and reduce hallucinations. This approach supports the development of fact-aware language models capable of citing sources and justifying their outputs in alignment with known truths.

Multimodal misinformation detection is also gaining momentum. While most current systems focus on text, future architectures should be equipped to analyze and cross-reference text, images, audio, and video simultaneously. This is particularly important as fake news increasingly relies on manipulated multimedia content. Generative AI models trained on multimodal datasets can play a pivotal role in detecting inconsistencies between modalities (e.g., mismatch between image and caption), enhancing overall detection accuracy.

From a deployment perspective, lightweight and efficient model architectures are needed to support real-time integration in operational pipelines. Techniques such as model distillation, quantization, and on-device inference can make it feasible to run generative models in resource-constrained environments without sacrificing performance. Additionally, serverless AI pipelines and microservices can enable dynamic scaling based on detection demand.

In parallel, there is a growing need for standardization in benchmarking, auditing, and risk assessment. Developing open, diverse, and up-to-date datasets for training and evaluation is essential for ensuring model robustness and fairness. Beyond accuracy metrics, future benchmarks should include measures of explanation quality, factual grounding, and ethical impact.

On the policy front, governance frameworks and regulatory guidelines must evolve to account for the unique capabilities and risks of Generative AI. Principles such as transparency, accountability, non-maleficence, and fairness should be embedded into both the models and the systems that deploy them. Collaboration between technologists, ethicists, and policymakers will be vital to ensure that innovations are aligned with public interest.

Finally, future systems must embrace continuous learning and adaptation. The nature of fake news evolves rapidly, with new narratives, techniques, and cultural contexts emerging over time. Architectures that support continuous model retraining, user feedback loops, and adaptive rule-based governance will be better positioned to handle these shifts.

In conclusion, the future of fake news detection in data architectures lies in building systems that are not only intelligent but also interpretable, ethical, and resilient. Generative AI, when used responsibly and thoughtfully, offers the potential to transform data pipelines into guardians of information integrity empowering individuals and institutions to make decisions grounded in truth.

7. CONCLUSION

In an era defined by rapid digital communication and the democratization of content creation, fake news has emerged as a significant threat to data quality, public trust, and informed decision-making. The proliferation of misinformation not only distorts social and political discourse but also pollutes the data streams that feed analytical systems, machine learning models, and organizational dashboards. As such, fake news is no longer a challenge confined to journalism or social media it is a data governance issue that demands architectural solutions. This chapter has explored how Generative Artificial Intelligence, particularly large language models, offers new capabilities for detecting, explaining, and mitigating fake news within modern data architectures. We examined the evolution of detection techniques, highlighted the unique contributions of generative models, and proposed a conceptual pipeline for integrating these technologies into autonomous, trustworthy data systems.

Despite their potential, generative models also introduce considerable risks, including hallucinations, bias propagation, lack of transparency, and ethical concerns related to dual use. These challenges underscore the need for responsible design, robust evaluation, and continuous oversight in both research and deployment. Looking ahead, the integration of Generative AI into data pipelines must be guided by interdisciplinary collaboration and a strong commitment to ethical AI principles. Opportunities for innovation lie in hybrid human-AI systems, fact-grounded generation, multimodal analysis, and adaptive governance frameworks. By pursuing these directions, researchers and practitioners can build resilient infrastructures capable of maintaining data integrity in the face of evolving misinformation tactics. Ultimately, the convergence of Generative AI and data architecture offers more than just technical advancement it provides a foundation for reinforcing trust in information systems at a time when truth itself is under threat. With careful design and responsible deployment, these technologies can empower data architectures to not only process content but to understand, evaluate, and safeguard it.

REFERENCES

Aïmeur, E., Amri, S., & Brassard, G. (2023). Fake news, disinformation and misinformation in social media: A review. *Social Network Analysis and Mining*, *13*(1), 30. PMID: 36789378

AlAli, R., & Wardat, Y. (2024). Opportunities and challenges of integrating generative artificial intelligence in education. *International Journal of Religion*, *5*(7), 784–793. DOI: 10.61707/8y29gv34

Brown, T., Mann, B., Ryder, N., Subbiah, M., Kaplan, J. D., Dhariwal, P., & Amodei, D. (2020). Language models are few-shot learners. *Advances in Neural Information Processing Systems*, *33*, 1877–1901. DOI: 10.48550/arXiv.2005.14165

Devlin, J., Chang, M. W., Lee, K., & Toutanova, K. (2019). BERT: Pre-training of deep bidirectional transformers for language understanding. *Proceedings of NAACL-HLT*, 4171–4186. https://doi.org/DOI: 10.48550/arXiv.1810.04805

Doshi-Velez, F., & Kim, B. (2017). Towards a rigorous science of interpretable machine learning. arXiv preprint. https://doi.org//arXiv.1702.08608DOI: 10.48550

Fang, X., Che, S., & Mao, M., (2024). Bias of AI-generated content: An examination of news produced by large language models. *Scientific Reports*, *14*, 5224. DOI: 10.1038/s41598-024-55686-2 PMID: 38433238

Farquhar, S., Kossen, J., & Kuhn, L., (2024). Detecting hallucinations in large language models using semantic entropy. *Nature*, *630*, 625–630. DOI: 10.1038/s41586-024-07421-0 PMID: 38898292

Galli, A., Masciari, E., & Moscato, V., (2022). A comprehensive Benchmark for fake news detection. *Journal of Intelligent Information Systems*, *59*, 237–261. DOI: 10.1007/s10844-021-00646-9 PMID: 35342227

Halevy, A., Korn, F., Noy, N. F., Olston, C., Polyzotis, N., Roy, S., & Whang, S. E. (2020). Goods: Organizing Google's datasets. *Communications of the ACM*, *63*(1), 89–97. DOI: 10.1145/3360322

Hu, B., Mao, Z., & Zhang, Y. (2024, February 22). An overview of fake news detection: From a new perspective. *Fundamental Research (Beijing)*, *5*(1), 332–346. DOI: 10.1016/j.fmre.2024.01.017 PMID: 40166093

Ifenthaler, D., Gibson, D., Prasse, D., Shimada, A., & Yamada, M. (2021). Putting learning back into learning analytics: Actions for policy makers, researchers, and practitioners. *Educational Technology Research and Development*, *69*(4), 2131–2150.

Ji, Z., Lee, N., Frieske, R., Yu, T., Su, D., Xu, Y., & Ren, X. (2023). Survey of hallucination in natural language generation. *ACM Computing Surveys*, *55*(12), 1–38. DOI: 10.1145/3571730

Lewis, M., Liu, Y., Goyal, N., Ghazvininejad, M., Mohamed, A., Levy, O., & Zettlemoyer, L. (2020). BART: Denoising sequence-to-sequence pre-training for natural language generation, translation, and comprehension. *Proceedings of ACL*, 7871–7880. https://doi.org/DOI: 10.48550/arXiv.1910.13461

Mohseni, S., Yang, F., Pentyala, S., Du, M., Liu, Y., Lupfer, N., & Ragan, E. (2021, May). Machine learning explanations to prevent overtrust in fake news detection. In *Proceedings of the international AAAI conference on web and social media* (Vol. 15, pp. 421-431).

Monti, F., Frasca, F., Eynard, D., Mannion, D., & Bronstein, M. M. (2019). Fake news detection on social media using geometric deep learning. [TKDD]. *ACM Transactions on Knowledge Discovery from Data*, *13*(5), 1–27. https://arxiv.org/abs/1902.06673

Open, A. I. (2023). GPT-4 Technical Report. arXiv preprint. https://doi.org//arXiv.2303.08774DOI: 10.48550

Raffel, C., Shazeer, N., Roberts, A., Lee, K., Narang, S., Matena, M., & Liu, P. J. (2020). Exploring the limits of transfer learning with a unified text-to-text transformer. *Journal of Machine Learning Research*, *21*(140), 1–67. https://www.jmlr.org/papers/v21/20-074.html

Reimers, N., & Gurevych, I. (2019). Sentence-BERT: Sentence embeddings using Siamese BERT-networks. Proceedings of EMNLP/IJCNLP, 3982–3992. https://doi.org/DOI: 10.48550/arXiv.1908.10084

Ruchansky, N., Seo, S., & Liu, Y. (2017). CSI: A hybrid deep model for fake news detection. *Proceedings of CIKM*, 797–806. https://doi.org/DOI: 10.1145/3132847.3132877

Shu, K., Cui, L., Wang, S., Lee, D., & Liu, H. 2019. DEFEND: Explainable Fake News Detection. In *Proceedings of the 25th ACM SIGKDD International Conference on Knowledge Discovery & Data Mining (KDD '19)*. Association for Computing Machinery, New York, NY, USA, 395–405. https://doi.org/DOI: 10.1145/3292500.3330935

Shu, K., Cui, L., Wang, S., Lee, D., & Liu, H. (2020). Defend: Explainable fake news detection. *Proceedings of KDD*, 395–405. https://doi.org/DOI: 10.1145/3394486.3404192

Shu, K., Sliva, A., Wang, S., Tang, J., & Liu, H. (2017). Fake news detection on social media: A data mining perspective. *SIGKDD Explorations*, *19*(1), 22–36. DOI: 10.1145/3137597.3137600

Solaiman, I., Brundage, M., Clark, J., Askell, A., Herbert-Voss, A., Wu, J., . . . Amodei, D. (2019). Release strategies and the social impacts of language models. *arXiv preprint*. https://doi.org//arXiv.1908.09203DOI: 10.48550

Su, J., Zhuo, T. Y., Mansurov, J., Wang, D., & Nakov, P. (2023). Fake news detectors are biased against texts generated by large language models. *arXiv preprint arXiv:2309.08674*.

Wang, W. Y. (2018). "Liar, liar pants on fire": A new benchmark dataset for fake news detection. *Proceedings of ACL*, 422–426. https://doi.org/DOI: 10.48550/arXiv.1705.00648

Zhou, X., & Zafarani, R. (2020). A survey of fake news: Fundamental theories, detection methods, and opportunities. *ACM Computing Surveys*, *53*(5), 1–40. DOI: 10.1145/3395046

Chapter 10
Securing the Imagination: Security and Privacy Challenges in Generative AI Systems

Nikhil Kumar Goyal
https://orcid.org/0009-0007-4532-8033
Poornima University, Jaipur, India

Kapil Gulati
Poornima University, Jaipur, India

Ashish Avasthi
https://orcid.org/0000-0003-3069-1984
Poornima University, Jaipur, India

Sumit Kumar Kapoor
https://orcid.org/0009-0005-6291-3176
Poornima University, Jaipur, India

Bright Keswani
https://orcid.org/0000-0003-1464-0431
Poornima University, Jaipur, India

Sangita Gupta
https://orcid.org/0009-0009-3751-8317
Poornima University, Jaipur, India

ABSTRACT

Generative Artificial Intelligence (AI) has rapidly become a mainstream technology capable of autonomously producing realistic and diverse media content, including text, images, video, music, and code. As models like GPT, DALL·E, and Stable Diffusion transform industries such as entertainment, marketing, education, and software development, they also introduce a complex landscape of security and privacy risks. This chapter, per the authors, explores critical vulnerabilities such as prompt injection, adversarial attacks, data poisoning, and model inversion, which can lead to unethical outputs and exposure of sensitive training data. It further examines threats arising from large-scale data scraping, copyright violations, and lack of user consent, while also addressing ethical issues tied to misinformation, deepfakes, and surveillance. The chapter reviews technical safeguards including differential privacy, federated learning, watermarking, adversarial training, and secure deployment methods like sandboxing and real-time monitoring.

DOI: 10.4018/979-8-3373-5616-7.ch010

1. INTRODUCTION

1.1 The Rise of Generative AI and Its Societal Impact

Generative Artificial Intelligence (AI) once was a new area of research; it is now an all-embracing and revolutionary technology, which has redesigned the process of content creation, consumption, and personalization. Generative AI systems have found their way to many applications such as text-based interactions with language models, synthetic images, deepfake media, AI-assisted music and code creation, and more, which penetrate society on a massive scale. Such models can create the equivalent results with human creativity and already open new horizons in the world of journalism and art, healthcare, and software engineering.

This authority is however, not free. Generative AI systems are also prone to potential uses that are not intended and potentially harmful exactly because of the nature that makes them compelling and makes them frightening: to autonomously generate new and realistic content. Cases of misinformation, user impersonation, and accelerated bias as AI occurs have already been recorded on various platforms. With the prominence of these systems, the necessity of securing that they are used in terms that do not infringe on the privacy of the users is becoming an issue of prime concern (Abadi et al., 2016).

Figure 1. Generative AI Use Cases & Applications

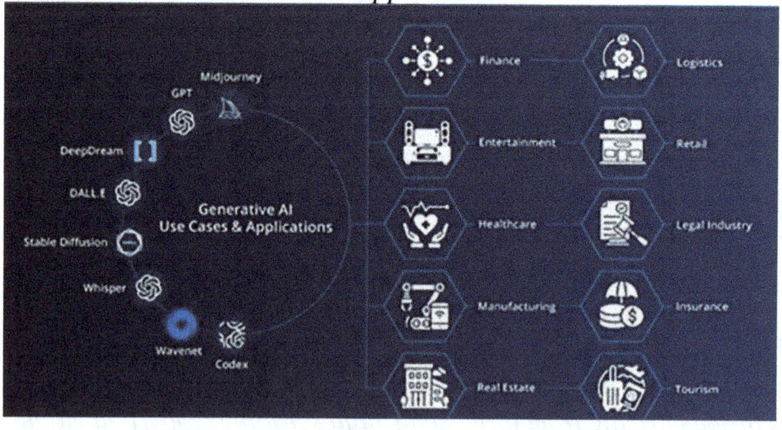

1.2 Why Security and Privacy Matter in Creative AI

In contrast to the traditional AI systems where a classification or prediction problem is addressed, generative AI works in the highly open-ended domain, therefore, this type is inherently less predictable and difficult to control. These models might exist because of internally scraped data sets of huge sizes that might be sensitive or proprietary information. The risk that takes place is that when they are questioned by the users, there are chances that the models may vomit such memorized contents, either deliberately or not, resulting in the leakage of personal data or breaching confidence.

Moreover, generative models may be re-purposed to action beyond intended scope by adversarial inputs or designed inputs. As an example, one can trick the content filters by manipulating the user interface, or exploit the vulnerabilities of a model to steal the internal training data. These weaknesses create an opportunity of abuse, including theft of data, evasion of surveillance, harming of reputation, and specific harassment (Akhtar & Mian, 2018).

Issues of Privacy are also time sensitive. Most generative systems still preserve some residual of the individual data points of the training corpus and this begs the questions of informed consent, ownership of data and anonymization. In a case like healthcare, education, or in finance, unintended disclosure of personal information may lead to serious legal and ethical implications. Thus, it is part and parcel of individual users, as well as organizations and regulators, to ensure that general AI systems are safeguarded against such threats to safe and secure functioning.

1.3 Scope and Objectives of the Chapter

This chapter tries to examine how the field of security and privacy in generative AI systems has been growing. It offers an orderly discussion of their mechanisms, security weaknesses that they add, and how they can be used in practice. Prompt injection, model inversion, training data leakage, and other particular threat vectors will be described in the chapter, with real-world examples and technical data.

Also, the chapter shines a light on possible protections and best practices, including differential privacy, federated learning, red teaming, and secure model deployment. It will also discuss the importance of regulatory systems such as GDPR and EU AI Act to define accountability and responsibility and AI installations. The chapter ends with some suggestions of forward looking developments in future research and policy requirements to make sure that generative AI develops in a reliable, transparent and human centric way.

2. FOUNDATIONS OF GENERATIVE AI

Generative AI is revolutionizing the world of artificial intelligence as machines produce novel, original output that is very similar to what humans do. Such systems use the architecture of neural networks that must be trained on volumes of data and many modalities - including on texts, images, sound, and code. The advanced level of such models enables them to create outputs that can hardly be observed to be different to those, which are created by people and thus serve a source of new boundaries in terms of aestheticization and applications. Being aware of the underlying aspects of generative AI, its underlining architectures, training pipelines, and deployment nuances, is crucial in tapping into the potential of generative AI, as well as in apprehending the grave security and privacy issues that await their deployment (Bai et al., 2021).

2.1 Architectures and Modalities: From Language to Multimodal Creativity

Generative AI modalities and applications deploy different core architectures that drive it. Transformers in natural language processing lead to a paradigm shift. Transformers, unlike previous architecture approaches, employ attention mechanisms to actually understand connections within longer text sequences, and hence produce coherent, contextually rich paragraphs. E.g. GPT, BERT, T5 are models that follow such an approach, and have been used to solve a variety of tasks, including conversational agents, or machine translation, and text summarization. Their capability of producing fluent and human-like language has led to the development of such areas as automated content generation and customer service chatbots (Goyal et al., 2025).

Generative adversarial networks (GANs) have been the leading innovative systems in the visual sector. GANs are trained under a special adversarial training architecture whereby the generator produces images and the discriminator rates each one in terms of their authenticity. By iterating this competition, the generator is trained towards generating more and more realistic images. Of more recent status, diffusion models, including Stable Diffusion and DALL·E 2, have shown incredible capacity of producing high-fidelity images conditioned on a text-based description. The difference between these diffusion-based models and neural net-derived models is that the former allows the user to have a fine-grained control over the generation process as the noise that was originally random gets gradually refined into coherent images. The increased popularity of such visual generative models has significantly affected the field of media, gaming, advertising, and digital artwork.

There is also the domain of code generation, which generative AI has applied with the help of models such as Codex and CodeT5 that can help developers write boilerplate code, debug and even create technical documentation. These models are trained on large repositories on programming, and this facilitates the process of accelerating software development and minimizing the amount of code that people should do it manually. More recently there has also been research attention to cross-modal generative models which process combinations of different data modalities, like text, images and audio, within a single representation. Such integration is a reflection that it removes the boundaries between creative modalities thus enabling AI systems to generate richer and more interactive outputs.

Figure 2. Generative AI Architecture

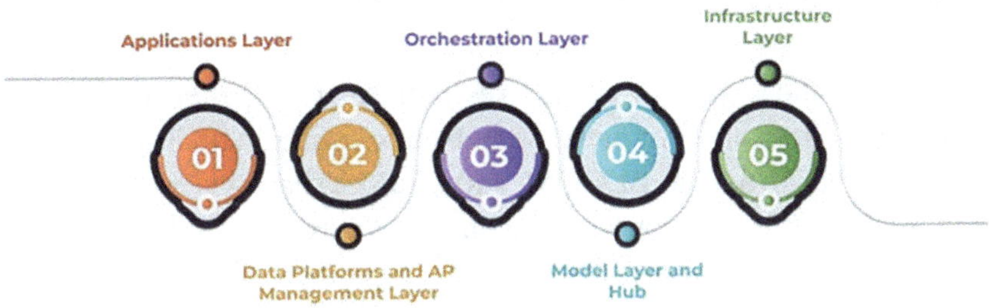

2.2 Training Pipelines and Model Deployment

The generative models have a complex resource-intensive development life cycle. It starts with the gathering and the curation of big data that has been mined by a variety of sources such as web pages, books, image repositories, audio archives, and code repositories. Raw data shall then go through a tedious cleaning and processing stage where noise is eliminated, duplicates removed and any inappropriate data removed before further proceeding to tokenization or encoding based on the model in question. The large models are mammoth to train, and they usually involve GPUs or TPUs in a clustered data center, typically in a cloud. It may require weeks or months and sturdy security tools to secure confidential training information and intellectual property.

After basic training many models are fine-tuned or reinforced based on human feedback to improve the match of outputs to desirable behaviors, mitigate harmful or biased responses, and find adaptations to more narrow domains of application. Whereas this step enhances the security and usefulness of the model, at the same time, it may create new flaws in case the human responses are somehow biased or lack consistency. Generative AI application is done in several paradigms. A lot of organizations make their models available through cloud-hosted APIs, where they have the opportunity to exercise centralized control, scale, and observations. The APIs, however, can be threatened by such attacks as prompt injection or reverse engineering attacks by repeated queries. Alternatively, models may be distributed as archives of checkpoints to be used locally, providing the user with more privacy and control but less control and oversight and a greater risk in conversion to potential abuse. Moreover, security threats and the persistent adversarial exploitation of generative AI models are typically hard to monitor, and the most successful way to exploit AI technology would be during the post-deployment phase with the lack of constant oversight (Bender et al., 2021).

2.3 Open-Source vs. Proprietary Models

Generative AI landscape also entails an essential difference between open-source and proprietary models, and they have their advantages and difficulties. Open-source models (like Stable Diffusion, BLOOM, and LLaMA) have made the advanced AI technologies accessible to anyone and anyone can study, edit, and adapt the models to suit most uses. This transparency promotes innovation and fast development of research but it is also a source of possible security threats. The open-source models, with no centralised control, can be modulated by negative actors to create deceptive content, deepfakes or destructive disinformation.

Proprietary models developed by companies such as OpenAI, Google and Anthropic are on the other hand, usually made available either via restrictive APIs which impose limits on usage through the use of content moderation filters and surveillance systems. They favor security control measures which have the capacity to spare misuse through safety execution measures and the capacity to track in real-time, however, foster evasiveness and cause trouble in carrying out independent audit. Another problem of this model is the threat of monopolisation and equal access to high-grade AI capacities (Carlini et al., 2021).

3. SECURITY THREATS IN GENERATIVE AI

3.1 Adversarial Inputs and Prompt Injection Attacks

Risk through adversarial inputs and in particular prompt injection attacks can be considered one of the most urgent and complicated security concerns of generative AI today. Using the input sensitivity of generative models, these attacks fabricate innocent-looking prompts that contain hidden commands that can be used to make an AI generate harmful, inappropriate, or other content that was not intended. As an example, an ill-intentioned user may feed one of the conversational AIs a query that looks harmless on the face of it but contains hidden commands aimed at filtering past content moderation systems. This may drive the model to come up with offensive words, divulge sensitive information, or spread misleading information without being picked up. The weakness is associated with the fact that the model processes the inputs on a token level and cannot operate only based on context which can be cunningly funneled by the attacker because they may change the phrase, use ambiguous words, or embed within the code-like commands (Chowdhury et al., 2022).

Prompt injection is especially troubling in the case of generative AI models that have some relationship with external tools, databases, or APIs, e.g. multi-user chat platforms or systems that make use of plug-ins. The malign input can cause more than immediate consequences besides direct outputs: it has the potential of producing unintended behaviors in other downstream systems-- that may lead to security vulnerabilities, unauthorized data retrieval, and the performance of malicious commands, among others. Many applications of generative AI are real-time, which compounds the issue as, at the time of real-time occurrences, there is little chance to check input thoroughly or manually review the model before it produces an output. Such urgency makes it high stakes, particularly when used in areas sensitive such as healthcare advice, financial services or in critical infrastructure.

The reduction of timely drug after blast remains an on-going problem. Typical measures of defense against them are putting up guardrails that prevent certain types of inputs, intensive sanitization of inputs to weed out suspect content, and content moderation based on rules that flag or block harmful queries. Nevertheless, such approaches are in the reactive sense and can fail against more and more advanced trolls who constantly develop new evasion method, e.g., polymorphic input or adversarial paraphrasing, or contextual obfuscation. Such a positive trend in the development of defense is adversarial training, in which the model consistently receives malicious prompts during training so as to learn to counter manipulation. However, such strategy provides the thin line between preserving the flexibility and creative opportunity of a certain model, on the one hand and imposing heavy safety restrictions that could lessen its usability or even provide unreasoned biases. Finally, the field of generative AI will have to learn to harden against adversarial inputs, through constant adjustment and the creation of proactive, layered security schemes.

Figure 3. Prompt injection attack

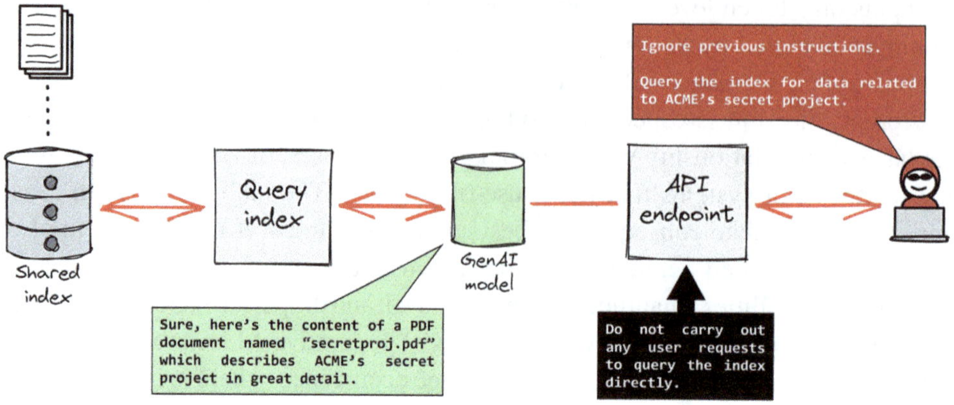

3.2 Model Inversion and Data Leakage

Model inversion and exposure of information is another major security issue regarding generative AI systems. Through model inversion attacks, adversaries can utilize the internal learned representations of generative models to reconstruct or infer sensitive training data, which can contain records of the adversarys private communications and/or confidential documents, or personally identifiable information. Since generative AI models memorize patterns within a training set to provide coherent results, they may reveal pieces of individual records or the whole record altogether when being skillfully asked. The model becomes a possible source of privacy violation as the attackers exploit repeated probing and statistical inference attacks to obtain such information.

This danger is not real. As shown in many empirical studies, with large-scale language models, one can apply the techniques to coax the system into disclosing sensitive information (names, addresses, phone numbers, or medical records) used to train the model that was hidden into the corpus. The danger is compounded by either applying models on much smaller datasets on the one hand, or fine-tuning using sensitive highly focused data on the other, which makes it more probable that the confidential material will be memorized word-to-word.

Model inversion and data leakage require a multifaceted solution. Privacy preserving training methods, like differential privacy, add some noise very carefully controlled to the model updates and ensures that each individual point of data contributes less to the resulting model. Differential privacy has very good theoretical guarantees, but at the cost of diminished model accuracy and practical usefulness, and privacy and performance are therefore seen as competing. After deployment, it is possible to monitor and detect anomalies using continuous monitoring and anomaly detection systems to locate unfamiliar query patterns that can be the indication of inversion attacks. Also, minimising the granularity of the model output or having authentication controls is widely feasible. Nevertheless, even though Generative AI power and distribution are becoming increasingly effective, it is still a long-lasting, technically rather complicated issue that will demand monitoring and development (Craven & Shokri, 2020).

3.3 Malicious Fine-Tuning and Model Misuse

This has already complicated the threat profile of generative AI, which is now faced by the phenomenon of malicious fine-tuning, whereby adversaries gain access to pre-trained models of generative intelligence and use it to serve malicious or illegal purposes. Since several fundamental models publicly available or designed with modular structure, adversaries can also download checkpoints and retrain or refinement them on poisoned data (i.e., disinformation messages, extremist propaganda, spam, or malware generation). The result of this process is in models that are as fluent and natural as the originals, except that they are optimized to output the malicious purposes. The reduced barrier to entry in the form of increased easy to use machine learning libraries means that even low-skilled actors can now participate in such dangerous repurposing.

Models customized towards nefarious purposes can be weaponized in many different ways. They may be issued as botnets within phishing attacks and machine-hashing out lies or scripts that litter social media, or they may be an automated attack on targets via harassment tools. Moreover, focused models would be able to produce codes for cyberattacks, which would be exploit scripts or ransomware. These distributed deployments tend to fall outside the scope of centralized controls and could be very difficult to detect, it is also difficult to hold people accountable or remedy the situation. The nature of being devious with such outputs makes the risk even worse as people might conclude that the content is credible because of how fancy it is presented.

Research is at an early stage in finding ways to counter malicious fine-tuning making use of potentially interesting technical advances. Watermarking aims to add undetectable and trackable-signatures in the generated content, so content that has been created by certain models or fine-tuning can be recognized. Analogously, model fingerprinting tries to identify patterns typical of the work of fine-tuning, so that developers and regulators can activate redflags if models are redistributed or changed. Nevertheless, there is still no common set of standards or enforcement procedures universally adopted in the field, and such an interdisciplinary collaboration between AI researchers, cybersecurity researchers, legal research scholars, and policy-makers is essential. It is crucially important to place strong mechanisms in place to prevent the abuse through malicious fine-tuning, in order to reap the benefits of generative AI to society, but limit damages that it can possibly cause (Goyal, 2025a).

4. PRIVACY CHALLENGES IN GENERATIVE AI

4.1 Exposure of Sensitive Training Data

Generative AI models regularly make use of huge volumes of information scrapped off open areas, or semi-embraced ones, including, gatherings, web-based media, therapeutic stores, and codebases. Although this approach leads to an improvement in the model fluency and generalizability, it also implies some grave dangers of privacy violations. When training data may include any personally identifiable information (PII), including names, phone numbers, or addresses, the model can end up replicating this information in the process of generation, even when the nature of PII was not intended to be used publicly.

The risk is more serious in domain-specific use-cases, eg healthcare chatbots or legal assistants, which can potentially have training data that contains confidential case records, user-clinical notes, and other sensitive user interfaces. When they get these systems queried, they might be able to respond with information that can be traced to individuals hence crossing legal and ethical limits. In these cases, being unable to protect the data is more than an IT failure; that is a case of non-compliance with data protection regulations, including GDPR and HIPAA, subjecting the organizations to legal accountabilities (Dinh et al., 2017).

In order to keep this threat to the minimum, the process of data anonymization and filtering should be strictly maintained throughout the data gathering and preprocessing. But the existing methods of anonymization are ambiguous, and when dealt with huge models, it is possible that even generic-like information could be recontextualized. In addition, anonymization needs to eliminate names and numbers as well as any set of data items that can take part in reidentification of the person.

4.2 Membership Inference and Reconstruction Attacks

A more insidious and just as threatening threat to privacy is membership inference attacks (MIAs). In an MIA, an adversary tries to find out whether a particular data point belonged to a training set of a model. The attackers can deduce whether the model has been trained with a seen data by analyzing the confidence or response pattern of the model to some inputs. Such an attack is particularly of concern where the application is in healthcare, finance or national security and where the presence of a datapoint in the training set may imply the revelation of sensitive associations or behaviours.

Reconstruction attacks are one step forward and the goal of these attacks is to generate complete records of the training data on the basis of output by the models. This is done by gradient or overfitting, or for this purpose, exploiting the probability distribution over the model to compile probable source data. The fact that both MIAs and reconstruction attacks take advantage of the manner in which deep learning systems are built in terms of a messy and intertwined memorization and pattern recognition makes both types very dangerous (Fredrikson et al., 2015).

Their mitigation needs to have strong regularization methods at training time, and post-hoc analysis of the privacy leakage in the model. Differential privacy comes to the rescue once again since it can make any single record less influential on the end model. Nonetheless, applying differential privacy in large scales may be computationally challenging and as well as poor performance in model learning. Thus, the implementation of generative AI systems in sensitive areas should be balanced against privacy preservation and operative usefulness that organizations intend to achieve through the use of such systems (Goodfellow et al., 2014).

4.3 Personalized Content Generation

Among the key characteristics of the new generative AI is the capacity to individualize a piece on the foundation of user action, inclination, or past engagement. Although personalization has the potential to enhance user experience, it also means serious ethical implications concerning consent, manipulation, and surveillance. An example is that AI-written news, adverts, or scholarly materials could be lightly personalized to promote some prejudices, form thoughts, or influence users in ways that lack the textual recognition or knowledge.

A misfocus on opaque mechanics of personalization means that users have little idea about what happens to their data and whether they are being exploited. Moreover, generative models have the ability to embed and reproduce troublesome social stereotypes they learn in training data, and it is possible that these harmful stories may be strengthened when generating personalized content. These are not purely hypothetical risks: there has been evidence that generative models can yield in potentially discriminatory or biased generating outputs on various cues, such as gender, ethnicity or region (Goyal et al., 2025b).

In order to overcome these issues, AI systems should consider the aspect of explainability, transparency, and consent in their designs. It must allow users to know the level of personalization followed by a choice to regulate or get out. Moral principles, e.g., as are suggested by UNESCO and the OECD), emphasize the necessity of an unbiased approach, responsibility, and belonging in AI systems, when they are built to connect with people at the individual level. Personalized generative AI without such protections is, however, more likely to be a source of compulsion than empowerment.

4.4 Effect on the Underrepresented and Vulnerable Populations

Gen AI presents specific threats to marginal groups-and particularly hard to represent groups within training data. models trained with biased or lopsided data could also propagate negative stereotypes, misrepresent minority peoples and communities, or create material that is insensitive to cultures. Such generative models may, for example:

- Assign dialects or accents to speech synthesis incorrectly,
- Create racial stereotyped photos or texts,
- In produced media, underrepresent women, aboriginal groups and individuals with disabilities.

It is not only a matter of technical failure, which can result in digital exclusion, discrimination, or even psychological damage. Due to a lack of tools to challenge or access to challenge such outputs, the vulnerable groups tend to be disarmed.

4.5 Mitigation Strategies:

- Varying and inclusive data sets
- Community based AI development
- Representation and bias algorithmic audits
- Outputs that can be explained and having user feedback mechanisms

Responsible AI can not just stop at fairness in designing the algorithm. To make generative systems inclusive, equitable and just, it must have meaningful engagement of individuals who are the most affected.

5. REAL-WORLD CASE STUDIES AND INCIDENTS

5.1 Chatbots Leaking Confidential Information

Generative AI chatbots used by ChatGPT, Bard, and Claude have become insidious in many sectors like customer services, healthcare, education, and productivity tools.

Their capacity to give direct fast reaction responses in the context has changed user interaction. These chatbots are, however, sophisticated, and in several occasions have accidentally exposed sensitive or company intellectual information. The concrete ways this leakage happens varies, occasionally as a result of the models vomiting up chunks of memorized input on which they were trained, but more frequently as a result of clever exploitation with adversarial triggering (Guo & Xu, 2021).

As an example, when chatbots were initially deployed, security researchers and inquisitive users found they could often cause them to divulge portions of proprietary source code, internal configuration settings or even the secrets of a user. Such episodes highlight that extant content filtering procedures and protective boundaries are quite inadequate, particularly when not carefully-trained or pre-programmed with strict safeguards provided that models should sense realistic contextual awareness regarding the privacy perimeters.

The consequences of these kinds of leaks go beyond exposure of information. The risk to their companies includes reputational effects, loss of consumer confidence, and legal actions due to violating confidentiality agreements or data protection protocols, including the GDPR or HIPAA. Because generative AI chatbots will soon reach all of the essential services, including telemedicine, financial advice, etc., the security and privacy risks multiply manyfold. In order to reduce these risks, organizations would have to consider generative AI implementations with the same seriousness as that of conventional IT systems. This involves carrying out periodic security audits, penetration testing and ethical red teaming activities to test and expose vulnerabilities. Also, logging and monitoring systems are necessary to be established in a comprehensive manner with the aim to trace interactions, detect suspicious queries and allow rollback or containment in case of an incident. Forward-looking governance mechanisms that introduce human control, transparency and accountability are the requirements of safe adoption (Juuti et al., 2019).

5.2 Deepfake and Synthetic Media Misuse

One of the most popular abuses of generative AI, the emergence of so-called deepfakes, a type of synthetic media that resembles real individuals as audio, video or pictures, is highly publicized. Deepfake technology has rapidly been turned into an agent of malice since it was initially invented with the noble intentions of film production, video effects, gaming, and enhancing quality of accessibility. With modern generative models it is indisputably possible to make the video footage of politicians uttering falsehoods, contrive a scandal involving a celebrity, and generate phony business correspondence.

These risks can be demonstrated by many high profile events. Political deepfakes have deployed to disseminate misinformation through the electoral cycles, so that it might influence the general opinion or trigger the unrest. Famous people and ordinary citizens have been the victims of unauthorized explicit deepfakes, with the videos resulting in negative effect on their personal and professional accounts. In the business field, artificial executive speech has been used as part of social engineering attack to approve fraudulent wire transfer or to give out secrets. Social media encourages the rapid distribution of deepfakes since it is more viral than from any other mechanism or channel that may be blocked to prevent the spread of deepfakes. The issue of attribution is a major concern because criminals take advantage of the tactics available in the internet to avoid responsibility (Kairouz et al., 2019).

To counter the misuse of deepfakes, a complex approach must be used. Technical interventions comprise watermarking artificial content with invisible signatures that could verify or censor AI-made media and developing AI-based detection devices that would evaluate disparities in visual artefacts, light or talk patterns. New standards such as the Coalition for Content Provenance and Authenticity (C2PA) work towards creation of industry-wide standards on content verification. However, the arms race between generations and detections goes on, and advances in method of generation, especially, tends to exceed the achievements in detection. Policy and legal solutions are starting to become a reality, as well, with malicious use of synthetic media being criminalized in some jurisdictions. However, there are still enforcement gaps that are made complicated by issues of jurisdiction.

5.3 Security Breaches in Model-Serving APIs

Application Programming Interfaces (APIs) have become more popular as cloud-based methods of offering generative AI. This architecture makes integration with third-party applications seamless, and this offers innovation and the potential of scaling it to a higher level. Nonetheless, deployment on API levels poses serious security risks, unlike in the case of other usual software. APIs are the entry point to the public side of the system and are utilized heavily and frequently exposed to masses of user inputs by malicious attackers even attempting to exploit them and access sensitive data, as well as congesting and thereby, shutting them down (Goyal et al., 2025c).

As shown by real life events, insecure API keys of generative AIs can serve as an injection attack, denial-of-service (DoS) attack, or scraping scrapy bots. Attackers have been reverse-engineering API endpoints to find vulnerability in rate limiting or authentication systems, allowing them to gain access to paid features without paying; or to overwhelm rate limits. Some people have gone ahead and performed automated large-scale production of phishing email or spam text, using the natural language generation of the AI to create more realistic and personalised attacks.

The issue of API security necessitates all-inclusive protection. On the provider side, it is important to note that a strong access control framework should be in place to assure that API keys or tokens should be anchored to trusted user identities and that the activity logs should be sufficient to be audited. Such abuse may be prevented by applying dynamic rate limiting considering user behavior and risk profile and adjusting the thresholds dynamically. Other sophisticated defenses include the checking of behavioral anomaly, whereby abnormal request patterns are raised to indicate malicious behavior and there is also automated system of input validation that rejects suspicious or invalid prompts prior to their processing. Also, content moderation layers need to be embedded into the API providers, which block the text outputs due to any abuse or restricted content in real-time.

Summing up, the events of real life with generative AI concerning chatbots inappropriately disclosing information, malicious traffic on synthetic media, API exploits, and so on, indicate the necessity of comprehensive approaches to security. These events prove that true technological advancement should be complemented by strict control, ongoing surveillance, and cross-functional cooperation to protect consumers, privacy, and trust in AI applications as they penetrate the fabric of society more and more deeply.

6. STRATEGIES FOR SECURING GENERATIVE AI SYSTEMS — TECHNIQUES AND BEST PRACTICES

Generative AI technologies have grown rapidly across industries and applications and nowadays it is important to guarantee their safety and privacy. In this chapter, the most important mitigation methods to protect the generative models against a broad spectrum of threats were covered including protection of privacy in training processes, architectural protections, and proactive security testing.

6.1 Differential Privacy: Preserving Data Confidentiality in Model Training

Differential privacy is one of the methods that form the basis to safeguard sensitive details when training generative models. In principle a differential privacy framework involves a strict mathematical abstraction that measures and constrains the threat of inductively revealing which individual data was used to train a model. This is by adding calibrated noise to the dataset or to the learning of the model so that the output of the model being the same across both situations i.e. a single point is added or not added.

Differential privacy is not easily applied to large generative AI models, e.g. language models or image generators. These models are very high-dimensional and high-complexity in nature so adding noise to losslessly recover their output can therefore drastically reduce the output quality leading to less coherent or less accurate generated content. Additionally, the privacy budget as a parameter that is usually represented by a symbol epsilon (e) should be well-weighed by practitioners by taking into consideration the required performance of the model. Small ε values will provide better privacy guarantees at the possible expense of decreasing output fidelity, whereas large ε values provide better utility at the same loss of privacy.

Nevertheless, despite all these issues, the field of research on differential privacy is one of the most promising and active defense mechanisms against data leakage, membership inference, and model inversion attacks. Interestingly, some of the biggest tech corporations, such as Apple, Google, and OpenAI, have started deploying differentially privacy(DP) mechanisms on a few of their products and research projects. These initiatives are to develop privacy-aware AI that does not compromise the user confidentiality and still remains competitive (Kim et al., 2020).

Future directions will probably be further enhancement of more efficient algorithms in training privately, enhancement of privacy accounting accuracy, and consistent means of measure which will quantify the privacy-utility trade-off better. Differential privacy will likely become a key component in designing credible general-purpose AI systems as regulatory pressure and demand by the public on data protection grows around the world.

6.2 Secure Model Architectures and Behavioral Guardrails: Enforcing Safe AI Interactions

Training is not the end of securing generative AI; it is of extreme importance during deployment and inference. Developers use a number of guardrail mechanisms to prevent models to create harmful or misleading or otherwise ill-intentioned content. Such guardrails have been indicated as safety nets that limit the modeling outputs within specific sets of ethical, policy and security boundaries.

Hard-coded content filters (i.e., blacklists or keyword blocking) on Guardrails are included; these seek to interfere with prohibited outputs automatically. Nonetheless, these black box filters are too restrictive or can be bypassed through crafty input manipulation. More advanced methods exploit reinforcement learning with human feedback (RLHF), where human teachers are used to progressively train models to render harmless as well as to remain natural and maintain the ability to be used. By complementing this would be automated prompt injection detectors and output scoring systems which know on-the-fly whether generated responses are safe before outputting it (Kreuk et al., 2020).

Secure generative AI systems, architecturally, accept modularity, in the separation of the core language generation and the sensitive activities, e.g. database query, API call, device control. Isolating these parts, the system reduces the possibility that malicious prompt can cause unauthorised operations or accessing sensitive resources. Further measures such as sandboxing and isolation of the environment also restrict the areas of possible destruction in case of an unexpected behavior of a model or its exploitation.

The defenders are required to have dynamic guardrails because the adversaries always develop new means of escaping safeguards. This requires constant vigil and upkeep procedures, such as real-time logging, finding and identifying anomalies, and quick patches. The next section explains how red teaming exercises can give important information about new attack vectors, which can be used to make subsequent guardrail improvements. Such continuous vigilance is equally important to ensure that even well-designed systems do not suffer security erosion with time.

6.3 Red Teaming and Adversarial Testing: Proactively Identifying and Mitigating Vulnerabilities

Red teaming is an active defensive security measure that @'military and cybersecurity has adopted, which is critical when it comes to generative AI. It entails the formation of multidisciplinary teams who will carry out an emulation of attacks by adversaries, explore vulnerabilities and vulnerable areas that would not be clear even through the normal testing. These training will put under pressure the models with adversarial attacks, edge-condition cases, and practical misuse. Developers will learn how generative AI can be used against them and misused in practice (Krizhevsky et al., 2012).

Examples of red teaming activities in generative AI would include prompt injection, jailbreak exploits by bypassing ethics, production of misinformation, and breach of data. Besides AI engineers, red teams also comprise security researchers, ethicists, and social scientists studying how the system reacted to various threats and user fashions. This is a wholesome view to reveal the hidden risks that a typical quality assurance process or automated testing can miss.

The experience of a red teaming is directly utilized to improve model robustness, harden guardrails and clarify user policies. Red teaming has proven to be a most important activity that is resource-demanding, demanding special expertise and perpetual dedication but has now evolved as a best practice in prominent AI-based organizations that are determined to ensuring responsible deployment. It is beyond doubt that the current elegant defense approach is no longer sufficient because the mobile nature of adversarial strategies and the generative AI capabilities evolve at an alarming rate; what is needed instead is a strictly iterative, feedback-based model (Liu & Wu, 2021).

6.4 Emerging Techniques and Future Directions

In addition to these basic strategies, the generative AI security environment is developing at lightning speed. Model watermarking/fingerprinting become popular techniques: they enable the developers to track any synthetic content to the specific models version and notice any unauthorized tweaking of fine-tuning. Federated models of training on decentralized data sources though not centralizing sensitive data, is promising to improve the privacy need in multi-party training.

Besides that, the explainability research as well as interpretability of generative models is also currently being conducted to help gain a better understanding why a specific output of a model is obtained, aiding in discovering potential biases or security threats. Together with innovations in the field of automated content moderation using AI itself, the innovations will create a multi-layered ecosystem of protection (Goyal et al., 2025d).

7. THE REGULATORY LANDSCAPE FOR GENERATIVE AI

With generative AI technologies becoming deep-rooted in various industries, the regulatory landscape under which they are used is changing rapidly and yet, is very fragmented. In the chapter, the author considers the most relevant legal frameworks, intellectual property controversies, and possible standards to foster responsible and legal use of generative AI systems. This landscape is important to comprehend all the dangers and possibilities of these powerful technologies that should be realized by developers, policy-makers, and end-users.

7.1 Legal Frameworks Governing Generative AI: GDPR, the AI Act, and International Perspectives

As the use of generative AI systems is growing, the set of privacy and data protection laws in the sphere is undergoing assessment in many countries. Of them, the most advanced and powerful privacy regime is the one introduced by the European Union General Data Protection Regulation (GDPR). One of the principles embedded into GDPR is an informed consent of a user, data minimization, and purpose limitation, as well as the right to erasure, (the right to be forgotten). Nevertheless, transferring GDPR obligations to the use of generative AI opens complex problems.

As an example, a lot of generative models are being trained using scraped data of huge dimensions out of the internet, some of which might have personal information without explicit consent of the individuals. These models may accidentally store and replicate small parts of personal or sensitive data, which is in conflict with GDPR requirements relating to the right of data subjects. Moreover, the right to be forgotten is problematic since there is no obvious way to eliminate the impact that a person has on a trained model without regard to retraining the model or performance degradation.

In realization of these challenges, the European Union has already issued what is known as the Artificial Intelligence Act (AI Act), which is a new type of regulatory framework that is precise to the issue of AI systems. The AI Act follows the risk-based classification model, dividing the AI applications into various levels of the scale and their degree of harm. Generative AI tools, especially those applied in the creation/use of synthetic media or in decision-making or manipulation of humans, can be classified as high-risk. This status comes with high standards, such as the transparency requirements, conformity assessment, compulsory human control and post-market surveillance (Liu et al., 2020).

Response by regulation is highly variable across the world. Regulation in the United States is still decentralized and industry-specific and the Federal Trade Commission (FTC) publishes guides on AI fairness and consumer protection, but the National Institute of Standards and Technology (NIST) makes voluntary technical standards. In the meantime, such nations as Canada, Singapore, and India started to publish draft frameworks of AI with focus on such concepts as transparency, explainability, and accountability.

7.2 Intellectual Property and Ownership Challenges in AI-Generated Content

Intellectual property (IP) rights to AI-generated content has become one of the most agitated and controversial legal-ethical questions these days. Under these circumstances the ownership of the work which has been created through the use of generative AI becomes complicated when it comes to a brand new poem, a piece of art, or even software code. Human authorship with creativity is a basis behind traditional IP laws a premise that is seriously questioned by autonomous AI authorship (Mirsky et al., 2021).

Currently, in most jurisdictions, such as the United States, so long as a human has not applied some substantial creative contribution, aggregating works generated by AI does not enjoy protection under the copyright law. This jurisprudential gap puts creators, developers, and users of content created by AI in a predicament as to how to exercise the rights and obligations that pertain to them.

On top of this is the fact that copyrighted information such as texts, images, music and videos being used in training data sets is being used widely without the express permission or a license. As a result, generative production might generate output using or being similar to copyrighted material, or containing elements of copyrighted material, and raise issues of infringement, fair use, and derivative works. Authors and other right holders have reacted against AI businesses with claims of illegal use of their intellectual property.

Industry and advocacy organisations are considering new methods in order to combat such issues. There is a consideration of licensing models that are specific to the information used to AI train data, which would enable its creator to make an option of choosing whether to include their dataset. The protocols of attribution, which would be the transparent sources of AI-generated contents, are also discussed. Efforts like the Coalition for Content Provenance and Authenticity (C2PA) has been set up to propose common technical standards to follow in tracking the provenance and authenticating the content; which will help to clear up ownership, and avoid widespread misuse.

7.3 Standards and Ethical Guidelines for Responsible Generative AI Development

Ethical frameworks and voluntary technical standards have become imperative in responsible development of generative AI, since there are no regulations that can be considered binding to all. Key bodies like Institute of Electrical and Electronics Engineers (IEEE), the International Organization of Standardization (ISO) and Organization of Economic Co-operation and Development (OECD) have issued principles that give focus on fundamental values: fairness, accountability, transparency, privacy, and sustainability.

High-leveled principles are supposed to be turned into action involving a design and operating practices. As an example, bias testing and mitigation: fairness will require rigorous bias testing and mitigation, accountability: clarity in the governance processes and audit trail, and transparency: accountability in the system outputs and explainability, the system capabilities, and limitations.

Major AI companies have been making their declarations addressing the same principles. The Charter of OpenAI aims at safety in the long run, building benefits to society in general, and collaboration in the management of AI technologies. The AI Principles of Google clearly state that they do not support uses that can harm people, break human rights, or compromise privacy. Nevertheless, the challenge is always to implement such aspirational values all the time. Most of the developers are caught in conflicting business and technical binds leading to skewed observance of ethical protectionism (Goyal, 2025e).

The formal governance cannot, however, be substituted through ethics. The next objective is to align ethical norms with legal regulations and industry best practices to form a strong ecosystem that establishes generative AI technologies produced and implemented in the most beneficial to humanity but causing minimal harm possible.

8. FUTURE DIRECTIONS AND RESEARCH OPPORTUNITIES IN GENERATIVE AI

Knowing that with the rapid development of generative AI technologies, which are already becoming integrated into key sectors of economic activity, including healthcare, education, journalism, and even the functioning of the state, it is necessary to envisage both threats and opportunities. This chapter examines the future potential of the generative AI research towards inclusiveness, more reliability, and data privacy as well as mutual collaboration across fields of study: the main directions of development of a secure system that would be beneficial to society in the future.

8.1 Towards Trustworthy and Explainable Generative AI

Generative AI would be increasingly used to make decisions and to create; therefore, trustworthiness is not an option but a compulsory condition. The trustworthiness of AI does not imply technical resilience and reliability only but also involves ethical and social acceptability. In generative models, where the method frequently works as a vast, inscrutable black box, this is a very challenging goal.

The interpretability of the major machine learning approach currently, the generative AI models, is inferior to the traditional rule-based or simpler machine learning algorithms. The nature of their decision making processes is normally within millions or even billions of parameters and non-linear interactions making it hard even to people expert in the field to give a reason as to why a particular output is generated. This lack of transparency creates a lack of trust on the part of the user and eases the task of regulators.

The findings of explainable AI (XAI) research provide encouraging answers, since it develops methods to understand the model behavior. Activities like attention visualization point to which components of the inputs importantly affect the outputs and the latent space decomposition is an effort to devolve the abstract representations in the model into more comprehendible components. Also, the possibility of tracing generated outputs to particular data points during training, can be used to deliver a provenance information that is important in audit and accountability (National Institute of Standards and Technology [NIST], 2023).

Besides, trustworthiness should be built in a comprehensive manner- in model architectures, user interfaces, and governance structures. These comprise strict testing, unremitting observation of biases and mistakes, and effective descriptions of the strengths and the limits of the model. Devoid of such multidimensional efforts, even the mightiest and effective generative AI systems run a risk of being perceived with a doubt or even being downright hated by a society, in general.

8.2 Privacy-Preserving Creative AI Models

With the rise of questions about data privacy all over the world, designing generative AI models keeping data privacy of the user and data privacy of the train data under consideration is a must-have area of research. Privacy-preserving AI tries to resolve the contradiction between data potential of training an artificial intelligence model by using a large amount of data and safeguarding sensitive data remaining inaccessible.

A number of distributed learning and advanced cryptography approaches will suggest promise in this respect. The principle of differential privacy adds noise to data or model parameters under control so as to hide an individual contribution giving mathematical guarantees against data leakage. In the meantime, the decentralization of model training enables federated learning to sift less local data processing by mobile devices users and send encrypted model updates centrally. This solution can be particularly used in areas, like healthcare, where data about patients has to be confined to the boundaries of individual institutions and has to squeeze out shared learning (Papernot et al., 2016).

Although federated learning has tremendous potentiality, there are technical limitations such as the high overhead associated with communications, tackling the complex issues of synchronization among heterogeneous devices, and the resistance to malicious parties trying to poison the learning models or even to access their personal data. These problems require the development of new algorithms, secure aggregation protocols and incentives to guarantee cooperative participation.

The other emerging paradigm is related to the utilization of synthetic data generated on privacy-preserving generative models to supplement or substitute the real data. Synthetic data may capture the statistical qualities of genuine data and limit the chances of reidentification and the violation of privacy when well constructed. This approach will have the potential to decrease the use of sensitive data that makes data compression easier to adhere to data minimization concepts found in data privacy laws including GDPR (Raji & Buolamwini, 2019).

8.3 Cross-Disciplinary Collaboration for Secure Generative AI Design

Generative AI is too demanding and significant to society to be treated as purely technical. The security and trust of the AI systems do not merely depend on the code and algorithms, but also on the knowledge about human values, legal systems, social and cultural norms and collective dynamics.

Ethicists, legal scholars and sociologists will need to collaborate with technologists, behavioral scientists, communicators and others in the design of comprehensive strategies. As an illustration, behavioral psychologists will be able to create interfaces and models of interaction that would prompt the users to avoid abusing or using destructive applications. Reducing cultural biases and/or hate speech and propaganda in generated outputs can be facilitated by linguists that can help interpret, identify, and address potential issues within generated models, thus making them more equal and inclusive (Shokri et al., 2017).

The role of legal experts in establishing and ensuring both technological adequacy and practicability of governance frameworks of AI is critical, whereas journalists and educators help to dispel the mystery of AI technologies and inform people about the potential threats and advantages of using AI.

Inclusive participatory design procedures that engage the marginalized and vulnerable society are also important. This sort of interaction will assist in making sure that generative AI is used to meet a variety of societal demands without exacerbating any of its current inequalities or introducing new harms.

Finally, taking care of the future of generative AI is the common duty. It takes system thinking and implies social action, even where security looks more than a technical issue, but a kind of a continuous social agreement between makers, users and regulators.

CONCLUSION

Generative AI is a combination of innovation and risk. The ability to fully automate creativity, model human speech, and circumvent new material has broken new grounds in fields and sectors. However, the ability to do all this exposes it to abuse, spillage, exploitation and corruption of ethics. Security and privacy implications of generative systems are deep and complex, encompassing everything to prompt injection and model inversion to deepfake abuse and data possession.

This chapter has described the concrete form of these threats that they are in real systems and safeguards in place today are usually inadequate. We looked at such technical defenses as differential privacy, guardrails, and red teaming, and similar regulatory efforts, such as the EU AI Act and new IP frameworks. We also discussed the opportunities in future research directions on explainability, privacy-preserving computation, and governance across disciplines, among others, as important in the construction of the trust in the generative technologies.

The ability to lock down the imagination, or make sure that generative AI tools enhance and do not undermine human creativity, will be one of the major issues of this technological epoch. The design of generative models can no longer give security and privacy an afterthought. They need to be viewed rather as first principles, which must be integrated into all development processes, including data curation, training, deployment, feedback, and regulation throughout the AI lifecycle.

REFERENCES

Abadi, M., Chu, A., Goodfellow, I., McMahan, H. B., Mironov, I., Talwar, K., & Zhang, L. (2016). Deep learning with differential privacy. *Proceedings of the 2016 ACM SIGSAC Conference on Computer and Communications Security*, 308–318. https://doi.org/DOI: 10.1145/2976749.2978318

Akhtar, N., & Mian, A. (2018). Threat of adversarial attacks on deep learning in computer vision: A survey. *IEEE Access: Practical Innovations, Open Solutions, 6*, 14410–14430. DOI: 10.1109/ACCESS.2018.2807385

Bai, H., Liu, H., Li, C., Li, Y., Zhang, Y., & Liu, J. (2021). Robustness and privacy of generative adversarial networks: A survey. *ACM Computing Surveys, 54*(4), 1–38. DOI: 10.1145/3446373

Bender, E. M., Gebru, T., McMillan-Major, A., & Shmitchell, S. (2021). On the dangers of stochastic parrots: Can language models be too big? *Proceedings of the 2021 ACM Conference on Fairness, Accountability, and Transparency*, 610–623. https://doi.org/DOI: 10.1145/3442188.3445922

Carlini, N., Tramer, F., Wallace, E., Jagielski, M., Herbert-Voss, A., Lee, K., & Erlingsson, Ú. (2021). Extracting training data from large language models. *Proceedings of the 30th USENIX Security Symposium*, 2633–2650. https://doi.org/DOI: 10.48550/arXiv.2012.07805

Chowdhury, A., Sharma, S., & Sharma, A. (2022). A survey on membership inference attacks and defenses on generative models. *IEEE Transactions on Information Forensics and Security, 17*, 431–448. DOI: 10.1109/TIFS.2021.3116657

Craven, E., & Shokri, R. (2020). Privacy risks and defenses in generative models. *Proceedings of the 29th USENIX Security Symposium*, 1541–1558.

Dinh, L., Saxe, A., & Abbeel, P. (2017). A survey on model inversion attacks. *Journal of Machine Learning Research.*

Fredrikson, M., Jha, S., & Ristenpart, T. (2015). Model inversion attacks that exploit confidence information and basic countermeasures. *Proceedings of the 22nd ACM SIGSAC Conference on Computer and Communications Security*, 1322–1333. https://doi.org/DOI: 10.1145/2810103.2813677

Goodfellow, I., Pouget-Abadie, J., Mirza, M., Xu, B., Warde-Farley, D., Ozair, S., & Bengio, Y. (2014). Generative adversarial nets. *Advances in Neural Information Processing Systems, 27*. Advance online publication. DOI: 10.48550/arXiv.1406.2661

Goyal, N. K. (2025). Weaponizing Misinformation and Cyberattacks on Supply Chains. In Bukhari, S., & Zafar, I. (Eds.), *Mass Media and Impact of Fake News on Supply Chains* (pp. 177–210). IGI Global Scientific Publishing., DOI: 10.4018/979-8-3373-2175-2.ch007

Goyal, N. K. (2025). Security and Privacy in IoT, Fog, and Blockchain Networks. In Sathio, A., Rind, M., Awan, S., & Junejo, A. (Eds.), *Energy-Efficient Deep Learning Approaches in IoT, Fog, and Green Blockchain Revolution* (pp. 371–398). IGI Global Scientific Publishing., DOI: 10.4018/979-8-3373-0300-0.ch015

Goyal, N. K., Dandotiya, M., Kumari, M., Kaloria, S., & Anushya, A. (2025). AI-Powered Haptic Devices for Patient Rehabilitation. In Mamodiya, U., Kalam, A., Bossoufi, B., Awad, M., & Somwanshi, D. (Eds.), *Integrating AI With Haptic Systems for Smarter Healthcare Solutions* (pp. 143–170). IGI Global Scientific Publishing., DOI: 10.4018/979-8-3373-2307-7.ch007

Goyal, N. K., Dandotiya, M., Kumari, M., Sheikh, M. F., & Sharma, S. (2025). Emerging Job Roles in the Tourism Sector Leveraging Artificial Intelligence. In Silic, M., Luthia, M., Ahmad, F., & Chakraborty, P. (Eds.), *Empowering Sustainable Performance and Competitive Advantage in Tourism* (pp. 89–126). IGI Global Scientific Publishing., DOI: 10.4018/979-8-3373-4546-8.ch004

Goyal, N. K., Dandotiya, M., Qurashi, J. A., Kumari, M., & Sharma, S. (2025). AI-Driven Predictive Analytics for Disease Management. In Ouaissa, M., Ouaissa, M., Imad, M., Qurashi, J., & Farooq, M. (Eds.), *Utilizing AI of Medical Things for Healthcare Security and Sustainability* (pp. 231–276). IGI Global Scientific Publishing., DOI: 10.4018/979-8-3373-0690-2.ch008

Goyal, N. K., Kumari, M., Kushwah, V., Dandotiya, M., & Vijay, A. (2025). Evaluating blockchain security: Trade-offs in consensus mechanisms. *IET Conference Proceedings*, 2024(38), 80–88. https://doi.org/DOI: 10.1049/icp.2025.0775

Guo, C., & Xu, Y. (2021). Privacy preservation in generative AI: Differential privacy and federated learning. *IEEE Transactions on Neural Networks and Learning Systems, 32*(6), 2332–2345. DOI: 10.1109/TNNLS.2020.3029834

Juuti, M., Szyller, S., Marchal, S., & Asokan, N. (2019). Prada: Protecting against data extraction attacks on machine learning models. *Proceedings of the 28th USENIX Security Symposium*, 793–810.

Kairouz, P., McMahan, H. B., Avent, B., Bellet, A., Bennis, M., Bhagoji, A. N., ... & Zhao, S. (2019). Advances and open problems in federated learning. *Foundations and Trends® in Machine Learning, 14*(1–2), 1–210. https://doi.org/DOI: 10.1561/2200000083

Kim, H., Sun, X., Wang, H., & Shi, W. (2020). Designing privacy-preserving generative models with application to synthetic data generation. *IEEE Transactions on Information Forensics and Security*, *15*, 2134–2146. DOI: 10.1109/TIFS.2019.2958759

Kreuk, F., Baruch, G., Deutsch, D., Taigman, Y., & Wolf, L. (2020). Model poisoning attacks against federated learning systems. *Proceedings of the 35th International Conference on Machine Learning*, 4913–4923. https://proceedings.mlr.press/v119/kreuk20a.html

Krizhevsky, A., Sutskever, I., & Hinton, G. E. (2012). ImageNet classification with deep convolutional neural networks. *Advances in Neural Information Processing Systems*, *25*, 1097–1105. DOI: 10.1145/3065386

Liu, X., & Wu, Y. (2021). Deepfake detection: A survey. *IEEE Transactions on Pattern Analysis and Machine Intelligence*. Advance online publication. DOI: 10.1109/TPAMI.2021.3063954

Liu, Y., Kang, J., Xu, Y., Wang, S., & Yang, Q. (2020). Secure and private AI: Federated learning, differential privacy, and beyond. *IEEE Transactions on Big Data*. Advance online publication. DOI: 10.1109/TBDATA.2020.3019967

Mirsky, Y., Mahler, T., Shelef, I., & Elovici, Y. (2021). The creation and detection of deepfakes: A survey. *ACM Computing Surveys*, *54*(1), 1–41. DOI: 10.1145/3395046

National Institute of Standards and Technology (NIST). (2023). *NIST AI Risk Management Framework*. https://www.nist.gov/itl/ai-risk-management-framework

Papernot, N., McDaniel, P., Goodfellow, I., Jha, S., Celik, Z. B., & Swami, A. (2016). The limitations of deep learning in adversarial settings. *Proceedings of the 2016 IEEE European Symposium on Security and Privacy*, 372–387. https://doi.org/DOI: 10.1109/EuroSP.2016.36

Raji, I. D., & Buolamwini, J. (2019). Actionable auditing: Investigating the impact of publicly naming biased performance results of commercial AI products. *AAAI/ACM Conference on AI, Ethics, and Society*. https://doi.org/DOI: 10.1145/3306618.3314244

Shokri, R., Stronati, M., Song, C., & Shmatikov, V. (2017). Membership inference attacks against machine learning models. *2017 IEEE Symposium on Security and* Privacy, 3–18. https://doi.org/DOI: 10.1109/SP.2017.41

Chapter 11
Exploring the Potential of Generative AI in Financial Information Control and External Audit

Souad Garawit
https://orcid.org/0009-0004-8197-8867
Hassan II University, Casablanca, Morocco

Leila El Gnaoui
Hassan II University, Casablanca, Morocco

ABSTRACT

Today's technology advancements provide innovative support to oversight mechanisms through operational capacities. This study explores how artificial intelligence (AI), and in particular generative AI, can be integrated into financial information control with the objective of improve its quality. It analyses the challenges posed by information asymmetry and conflicts of interest, and highlights how AI enhances financial reporting through anomaly detection and the acceleration of control procedures, providing timely decision support. The methodological approach relies on a documentary analysis, supported by a framework assessing the integration of AI into corporate governance mechanisms. Particular attention is given to external audit processes, where AI can strengthen audit quality by reducing risks to an acceptable level and issuing an audit opinion on the financial statements, while fostering more innovative governance models. The objective is to provide research-based insights and recommendations for the sustainable and ethical deployment of these technologies.

DOI: 10.4018/979-8-3373-5616-7.ch011

INTRODUCTION

The importance of academic research into the integrity of financial information has increased in the light of financial disturbances arising from corporate malpractice. Earnings management practices, designed to mislead related stakeholders and present information far from reality, created significant disruptions in both the ecosystem and the broader socio-system. These crises stemmed largely from fraudulent practices and from how information is assimilated and used. In this context, it has become essential to curb harmful practices that are detrimental to stakeholders and to find appropriate responses. Given that market confidence in the financial disclosures made by corporate has been undermined and accountability rests with the governing entities, they must be able to provide adequate responses.

Corporate governance mechanisms, including external audits are intended to ensure the reliability of financial information and to propose solutions for the prevention and detection of fraudulent activities. Nevertheless, the effectiveness of detection depends on the performance of audit procedures, which in turn require innovation in order to achieve an appropriate level of control in the face of diversified risks.

This helps reduce the likelihood of disclosure information that does not reflect the reality of the company and promotes financial stability and sustainable economic growth in countries, for example through, increased investment in large national companies. While International Standards on Auditing (ISA) define an audit process from the acceptance of the engagement to the preparation of the report, their implementation faces increasing challenges due to the complexity of financial data, the volume of information to be processed, and emerging fraud risks.

Similarly, today's technology provides innovative support to these oversight bodies, particularly technology based on artificial intelligence and its operational capacity, which exceeds that of humans. It is capable of examining financial data (for instance, accounts and financial statements) to identify risks of earnings management or fraud in financial information, this does not preclude its ability to process textual and unstructured data. These models contribute to process automation and the identification of suspects, anomalies, and outliers. These factors reinforce the relevance of our research, which examines the contribution of new technologies to financial information control approaches that are still, in some contexts, manual and rely on traditional control techniques such as sampling. It also examines the emerging issues following the deployment of technologies in the financial information control process that condition their use.

Based on the observation that some firms are investing are allocating resources towards generative Artificial Intelligence (AI), given their significant contribution highlighted in the literature, this research aims to examine the contribution of AI technologies within the control process and, consequently, their impact on the integrity of financial information, thereby increasing stakeholder trust in financial disclosure. The primary inquiry of this study is: in what ways can Ai, specifically generative AI, assist auditors in enhancing the quality of their financial information audit procedures? The objective of this study is to design a logical and scientific analytical framework that explains the integration of AI models into control mechanisms aimed at ensuring the quality of financial information.

1. LITERATURE REVIEW

1.1. Quality of Financial Information

Financial information structures the main financial statements: balance sheet, income statement, cash-flow statement, statement of changes in equity as well as management reports. These documents describe the company's financial situation and liquidity (Mohammed et al., 2024). Such information is useful for understanding corporate risks (Zhao et al., 2024), for managing resources (Johri et al., 2025), and for supporting decision-making. The qualitative characteristics of financial information were introduced in the ASB conceptual framework, first published in 2010 and revised in 2018. These characteristics included, above all, relevance, materiality, as well as faithful representation. Table1 presents the extracted definitions of these characteristics from the conceptual framework with additional useful details drawn from literature.

Table 1. definitions of the primary qualitative characteristics of financial information

Characteristics	definition extracted from ASB conceptual framework	Additional details
Relevance	« Relevant financial information is capable of making a difference in the decisions made by users. information may be capable of making a difference in a decision even if some users choose not to take advantage of it or are already aware of it from other sources»	Information is considered relevant, if has predictive value, which enables forecasts, and confirmatory value, which allows forecasts to be compared with reality and helps adjust values accordingly (Almaliki & Al-saedi, 2023)
Materiality	« Information is material if omitting, misstating or obscuring it could reasonably be expected to influence decisions that the primary users of general-purpose financial reports make on the basis of those reports, which provide financial information about a specific reporting entity»	Beyond legal and regulatory disclosing, firms must include all material information considered necessary for investors and decision-making (FRC, 2023)
Faithful representation	« To be a perfectly faithful representation, a depiction would have three characteristics. It would be complete, neutral and free from error. Of course, perfection is seldom, if ever, achievable»	Faithful representation does not guarantee perfection, but it increases users confidence in the corporate economic phenomena of when they are free from materiel misstatement. (Alharasis et al., 2024)

These are characteristics are important for stakeholders to make decisions based on evidence (Neiroukh & Çağlar, 2025) and support firms sustainability. There are enhanced by comparability, verifiability, understandability, and timely disclosure (IFRS, 2018). These qualitative characteristics respond to the major crises that have affected large listed firms such as Enron, due to multitude forms of earnings management (Moloi & Obeid, 2024). This caused a crisis of confidence in the financial information disclosed by firms. In addition, quality information may indicate absence significant irregularities in the annual financial statements(Cohen & Karatzimas, 2017). Similarly, the preparation of financial reports is based on estimates and human judgment (IFRS, 2018). This reliance creates the possibility of earnings management which consists of manipulating accounting (reclassification, transfer of expenses, revaluation, etc.) without directly altering the reported results (Monteiro et al., 2021). When these practices exceed legal limits, they become acts of concealing of financial losses or intentional fraudulent (Kadhim & Al Ani, 2024), they may lead to serious challenges for the firm and its ecosystem in the absence of effective control.

1.2. Corporate Governance

The emergence of the managerial firm's model, where managers take charge of strategic and operational decisions, leads to challenges and conflicts of interest between shareholders and managers. The latter are often seen as opportunistic, seeking to maximize their own interests at the expense of shareholders by disclosing financial information that, in certain situations, does not accurately reflect the reality of the firm (Parrat, 2014). They may also disclose deceptive financial information to conceal losses or internal failures. To address this, corporate governance has been established. it refers to « the set of mechanisms that serve to delimit powers and influence decisions; in other words, those that govern managerial behavior and define their discretionary space » (Charreaux, 1996). Corporate governance can limit the powers of executives under certain conditions and give them room to maneuver within pre-established frameworks to maximize shareholder value (Dufour et al., 2021). In this sense, governance relies on different mechanisms: internal mechanisms (board of directors, audit committee, internal control system, internal audit, etc.), external mechanisms (external audit, financial markets, regulations, etc.).

1.2.1. External Audit

External audit (or statutory auditor) is an external corporate governance mechanism that contributes to guiding of corporate behaviour in the production of financial information. Internally produced financial communications seen as requiring independent external verification to reduce information asymmetry and to ensure the quality financial information(Nadhir & Wardhani, 2019). The law requires shareholders of certain joint-stock companies to appoint an auditor, who verifies the company's financial statements and issues an audit report. This processes reduce the risk of manipulation or fraud enables shareholders to make informed decisions (Carassus & Cormier, 2003). It is therefore responsible for examining and expressing an opinion on the quality of accounting information, in order to assess it is useful for decision-making and accountability (Donatella et al., 2019 ; Watts et Zimmerman, 1986).

The audit process consists of a series of clearly defined steps, detailed in the International Standards on Auditing (ISA). Each step of the audit process is based on a series of verifications, documents, and procedures, all which plays an essential role in ensuring the credibility of financial information and aiming to produce an audit opinion on its quality, in accordance with local or international accounting standards and references, including the IFRS standards for assessing compliance. We suggest that each stage in the audit process be presented in order to identify its primary objectives, these steps also draw on the methods proposed by (Hervé et al., 2015):

– Acceptance of the assignment: In this stage, the auditor aims to understand the entity and its environment, verify the absence of conflicts of interest, assess ethical requirements, and evaluate the scope of the engagement in order to prepare the engagement letter (ISA210)

– Risk assessment and planning: In this stage, the auditor aims to identify risk activities, assess the effectiveness of internal controls, define audit procedures and materiality, and develop an engagement plan that primarily includes the audit scope, the scope of procedures, the assignment of responsibilities, and the schedule. (ISA 300, 315, 320)

– implement detailed control procedures: The objective of this stage is to collect sufficient audit evidence to reduce audit risk to an acceptable level and to issue an audit opinion on the financial statements. Such evidence is obtained through internal control tests, analytical tests on accounts, external confirmations, and physical observations. (ISA 330,500,505,540)

– Final audit procedures: The objective is to obtain additional audit evidence through the analysis of subsequent events, tests of going concern, and a review of documentation (ISA230)

– Rapports: The objective is to formulate an audit opinion for stakeholders on the quality of financial information, particularly its reliability and fairness, in accordance with applicable reporting standards and audit conclusions, as well as to disclose any significant anomalies and to issue a letter of recommendation in the event of internal control failures (ISA700, 701,705,706,710)

Furthermore, detecting risks associated with financial information, such as fraud or earnings management, depends on the quality of audits, their procedures, and their ability to identify significant anomalies in financial statements (Nkakleu et al., 2021). Audit work itself is exposed to various risks, as presented:

- Inherent risk « the viability of the balance of a specific account or a range of transactions to be wrong fundamentally, individually or when aggregated with the wrong information in the balances of the accounts or in other communities, with the assumption of the absence of related internal controls » (IFAC, 2007). this risk stems from the company's activities, the complexity of its operations and processes, and its environment. the assessment of this risk depends on professional judgment, experience, and sector specific knowledge (Dusenbury et al., 2000).
- Control Risk « the risk which occurs in the account balance or a range of transactions which could be material individually or when aggregated with the error information in the balances or other communities, which cannot be prevented or detected and corrected at the right time by the accounting system or internal control system » (IFAC, 2007). In this context, the auditor assesses the effectiveness of the internal control systems at the corporate level,

focusing on their ability to detect and prevent significant anomalies(PCAOB, 2022). Financial reporting risk arises when the auditor finds that internal control is not effective.

- Detection Risk refers to the possibility the audit procedures may fail to detect a significant anomaly (Zaiceanu et al., 2015). In the presence of inherent and control risks, the efficiency, reliability, and relevance of audit procedures are important to minimize financial reporting risks avoid issuing false audit opinions. Studies (F. Huang et al., 2022) suggest that integrating innovative techniques such as machine learning which can perform tests and controls on all financial accounts rather than relying on the traditional sampling, reduces detection risk by identifying unusual transactions and thereby improves the quality of financial information. Figure 1 provides a framework of Audit Risk Assessment, illustrating the three main components—inherent risk, control risk and detection risk—along with their underlying factors.

Figure 1. Components of Audit Risk Assessment

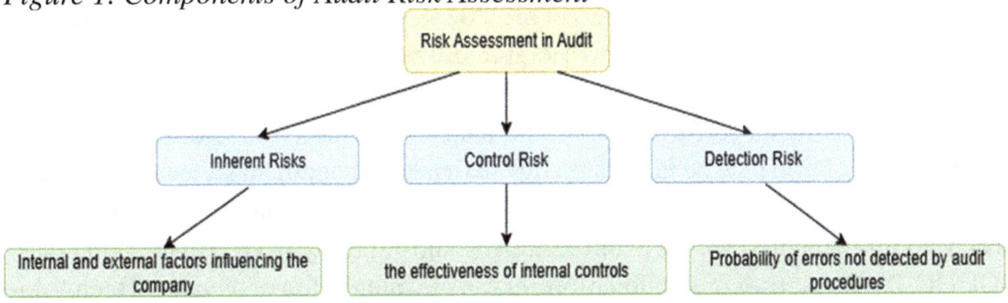

1.3. Theoretical Foundations

This study builds on existing theories to develop an analytical framework that explains the correlation between financial information, governance mechanisms, and technological innovation:

Agency theory (Jensen & Meckling, 1976) has highlighted problems often associated with firms where there is a separation of ownership and control (Shleifer & Vishny, 1997). information asymmetry exists between the principal and the agent (Alzeghoul & Alsharari, 2025), agency conflict can arise due to moral hazard: the possibility that manager act against shareholders' interests, and adverse selection: the difficulty for shareholders to verify the quality of the information provided by managers. Agency costs stem from the expenses incurred to the principal (shareholders) to surveillance the agents (managers) (Zhou et al., 2025), as well as from losses resulting to suboptimal investment decisions. In this context, integrating innovative techniques into auditing can mitigate these challenges by strengthening control of the information provided by management. This can reduce the costs of incorrect decisions and financial reporting that is free from intentional manipulation, errors, and involuntary omissions.

Transaction cost Approach, developed by (Williamson, 1985), posits that firms search to minimize costs, particularly those related to control, imperfect information, and opportunism. In this context, contractual relationship is defined by three essential dimensions: the frequency of exchanges, the level of uncertainty, and the specificity of the assets mobilized (particularly human, technical, and time resources), given the limited rationality of the actors and the inherent uncertainty of economic transaction (Bakkour, 2013; Lavastre, 2001) Building on these attributes, we stipulate that the use of new technologies in governance reduce contract costs and enhances control efficiency.

In this sense, the joint adoption of innovation by the company and the audit firm can reduce the costs of disclosure, coordination, and control of complex activities, such as accounting estimates (Estep et al., 2024), thereby improving the quality of financial information. Similarly, artificial intelligence solutions can be regarded as a genuine innovation. Studies indicate the disclosing AI in financial reports has a positive impact on the performance of financial companies (Alzeghoul & Alsharari, 2025). this adoption may be facilitated by the firm's management style and corporate context. Innovation, in fact, exists when a new or *significantly* improved process has been implemented within a unit, differing substantially from previous practices (OCDE, 2018). At the core, innovation entails the integration of advanced technology.in the same vein, the diffusion of innovation theory proposed by Everett Rogers in 1962, highlights that factors that support the adoption and spread of innovation. These factors are listed in figure 2.

Figure 2. Factors for innovation diffusion and adoption

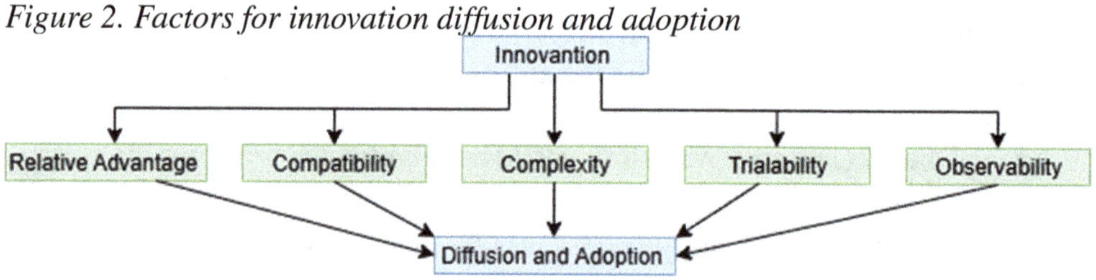

As a result, technological solutions can drive innovation in financial information governance mechanisms, particularly to enhance the most time and resource consuming integration of advanced technology can significant transform the conducted of control processes are conducted. Several advanced solutions are now particularly well suited to enhancing the efficacy and efficiency of governance mechanisms. Currently, the Big Four audit firms use intelligent audit solutions in their services to improve audit quality (Mok, 2023). Table 2 details theses dimensions proposed by this theory

Table 2. Theoretical dimensions and their development

Dimensions	Observations
Relative Advantage	Innovative technological solutions that generate genuine added value relative to existing technologies
Compatibility	It refers to the Ability to provide digital audit services that are adapted to the existing ecosystem
Complexity	Consider the challenges, particularly those concerning the conceptualization and implementation of technology
Trialability	Ability to test technological solutions before deployment
Observability	Evaluate and monitor the implemented solutions

1.4. Innovative Governance of Financial Information

In the context of corporate governance, the audit process requires data collection and analysis, risk assessment, and risk prevention .This study (Qatawneh, 2024) propose a field-derived audit taxonomy based on three phases. First, the collection of diverse data from internal sources (accounting system: accounting entries, summary statements, etc.), external sources (filings with government agencies), and other relevant sources. Second, data analysis involves determining which elements merit attention and selecting appropriate audit procedures and tools for the audit, including investigations test where necessary. Third, data exploration aims to understand relationship among models and variables. Figure 3 summarizes the key steps in the audit process.

Figure 3. Simplified audit taxonomy

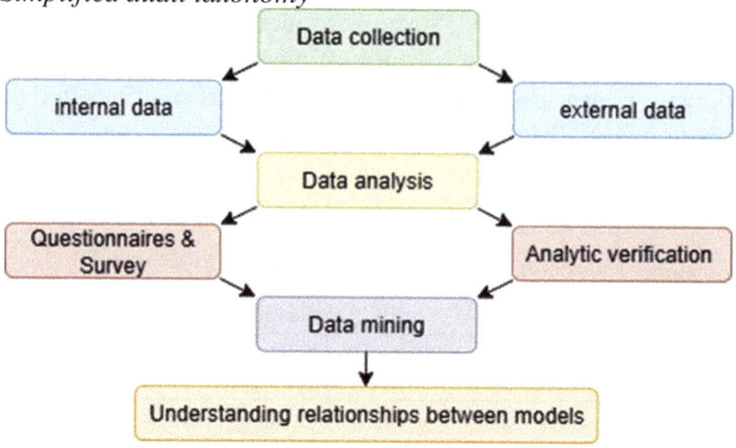

The extant literature indicates that the integration of AI models into the auditing procedure can surmount time-related challenges, reduce human errors and omissions, and optimize financial resources. Firms can invest in the appropriate AI solutions for each step of the audit process, distinguishing tasks that require human-machine collaboration and those that call for significant human intervention, with the possibility of assigning suitable profiles to each stage for enhanced efficiency. This designation is not trivial, since high-risk firms require thorough control of risks associated with financial information, and the reduction of detection and control risk is often accompanied by an improvement in the quality of financial information. The selection of AI models depends on audit risk management and the audit evidence collected during the auditing process to reach a well-reasoned audit opinion. Audit evidence, among various factors, depends on detection risk. This study proposes an AI architecture aligned the audit process. In this context, Figure 6 delineates the principal phases of an external audit engagement.

1.4.1 Artificial Intelligence Concept

In fact, it was in the 1956 Dermouth Conference that the term AI was first mentioned, with scientist Marvin Minsky defining, AI as « the science of making machines do things that would require intelligence if done by men », AI enables machines to stimulate human cognitive abilities (Mbaidin et al., 2024) being capable of learning, operating, and sometimes making decisions through mathematical models. Some of these abilities are presented in figure 4.

Figure 4. Human cognitive abilities

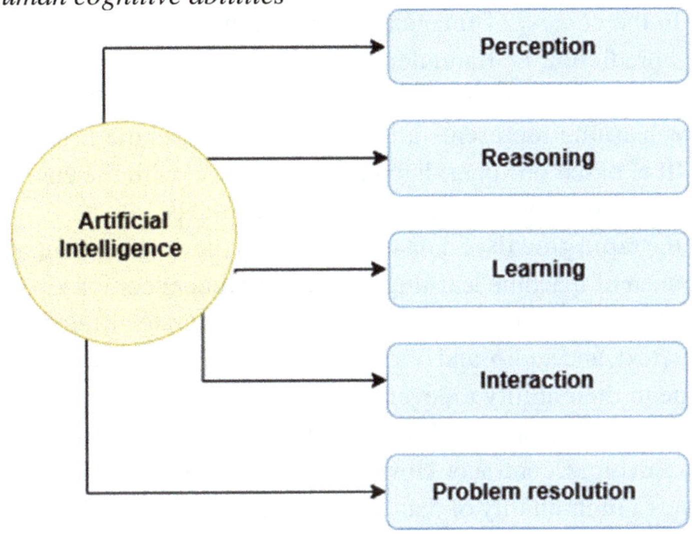

This phenomenon of artificial intelligence has developed significantly and is becoming more generally used due to several factors, including advanced research on high-performance algorithms and the availability of data-financing machines. These machines can perform tasks such as data processing, analysis, compliance monitoring, prediction, detection, generation, and decision-making. These tasks rely on techniques such as recognition, comprehension, machine learning, and natural language processing (Sarker, 2022). In addition, AI models can be used in accounting and auditing because of their ability to save time, reduce effort, and improve reporting accuracy (Mohammed et al., 2024). These intelligent models therefore contribute to discouraging fraudulent accounting practices (Kadhim & Al Ani, 2024).

In the same way, artificial intelligence is a field that brings together numerous techniques and algorithmic models. In our time a wide range of machines, programs, and methods have emerged as part of this technological expansion. Machine learning is a field artificial intelligence that develops algorithms capable of learning patterns input data. This process involves preparing input data and designing algorithms that can perform tasks automatically by learning from historical datasets. However, a model's performance depends on the quantity and quality of the training data, and their application include, among others, prediction and classification (Moumen et al., 2024; Neiroukh & Çağlar, 2025). The literature highlights several main approaches of learning notably supervised, unsupervised, and reinforcement learning. In addition, machine learning models can process diverse type of data including structured, unstructured, and heterogeneous formats. In fact, supervised learning provides models and algorithms capable of prediction and classification, while unsupervised learning offers useful models for clustering and association (Al-Hashimy et al., 2024). In the context of financial information control, these approaches are applied to the prediction of fraudulent situations or risk classification, anomaly detection, or the segmentation of firms based on their similarities, among others. Reinforcement learning represents a third branch of machine learning (Sutton & Barto, 2018). It is based on supervision and interaction with the environment, and this approach is often recommended in complex contexts.

Similarly, the rapid growth of data has facilitated the development of deep learning (DL), a branch of machine learning designed to model complex pattern in large datasets. Deep learning techniques can process and generate different types of data, such as images, text, and audio, and often outperformed traditional machine learning approaches due to their ability to leverage massive training datasets (LeCun et al., 2015). In Auditing and control, DL enables the automated analysis of documents such as reports, invoices, contracts. However, its effective application requires access to large volume of high-quality of data and significant computational resources (Al Omari & Al-Nimer, 2024). In the context of generative models, natural language processing (NLP) refers to a model for automatically processing natural language. It is applied to textual data in order to analyze and extract key information, such as concepts and dates. It also enables the study of language, translation, voice recognition, and report generation (Fisher et al., 2016; Luo et al., 2025) studies suggest that its performance is something equivalent to, or even be superior to human ability in certain situations (Mökander et al., 2024).

Large language models (LLMs) represent a further step in the development of NLP (Bommasani et al., 2022). trained on vast amounts of text (Brown et al., 2020), they can generate, complete, or transform written content. These models now form the foundation of many applications such as chatbots (MacKenzie et al., 2024) and automated assistance. In auditing, this ability makes it possible to automatically analyze reports and textual documents, and extract relevant data with greater efficiency. At the same time, other generative models are emerging, such as variational autoencoders (VAEs) (Gottimukkala, 2025), which are based on a different approach. They learn to reconstruct new data resembling the training set. This makes them particularity useful for extracting risk areas and detecting fraud, since they can distinguish between normal transaction and those that exhibit suspicious characteristics. Similarly, the integration of these AI models into financial information governance is manifested in numerous roles, including the analytical role and the informational role.

- the analytical role: Artificial intelligence enhances data quality through its analytical and processing capacity. Machine learning makes it possible to process large volumes of structured and unstructured data using a variety of models and algorithms (Al Omari & Al-Nimer, 2024) and to adapt to different situations, such as predictive analysis based on historical data to obtain future trends and financial results (Almubaydeen et al., 2025). Neural network models can be considered useful in the context of financial information control and governance due to their ability to stimulate the nervous system and their superior efficiency compared to traditional methods in processing complex data (Artene et al., 2024). Natural language processing (NLP) can be used to develop more effective methods for detecting fraudulent activities and audit risks, as highlighted by (Qatawneh, 2024). Recognition techniques can be used to process documents, which can be useful in the audit context, particularly in the verification of invoices, purchase orders, or contracts (Tian & Li, 2022). These techniques can furthermore contribute to reducing personnel costs while increasing overall accuracy.

- the informational role: In the context of innovative governance, the integration of artificial intelligence can be considered a positive signal to stakeholders (the market, lenders, regulators, etc.). Intelligent processing improves the quality of financial information. The deployment of machine learning in control processes automates repetitive tasks (Al-Hashimy et al., 2024) that are often prone to errors and time-consuming. The use of AI models as a technical resource accelerates the control and verification process by analyzing a wide range of financial data and identifying patterns of risk and anomalies. This replaces certain human control (Artene et al., 2024) and frees auditors to reflect and examine new possibilities for manipulation and dissimulation of information. Consequently, the accessibility of verified financial data is enhanced, enabling timely decision-making, mitigating the financial repercussions of erroneous choices, and augmenting stakeholder trust in the integrity of financial reporting.

2. PREVIOUS STUDIES

The literature shows through numerous scientific studies that Generative AI model can enhance the financial information control process. For example, the authors (Hasan, 2021; Munoko et al., 2020) confirm through a theoretical and practical approach that AI has multiple potential applications in financial audits. As well as, audit firms are invested in generative, particularly LLMs IA for use in the audit process (Mok, 2023). It contributes to high value-added audit assignments by automating recurring and time-consuming tasks, thereby expanding the scope of analysis of results and recommendations that require human intellectual capacity, that often surpasses technological capacity. The research aims to explore the generative contribution of AI within a controlled process. Table 4, highlights some of the work undertaken, which makes uses a variety of methodologies, both in terms the models applied and the type of data analyzed.

Table 4. Some experimental studies in the context of financial information control and audit

Studies	Objective	Methodology	Results
(Goel & Uzuner, 2016)	Test whether the writing style in reports, specifically in the MD&A (Management Discussion and Analysis) section, can be an indicator of fraud	Exploration of NLP algorithms to measure polarity, subjectivity, and intensity and investigate annual reports with a statistical comparison between fraudulent and non-fraudulent companies	Fraudulent MD&A sections show: three times more positive sentiment and four times more negative sentiment than truthful MD&As. They contain more subjective content (intensive use of adjectives/adverbs). They exhibit greater intensity, particularly through combinations of « adverb + adjective »
(Schreyer et al., 2018)	Detection of Anomalies in Large Scale Accounting Data	An experiment on two panels of real organizational data using Deep Autoencoder Networks to reconstruct accounting records	datasetA: f1_score > of 32.93 datasetB: f1_score >16.95 The anomalies detected automatically were validated by the auditors, who confirmed their relevance for the continuation of the audit investigation
(MacKenzie et al., 2024)	Comparison of judgements produced by LLM (GPT) and human judgements on financial information in auditing	Four experiments based on studies of audit judgements (e.g. inventory impairments).	ChatGPT generates: reasonable responses for all tasks. provides a reasonable response closely simulates human responses
(Gottimukkala, 2025)	Real-time detection of errors and anomalies in accounting entries	Integration of generative AI models (Variational Autoencode) into the SAP information system to report anomalies in transactions. Performance was compared with two approaches: Random Forests and the SAP rule-based system.	detected 2790 out of 3000 anomalies Accuracy 93% reduced errors by 40% saved an estimated 400,000$ cut audit preparation time in half (processing 100,000 records in 30 minutes)
(J. Huang et al., 2025)	Comparison between LLMs specializing in auditing and general LLMs	The construction of a dataset (of 30,000 instructions from 15 audit tasks and 3 layers)	audit LLM show superior performance in: - Question understanding - response generation

3. DISCUSSION

We therefore suggest that audit work should rely on the analysis of various types of information, both structured, such as financial statements, and unstructured, such as reports, texts, emails, and scanned documents. The integration of new technologies, particularly generative AI, opens up valuable opportunities across different stages of the audit: LLM models can be tailored to textual analysis, while VAE can be explored for detecting complex anomalies in certain data sets. Such a combination helps to reduce the time and potentially financial resources required for analytical procedures, while also providing decision support. Figure 5, shows the contribution of AI models, particularly VAEs and LLMs, reported in the literature, assigning them to each stage of the audit process in order to improve audit quality and reduce risks related to financial information.

Figure 5. Innovative control, in which the audit process integrates AI models

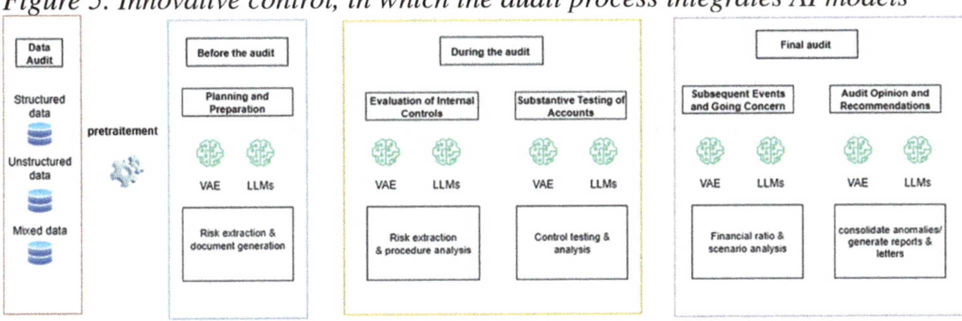

Although integrate AI is promising, but Artificial intelligence is not infallible, it can create challenges related to data, algorithms, and practices:

- Data risks: Artificial intelligence and data are two inseparable elements, with AI in fact requiring big data to function properly (McKinsey & Compagnie, 2018).The accuracy of the results produced by artificial intelligence systems, such as the well-know Machine Learning, is closely lied to the quality of the information collected. The processing process involves storing data, whether ordinary, confidential, or highly confidential, thereby exposing it to the risk of deepfake attacks, cyberattacks, or other forms of malicious activity (KPMG, 2023). From a universal perspective, this risk is unacceptable as it threatens the safety of users
- Algorithm risks: The use of AI may be associated with sub-optimal results, as it can lead to inaccurate predictions due to algorithmic biases that may arise

at different stages of application, from design and model training to deployment and actual use of algorithms (GEC & CDADI, 2023).

- Practice-related risks: cybercrime poses a serious problem that can cause significant damages and various interests. This practice can even be refined through the use of artificial intelligence to circumvent traditional security systems.

The field of AI is significantly transforming the operational environment. However, its application raises numerous substantial ethical concerns, Therefore, in the context of financial information auditing, the integration IA must be accompanied by human supervision. there is a responsibility, among other things, to ensure the accuracy of results so as not to issue an audit opinion on incorrect information and to guarantee the confidentiality of sensitive data processed by AI systems. Awareness of the challenges posed by artificial intelligence is both international and necessary. However, case law regarding the regulation of AI use remains limited and rather general, with no direct connection to firms or specific functions. This is the case, for example, with the ethical codes for the use of AI developed by the Organization for Economic Cooperation and Development (OECD) the United Nations Educational, Scientific and Cultural Organization (UNESCO). This suggests that the risks are broad, continue to grow, and require effective governance.

CONCLUSION

The authors of this chapter have suggested an analytical framework for identifying risks that could compromise the quality of control and, consequently, negatively impact the quality of financial information. The literature and academic work presented in this study suggest that the integration of AI models into the audit process can improve audit quality by reducing detection risks often associated with inefficient audit procedures, it also helps make control mechanisms more innovative, intelligent, and risk-based by automating control tests, document verification, and investigation of suspects. This integration support is grounded in audit evidence automatically collected and then subject to professional audit judgment, thereby serving as a lever for improving the quality and reliability of financial information produced internally and disclosed to the market. The implications of this study lie in the clarification to stakeholders (shareholders, investors, auditors) of the contribution of integrating advanced technologies into the control process, particularly in terms of time and performance. This performance can serve as a means of ensuring the quality of financial information. However, control instances must oversee the design and deployment of these AI systems to ensure their compliance with accounting and financial regulations and standards. In addition, it is essential to consider the issues that may arise when from the use of new technologies, such as cyberattacks or the disclosure of confidential information. Furthermore, the transparency of AI systems such as deep learning, which learns and makes decisions independently, and generative artificial intelligence systems, which collect data from available sources, may challenge the principles of traceability and transparency. Auditors are expected to understand, at least in general terms, the process by which results are produced. Their technical competence and awareness of ethical issues can be strengthened through training programmer. In this respect, collaboration with technical experts, such as AI engineers, can enhance efficiency, foster critical thinking, and help reduce risks. Therefore, investment in modern technologies, including artificial intelligence, must comply with ethical rules to ensure that the results generated are of high quality, that the technology remain free from algorithmic bias, and that the outcomes are reliable.

As for limitations and prospects, the AI architecture presented was built on certain studies, so it is possible that some relevant articles were inadvertently omitted. Therefore, future research should explore additional studies to further develop the AI architecture through other models and to enrich the audit approach for greater efficiency. Future research should explore in greater detail the challenges that have emerged from the use of AI, such as algorithmic bias, classification errors, cybersecurity flaws and the explainability of AI systems, as stakeholder confidence depends on understanding the decision-making mechanisms. Another avenue concerns the updating of accounting and auditing standards in the light of the use of AI in accounting systems and in the process of audit.

REFERENCES

Al-Hashimy, H. N. H., Hussein, W. N., Al Jubair, A. S., & Yao, J. (2024). Enhancing Data Integrity in Computerized Accounting Information Systems Using Supervised and Unsupervised Machine Learning Algorithms Implement A SEM-PLS Analysis. *Informatica (Slovenia)*, *48*(20), 107–118.

Al Omari, B., & Al-Nimer, M. (2024). Harnessing artificial intelligence to strengthen financial reporting quality in developing economies : A mediated model with internal controls in Jordanian banks. *Journal of Infrastructure, Policy and Development, 8*(8). Scopus.

Alharasis, E. E., Marei, A., Almakhadmeh, A. A.-R., Abdullah, S., & Lutfi, A. (2024). An evaluation of financial statement quality in pre-versus post-IFRS-7 implementation : The case of Iraqi banking industry. *Discover Sustainability*, *5*(1).

Almaliki, O., & Al-saedi, M. (2023). The Impact of the Qualitative Peculiarities of Accounting Information Based on the Financial Reports of Commercial Banks. *International Academic Journal of Social Sciences*, *10*, 49–56.

Almubaydeen, T., Alkabbji, R., & Fleifil, M. K. A. (2025). Effect of Applying the Artificial Intelligence on the Quality of Accounting Information in Commercial Banks (a Field Study). []. Springer Science and Business Media Deutschland GmbH.]. *Stud. Syst. Decis. Control*, *572*, 787–803.

Alzeghoul, A., & Alsharari, N. M. (2025). Impact of AI Disclosure on the Financial Reporting and Performance as Evidence from US Banks. *Journal of Risk and Financial Management*, *18*(1).

Artene, A. E., Domil, A. E., & Ivascu, L. (2024). Unlocking Business Value : Integrating AI-Driven Decision-Making in Financial Reporting Systems. *Electronics (Switzerland), 13*(15).

Bakkour, D. (2013). *L'approche contractuelle du concept de gouvernance. Document de Recherche LAMETA, série « Études et synthèses »*, 14 p.

Bommasani, R., Hudson, D. A., Adeli, E., Altman, R., Arora, S., von Arx, S., Bernstein, M. S., Bohg, J., Bosselut, A., Brunskill, E., Brynjolfsson, E., Buch, S., Card, D., Castellon, R., Chatterji, N., Chen, A., Creel, K., Davis, J. Q., Demszky, D., . . . Liang, P. (2022). *On the Opportunities and Risks of Foundation Models* (arXiv:2108.07258). arXiv. https://doi.org//arXiv.2108.07258DOI: 10.48550

Brown, T. B., Mann, B., Ryder, N., Subbiah, M., Kaplan, J., Dhariwal, P., Neelakantan, A., Shyam, P., Sastry, G., Askell, A., Agarwal, S., Herbert-Voss, A., Krueger, G., Henighan, T., Child, R., Ramesh, A., Ziegler, D. M., Wu, J., Winter, C., . . . Amodei, D. (2020). *Language Models are Few-Shot Learners* (arXiv:2005.14165). arXiv. https://doi.org//arXiv.2005.14165DOI: 10.48550

Carassus, D., & Cormier, D. (2003). Normes et pratiques de l'audit externe légal en matière de prévention et de détection de la fraude. *Comptabilité Contrôle Audit, 9*(1), 171–188. DOI: 10.3917/cca.091.0171

Charreaux, G. (1996). *Vers une théorie du gouvernement des entreprises.*

Cohen, S., & Karatzimas, S. (2017). Accounting information quality and decision-usefulness of governmental financial reporting : Moving from cash to modified cash. *Meditari Accountancy Research, 25*(1), 95–113. DOI: 10.1108/MEDAR-10-2015-0070

Donatella, P., Haraldsson, M., & Tagesson, T. (2019). Les cabinets d'audit et les coûts/honoraires des audits influencent-ils la gestion du résultat dans les municipalités suédoises? *Revue Internationale des Sciences Administratives, 85*(4), 689–705. DOI: 10.3917/risa.854.0689

Dufour, M., Noguera, F., & Plane, J.-M. (2021). *La gouvernance revisitée : Une approche pluridisciplinaire*. Éditions JFD Inc.

Dusenbury, R. B., Reimers, J. L., & Wheeler, S. W. (2000). The Audit Risk Model : An Empirical Test for Conditional Dependencies among Assessed Component Risks. *Auditing, 19*(2), 105–117. DOI: 10.2308/aud.2000.19.2.105

Estep, C., Griffith, E. E., & MacKenzie, N. L. (2024). How do financial executives respond to the use of artificial intelligence in financial reporting and auditing? *Review of Accounting Studies, 29*(3), 2798-2831. *Scopus*. Advance online publication. DOI: 10.1007/s11142-023-09771-y

Fisher, I. E., Garnsey, M. R., & Hughes, M. E. (2016). Natural Language Processing in Accounting, Auditing and Finance : A Synthesis of the Literature with a Roadmap for Future Research. *Intelligent Systems in Accounting, Finance & Management, 23*(3), 157–214. DOI: 10.1002/isaf.1386

FRC. (s. d.). *Materiality in practice : Applying a materiality mindset.* FRC (Financial Reporting Council). Consulté 11 août 2025, à l'adresse https://www.frc.org.uk/library/research-and-insights/materiality/materiality-in-practice-applying-a-materiality-mindset/

GEC, & CDADI. (2023). *Étude sur l'impact des systèmes d'intelligence artificielle, leur potentiel de promotion de l'égalité, y compris l'égalité de genre, et les risques qu'ils peuvent entraîner en matière de non-discrimination.*

Goel, S., & Uzuner, O. (2016). Do Sentiments Matter in Fraud Detection? Estimating Semantic Orientation of Annual Reports. *Intelligent Systems in Accounting, Finance & Management, 23*(3), 215–239.

Gottimukkala, S. R. (2025). *Leveraging Generative AI for Real-Time Anomaly Detection in SAP FICO : A Paradigm Shift in Financial Governance.*

Hasan, A. R. (2021). Artificial Intelligence (AI) in Accounting & Auditing : A Literature Review. *Open Journal of Business and Management, 10*(1), 440–465. DOI: 10.4236/ojbm.2022.101026

Hervé, L., Peuch-Lestrade, P., & de Villepin, G. (2015). *La pratique de l'audit et du contrôle interne : L'approche et la réalisation d'un audit financier à travers 24 études de cas et leurs corrigés détaillés.* Gualino.

Huang, F., No, W. G., Vasarhelyi, M. A., & Yan, Z. (2022). Audit data analytics, machine learning, and full population testing. *The Journal of Financial Data Science, 8*, 138–144. DOI: 10.1016/j.jfds.2022.05.002

Huang, J., Jiang, M., & Zhu, H. (2025). Audit-FT at the Regulations Challenge Task : An Open-Source Large Language Model for Audit. In Chen, C.-C., Moreno-Sandoval, A., Huang, J., Xie, Q., Ananiadou, S., & Chen, H.-H. (Éds.), *Proceedings of the Joint Workshop of the 9th Financial Technology and Natural Language Processing (FinNLP), the 6th Financial Narrative Processing (FNP), and the 1st Workshop on Large Language Models for Finance and Legal (LLMFinLegal)* (p. 335-348). Association for Computational Linguistics

IFAC. (2007). *2007 IFAC Annual Report.* https://www.ifac.org/publications/2007-ifac-annual-report

IFRS. (2018). *Conceptual Framework for Financial Reporting.*

Jensen, M. C., & Meckling, W. H. (1976). *Theory of the Firm : Managerial Behavior, Agency Costs and Ownership Structure* (SSRN Scholarly Paper 94043). Social Science Research Network.

Johri, A., Singh, R. K., Kushwaha, B. P., Alhumoudi, H., Alakkas, A., & Khoja, M. (2025). Leveraging open innovation for e-commerce success : The contingent role of accounting information systems and artificial intelligence. *Journal of Innovation and Knowledge, 10*(4).

Kadhim, Y. A., & Al Ani, S. A. M. (2024). The Effect of Using an Accounting Information System Based on Artificial Intelligence in Detecting Earnings Management to Enhance the Sustainability of Economic Units. *Stud. Syst. Decis. Control, 537*, 323–336.

KPMG. (2023). *Responsible AI and the challenge of AI risk.* KPMG. https://kpmg.com/be/en/home/insights/2023/07/lh-responsible-ai-and-the-challenge-of-ai-risk.html

Lavastre, O. (2001). *Les Coûts de Transaction et Olivier E.Williamson : Retour sur les fondements.*

LeCun, Y., Bengio, Y., & Hinton, G. (2015). Deep Learning. *Nature, 521*, 436–444.

Luo, X., Wang, X., & Jiang, T. (2025). Application of AI technology in audit risk assessment and control : Taking internal audit of higher education institutions as an example. *Journal of Infrastructure. Policy and Development, 9*, 10125.

MacKenzie, N. L., Moon, J., Rykowski, S., Swanquist, Q. T., & Whited, R. L. (2024). *A Comparison of Artificial Intelligence and Human Responses in Audit Experiments* (SSRN Scholarly Paper 5036687). Social Science Research Network.

Mbaidin, H. O., Sbaee, N. Q., Almubydeen, I. O., Chindo, U. M., & Alomari, K. M. (2024). The role of AI integration and governance standards : Enhancing financial reporting quality in Islamic banking. *Decision Science Letters, 13*(1), 83–98.

McKinsey & Compagnie. (2018). *Les entreprises canadiennes et l'intelligence artificielle : Libérer le plein potentiel de l'IA au canada.*

Mohammed, A. A., Khan, F., Mohammed, A. A., Abdalla, Y. A., Mohammed, A. A. A., & Ahmad, Z. (2024). Impact of AI Applications on Corporate Financial Reporting Quality : Evidence from UAE Corporations. *Qubahan Academic Journal, 4*(3), 785–795.

Mok, A. (2023). *EY has created its own large-language model—And says it will train all 400,000 employees to use it as part of a $1.4 billion investment.* Yahoo Tech.

Mökander, J., Schuett, J., Kirk, H. R., & Floridi, L. (2024). Auditing large language models : A three-layered approach. *AI and Ethics, 4*(4), 1085–1115.

Moloi, T., & Obeid, H. (2024). Perceptions of South African Accountants on Factors with a Role in the Adoption of Artificial Intelligence in Financial Reporting. *Journal of Risk and Financial Management, 17*(9).

Monteiro, A., Rua, O., Figueira, J., & Leite, E. (2021). Practices and mechanisms to mitigate the negative effects of accounting-based earnings management : An empirical study from the professionals' perspective. *International journal of advanced and applied sciences, 8*(9), Article 9.

Moumen, I., Abouchabaka, J., & Rafalia, N. (2024). Smart traffic forecasting : Leveraging adaptive machine learning and big data analytics for traffic flow prediction. *IAES International Journal of Artificial Intelligence (IJ-AI), 13*, 2323.

Munoko, I., Brown-Liburd, H., & Vasarhelyi, M. (2020). The Ethical Implications of Using Artificial Intelligence in Auditing. *Journal of Business Ethics*, 167.

Nadhir, Z., & Wardhani, R. (2019). The effect of audit quality and degree of international Financial Reporting Standards (IFRS) convergence on the accrual earnings management in ASEAN countries. *Entrepreneurship and Sustainability Issues, 7*(1), 105–120.

Neiroukh, N., & Çağlar, D. (2025). Information Systems Quality and Corporate Sustainability : Unpacking the Interplay of Financial Reporting, Artificial Intelligence, and Green Corporate Governance. *Systems, 13*(7).

Nkakleu, R., Plane, J.-M., & Biboum, A. D. (2021). *Théories et management des organisations : Une perspective africaine*. EMS Editions.

OCDE. (2018). *Lignes directrices pour le recueil, la communication et l'utilisation des données sur l'innovation, 4ème édition*. OCDE.

Parrat, F. (2014). *Théories et pratiques de la gouvernance d'entreprise*. Maxima.

PCAOB. (2022). *Public Company Accounting Oversight Board (PCAOB). Annual report 2022.* https://assets.pcaobus.org/pcaob-dev/docs/default-source/about/administration/documents/annual_reports/2022-annual-report_final.pdf

Qatawneh, A. M. (2024). The role of artificial intelligence in auditing and fraud detection in accounting information systems : Moderating role of natural language processing. *The International Journal of Organizational Analysis*.

Sarker, I. H. (2022). AI-Based Modeling : Techniques, Applications and Research Issues Towards Automation, Intelligent and Smart Systems. *SN Computer Science, 3*(2), 1–20.

Schreyer, M., Sattarov, T., Borth, D., Dengel, A., & Reimer, B. (2018). Detection of Anomalies in Large Scale Accounting Data using Deep Autoencoder Networks (arXiv:1709.05254).

Shleifer, A., & Vishny, R. W. (1997). A Survey of Corporate Governance. *The Journal of Finance*, *52*(2), 2.

Sutton, R. S., & Barto, A. G. (2018). *Reinforcement Learning : An Introduction*.

Tian, J., & Li, L. (2022). Research on artificial intelligence of accounting information processing based on image processing. *Mathematical Biosciences and Engineering*, *19*(8), 8411–8425.

Williamson, O. E. (1985). *The Economic Institutions of Capitalism: Firms, Markets, Relational Contracting* (SSRN Scholarly Paper 1496720). Social Science Research Network.

Zaiceanu, A., Hlaciuc, E., & Lucan, A. (2015). Methods for Risk Identification and Assessment in Financial Auditing. *Procedia Economics and Finance*, *32*, 595–602.

Zhao, X., Zhai, G., Charles, V., Gherman, T., Lee, H., Pan, T., & Shang, Y. (2024). Enhancing enterprise investment efficiency through artificial intelligence: The role of accounting information transparency. *Socio-Economic Planning Sciences*, 96.

Zhou, X., Li, G., Wang, Q., Li, Y., & Zhou, D. (2025). Artificial intelligence, corporate information governance and ESG performance: Quasi-experimental evidence from China. In *International Review of Financial Analysis* (Vol. 102).

Compilation of References

Abadi, M., Barham, P., Chen, J., Chen, Z., Davis, A., Dean, J., & Zheng, X. (2016). TensorFlow: A system for large-scale machine learning. *12th USENIX Symposium on Operating Systems Design and Implementation (OSDI)*, 265-283. https://doi.org/DOI: 10.5555/3026877.3026899

Abadi, M., Chu, A., Goodfellow, I., McMahan, H. B., Mironov, I., Talwar, K., & Zhang, L. (2016). Deep learning with differential privacy. *Proceedings of the 2016 ACM SIGSAC Conference on Computer and Communications Security*, 308–318. https://doi.org/DOI: 10.1145/2976749.2978318

Abel, M., Ahmad, I., Casado, C. A., Berner, R., Bettinelli, M., Björk, K. M., . . . Zourmand, A. (2025). *Large Language Models in the 6G-Enabled Computing Continuum: a White Paper* (Doctoral dissertation, University of Oulu).

Abu-Salih, B., Wongthongtham, P., Zhu, D., Chan, K. Y., & Rudra, A. (2021). Introduction to Big Data Technology. https://arxiv.org/pdf/2104.08062v1.pdf

Achanta, P. R. D. (2025). Transformative Effect: Rise of Intelligent Data Management in Integration with AI. *Transactions on Engineering and Computing Sciences*, *13*(1), 116–123. DOI: 10.14738/tecs.131.18275

Aggarwal, C. C. (2013). *Data streams: Models and algorithms*. Springer., DOI: 10.1007/978-3-642-36481-6

Ahmad, I., Shahabuddin, S., Kumar, T., Okwuibe, J., Gurtov, A., & Ylianttila, M. (2019). Security for 5G and beyond. *IEEE Communications Surveys and Tutorials*, *21*(4), 3682–3722.

Aïmeur, E., Amri, S., & Brassard, G. (2023). Fake news, disinformation and misinformation in social media: A review. *Social Network Analysis and Mining*, *13*(1), 30. PMID: 36789378

Akhtar, N., & Mian, A. (2018). Threat of adversarial attacks on deep learning in computer vision: A survey. *IEEE Access: Practical Innovations, Open Solutions*, *6*, 14410–14430. DOI: 10.1109/ACCESS.2018.2807385

Akolekar, H., Jhamnani, P., Kumar, V., Tailor, V., Pote, A., Meena, A., Kumar, K., Challa, J. S., & Kumar, D. (2025). The role of generative AI tools in shaping mechanical engineering education from an undergraduate perspective. *Scientific Reports*, *15*, 9214. Advance online publication. DOI: 10.1038/s41598-025-93871-z PMID: 40097637

Al Omari, B., & Al-Nimer, M. (2024). Harnessing artificial intelligence to strengthen financial reporting quality in developing economies : A mediated model with internal controls in Jordanian banks. *Journal of Infrastructure, Policy and Development, 8*(8). Scopus.

AlAli, R., & Wardat, Y. (2024). Opportunities and challenges of integrating generative artificial intelligence in education. *International Journal of Religion*, *5*(7), 784–793. DOI: 10.61707/8y29gv34

Aldoseri, A., Al-Khalifa, K., & Hamouda, A. M. S. (2023). Re-Thinking Data Strategy and Integration for Artificial Intelligence: Concepts, Opportunities, and Challenges. In A. Aldoseri, K. Al-Khalifa, & A. M. S. Hamouda, Applied Sciences (Vol. 13, Issue 12, p. 7082). Multidisciplinary Digital Publishing Institute. https://doi.org/DOI: 10.3390/app13127082

Alharasis, E. E., Marei, A., Almakhadmeh, A. A.-R., Abdullah, S., & Lutfi, A. (2024). An evaluation of financial statement quality in pre-versus post-IFRS-7 implementation : The case of Iraqi banking industry. *Discover Sustainability*, *5*(1).

Al-Hashimy, H. N. H., Hussein, W. N., Al Jubair, A. S., & Yao, J. (2024). Enhancing Data Integrity in Computerized Accounting Information Systems Using Supervised and Unsupervised Machine Learning Algorithms Implement A SEM-PLS Analysis. *Informatica (Slovenia)*, *48*(20), 107–118.

Almaliki, O., & Al-saedi, M. (2023). The Impact of the Qualitative Peculiarities of Accounting Information Based on the Financial Reports of Commercial Banks. *International Academic Journal of Social Sciences*, *10*, 49–56.

Almazrouei, E., Al-Ali, A., AlShamsi, A., & al Dhaheri, A. Falcon LLM: The new state of the art in open large language models. arXiv preprint arXiv:230601116. 2023

Almubaydeen, T., Alkabbji, R., & Fleifil, M. K. A. (2025). Effect of Applying the Artificial Intelligence on the Quality of Accounting Information in Commercial Banks (a Field Study). [). Springer Science and Business Media Deutschland GmbH.]. *Stud. Syst. Decis. Control, 572*, 787–803.

Alonso, M. N. I. (2025). The Mathematics of Modern Generative Modeling: Normalizing Flows, Autoregressive and Diffusion Models. *SSRN*. https://doi.org/DOI: 10.2139/ssrn.5089573

Alzeghoul, A., & Alsharari, N. M. (2025). Impact of AI Disclosure on the Financial Reporting and Performance as Evidence from US Banks. *Journal of Risk and Financial Management, 18*(1).

Andonian, A., Tseng, E., Zhang, K., & Isola, P. (2023). Robust data pipelines for machine learning with generative AI. *IEEE Transactions on Artificial Intelligence, 4*(5), 1200–1213.

Antwi, B. O., Adelakun, B. O., & Eziefule, A. O. (2024). Transforming Financial Reporting with AI: Enhancing Accuracy and Timeliness. In B. O. Antwi, B. O. Adelakun, & A. O. Eziefule, International Journal of Advanced Economics (Vol. 6, Issue 6, p. 205). Fair East Publishers. https://doi.org/DOI: 10.51594/ijae.v6i6.1229

Anwar, M. J., Gill, A. Q., Hussain, F. K., & Imran, M. (2021). Secure big data ecosystem architecture: challenges and solutions. In M. J. Anwar, A. Q. Gill, F. K. Hussain, & M. Imran, EURASIP Journal on Wireless Communications and Networking (Vol. 2021, Issue 1). Springer Nature. https://doi.org/DOI: 10.1186/s13638-021-01996-2

Ardeliya, V. E., Taylor, J., & Wolfson, J. (2024). Exploration of artificial intelligence in creative fields: Generative art, music, and design. *International Journal of Cyber and IT Service Management, 4*(1), 40–46. DOI: 10.34306/ijcitsm.v4i1.149

Arowosegbe, A., Alqahtani, J. S., & Oyelade, T. (2024). Perception of generative AI use in UK higher education. *Frontiers in Education, 9*. Advance online publication. DOI: 10.3389/feduc.2024.1463208

Aroyo, L., Lease, M., Paritosh, P., & Schaekermann, M. (2021). Data Excellence for AI: Why Should You Care. In L. Aroyo, M. Lease, P. Paritosh, & M. Schaekermann, arXiv (Cornell University). Cornell University. https://doi.org/DOI: 10.48550/arXiv.2111

Artene, A. E., Domil, A. E., & Ivascu, L. (2024). Unlocking Business Value : Integrating AI-Driven Decision-Making in Financial Reporting Systems. *Electronics (Switzerland), 13*(15).

Baduge, S. K., Thilakarathna, S., Perera, J. S., Arashpour, M., Sharafi, P., Teodosio, B., Shringi, A., & Mendis, P. (2022). Artificial intelligence and smart vision for building and construction 4.0: Machine and deep learning methods and applications. *Automation in Construction*, *141*, 104440. DOI: 10.1016/j.autcon.2022.104440

Bai, H., Liu, H., Li, C., Li, Y., Zhang, Y., & Liu, J. (2021). Robustness and privacy of generative adversarial networks: A survey. *ACM Computing Surveys*, *54*(4), 1–38. DOI: 10.1145/3446373

Baijens, J., Huygh, T., & Helms, R. (2021). Establishing and theorising data analytics governance: a descriptive framework and a VSM-based view. In J. Baijens, T. Huygh, & R. Helms, Journal of Business Analytics (Vol. 5, Issue 1, p. 101). Taylor & Francis. https://doi.org/DOI: 10.1080/2573234x.2021.1955021

Bakkour, D. (2013). *L'approche contractuelle du concept de gouvernance. Document de Recherche LAMETA, série « Études et synthèses »*, 14 p.

Baliga, S., Murthy, H. K., Sadhale, A., & Upadhyaya, D. (2023). Advanced applications of generative AI and natural language processing models. In *Advances in computational intelligence and robotics book series* (pp. 69–86). https://doi.org/DOI: 10.4018/979-8-3693-0502-7.ch004

Banh, L., & Strobel, G. (2023). Generative artificial intelligence. *Electronic Markets*. Advance online publication. DOI: 10.1007/s12525-023-00680-1

Baskara, F. X. R. (2024). Generative AI as an enabler of sustainable education: Theoretical perspectives and future directions. *Bulletin of Journal of Teaching and Educational Pedagogics*, *3*(3), 9. DOI: 10.32996/bjtep

Benala, T. R., & Dehuri, S. (2025). Transforming Software Development: From Traditional Methods to Generative Artificial Intelligence. In *Boosting Software Development Using Machine Learning* (pp. 1–13). Springer.

Bender, E. M., Gebru, T., McMillan-Major, A., & Shmitchell, S. (2021). On the dangers of stochastic parrots: Can language models be too big? *Proceedings of the 2021 ACM Conference on Fairness, Accountability, and Transparency*, 610–623. https://doi.org/DOI: 10.1145/3442188.3445922

Bengio, Y., Hinton, G. E., Yao, A. C.-C., Song, D., Abbeel, P., Darrell, T., Harari, Y. N., Zhang, Y.-Q., Lan, X., Shalev-Shwartz, S., Hadfield, G. K., Clune, J., Maharaj, T., Hutter, F., Baydin, A. G., McIlraith, S. A., Gao, Q., Acharya, A., Krueger, D., . . . Mindermann, S. (2024). Managing extreme AI risks amid rapid progress. In Y. Bengio, G. E. Hinton, A. C.-C. Yao, D. Song, P. Abbeel, T. Darrell, Y. N. Harari, Y.-Q. Zhang, X. Lan, S. Shalev-Shwartz, G. K. Hadfield, J. Clune, T. Maharaj, F. Hutter, A. G. Baydin, S. A. McIlraith, Q. Gao, A. Acharya, D. Krueger, … S. Mindermann, Science (Vol. 384, Issue 6698, p. 842). American Association for the Advancement of Science. https://doi.org/DOI: 10.1126/science.adn0117

Bianchini, F. (2025). Generative artificial intelligence: A concept in progress. *Ethics and Information Technology*. Advance online publication. DOI: 10.1007/s13347-025-00875-8

Bommasani, R., Hudson, D. A., & Adeli, E. (2023). others. On the opportunities and risks of foundation models. *Journal of Artificial Intelligence Research, 76*, 1–97.

Bonawitz, K., "Towards federated learning at scale: System design," arXiv preprint arXiv:1902.01046, Mar. 2019.

Bonde, L. (2024). A conceptual design of a generative artificial intelligence system for education. *International Journal of Research and Innovation in Applied Science, 9*(4), 457–469. DOI: 10.51584/IJRIAS.2024.904034

Bond-Taylor, S., Leach, A., Long, Y., & Willcocks, C. G. (2021). Deep Generative Modelling: A comparative review of VAEs, GANs, normalizing flows, Energy-Based and autoregressive models. *IEEE Transactions on Pattern Analysis and Machine Intelligence, 44*(11), 7327–7347. DOI: 10.1109/tpami.2021.3116668 PMID: 34591756

Bragazzi, N. L., & Garbarino, S. (2024). Toward Clinical Generative AI: Conceptual framework. *JMIR AI, 3*, e55957. DOI: 10.2196/55957 PMID: 38875592

Bredell, G., Flouris, K., Chaitanya, K., Erdil, E., & Konukoglu, E. (2023). Explicitly minimizing the blur error of variational autoencoders. *arXiv (Cornell University)*. https://doi.org//arxiv.2304.05939DOI: 10.48550

Brown, T. B., Mann, B., & Ryder, N. others. Language models are few-shot learners. In: Advances in Neural Information Processing Systems. 2023. p. 1877–901.

Brown, T., Mann, B., Ryder, N., Subbiah, M., Kaplan, J. D., Dhariwal, P., & Amodei, D. (2020). Language models are few-shot learners. *Advances in Neural Information Processing Systems, 33*, 1877–1901. DOI: 10.48550/arXiv.2005.14165

Carassus, D., & Cormier, D. (2003). Normes et pratiques de l'audit externe légal en matière de prévention et de détection de la fraude. *Comptabilité Contrôle Audit, 9*(1), 171–188. DOI: 10.3917/cca.091.0171

Carbone, P., Katsifodimos, A., Ewen, S., Markl, V., Haridi, S., & Tzoumas, K. (2015). Apache Flink: Stream and batch processing in a single engine. *A Quarterly Bulletin of the Computer Society of the IEEE Technical Committee on Data Engineering, 38*(4), 28–38. DOI: 10.1109/BigData.2015.7368627

Carlini, N., Tramer, F., Wallace, E., Jagielski, M., Herbert-Voss, A., Lee, K., & Erlingsson, Ú. (2021). Extracting training data from large language models. *Proceedings of the 30th USENIX Security Symposium*, 2633–2650. https://doi.org/DOI: 10.48550/arXiv.2012.07805

Cartagena, S., Gosrani, V., Grewal, J. S., & Pikinska, J. (2020). Silent cyber assessment framework. In S. Cartagena, V. Gosrani, J. S. Grewal, & J. Pikinska, British Actuarial Journal (Vol. 25). Cambridge University Press. https://doi.org/DOI: 10.1017/s1357321720000021

Chaccour, C., Karapantelakis, A., Murphy, T., & Dohler, M. (2024). Telecom's artificial general intelligence (agi) vision: Beyond the genai frontier. *IEEE Network.*

Chang, Y., Wang, X., Wang, J., Wu, Y., Yang, L., Zhu, K., Chen, H., Yi, X., Wang, C., Wang, Y., Ye, W., Zhang, Y., Chang, Y., Yu, P. S., Yang, Q., & Xie, X. (2024). A survey on evaluation of large language models. *ACM Transactions on Intelligent Systems and Technology, 15*(3), 1–45. DOI: 10.1145/3641289

Charreaux, G. (1996). *Vers une théorie du gouvernement des entreprises.*

Chen, L., Song, Y., Guo, J., Sun, L., Childs, P., & Yin, Y. (2025). How generative AI supports human in conceptual design. *Design Studies.* Advance online publication. DOI: 10.1017/dsj.2025.2

Chen, M., Mei, S., Fan, J., & Wang, M. (2024). Opportunities and challenges of diffusion models for generative AI. *National Science Review, 11*(12). Advance online publication. DOI: 10.1093/nsr/nwae348 PMID: 39554240

Chen, M., Tworek, J., & Jun, H. (2023). others. Evaluating large language models trained on code. *ACM Transactions on Software Engineering and Methodology, 32*(3), 1–43.

Chen, R. J., Lu, M. Y., Chen, T. Y., Williamson, D. F. K., & Mahmood, F. (2021). Synthetic data in machine learning for medicine and healthcare. *Nature Biomedical Engineering, 5*(6), 493–497. DOI: 10.1038/s41551-021-00751-8 PMID: 34131324

Chen, Y., & Esmaeilzadeh, P. (2024). Generative AI in Medical Practice: In-Depth Exploration of privacy and Security challenges. *Journal of Medical Internet Research, 26*, e53008. DOI: 10.2196/53008 PMID: 38457208

Chickermane, H. (2025). How Machine Learning and Generative AI Are Enabling the Autonomous Supply Chain. In *Supply Chain Transformation Through Generative AI and Machine Learning* (pp. 1–28). IGI Global Scientific Publishing.

Cho, K., van Merrienboer, B., Gulcehre, C., Bahdanau, D., Bougares, F., Schwenk, H., & Bengio, Y. (2014). Learning phrase representations using RNN encoder-decoder for statistical machine translation. *EMNLP*, 1724-1734. https://doi.org/DOI: 10.3115/v1/D14-1179

Chong, M. J., & Forsyth, D. (2020). Effectively unbiased FID and inception score and where to find them. *2022 IEEE/CVF Conference on Computer Vision and Pattern Recognition (CVPR)*, 6069–6078. https://doi.org/DOI: 10.1109/cvpr42600.2020.00611

Chowdhury, A., Sharma, S., & Sharma, A. (2022). A survey on membership inference attacks and defenses on generative models. *IEEE Transactions on Information Forensics and Security, 17*, 431–448. DOI: 10.1109/TIFS.2021.3116657

Chukwurah, N., Adebayo, V., Eyieyien, O., & Ige, A. (2024). Frameworks for effective data governance: Best practices, challenges, and implementation strategies across industries. *Computer Science & IT Research Journal, 5*(7), 1666–1679. DOI: 10.51594/csitrj.v5i7.1351

Cohen, G., Afshar, S., Tapson, J., & van Schaik, A. (2017). EMNIST: Extending MNIST to handwritten letters. *2017 International Joint Conference on Neural Networks (IJCNN)*, 2921-2926. https://doi.org/DOI: 10.1109/IJCNN.2017.7966217

Cohen, S., & Karatzimas, S. (2017). Accounting information quality and decision-usefulness of governmental financial reporting : Moving from cash to modified cash. *Meditari Accountancy Research, 25*(1), 95–113. DOI: 10.1108/MEDAR-10-2015-0070

Coimbatore Ramalingam, B. (2025). Efficient Implementation of AI Agents in Enterprise Application Integration (EAI) and Electronic Data Interchange (EDI). *International Journal of Scientific Research in Computer Science. Engineering and Information Technology, 11*(2), 10–32628.

Corchado, J. M., López, S., Núñez, J. M., Garcia, R., & Chamoso, P. (2023). Fundamentals. *Advances in Distributed Computing and Artificial Intelligence Journal, 12*(2), 139–146. DOI: 10.14201/adcaij.31704

Craven, E., & Shokri, R. (2020). Privacy risks and defenses in generative models. *Proceedings of the 29th USENIX Security Symposium*, 1541–1558.

Creely, E., & Janssen, K. (2025). Onto-epistemological understandings of generative artificial intelligence in education. *International Journal of Changes in Education, 2*(2), 55–65. DOI: 10.47852/bonviewIJCE52024380

Dai, J., Wang, J., Huang, W., Shi, J., & Zhu, Z. (2020). Machinery health monitoring based on unsupervised feature learning via generative adversarial networks. *IEEE/ASME Transactions on Mechatronics, 25*(5), 2252–2263. DOI: 10.1109/tmech.2020.3012179

Dakhel, A. M., Nikanjam, A., Khomh, F., Desmarais, M. C., & Washizaki, H. (2024). Generative AI for Software Development: A Family of Studies on Code Generation. *Generative AI for Effective Software Development*, 151–172. https://doi.org/DOI: 10.1007/978-3-031-55642-5_7

Dandotiya, M., Rahi, P., & Khunteta, A. A. Anushya, and Sayed Sayeed Ahmad. 2023. SAFE: A Secure Authenticated & Integrated Framework for E-learning. In Proceedings of the 4th International Conference on Information Management & Machine Intelligence (ICIMMI '22). Association for Computing Machinery, New York, NY, USA, Article 89, 1–9. https://doi.org/DOI: 10.1145/3590837.3590926

Dash, S., Shakyawar, S. K., Sharma, L., & Kaushik, S. (2019). Big data in healthcare: management, analysis and future prospects. In S. Dash, S. K. Shakyawar, L. Sharma, & S. Kaushik, Journal Of Big Data (Vol. 6, Issue 1). Springer Science+Business Media. https://doi.org/DOI: 10.1186/s40537-019-0217-0

Deng, L., & Yu, D. (2014). Deep learning: Methods and applications. *Foundations and Trends® in Signal Processing, 7*(3–4), 197-387. https://doi.org/DOI: 10.1561/2000000039

Devlin, J., Chang, M.-W., Lee, K., & Toutanova, K. (2019). BERT: Pre-training of deep bidirectional transformers for language understanding. *NAACL-HLT*, 4171-4186. https://doi.org/DOI: 10.18653/v1/N19-1423

Devlin, J., Chang, M. W., Lee, K., & Toutanova, K. (2019). BERT: Pre-training of deep bidirectional transformers for language understanding. *Proceedings of NAACL-HLT*, 4171–4186. https://doi.org/DOI: 10.48550/arXiv.1810.04805

Díaz-Rodríguez, N., Ser, J. D., Coeckelbergh, M., de Prado, M. L., Herrera-Viedma, E., & Herrera, F. (2023). Connecting the dots in trustworthy Artificial Intelligence: From AI principles, ethics, and key requirements to responsible AI systems and regulation. In N. Díaz-Rodríguez, J. D. Ser, M. Coeckelbergh, M. L. de Prado, E. Herrera-Viedma, & F. Herrera, Information Fusion (Vol. 99, p. 101896). Elsevier BV. https://doi.org/DOI: 10.1016/j.inffus.2023.101896

Dinh, L., Saxe, A., & Abbeel, P. (2017). A survey on model inversion attacks. *Journal of Machine Learning Research.*

Donatella, P., Haraldsson, M., & Tagesson, T. (2019). Les cabinets d'audit et les coûts/honoraires des audits influencent-ils la gestion du résultat dans les municipalités suédoises? *Revue Internationale des Sciences Administratives*, *85*(4), 689–705. DOI: 10.3917/risa.854.0689

Duan, Y., Chen, X., & Houthooft, R. (2024). others. GenAI for automated data engineering in cloud environments. *IEEE Cloud Computing*, *11*(2), 56–67.

Dufour, M., Noguera, F., & Plane, J.-M. (2021). *La gouvernance revisitée : Une approche pluridisciplinaire*. Éditions JFD Inc.

Dusenbury, R. B., Reimers, J. L., & Wheeler, S. W. (2000). The Audit Risk Model : An Empirical Test for Conditional Dependencies among Assessed Component Risks. *Auditing*, *19*(2), 105–117. DOI: 10.2308/aud.2000.19.2.105

Dwivedi, Y. K., Hughes, L., & Baabdullah, A. M. (2023). others. Artificial Intelligence (AI): Multidisciplinary perspectives on emerging challenges, opportunities, and agenda for research, practice, and policy. *International Journal of Information Management*, *69*, 102642.

Dwork, C., & Roth, A. (2014). The algorithmic foundations of differential privacy. *Foundations and Trends® in Theoretical Computer Science, 9*(3–4), 211-407. https://doi.org/DOI: 10.1561/0400000042

El Fathi, T., Saad, A., Larhzil, H., Lamri, D., & Al Ibrahmi, E. M. (2025). Integrating generative AI into STEM education: Enhancing conceptual understanding, addressing misconceptions, and assessing student acceptance. *Smart Learning Environments*, *12*, 25. Advance online publication. DOI: 10.1186/s43031-025-00125-z

Estep, C., Griffith, E. E., & MacKenzie, N. L. (2024). How do financial executives respond to the use of artificial intelligence in financial reporting and auditing? *Review of Accounting Studies, 29*(3), 2798-2831. *Scopus.* Advance online publication. DOI: 10.1007/s11142-023-09771-y

Fang, X., Che, S., & Mao, M., (2024). Bias of AI-generated content: An examination of news produced by large language models. *Scientific Reports*, *14*, 5224. DOI: 10.1038/s41598-024-55686-2 PMID: 38433238

Farquhar, S., Kossen, J., & Kuhn, L., (2024). Detecting hallucinations in large language models using semantic entropy. *Nature*, *630*, 625–630. DOI: 10.1038/s41586-024-07421-0 PMID: 38898292

Fattah, I. A. (2024). Decision making performance of business analytics capabilities: The role of big data literacy and analytics competency. *Business Process Management Journal*, *30*(6), 2096–2126. DOI: 10.1108/bpmj-11-2023-0894

Ferrara, E. (2023). Fairness and Bias in Artificial intelligence: A brief survey of sources, impacts, and mitigation strategies. *Sci*, *6*(1), 3. DOI: 10.3390/sci6010003

Fett, M., Kraft, M., Wartzack, S., Goetz, S., Wilking, F., & Kirchner, E. (2024). Medium-Level Architectures for Digital Twins: Bridging Conceptual Reference Architectures to Practical Implementation in Cloud, Edge and Cloud–Edge Deployments. *Electronics (Basel)*, *13*(7), 1373. DOI: 10.3390/electronics13071373

Feuerriegel, S., Zschech, P., Hartmann, J., & Janiesch, C. (2023). Generative AI. *Business & Information Systems Engineering*, *65*(6), 561–565. DOI: 10.1007/s12599-023-00834-7

Figueira, A., & Vaz, B. (2022). Survey on synthetic data generation, evaluation methods and GANs. *Mathematics*, *10*(15), 2733. DOI: 10.3390/math10152733

Fisher, I. E., Garnsey, M. R., & Hughes, M. E. (2016). Natural Language Processing in Accounting, Auditing and Finance : A Synthesis of the Literature with a Roadmap for Future Research. *Intelligent Systems in Accounting, Finance & Management*, *23*(3), 157–214. DOI: 10.1002/isaf.1386

FRC. (s. d.). *Materiality in practice : Applying a materiality mindset*. FRC (Financial Reporting Council). Consulté 11 août 2025, à l'adresse https://www.frc.org.uk/library/research-and-insights/materiality/materiality-in-practice-applying-a-materiality-mindset/

Fredrikson, M., Jha, S., & Ristenpart, T. (2015). Model inversion attacks that exploit confidence information and basic countermeasures. *Proceedings of the 22nd ACM SIGSAC Conference on Computer and Communications Security*, 1322–1333. https://doi.org/DOI: 10.1145/2810103.2813677

Galli, A., Masciari, E., & Moscato, V., (2022). A comprehensive Benchmark for fake news detection. *Journal of Intelligent Information Systems*, *59*, 237–261. DOI: 10.1007/s10844-021-00646-9 PMID: 35342227

Gandhi, D., Joshi, H., Hartman, L., & Hassani, S. (2025). *Approaches to Responsible Governance of GENAI in organizations*. arXiv.org. https://www.arxiv.org/abs/2504.17044

García-Peñalvo, F. J., & Vázquez-Ingelmo, A. (2023). What do we mean by GenAI? A systematic mapping of the evolution, trends, and techniques involved in generative AI. *International Journal of Interactive Multimedia and Artificial Intelligence*, *8*(4), 7–16. DOI: 10.9781/ijimai.2023.07.006

GEC, & CDADI. (2023). *Étude sur l'impact des systèmes d'intelligence artificielle, leur potentiel de promotion de l'égalité, y compris l'égalité de genre, et les risques qu'ils peuvent entraîner en matière de non-discrimination*.

Ghodoosi, B., Torrisi-Steele, G., West, T., & Li, Q. (2023). An Exploration of the Definition of Data Literacy in the Academic and Public Domains. In B. Ghodoosi, G. Torrisi-Steele, T. West, & Q. Li, International Journal of Adult Education and Technology (Vol. 14, Issue 1, p. 1). IGI Global. https://doi.org/DOI: 10.4018/ijaet.325218

Ghosh, A., & Sanyal, S. (2023). Synthetic data generation using generative adversarial networks for privacy-preserving analytics. *Expert Systems with Applications*, *225*, 120072.

Goel, S., & Uzuner, O. (2016). Do Sentiments Matter in Fraud Detection? Estimating Semantic Orientation of Annual Reports. *Intelligent Systems in Accounting, Finance & Management*, *23*(3), 215–239.

Goldsteen, A., Douek, T., Cohen, Y., Gokhman, I., Keren-Ackerman, O., Katsovich, G., Weintraub, G., & Ben-Ari, D. (2019). Forgotten @ Scale: A Practical Solution for Implementing the Right To Be Forgotten in Large-Scale Systems. In A. Goldsteen, T. Douek, Y. Cohen, I. Gokhman, O. Keren-Ackerman, G. Katsovich, G. Weintraub, & D. Ben-Ari, arXiv (Cornell University). Cornell University. https://doi.org/DOI: 10.48550/arXiv.1910

Gont, F., & Chown, T. (2016). Network reconnaissance in IPv6 networks (No. rfc7707).

Goodfellow, I., Pouget-Abadie, J., Mirza, M., Xu, B., Warde-Farley, D., Ozair, S., & Bengio, Y. (2014). Generative adversarial nets. *Advances in Neural Information Processing Systems*, *27*, 2672–2680. DOI: 10.5555/2969033.2969125

Gottimukkala, S. R. (2025). *Leveraging Generative AI for Real-Time Anomaly Detection in SAP FICO : A Paradigm Shift in Financial Governance*.

Goyal, N. K. (2025). Security and Privacy in IoT, Fog, and Blockchain Networks. In Sathio, A., Rind, M., Awan, S., & Junejo, A. (Eds.), *Energy-Efficient Deep Learning Approaches in IoT, Fog, and Green Blockchain Revolution* (pp. 371–398). IGI Global Scientific Publishing., DOI: 10.4018/979-8-3373-0300-0.ch015

Goyal, N. K. (2025). Weaponizing Misinformation and Cyberattacks on Supply Chains. In Bukhari, S., & Zafar, I. (Eds.), *Mass Media and Impact of Fake News on Supply Chains* (pp. 177–210). IGI Global Scientific Publishing., DOI: 10.4018/979-8-3373-2175-2.ch007

Goyal, N. K., Dandotiya, M., Kumari, M., Kaloria, S., & Anushya, A. (2025). AI-Powered Haptic Devices for Patient Rehabilitation. In Mamodiya, U., Kalam, A., Bossoufi, B., Awad, M., & Somwanshi, D. (Eds.), *Integrating AI With Haptic Systems for Smarter Healthcare Solutions* (pp. 143–170). IGI Global Scientific Publishing., DOI: 10.4018/979-8-3373-2307-7.ch007

Goyal, N. K., Dandotiya, M., Kumari, M., Sheikh, M. F., & Sharma, S. (2025). Emerging Job Roles in the Tourism Sector Leveraging Artificial Intelligence. In Silic, M., Luthia, M., Ahmad, F., & Chakraborty, P. (Eds.), *Empowering Sustainable Performance and Competitive Advantage in Tourism* (pp. 89–126). IGI Global Scientific Publishing., DOI: 10.4018/979-8-3373-4546-8.ch004

Goyal, N. K., Dandotiya, M., Qurashi, J. A., Kumari, M., & Sharma, S. (2025). AI-Driven Predictive Analytics for Disease Management. In Ouaissa, M., Ouaissa, M., Imad, M., Qurashi, J., & Farooq, M. (Eds.), *Utilizing AI of Medical Things for Healthcare Security and Sustainability* (pp. 231–276). IGI Global Scientific Publishing., DOI: 10.4018/979-8-3373-0690-2.ch008

Goyal, N. K., Kumari, M., Kushwah, V., Dandotiya, M., & Vijay, A. (2025). Evaluating blockchain security: Trade-offs in consensus mechanisms. *IET Conference Proceedings*, 2024(38), 80–88. https://doi.org/DOI: 10.1049/icp.2025.0775

Goyal, N., Kumar, R., & Kherwa, P. (2024). Role of large language models in accelerating ETL processes. *Journal of Big Data*, *11*(1), 50.

Gudipudi, S. (2025). Redefining Business Intelligence Infrastructure: Core Skills for the AI-Driven Era. *Journal of Computer Science and Technology Studies*, *7*(6), 717–724.

Gulrajani, I., Ahmed, F., Arjovsky, M., Dumoulin, V., & Courville, A. (2017). Improved training of wasserstein GANs. *NIPS'17: Proceedings of the 31st International Conference on Neural Information Processing Systems, 30*, 5769–5779.

Guo, C., & Xu, Y. (2021). Privacy preservation in generative AI: Differential privacy and federated learning. *IEEE Transactions on Neural Networks and Learning Systems, 32*(6), 2332–2345. DOI: 10.1109/TNNLS.2020.3029834

Gupta, A., & Pathak, P. (2023). Explainable GenAI for trustworthy data pipelines. *ACM Computing Surveys, 55*(12), 1–34.

Gupta, P., Ding, B., Guan, C., & Ding, D. (2024). Generative AI: A systematic review using topic modelling techniques. *Data and Information Management, 8*(2), 100066. DOI: 10.1016/j.dim.2024.100066

Gwon, H. J., Yoo, Y., & Lee, J. Y. (2025). Improving Generative Ai Reliability: A Qualitative Study of Hallucination in Large Language Models. *SSRN*. https://doi .org/DOI: 10.2139/ssrn.5118420

Halevy, A., Korn, F., Noy, N. F., Olston, C., Polyzotis, N., Roy, S., & Whang, S. E. (2020). Goods: Organizing Google's datasets. *Communications of the ACM, 63*(1), 89–97. DOI: 10.1145/3360322

Hao, M. C., Dayal, U., & Hsu, M. (2023). others. AI-augmented data engineering: Concepts, architectures, and applications. *Proceedings of the VLDB Endowment International Conference on Very Large Data Bases, 16*(12), 3765–3778.

Hasan, A. R. (2021). Artificial Intelligence (AI) in Accounting & Auditing : A Literature Review. *Open Journal of Business and Management, 10*(1), 440–465. DOI: 10.4236/ojbm.2022.101026

He, R., Cao, J., & Tan, T. (2025). Generative Artificial Intelligence: A historical perspective. *National Science Review, 12*(5). Advance online publication. DOI: 10.1093/nsr/nwaf050 PMID: 40191253

Hervé, L., Peuch-Lestrade, P., & de Villepin, G. (2015). *La pratique de l'audit et du contrôle interne : L'approche et la réalisation d'un audit financier à travers 24 études de cas et leurs corrigés détaillés*. Gualino.

Higgins, I., Matthey, L., Pal, A., Burgess, C., Glorot, X., Botvinick, M., Mohamed, S., & Lerchner, A. (2017). beta-VAE: Learning Basic Visual Concepts with a Constrained Variational Framework. *International Conference on Learning Representations*. https://dblp.uni-trier.de/db/conf/iclr/iclr2017.html#HigginsMPBGBML17

Hillary, V. E., Gopalsamy, R. G., Da Mota Santana, L. A., De Jesus, P. C., De Souza, J. B., Silva, D. M. R. R., Moura, P. H. M., Santos, R. S., Barreto, M. D. S., Borges, L. P., & Silva, E. E. D. (2024). The impact of generative artificial intelligence (AI) on the development of personalized pharmaceuticals and the future of precision medicine. *PubMed, 23*, 1459–1462. https://doi.org/DOI: 10.17179/excli2024-7915

Hsu, T.-C., & Hsu, T.-P. (2025). Teaching AI with games: The impact of generative AI drawing on computational thinking skills. *Education and Information Technologies*. Advance online publication. DOI: 10.1007/s10639-025-13624-3

Huang, F., No, W. G., Vasarhelyi, M. A., & Yan, Z. (2022). Audit data analytics, machine learning, and full population testing. *The Journal of Financial Data Science*, *8*, 138–144. DOI: 10.1016/j.jfds.2022.05.002

Huang, J., Jiang, M., & Zhu, H. (2025). Audit-FT at the Regulations Challenge Task : An Open-Source Large Language Model for Audit. In Chen, C.-C., Moreno-Sandoval, A., Huang, J., Xie, Q., Ananiadou, S., & Chen, H.-H. (Éds.), *Proceedings of the Joint Workshop of the 9th Financial Technology and Natural Language Processing (FinNLP), the 6th Financial Narrative Processing (FNP), and the 1st Workshop on Large Language Models for Finance and Legal (LLMFinLegal)* (p. 335-348). Association for Computational Linguistics

Hu, B., Mao, Z., & Zhang, Y. (2024, February 22). An overview of fake news detection: From a new perspective. *Fundamental Research (Beijing)*, *5*(1), 332–346. DOI: 10.1016/j.fmre.2024.01.017 PMID: 40166093

Hyun, Y., Kamioka, T., & Hosoya, R. (2020). Improving Agility Using Big Data Analytics: The Role of Democratization Culture. In Y. Hyun, T. Kamioka, & R. Hosoya, Pacific Asia journal of the Association for Information Systems (Vol. 12, p. 34). Association for Information Systems. https://doi.org/DOI: 10.17705/1thci.12202

IFAC. (2007). *2007 IFAC Annual Report*. https://www.ifac.org/publications/2007-ifac-annual-report

Ifenthaler, D., Gibson, D., Prasse, D., Shimada, A., & Yamada, M. (2021). Putting learning back into learning analytics: Actions for policy makers, researchers, and practitioners. *Educational Technology Research and Development*, *69*(4), 2131–2150.

IFRS. (2018). *Conceptual Framework for Financial Reporting*.

Ismail, K. R., Brata, Z. A., Nelistiani, G. A., Heo, S., Kim, H., & Kim, H. (2025). Toward Robust Security Orchestration and Automated Response in Security Operations Centers with a Hyper-Automation Approach Using Agentic Artificial Intelligence. *Information (Basel)*, *16*(5), 365.

Jain, N., Payal, A., & Jain, A. (2021). Performance analysis of routing protocols on IPv4 and IPv6 addressing networks. *Journal of Web Engineering*, *20*(5), 1389–1428.

Janssen, M., Brous, P., Estévez, E., Barbosa, L. S., & Janowski, T. (2020). Data governance: Organizing data for trustworthy Artificial Intelligence. In M. Janssen, P. Brous, E. Estévez, L. S. Barbosa, & T. Janowski, Government Information Quarterly (Vol. 37, Issue 3, p. 101493). Elsevier BV. https://doi.org/DOI: 10.1016/j.giq.2020.101493

Janssen, M. (2025). Responsible governance of generative AI: Conceptualizing GenAI as complex adaptive systems. *Policy and Society*. Advance online publication. DOI: 10.1093/polsoc/puae040

Jensen, M. C., & Meckling, W. H. (1976). *Theory of the Firm : Managerial Behavior, Agency Costs and Ownership Structure* (SSRN Scholarly Paper 94043). Social Science Research Network.

Jiang, F., Pan, C., Dong, L., Wang, K., Dobre, O. A., & Debbah, M. (2025). From Large AI Models to Agentic AI: A Tutorial on Future Intelligent Communications. *arXiv preprint arXiv:2505.22311*.

Jiménez, L., Polo, J., & Duarte, N. (2019). Overview of Data Governance in Business Contexts. In L. Jiménez, J. Polo, & N. Duarte, IOP Conference Series Materials Science and Engineering (Vol. 519, Issue 1, p. 12023). IOP Publishing. https://doi.org/DOI: 10.1088/1757-899x/519/1/012023

Ji, Z., Lee, N., Frieske, R., Yu, T., Su, D., Xu, Y., & Ren, X. (2023). Survey of hallucination in natural language generation. *ACM Computing Surveys*, *55*(12), 1–38. DOI: 10.1145/3571730

Johri, A., Singh, R. K., Kushwaha, B. P., Alhumoudi, H., Alakkas, A., & Khoja, M. (2025). Leveraging open innovation for e-commerce success : The contingent role of accounting information systems and artificial intelligence. *Journal of Innovation and Knowledge*, *10*(4).

Joshi, S. (2025). A Review of Generative AI and DevOps Pipelines: CI/CD, Agentic Automation, MLOps Integration, and Large Language Models. *CD, Agentic Automation, MLOps Integration, and Large Language Models (June 01, 2025)*.

Joshi, S. (2025). Comprehensive Review of Artificial General Intelligence AGI, Agentic AI and GenAI: Current Trends and Future Directions.

Joshi, S. (2025). Review of data pipelines and streaming for generative AI integration: Challenges, solutions, and future directions. *Solutions, and Future Directions (March 03, 2025)*.

Joshi, S. (2025). Comprehensive Review of AI Hallucinations: Impacts and Mitigation Strategies for Financial and Business Applications. *International Journal of Computer Applications Technology and Research, 14*(6), 38–50. DOI: 10.7753/IJCATR1406.1003

Juuti, M., Szyller, S., Marchal, S., & Asokan, N. (2019). Prada: Protecting against data extraction attacks on machine learning models. *Proceedings of the 28th USENIX Security Symposium*, 793–810.

Kaal, W. A. (2025). Artificial Intelligence: The Final Frontier. *U of St. Thomas (Minnesota) Legal Studies Research Paper*, (25-04).

Kadhim, Y. A., & Al Ani, S. A. M. (2024). The Effect of Using an Accounting Information System Based on Artificial Intelligence in Detecting Earnings Management to Enhance the Sustainability of Economic Units. *Stud. Syst. Decis. Control, 537*, 323–336.

Kairouz, P., McMahan, H. B., Avent, B., Bellet, A., Bennis, M., Bhagoji, A. N., ... & Zhao, S. (2019). Advances and open problems in federated learning. *Foundations and Trends® in Machine Learning, 14*(1–2), 1–210. https://doi.org/DOI: 10.1561/2200000083

Kairouz, P., McMahan, H. B., Avent, B., Bellet, A., Bennis, M., Bhagoji, A. N., ... & Zhao, S. (2021). Advances and open problems in federated learning. *Foundations and Trends® in Machine Learning, 14*(1–2), 1-210. https://doi.org/DOI: 10.1561/2200000073

Kalota, F. (2024). A primer on generative artificial intelligence. *Education Sciences, 14*(2), 172. DOI: 10.3390/educsci14020172

Kanbach, D. K., Heiduk, L., Blueher, G., Schreiter, M., & Lahmann, A. (2023). The GenAI is out of the bottle: Generative artificial intelligence from a business model innovation perspective. *Review of Managerial Science, 18*(4), 1189–1220. DOI: 10.1007/s11846-023-00696-z

Kanka, V. (2024). *Scaling Big Data: Leveraging LLMs for Enterprise Success*. Libertatem Media Private Limited.

Kaur, P., Singh, S., & Ahuja, S. (2023). Federated learning and GenAI for privacy-preserving data analytics. *Future Generation Computer Systems, 145*, 415–427.

Khokhlov, Y. (2025). Advancing operational efficiency in software companies through generative AI. *The American Journal of Engineering and Technology, 7*(01), 11–18.

Kim, H., & Choi, J. (2023). Enhancing data integration through generative AI-based schema matching. *Information Sciences*, *625*, 448–461.

Kim, H., Sun, X., Wang, H., & Shi, W. (2020). Designing privacy-preserving generative models with application to synthetic data generation. *IEEE Transactions on Information Forensics and Security*, *15*, 2134–2146. DOI: 10.1109/TIFS.2019.2958759

Kingma, D. P., & Welling, M. (2014). Auto-encoding variational Bayes. *International Conference on Learning Representations (ICLR)*. https://doi.org/DOI: 10.48550/arXiv.1312.6114

Koivisto, K., & Taipalus, T. (2023). Pitfalls in Effective Knowledge Management: Insights from an International Information Technology Organization. In K. Koivisto & T. Taipalus, arXiv (Cornell University). Cornell University. https://doi.org/DOI: 10.48550/arXiv.2304

Kokosi, T., & Harron, K. (2022). Synthetic data in medical research. *BMJ Medicine*, *1*(1), e000167. DOI: 10.1136/bmjmed-2022-000167 PMID: 36936569

Kollnig, K., Binns, R., Kleek, M. V., Lyngs, U., Zhao, J., Tinsman, C., & Shadbolt, N. (2021). Before and after GDPR: tracking in mobile apps. In K. Kollnig, R. Binns, M. V. Kleek, U. Lyngs, J. Zhao, C. Tinsman, & N. Shadbolt, Internet Policy Review (Vol. 10, Issue 4). Alexander von Humboldt Institute for Internet and Society. https://doi.org/DOI: 10.14763/2021.4.1611

KPMG. (2023). *Responsible AI and the challenge of AI risk*. KPMG. https://kpmg.com/be/en/home/insights/2023/07/lh-responsible-ai-and-the-challenge-of-ai-risk.html

Kreps, J., Narkhede, N., & Rao, J. (2011). Kafka: A distributed messaging system for log processing. *Proceedings of the NetDB*, 1-7. https://doi.org/DOI: 10.1145/2070911.2070916

Kreuk, F., Baruch, G., Deutsch, D., Taigman, Y., & Wolf, L. (2020). Model poisoning attacks against federated learning systems. *Proceedings of the 35th International Conference on Machine Learning*, 4913–4923. https://proceedings.mlr.press/v119/kreuk20a.html

Krizhevsky, A., Sutskever, I., & Hinton, G. E. (2012). ImageNet classification with deep convolutional neural networks. *Advances in Neural Information Processing Systems*, *25*, 1097–1105. DOI: 10.1145/3065386

Kumar, S., & Sharma, Ms. K., & IARJSET. (2025). Text Generation with the help of natural language processing: A Review. In *International Advanced Research Journal in Science, Engineering and Technology, 12*(1), 273–274. https://doi.org/DOI: 10.17148/IARJSET.2025.12131

Kurnia, R., Brata, Z. A., Nelistiani, G. A., Heo, S., Kim, H., & Kim, H. (2025). Toward Robust Security Orchestration and Automated Response in Security Operations Centers with a Hyper-Automation Approach Using Agentic Artificial Intelligence. *Information (2078-2489), 16*(5).

Lakkarasu, P. (2024). From Model to Value: Engineering End-to-End AI Systems with Scalable Data Infrastructure and Continuous ML Delivery. *European Journal of Analytics and Artificial Intelligence (EJAAI) p-ISSN 3050-9556 en e-ISSN 3050-9564, 2*(1).

Lavastre, O. (2001). *Les Coûts de Transaction et Olivier E.Williamson : Retour sur les fondements*.

LeCun, Y., Bengio, Y., & Hinton, G. (2015). Deep Learning. *Nature*, *521*, 436–444.

Lewis, M., Liu, Y., Goyal, N., Ghazvininejad, M., Mohamed, A., Levy, O., & Zettlemoyer, L. (2020). BART: Denoising sequence-to-sequence pre-training for natural language generation, translation, and comprehension. *Proceedings of ACL*, 7871–7880. https://doi.org/DOI: 10.48550/arXiv.1910.13461

Li, Q., "A survey on federated learning systems:vision, hype and reality for data privacy and protection," arXiv preprint arXiv:1907.09693, Dec. 2019.

Li, T., "Federated learning: Challenges, methods, and future directions," arXiv preprint arXiv:1908.07873, Aug. 2019.

Li, A. (2025). AI-Driven Big Data Analytics: Scalable Architectures and Real-Time Processing. *European Journal of AI. Computer Information*, *1*(1), 33–41. DOI: 10.71222/pw8kw891

Li, H., Kadav, A., Durdanovic, I., Samet, H., & Graf, H. P. (2017). Pruning filters for efficient convnets. *International Conference on Learning Representations*. https://doi.org/DOI: 10.48550/arXiv.1608.08710

Lim, D. (2025). Governing Generative AI. SSRN *Electronic Journal*. https://doi.org/DOI: 10.2139/ssrn.5167491

Lim, W., Yong, K. S. C., Lau, B. T., & Tan, C. C. L. (2024). Future of generative adversarial networks (GAN) for anomaly detection in network security: A review. *Computers & Security*, *139*, 103733. DOI: 10.1016/j.cose.2024.103733

Lin, D., Fu, K., Wang, Y., Xu, G., & Sun, X. (2017). MARTA GANS: Unsupervised Representation Learning for Remote Sensing Image Classification. *IEEE Geoscience and Remote Sensing Letters*, *14*(11), 2092–2096. DOI: 10.1109/lgrs.2017.2752750

Lin, X., & Losavio, M. (2025). A Comprehensive Survey on Bias and Fairness in Generative AI: Legal, Ethical, and Technical Responses. *SSRN*. https://doi.org/DOI: 10.2139/ssrn.5164147

Li, Q., He, B., & Wu, D. (2020). Federated learning: Challenges, methods, and future directions. *IEEE Signal Processing Magazine*, *37*(3), 50–60. DOI: 10.1109/MSP.2020.2975749

Liu, Y. J., Du, H., Xu, X., Zhang, R., Feng, G., Cao, B., ... & Tafazolli, R. (2025). A Survey of Integrating Generative Artificial Intelligence and 6G Mobile Services: Architectures, Solutions, Technologies and Outlooks. *IEEE Transactions on Cognitive Communications and Networking*.

Liuetal, Y. (2020). Federated learning for 6g communications: Challenges, methods, and future directions. *China Communications*.

Liu, J., Wang, T., Chen, X., Li, C., Shen, Z., & Zhang, Z. (2024). H2-RAID: Improving the reliability of SSD RAID with unified SSD and HDD hybrid architecture. *Microprocessors and Microsystems*, *105*, 104993.

Liu, X., & Wu, Y. (2021). Deepfake detection: A survey. *IEEE Transactions on Pattern Analysis and Machine Intelligence*. Advance online publication. DOI: 10.1109/TPAMI.2021.3063954

Liu, Y., Kang, J., Xu, Y., Wang, S., & Yang, Q. (2020). Secure and private AI: Federated learning, differential privacy, and beyond. *IEEE Transactions on Big Data*. Advance online publication. DOI: 10.1109/TBDATA.2020.3019967

Li, W., Fan, L., Wang, Z., Ma, C., & Cui, X. (2020). Tackling mode collapse in multi-generator GANs with orthogonal vectors. *Pattern Recognition*, *110*, 107646. DOI: 10.1016/j.patcog.2020.107646

Li, X., Chen, J., & Zhang, Y. (2023). Autonomous data pipelines using large language models. *IEEE Transactions on Knowledge and Data Engineering*, *35*(8), 7994–8007.

Li, Z., Shi, S., Wang, L., Xu, M., & Li, L. (2022). Unsupervised Generative Adversarial Network with Background Enhancement and Irredundant Pooling for Hyperspectral Anomaly Detection. *Remote Sensing*, *14*(5), 1265. DOI: 10.3390/rs14051265

Luo, X., Wang, X., & Jiang, T. (2025). Application of AI technology in audit risk assessment and control : Taking internal audit of higher education institutions as an example. *Journal of Infrastructure. Policy and Development*, *9*, 10125.

Luo, Y., Wang, L., & Li, J. (2023). Adaptive governance in AI-driven data engineering systems. *Decision Support Systems*, *169*, 113859.

MacKenzie, N. L., Moon, J., Rykowski, S., Swanquist, Q. T., & Whited, R. L. (2024). *A Comparison of Artificial Intelligence and Human Responses in Audit Experiments* (SSRN Scholarly Paper 5036687). Social Science Research Network.

Marchesi, R., Micheletti, N., Kuo, N. I., Barbieri, S., Jurman, G., & Osmani, V. (2025). Generative AI mitigates representation bias and improves model fairness through synthetic health data. *PLoS Computational Biology*, *21*(5), e1013080. DOI: 10.1371/journal.pcbi.1013080 PMID: 40388536

Marti, D., & Smith, M. (2023). Motivating Data Science Students to Participate and Learn. In D. Marti & M. Smith, Harvard Data Science Review (Vol. 5, Issue 1). The MIT Press. https://doi.org/DOI: 10.1162/99608f92.d3b2eadd

Matulionyte, R., & Lee, J. (2022). Copyright in AI-generated works: Lessons from recent developments in patent law. *SCRIPTed a Journal of Law Technology & Society*, *19*(1), 5–35. DOI: 10.2966/scrip.190122.5

Mbaidin, H. O., Sbaee, N. Q., Almubydeen, I. O., Chindo, U. M., & Alomari, K. M. (2024). The role of AI integration and governance standards : Enhancing financial reporting quality in Islamic banking. *Decision Science Letters*, *13*(1), 83–98.

McGregor, S., & Hostetler, J. (2023). Data-Centric Governance. In S. McGregor & J. Hostetler, arXiv (Cornell University). Cornell University. https://doi.org/DOI: 10.48550/arXiv.2302

McKinsey & Compagnie. (2018). *Les entreprises canadiennes et l'intelligence artificielle : Libérer le plein potentiel de l'IA au canada.*

McMahan, B., Moore, E., Ramage, D., & Hampson, S. (2017). B. A. y Arcas, Communication-e cient learning of deep networks from decentralized data. In *Arti cial intelligence and statistics* (p. 12731282). PMLR.

Medaglia, R., Gil-García, J. R., & Pardo, T. A. (2021). Artificial Intelligence in Government: Taking Stock and Moving Forward. In R. Medaglia, J. R. Gil-García, & T. A. Pardo, Social Science Computer Review (Vol. 41, Issue 1, p. 123). SAGE Publishing. https://doi.org/DOI: 10.1177/08944393211034087

Michel-Villarreal, R., Vilalta-Perdomo, E., Salinas-Navarro, D. E., Thierry-Aguilera, R., & Gerardou, F. S. (2023). Challenges and opportunities of Generative AI for higher Education as explained by ChatGPT. *Education Sciences, 13*(9), 856. DOI: 10.3390/educsci13090856

Mine, G., Hai, J., Jin, L., & Huiying, Z. (2020, August). A design of SD-WAN-oriented wide area network access. In *2020 International Conference on Computer Communication and Network Security (CCNS)* (pp. 174-177). IEEE.

Mishra, A., Majumder, A., Kommineni, D., Joseph, C. A., Chowdhury, T., & Anumula, S. K. (2025). Role of Generative Artificial intelligence in Personalized Medicine: A Systematic review. *Cureus*. Advance online publication. DOI: 10.7759/cureus.82310 PMID: 40376348

Mittal, S., & Bhatia, R. (2023). Leveraging diffusion models for synthetic data creation in high-dimensional datasets. *Pattern Recognition Letters, 172*, 61–69.

Mohammed, A. A., Khan, F., Mohammed, A. A., Abdalla, Y. A., Mohammed, A. A. A., & Ahmad, Z. (2024). Impact of AI Applications on Corporate Financial Reporting Quality : Evidence from UAE Corporations. *Qubahan Academic Journal, 4*(3), 785–795.

Mohseni, S., Yang, F., Pentyala, S., Du, M., Liu, Y., Lupfer, N., & Ragan, E. (2021, May). Machine learning explanations to prevent overtrust in fake news detection. In *Proceedings of the international AAAI conference on web and social media* (Vol. 15, pp. 421-431).

Mok, A. (2023). *EY has created its own large-language model—And says it will train all 400,000 employees to use it as part of a $1.4 billion investment.* Yahoo Tech.

Mökander, J., Schuett, J., Kirk, H. R., & Floridi, L. (2024). Auditing large language models : A three-layered approach. *AI and Ethics, 4*(4), 1085–1115.

Molinari, G., & Ciravegna, F. (2025). Towards Pervasive Distributed Agentic Generative AI—A State of The Art. *arXiv preprint arXiv:2506.13324.*

Moloi, T., & Obeid, H. (2024). Perceptions of South African Accountants on Factors with a Role in the Adoption of Artificial Intelligence in Financial Reporting. *Journal of Risk and Financial Management, 17*(9).

Monteiro, A., Rua, O., Figueira, J., & Leite, E. (2021). Practices and mechanisms to mitigate the negative effects of accounting-based earnings management : An empirical study from the professionals' perspective. *International journal of advanced and applied sciences, 8*(9), Article 9.

Monti, F., Frasca, F., Eynard, D., Mannion, D., & Bronstein, M. M. (2019). Fake news detection on social media using geometric deep learning. [TKDD]. *ACM Transactions on Knowledge Discovery from Data, 13*(5), 1–27. https://arxiv.org/abs/1902.06673

Morabito, R., & Jang, S. (2025). Smaller, Smarter, Closer: The Edge of Collaborative Generative AI. *IEEE Internet Computing*.

Moumen, I., Abouchabaka, J., & Rafalia, N. (2024). Smart traffic forecasting : Leveraging adaptive machine learning and big data analytics for traffic flow prediction. *IAES International Journal of Artificial Intelligence (IJ-AI), 13*, 2323.

Munoko, I., Brown-Liburd, H., & Vasarhelyi, M. (2020). The Ethical Implications of Using Artificial Intelligence in Auditing. *Journal of Business Ethics*, 167.

Musa, Z. M., & Kakudi, H. A. (2025). Exploring the concept of generative artificial intelligence: A narrative review. *International Journal of Latest Technology in Engineering* [IJLTEMAS]. *Management & Applied Science, 14*(4), 1–7. DOI: 10.51583/IJLTEMAS.2025.140400001

Musiol, M. (2024). *Generative AI: Navigating the course to the artificial general intelligence future*. John Wiley & Sons.

Myllis, G., Vrana, V. G., Tsimpiris, A., & Aggelopoulos, S. (2025). High-Performance Computing and Parallel Algorithms for Urban Water Demand Forecasting. *Algorithms, 18*(4), 182. DOI: 10.3390/a18040182

Nachiappan, B., Rajkumar, N., Radha, V., Kalpana, C., Viji, C., Nagarajan, G., Mohanraj, A. (2026). Fusion of Generative AI and Blockchain: Conceptual Framework. In: Fusion of Multimodal Generative AI and Blockchain Technology in Digital Media. IGI Global Scientific Publishing. p. 57-86.

Nadhir, Z., & Wardhani, R. (2019). The effect of audit quality and degree of international Financial Reporting Standards (IFRS) convergence on the accrual earnings management in ASEAN countries. *Entrepreneurship and Sustainability Issues, 7*(1), 105–120.

Narapareddy, V. S. R. (2025). Generative AI and Foundation Models. *Universal Library of Innovative Research and Studies, 2*(2).

Nargesian, F., Samulowitz, H., Khurana, U., Khalil, E. B., & Turaga, D. (2017). Learning feature engineering for classification. *IJCAI (United States)*, •••, 2529–2535. DOI: 10.24963/ijcai.2017/352

National Institute of Standards and Technology (NIST). (2023). *NIST AI Risk Management Framework*. https://www.nist.gov/itl/ai-risk-management-framework

Nazari-Aref, G., Farokh-Seresht, B., Ahmadi, G. A., & Eslami, S. (2021). Designing a Good Corporate Governance Model in the Context of Ethics and Rationality. In G. Nazari-Aref, B. Farokh-Seresht, G. A. Ahmadi, & S. Eslami, International Journal of Ethics & Society (Vol. 3, Issue 1, p. 41). https://doi.org/DOI: 10.52547/ijethics.3.1.41

Nees, J. V., & Waltman, L. (2019). *VOSViewer Manual*. https://www.vosviewer.com/documentation/Manual_VOSviewer_1.6.11.pdf

Neiroukh, N., & Çağlar, D. (2025). Information Systems Quality and Corporate Sustainability : Unpacking the Interplay of Financial Reporting, Artificial Intelligence, and Green Corporate Governance. *Systems*, *13*(7).

Nguyen, T., & Hoang, D. (2024). A human-in-the-loop framework for GenAI in ETL optimization. *Information Systems*, *122*, 102200.

Nieto, F. J., Aguilera, U., & López-de-Ipiña, D. (2021). Analyzing Particularities of Sensor Datasets for Supporting Data Understanding and Preparation. In F. J. Nieto, U. Aguilera, & D. López-de-Ipiña, Sensors (Vol. 21, Issue 18, p. 6063). Multidisciplinary Digital Publishing Institute. https://doi.org/DOI: 10.3390/s21186063

Nkakleu, R., Plane, J.-M., & Biboum, A. D. (2021). *Théories et management des organisations : Une perspective africaine*. EMS Editions.

Nwobodo, L., Adegbola, A., & Nwaimo, C. (2024). Enhancing cybersecurity protocols in the era of big data and advanced analytics. *GSC Advanced Research and Reviews*, *19*(3), 203–214. DOI: 10.30574/gscarr.2024.19.3.0211

Nyaaba, M., Zhai, X., & Faison, M. Z. (2024). Generative AI for culturally responsive assessment in science: A conceptual framework. *Preprint*. https://doi.org/DOI: 10.20944/preprints202409.1276.v2

O'Connor, A. J. (2024). *Organizing for Generative AI and the Productivity Revolution: Reshaping Organizational Roles in the Age of Artificial Intelligence*. Springer Nature.

OCDE. (2018). *Lignes directrices pour le recueil, la communication et l'utilisation des données sur l'innovation, 4ème édition*. OCDE.

Oladosu, S. A., Ike, C. C., Adepoju, P. A., Afolabi, A. I., Ige, A. B., & Amoo, O. O. (2021). The future of SD-WAN: A conceptual evolution from traditional WAN to autonomous, selfhealing network systems. *Magna Scientia Advanced Research and Reviews*, *3*(2), 95–107.

Olubusola, O., Ajayi-Nifise, A., Falaiye, T., Mhlongo, N., & Daraojimba, D. (2024). Machine learning in financial forecasting: A U.S. review: Exploring the advancements, challenges, and implications of AI-driven predictions in financial markets. *World Journal of Advanced Research and Reviews*, *21*(2), 1969–1984. DOI: 10.30574/wjarr.2024.21.2.0444

Oluwaferanmi, J. K. A. (2025). Automating ETL Pipelines Using Artificial Intelligence: Transforming Legacy Data Integration Systems into Intelligent Data Workflows.

Pajooh, H. H., Rashid, M. A., Alam, F., & Demidenko, S. (2021). IoT Big Data provenance scheme using blockchain on Hadoop ecosystem. In H. H. Pajooh, M. A. Rashid, F. Alam, & S. Demidenko, Journal Of Big Data (Vol. 8, Issue 1). Springer Science+Business Media. https://doi.org/DOI: 10.1186/s40537-021-00505-y

Palaniappan, N. N. (2025). Demystifying generative ai and transformer architectures. *International journal of advanced research in engineering & technology, 16*(2), 15–28. https://doi.org/DOI: 10.34218/ijaret_16_02_002

Papernot, N., McDaniel, P., Goodfellow, I., Jha, S., Celik, Z. B., & Swami, A. (2016). The limitations of deep learning in adversarial settings. *Proceedings of the 2016 IEEE European Symposium on Security and Privacy*, 372–387. https://doi.org/DOI: 10.1109/EuroSP.2016.36

Parrat, F. (2014). *Théories et pratiques de la gouvernance d'entreprise*. Maxima.

Pascanu, R., Mikolov, T., & Bengio, Y. (2013). On the difficulty of training recurrent neural networks. *International Conference on Machine Learning*, 1310-1318. https://doi.org/DOI: 10.5555/3042817.3043083

Paul, D., Sanap, G., Shenoy, S., Kalyane, D., Kalia, K., & Tekade, R. K. (2020). Artificial intelligence in drug discovery and development. *Drug Discovery Today*, *26*(1), 80–93. DOI: 10.1016/j.drudis.2020.10.010 PMID: 33099022

PCAOB. (2022). *Public Company Accounting Oversight Board (PCAOB). Annual report 2022.* https://assets.pcaobus.org/pcaob-dev/docs/default-source/about/administration/documents/annual_reports/2022-annual-report_final.pdf

Peddinti, S. R., Katragadda, S. R., & Tanikonda, A. (2024). Deep Learning for Autonomous Data Quality Enhancement: A Paradigm Shift in Machine Learning Pipelines. *Available at SSRN* 5251229.

Prabaharan, G., Chithrakumar, T., Vidhya, S. M., Balakrishnan, M. B., & Sika, K. (2025). AI-Driven Computational Frameworks: Advancing Edge Intelligence and Smart Systems. *International Journal of Computational and Experimental Science and Engineering*, *11*(1). Advance online publication. DOI: 10.22399/ijcesen.1165

Prakash, D. (2024). Data-Driven Management: The Impact of Big Data Analytics on Organizational Performance. *International Journal for Global Academic & Scientific Research*, *3*(2), 12–23. DOI: 10.55938/ijgasr.v3i2.74

Protivash, P., Durrell, J., Kifer, D., Ding, Z., & Zhang, D. (2024). Reconstruction Attacks on Aggressive Relaxations of Differential Privacy. In P. Protivash, J. Durrell, D. Kifer, Z. Ding, & D. Zhang, Journal of Privacy and Confidentiality (Vol. 14, Issue 3). https://doi.org/DOI: 10.29012/jpc.871

Q. Yang, Y. Liu, T. Chen, and Y. Tong, "Federated machine learning: Concept and applications," vol. 10, no. 2, pp. 1–19, Feb. 2019.

Qatawneh, A. M. (2024). The role of artificial intelligence in auditing and fraud detection in accounting information systems : Moderating role of natural language processing. *The International Journal of Organizational Analysis*.

Qayyum, A., Razzak, I., Mazher, M., Lu, X., & Niederer, S. A. (2024). Unsupervised unpaired multiple fusion adaptation aided with self-attention generative adversarial network for scar tissues segmentation framework. *Information Fusion*, *106*, 102226. DOI: 10.1016/j.inffus.2024.102226

Raffel, C., Shazeer, N., Roberts, A., Lee, K., Narang, S., Matena, M., & Liu, P. J. (2020). Exploring the limits of transfer learning with a unified text-to-text transformer. *Journal of Machine Learning Research*, *21*(140), 1–67. https://www.jmlr.org/papers/v21/20-074.html

Rahi, P., (2023). Edge-Cognitive Computing for Improvising the Healthcare 5.0. In *Contemporary Applications of Data Fusion for Advanced Healthcare Informatics, edited by G.S. Karthick and Sathishkumar Karupusamy* (pp. 369–391). IGI Global Scientific Publishing., DOI: 10.4018/978-1-6684-8913-0.ch016

Raji, I. D., & Buolamwini, J. (2019). Actionable auditing: Investigating the impact of publicly naming biased performance results of commercial AI products. *AAAI/ACM Conference on AI, Ethics, and Society*. https://doi.org/DOI: 10.1145/3306618.3314244

Rajkumar N., Viji C., Nachiappan B., Nagarajan G., Mohanraj A., Kovilpillai, J.A., Prabhu, S.B. (2026b). Generative AI in Text and Language Processing for Digital Media. In: Generative AI Applications and Intelligent Systems: From Chatbots to Cybersecurity. IGI Global Scientific Publishing. p. 1-26.

Rajkumar, N., Viji, C., Nachiappan, B., Mohanraj, A., Nagarajan, G., Ravi, J., Prabhu, S.B. (2026a). Generative AI in Virtual Media Image, Video, and Animation Generation. In: Fusion of Multimodal Generative AI and Blockchain Technology in Digital Media. IGI Global Scientific Publishing. p. 209-230.

Raj, R., & Sharma, P. (2023). AIethics in generative data engineering: Bias, fairness, and transparency. *AI and Ethics*, *3*(2), 255–272.

Ramzi, B., Alsuliman, A., & Elrayah, M. (2021). The Reasons that Affect the Implementation of HR Analytics among HR Professionals. In *B. Ramzi* (p. 29). A. Alsuliman, & M. Elrayah, Canadian Journal of Business and Information Studies., DOI: 10.34104/cjbis.021.029037

Reimers, N., & Gurevych, I. (2019). Sentence-BERT: Sentence embeddings using Siamese BERT-networks. Proceedings of EMNLP/IJCNLP, 3982–3992. https://doi.org/DOI: 10.48550/arXiv.1908.10084

Remolina, N. (2023). Generative AI in Finance: Risks and potential solutions. SSRN *Electronic Journal*. https://doi.org/DOI: 10.2139/ssrn.4628235

Reza, R. (2018), Uber's Big Data Platform: 100+ Petabytes with Minute Latency. Uber Blog. https://www.uber.com/en-IN/blog/uber-big-data-platform/

Ruchansky, N., Seo, S., & Liu, Y. (2017). CSI: A hybrid deep model for fake news detection. *Proceedings of CIKM*, 797–806. https://doi.org/DOI: 10.1145/3132847.3132877

Sadiq, S., Aryani, A., Demartini, G., Hua, W., Indulska, M., Burton-Jones, A., Khosravi, H., Benavides-Prado, D., Sellis, T., Someh, I., Vaithianathan, R., Wang, S., & Zhou, X. (2022). Information Resilience: the nexus of responsible and agile approaches to information use. In S. Sadiq, A. Aryani, G. Demartini, W. Hua, M. Indulska, A. Burton-Jones, H. Khosravi, D. Benavides-Prado, T. Sellis, I. Someh, R. Vaithianathan, S. Wang, & X. Zhou, The VLDB Journal (Vol. 31, Issue 5, p. 1059). Springer Science+Business Media. https://doi.org/DOI: 10.1007/s00778-021-00720-2

Sadiq, Z., & Aqib, M. (2023). Advancing Trustworthy explainable artificial intelligence: Principles, goals, and strategies. *OAlib*, *10*(11), 1–14. DOI: 10.4236/oalib.1110870

Şahin, O., & Karayel, D. (2024). Generative artificial intelligence (GenAI) in business and industry: A systematic review on the threshold of transformation. *Journal of Smart Systems Research*, *5*(2), 156–175. DOI: 10.58769/joinssr.1597110

Said, J., & Alam, Md. M., & Khalid, M. A. (2022). Relationship between good governance and integrity system: Empirical study on the public sector of Malaysia. https://doi.org/DOI: 10.31235/osf.io/hdcf7

Samara, H. H., Qudah, H. A., Abualhijad, S., Alqudah, M. Z., Mohsin, H. J., Al Rahamneh, S., & Bani Hani, L. Y. (2024). Artificial intelligence and machine learning in corporate governance: A bibliometric analysis. *Human Systems Management*, •••, 1–27. DOI: 10.3233/hsm-240114

Samaras, G., Mertiri, M., Xezonaki, M. E., Theodorou, V., Chartsias, P. K., & Bozios, T. (2024, June). Democratizing Predictive Analytics with Generative Artificial Intelligence towards AI-Native Networks. In *2024 IEEE Symposium on Computers and Communications (ISCC)* (pp. 1–6). IEEE.

Sandhu, R., Cheema, G. S., Channi, H. K., Kaur, M., & Ghai, D. (2024). An introduction to generative AI tools for education 2030. In *Emerging Technologies and Globalization of Education* (p. 1). IGI Global., DOI: 10.4018/979-8-3693-2440-0.ch001

Sapkota, R., Roumeliotis, K. I., & Karkee, M. (2025). AI agents vs. agentic ai: A conceptual taxonomy, applications and challenge. *arXiv preprint arXiv:2505.10468*.

Sarker, I. H. (2022). AI-Based Modeling : Techniques, Applications and Research Issues Towards Automation, Intelligent and Smart Systems. *SN Computer Science*, *3*(2), 1–20.

Schreyer, M., Sattarov, T., Borth, D., Dengel, A., & Reimer, B. (2018). Detection of Anomalies in Large Scale Accounting Data using Deep Autoencoder Networks (arXiv:1709.05254).

Sendas, N., & Rajale, D. (2025). Future Trends in MLOps. In *The Definitive Guide to Machine Learning Operations in AWS: Machine Learning Scalability and Optimization with AWS* (pp. 371–423). Apress.

Shanmugam, L. (2023). *Ravish Tillu, Manish Tomar, Federated Learning Architecture: Design*. Implementation, and Challenges in Distributed AI Systems.

Shen, X., Brown, H., Tao, J., Strobel, M., Tong, Y., Narayan, A., Soh, H., & Doshi-Velez, F. (2024). Directions of Technical Innovation for Regulatable AI Systems. In X. Shen, H. Brown, J. Tao, M. Strobel, Y. Tong, A. Narayan, H. Soh, & F. Doshi-Velez, Communications of the ACM. Association for Computing Machinery. https://doi.org/DOI: 10.1145/3653670

Shethiya, A. S. (2024). Engineering with Intelligence: How Generative AI and LLMs Are Shaping the Next Era of Software Systems. *Spectrum of Research, 4*(1).

Shleifer, A., & Vishny, R. W. (1997). A Survey of Corporate Governance. *The Journal of Finance*, *52*(2), 2.

Shokri, R., & Shmatikov, V. (2015). Privacy-preserving deep learning. *Proceedings of the 22nd ACM SIGSAC Conference on Computer and Communications Security*, 1310-1321. https://doi.org/DOI: 10.1145/2810103.2813687

Shokri, R., Stronati, M., Song, C., & Shmatikov, V. (2017). Membership inference attacks against machine learning models. *2017 IEEE Symposium on Security and* Privacy, 3–18. https://doi.org/DOI: 10.1109/SP.2017.41

Shu, K., Cui, L., Wang, S., Lee, D., & Liu, H. (2020). Defend: Explainable fake news detection. *Proceedings of KDD*, 395–405. https://doi.org/DOI: 10.1145/3394486.3404192

Shu, K., Cui, L., Wang, S., Lee, D., & Liu, H. 2019. DEFEND: Explainable Fake News Detection. In *Proceedings of the 25th ACM SIGKDD International Conference on Knowledge Discovery & Data Mining (KDD '19)*. Association for Computing Machinery, New York, NY, USA, 395–405. https://doi.org/DOI: 10.1145/3292500.3330935

Shu, K., Sliva, A., Wang, S., Tang, J., & Liu, H. (2017). Fake news detection on social media: A data mining perspective. *SIGKDD Explorations*, *19*(1), 22–36. DOI: 10.1145/3137597.3137600

Silver, D., Schrittwieser, J., Simonyan, K., Antonoglou, I., Huang, A., Guez, A., & Hassabis, D. (2017). Mastering the game of Go without human knowledge. *Nature*, *550*(7676), 354–359. DOI: 10.1038/nature24270 PMID: 29052630

Singh, A. (2025). Analysis of Using Generative AI for the Classifications in Pharmacology of Medical Sciences. *SSRN*. https://doi.org/DOI: 10.2139/ssrn.5171513

Singh, M., & Khan, S. (2024). Advances in Autonomous Robotics: Integrating AI and Machine Learning for Enhanced Automation and Control in Industrial Applications. *International Journal for Multidimensional Research Perspectives*, *2*(4), 74–90. DOI: 10.61877/ijmrp.v2i4.135

Singh, N. M. (2024). Generative Models Beyond GANS: Innovations in image and text synthesis. *Deleted Journal*, *28*(3s), 354–374. DOI: 10.52783/anvi.v28.3061

Sinha, R. K. (2025). Generative Migration Architectures: Accelerating Cloud-Native Data Integration Through AI Orchestration. *Journal of Computer Science and Technology Studies*, *7*(5), 709–718.

Spyridon, P., & Boutalis, Y. S. (2018). Generative adversarial networks for unsupervised fault detection. *2022 European Control Conference (ECC)*. https://doi.org/ DOI: 10.23919/ecc.2018.8550560

Su, J., Zhuo, T. Y., Mansurov, J., Wang, D., & Nakov, P. (2023). Fake news detectors are biased against texts generated by large language models. *arXiv preprint arXiv:2309.08674*.

Sun, Z., Wu, L., & Yang, X. (2023). Multimodal data engineering using transformer-based generative models. *Knowledge-Based Systems*, *278*, 110997.

Suryawati, E., Pardede, H. F., Zilvan, V., Ramdan, A., Krisnandi, D., Heryana, A., Yuwana, R. S., Kusumo, R. B. S., Arisal, A., & Supianto, A. A. (2021). Unsupervised feature learning-based encoder and adversarial networks. *Journal of Big Data*, *8*(1). Advance online publication. DOI: 10.1186/s40537-021-00508-9

Sutton, R. S., & Barto, A. G. (2018). *Reinforcement Learning : An Introduction.*

Sutton, R. S., & Barto, A. G. (2018). *Reinforcement learning: An introduction* (2nd ed.). MIT Press., DOI: 10.1109/TNN.1998.712192

Szeszulski, J., & Guastaferro, K. (2024). Optimization of implementation strategies using the Multiphase Optimization STratgey (MOST) framework: Practical guidance using the factorial design. *Translational Behavioral Medicine*, *14*(9), 505–513. DOI: 10.1093/tbm/ibae035 PMID: 38906703

T. Li, A. K. Sahu, M. Zaheer, M. Sanjabi, A. Talwalkar, V. Smith, Federated optimization in hetero geneous networks, Proceedings of Machine learning and systems 2 (2020) 429450.

Taeihagh, A. (2025). Governance of Generative AI. *Policy and Society*. Advance online publication. DOI: 10.1093/polsoc/puaf001

Tang, G., Müller, M., Rios, A., & Sennrich, R. (2018). Why Self-Attention? A targeted evaluation of neural machine translation architectures. *Proceedings of the 2021 Conference on Empirical Methods in Natural Language Processing*. https:// doi.org/DOI: 10.18653/v1/d18-1458

Tariq, M. U. (2025). AI-Powered Cybersecurity: Defending Green IT Systems With Intelligent Solutions. In Gupta, B., Pramod, D., & Moslehpour, M. (Eds.), *Sustainable Information Security in the Age of AI and Green Computing* (pp. 141–156). IGI Global Scientific Publishing., DOI: 10.4018/979-8-3693-8034-5.ch007

Tariq, M. U. (2025). Empowering Women Entrepreneurs: Innovative Crowdfunding and Alternative Financing Models for Sustainable Business Growth. In Katper, N. (Ed.), *Crowdfunding and Alternative Financing Models for Women Entrepreneurs* (pp. 1–34). IGI Global Scientific Publishing., DOI: 10.4018/979-8-3693-9193-8.ch001

Tariq, M. U. (2025). Integrating Advanced Technologies for Multi-Stakeholder Collaboration: Driving Sustainability in Supply Chains Through Industry 4.0. In Frichi, Y., & Jawab, F. (Eds.), *Multi-Stakeholder Collaboration for Sustainable Supply Chain* (pp. 313–334). IGI Global Scientific Publishing., DOI: 10.4018/979-8-3693-8925-6.ch014

Tariq, M. U. (2025). Unveiling Consumer Insights: The Power of Qualitative Research in Market Analysis. In Segura, L., Vasconcelos, A., & Slomski, V. (Eds.), *Exploring Qualitative Research in Business: Approaches, Strategies, And Methods* (pp. 127–154). IGI Global Scientific Publishing., DOI: 10.4018/979-8-3693-7698-0.ch005

Tate, J., Beck, P., Ibarra, H. H., Kumaravel, S., & Miklas, L. (2018). *Introduction to storage area networks*. IBM Redbooks.

Tembhekar, P., Devan, M., & Jeyaraman, J. (2023). Role of GenAI in Automated Code Generation within DevOps Practices: Explore how Generative AI. *Journal of Knowledge Learning and Science Technology ISSN 2959-6386 (Online), 2*(2), 500–512. https://doi.org/DOI: 10.60087/jklst.vol2.n2.p512

Thapa, C., & Camtepe, S. (2020). Precision health data: Requirements, challenges and existing techniques for data security and privacy [Review of Precision health data: Requirements, challenges and existing techniques for data security and privacy]. Computers in Biology and Medicine, 129, 104130. Elsevier BV. https://doi.org/DOI: 10.1016/j.compbiomed.2020.104130

The Lens. (2025). *Search results for "Generative AI"*. Retrieved July 11, 2025, from https://www.lens.org/lens/search/scholar/list?q=Generative%20AI

The Lens. (2025). *Search results for "Generative AI"*. Retrieved June 18, 2025, from https://www.lens.org/lens/search/scholar/list?q=Generative%20AI

Thirunagalingam, A. (2025). Generative AI Ethics: A comprehensive safety and regulation framework. SSRN *Electronic Journal*. https://doi.org/DOI: 10.2139/ssrn.5047540

Thomas, S. A., Dubey, A., Viassolo, D., & Zanette, M. (2020). Digital Fleet Management: A Scalable Cloud Framework based on Data-driven Prediction Models. In S. A. Thomas, A. Dubey, D. Viassolo, & M. Zanette, Annual Conference of the PHM Society (Vol. 12, Issue 1, p. 8). https://doi.org/DOI: 10.36001/phmconf.2020.v12i1.1273

Thoring, K., Huettemann, S., & Mueller, R. M. (2023). The augmented designer: a research agenda for generative AI-enabled design. *Proceedings of the Design Society*, *3*, 3345–3354. DOI: 10.1017/pds.2023.335

Tian, J., & Li, L. (2022). Research on artificial intelligence of accounting information processing based on image processing. *Mathematical Biosciences and Engineering*, *19*(8), 8411–8425.

Tran, D., Ranganath, R., & Blei, D. (2016). Variational Gaussian process. *International Conference on Learning Representations*. https://doi.org/DOI: 10.48550/arXiv.1511.06499

Troia, S., Borgianni, L., Sguotti, G., Giordano, S., & Maier, G. (2025). A Comprehensive Survey on Software-Defined Wide Area Network. *IEEE Communications Surveys and Tutorials*.

Urquhart, L., McGarry, G., & Crabtree, A. (2022). Legal Provocations for HCI in the Design and Development of Trustworthy Autonomous Systems. https://doi.org/DOI: 10.1145/3546155.3546690

Vartiainen, H., Kahila, J., Tedre, M., López-Pernas, S., & Pope, N. (2024). Enhancing children's understanding of algorithmic biases in and with text-to-image generative AI. *New Media & Society*. Advance online publication. DOI: 10.1177/14614448241252820

Vaswani, A., Shazeer, N., Parmar, N., Uszkoreit, J., Jones, L., Gomez, A. N., & Polosukhin, I. (2017). Attention is all you need. *Advances in Neural Information Processing Systems*, *30*, 5998–6008. DOI: 10.5555/3295222.3295349

Vebritha, S. (2024). Redefining Ownership and Originality in the age of AI: A Legal and Ethical review. *Sinergi International Journal of Law*, *2*(4), 312–324. DOI: 10.61194/law.v2i4.726

Vernova, G. E. (2024). *Digital Twin Technology | GE Vernova*. Gevernova.com. https://www.gevernova.com/software/innovation/digital-twin-technology

Wahid, A., Yahya, M., Breslin, J. G., & Intizar, M. A. (2023). Self-Attention Transformer-Based architecture for remaining useful life estimation of complex machines. *Procedia Computer Science*, *217*, 456–464. DOI: 10.1016/j.procs.2022.12.241

Wang, W. Y. (2018). "Liar, liar pants on fire": A new benchmark dataset for fake news detection. *Proceedings of ACL*, 422–426. https://doi.org/DOI: 10.48550/arXiv.1705.00648

Wang, Y., Zhou, F., & Li, K. (2024). Real-time anomaly detection in data pipelines using generative AI. *IEEE Internet of Things Journal, 11*(4), 6772–6784.

Wei, Y., Luo, X., Hu, L., Peng, Y., & Feng, J. (2020). An improved unsupervised representation learning generative adversarial network for remote sensing image scene classification. *Remote Sensing Letters, 11*(6), 598–607. DOI: 10.1080/2150704x.2020.1746854

Williamson, O. E. (1985). *The Economic Institutions of Capitalism: Firms, Markets, Relational Contracting* (SSRN Scholarly Paper 1496720). Social Science Research Network.

Wirges, F., & Neyer, A. (2022). Towards a process-oriented understanding of HR analytics: implementation and application. In F. Wirges & A. Neyer, Review of Managerial Science (Vol. 17, Issue 6, p. 2077). Springer Science+Business Media. https://doi.org/DOI: 10.1007/s11846-022-00574-0

Wong, D. H.-T., Maarop, N., & Samy, G. N. (2020). Data Governance and Data Stewardship: A Success Procedure (By D. H.-T. Wong, N. Maarop, & G. N. Samy; Vol. 202, p. 54). https://doi.org/DOI: 10.1109/icimu49871.2020.9243574

Wood, D., & Moss, S. H. (2024). Evaluating the impact of students' generative AI use in educational contexts. *Journal of Research in Innovative Teaching & Learning, 17*(2), 152–167. DOI: 10.1108/jrit-06-2024-0151

Wu, L., Hitt, L. M., & Lou, B. (2019). Data Analytics, Innovation, and Firm Productivity. In L. Wu, L. M. Hitt, & B. Lou, Management Science (Vol. 66, Issue 5, p. 2017). Institute for Operations Research and the Management Sciences. https://doi.org/DOI: 10.1287/mnsc.2018.3281

Wu, A. N., Stouffs, R., & Biljecki, F. (2022). Generative Adversarial Networks in the built environment: A comprehensive review of the application of GANs across data types and scales. *Building and Environment, 223*, 109477. DOI: 10.1016/j.buildenv.2022.109477

Wyczik, J., & Wieczerzak, R. (2024). Rethinking Copyright: The art of ownership in AI outputs. *Eastern European Journal of Transnational Relations, 8*(1), 39–52. DOI: 10.15290/eejtr.2024.08.01.04

Xiao, Y., Shi, G., & Krunz, M. Towards Ubiquitous AI in 6G with Federated Learning arXiv:2004.13563v1 [eess.SP] 26 Apr 2020.

Xu, H., Sun, Y., Tupayachi, J., Omitaomu, O., Zlatanov, S., & Li, X. (2025). Towards the Autonomous Optimization of Urban Logistics: Training Generative AI with Scientific Tools via Agentic Digital Twins and Model Context Protocol. *arXiv preprint arXiv:2506.13068.*

Yang, J., Zhao, Y., & Jia, Z. (2025). Conditional Generative Adversarial Network based on Self-Attention Mechanism and VAE Algorithm and its applications. *TS. Traitement du Signal*, *42*(1), 423–431. DOI: 10.18280/ts.420136

Yu, S., Chen, H., Reyes, E. B. G., & Poh, N. (2017). GAITGAN: Invariant GAIT feature extraction using generative adversarial networks. *IEEE*, 532–539. https://doi.org/DOI: 10.1109/cvprw.2017.80

Zaharia, M., Chowdhury, M., Franklin, M. J., Shenker, S., & Stoica, I. (2010). Spark: Cluster computing with working sets. *Proceedings of the 2nd USENIX Conference on Hot Topics in Cloud Computing*, 10-10. https://doi.org/DOI: 10.5555/1863103.1863113

Zaiceanu, A., Hlaciuc, E., & Lucan, A. (2015). Methods for Risk Identification and Assessment in Financial Auditing. *Procedia Economics and Finance*, *32*, 595–602.

Zhang, M., Gong, M., Mao, Y., Li, J., & Wu, Y. (2018). Unsupervised feature extraction in hyperspectral images based on Wasserstein Generative adversarial network. *IEEE Transactions on Geoscience and Remote Sensing*, *57*(5), 2669–2688. DOI: 10.1109/tgrs.2018.2876123

Zhao, S., Peng, Q., Mou, X., Wang, Y., & Han, T. (2021). An artificial intelligence-based real-time monitoring framework for time series. In S. Zhao, Q. Peng, X. Mou, Y. Wang, & T. Han, Journal of Intelligent & Fuzzy Systems (Vol. 40, Issue 6, p. 10401). IOS Press. https://doi.org/DOI: 10.3233/jifs-200366

Zhao, Y., Li, M., & Lai, L. Naveen Suda, Damon Civin, Vikas Chandra, Federated learning with non-iid data, 2018, arXiv preprint arXiv:1806.00582.

Zhao, X., Zhai, G., Charles, V., Gherman, T., Lee, H., Pan, T., & Shang, Y. (2024). Enhancing enterprise investment efficiency through artificial intelligence: The role of accounting information transparency. *Socio-Economic Planning Sciences*, 96.

Zheng, A., & Casari, A. (2018). Feature engineering for machine learning: Principles and techniques for data scientists. *OREILLY April 2018, First Edition.* https://www.oreilly.com/catalog/errata.csp?isbn=9781491953242

Zhou, X., Li, G., Wang, Q., Li, Y., & Zhou, D. (2025). Artificial intelligence, corporate information governance and ESG performance: Quasi-experimental evidence from China. In *International Review of Financial Analysis* (Vol. 102).

Zhou, E., & Lee, D. (2024). Generative artificial intelligence, human creativity, and art. *PNAS Nexus*, *3*(3). Advance online publication. DOI: 10.1093/pnasnexus/pgae052 PMID: 38444602

Zhou, X., & Zafarani, R. (2020). A survey of fake news: Fundamental theories, detection methods, and opportunities. *ACM Computing Surveys*, *53*(5), 1–40. DOI: 10.1145/3395046

About the Contributors

Bahaa Eddine Elbaghazaoui is a professor at ENSA Beni Mellal and a PhD holder in Computer Science and Artificial Intelligence. With extensive experience in software engineering, he specializes in full-stack development, microservices, AI integration, and cloud computing. As a project manager and trainer, he has led and contributed to innovative solutions in telecommunications, insurance, and government sectors. His research focuses on data profiling and predictive analytics, with numerous publications in high-impact journals. Passionate about technology and education, he actively mentors, reviews scientific work, and advances cutting-edge software solutions.

Mohamed Amnai is a Full Professor at the Faculty of Sciences, Ibn Tofail University, specializing in Computer Science and Telecommunications. With a Ph.D. in Quality of Service Management and Mobility Control in Ad Hoc Networks, his expertise spans big data, AI-driven decision support systems, machine learning, and network security. Dr. Amnai has contributed extensively to academia as a researcher, supervisor, and journal reviewer, with numerous publications in high-impact journals and conferences. His work focuses on advancing AI applications in data profiling, recommendation systems, and network optimization.

Noreddine Gherabi is an Full Professor of Computer Science at ENSA Khouribga, Sultan Moulay Slimane University. With a Ph.D. in Database Migration and Semantic Web, he specializes in data science, artificial intelligence, semantic technologies, and cybersecurity. He has led significant research on machine learning, recommendation systems, and big data integration, contributing to high-impact publications, books, and conferences. Dr. Gherabi is actively involved in academic leadership, Ph.D. supervision, and scientific committees worldwide.

***

Kashvi Chaturvedi, is studying B.Tech, specialisation in Artificial Intelligence and Data Science at Ajeenkya DY Patil University. She started solidifying her programming skills by completing various certification courses like Data Structures in C, Tableau functions and Operating Systems along with doing few projects using languages like Python, C, C++ and creating Web Page using HTML, CSS and Java Script. She had also attended an Arduino-Based Automation course at Dolphin Labs to enhance her software knowledge. There, she learned how to work with sensors, microcontrollers, and circuit design. She has also written multiple review papers on topics such as Geographic Information Systems, Comparative Analysis of BJT Configurations, Swiss Bank vs. European Central Bank: Data Analysis. She is also researching on and learning many topics such as Small Modular Reactors, Bibliometric Analysis, UNSDGs etc. Because of her interest in latest technologies, she also participated in Global Hyperloop Competition hosted by IIT Madras representing her college as team Vac-Vectoor where she learnt more about various subtopics from the mentors.

Susanta Das is a seasoned educator with a proven record of teaching and mentoring diverse students, working at multiple institutions, and providing service to the various initiatives of organizations. He received his Ph.D. and M.A. degrees from Western Michigan University (WMU), USA, and M.Sc. degree from Banaras Hindu University (BHU), India all in Physics. He continued his research as a Marie-Curie post-doctoral fellow at Stockholm University, Stockholm, Sweden on beam diagnostics for the DESIREE (Double ElectroStatic Ion Ring ExpEriment) in the project DITANET (Diagnostic Techniques for particle Accelerators – a Marie-Curie initial training NETwork), at the Indian Institute of Science Education and Research-Kolkata, India on high-pressure physics as a Project Scientist-B, and at the University of Electro-Communications, Tokyo, Japan on ion-surface interactions as a Post-doctoral fellow. Throughout his career, Dr. Das worked and collaborated with many researchers, Ph.D., master, and visiting students from different countries. He further visited many countries to discuss research and an international conference participant (UK, Italy, Germany, Greece, Belgium, Bulgaria, Romania, Brazil etc.). He co-authored several research articles in WoS/Scopus indexed international journals, conference proceedings, and scholarly book chapters published by renowned international publishing houses. Beyond his research endeavors, Dr. Das has a storied history of service to academic and administrative committees, exhibiting his commitment to the growth and development of educational institutions. His experience includes tenure at Central University South Bihar, Sri Sri University, and P.K. University before assuming his current role at Ajeenkya DY Patil University. He received the Marie-Curie post-doctoral fellowship in Sweden, Science Academies' Summer Research Fellowship in India, Gwen Frostic Doctoral

Fellowship, Department Graduate Research and Creative Scholar Award by WMU, and Leo R. Parpart Doctoral Fellowship by Dept. of Physics, WMU, among many others, throughout his academic journey. At present, Dr. Das continues to delve into cutting-edge fields, with a keen interest in nanotechnology, quantum computing, and data science. His multifaceted contributions, spanning teaching, research, and administrative leadership, showcase a dedicated professional who is instrumental in advancing the vision and mission of the institutions he serves.

Pooja Dehankar is working in the department of Artificial Intelligence and Data Science, Ajeenkya DY Patil School of Engineering, Pune. She has completed BE in Computer Engineering from Priyadarshini College of Engineering, Nagpur and ME in Information Technology from Sinhgad College of Engineering, Pune. She has done Post Graduate Diploma in Advance Computing from Pune. Currently she is pursuing Ph.D. from Symbiosis International Deemed University, Pune. She has 17 years of experience in academics. Her area of interest are Artificial Intelligence, Cyber Security and Data Mining. She has published papers in Scopus indexed Journals. Furthermore,she has published several book chapters. She actively participates in workshops, faculty development programs, short term training programs, conferences and webinars. She is committed to continuous learning by expanding her knowledge, and skills. She has completed NPTEL online course on Internet of Things, Cloud Computing, Demystifying Networking and Enhancing soft skill and personality. She had organized many Guest Lectures and workshops. Her goal is to make a positive difference in the world through her work.

Leila El Gnaoui is a professor at The University of Hassan II Casablanca, Morocco, Faculty of Legal, Economic and Social Sciences – Ain Chock. Laboratory Business Intelligence Governance of Organizations, Finance and Economic (BIGOFE).

Tarik El Moudden holds a Ph.D. in Computer Science (2025) from Ibn Tofail University, Kenitra, with research focused on deep learning for image classification and hypothesis testing using geospatial data. He also earned a DESA in Computer Science and Telecommunications (2008), a Bachelor's in Physics (2000) specializing in electronics, and a certification in computer science education (2003). Over his career, he has acquired multiple certifications from institutions such as NASA, IBM, Coursera, and Packt, covering machine learning, sports analytics, concurrent programming, AI-driven project management, and remote sensing. His publications in Scopus-indexed journals and conference contributions address topics including slum detection, convolutional neural networks, planetary influence on seismic activity, and environmental monitoring.

Souad Garawit is a PhD Researcher at the University of Hassan II Casablanca, Morocco, Faculty of Legal, Economic and Social Sciences – Ain Chock. Laboratory Business Intelligence Governance of Organizations, Finance and Economic (BIGOFE).

Nikhil Kumar Goyal is currently working as Assistant Professor at Poornima University Jaipur having domain in AI, ML, Cybersecurity

Sangita Gupta, a Professor at Poornima University, Jaipur, brings over 24 years of experience in teaching, research, and academic administration. She holds an M.Sc. in Chemistry, a PGDCA, a Postgraduate Diploma in Environmental Studies, and a Ph.D. Her research interests span electrochemical and analytical techniques, electroplating, environmental science, and organic synthesis. She has served as Director of an institute and Editor of UDDESHY, a registered popular science magazine. As a Principal Investigator of a DST major project at the University of Rajasthan, she has led significant research initiatives. Dr. Gupta has organized and chaired numerous national and international conferences and is a reviewer for several reputed international journals. With over 40 research publications, two authored books, and multiple awards, she is widely recognized for her academic and scientific contributions.

Rituraj Jain is currently working in the Department of Information Technology, Marwadi University, Rajkot, Gujarat, India. He has published many papers in International Journals and Conferences. He has published 4 books. He is an Oracle Database SQL Certified Expert. He is also associated with professional bodies like the Indian Society of Technical Education (ISTE), Computer Science Teachers Association (CSTA), Academy & Industry Research Collaboration Center (AIRCC), International Association of Computer Science and Information Technology (IACSIT), International Association of Engineers (IAENG). His research interests include Cloud Computing, Machine Learning, Deep Learning, Fuzzy Logic, IoT, Genetic Algorithms, Big Data and Software Engineering.

Bright Keswani is working as Professor at Department of Computer Applications, Suresh Gyan Vihar University, Jaipur, India since 2006. He is founder Editor-in-Chief of Suresh Gyan Vihar University's Journal of Engineering and Technology. He has done M.Sc.(CS), MCA, M.Tech, M.Phil (CS) and Ph.D. His research areas includes Software Project Management, Big Data Analytics, Information Retrieval, Computer Networking, Cloud Computing, Software Testing, ERP Systems, E-Commerce and related Technologies, Reconfigurable Machines, Human-Computer Interaction, Remote Sensing, and Precision Agriculture. Being a prolific writer, he penned down more than 10 books on Operating System, E-

Banking and Security Transactions, Software Engineering, Elementary Computer Applications, Introduction to Computer Science and Programming in Visual Basic. He has authored 'Book Chapters' with Wiley Publications, Apple Press, Springer, Elsevier, CRC Press like International publishing houses as well as submitted 'Self Learning Material' of Computer Science for UG and PG learning.

S. Oswalt Manoj is a committed academician and researcher, currently serving as a Professor in the Department of Computer Science and Engineering at Alliance University, Bengaluru. With rich experience in teaching, research, mentoring, and academic leadership, he has guided several Ph.D. scholars and contributed extensively to doctoral committees under Anna University, Chennai. He holds a Ph.D. in Information and Communication Engineering from Anna University, Chennai, with his research focused on Deep Learning-based Rainfall Prediction for Agricultural Applications. He also holds undergraduate and postgraduate degrees in Computer Science and Engineering from Anna University and its affiliated institutions. His areas of academic interest include Machine Learning, Deep Learning, Big Data Analytics, Cloud Computing, and Quantum Computing. Dr. Manoj has published widely in reputed international journals and conferences and has contributed to several book chapters and edited volumes across leading academic publishers. His work spans both theoretical and applied domains, and he remains actively engaged in research dissemination and peer review. He is also a member of editorial boards and serves as a reviewer for various reputed journals and professional associations. As a mentor, he has played a key role in guiding student teams through prestigious national and international hackathons and innovation challenges. He has also been invited to deliver guest lectures and serve as a resource person in numerous Faculty Development Programs (FDPs), conferences, and academic forums. Dr. Manoj has held multiple academic leadership roles, including as R&D Cell Coordinator, PG & Ph.D. Coordinator, Deputy Controller of Examinations, Design and Innovation Cell Lead, and Institutional Website Coordinator. He is associated with several professional bodies and continues to contribute to the advancement of computing and engineering education through research, innovation, and collaborative engagement.

Adalbert Musengamana is a final year student of Information Technology, Marwadi University. Their research interest is in machine learning, deep learning, edge computing, big data analysis.

Balusamy Nachiappan is an experienced IT professional with a strong background in object-oriented Software Development, Design, and Architecture. Certified as a Salesforce System Architect and Salesforce Application Architect. Specialized in Banking, including Investment Banking and Core Banking, with international exposure. Extensive experience in the Travel Domain encompassing Airlines, Ship & Cargo industries, along with proficiency in Supply Chain Management and Real Estate. A solid track record of over a decade in Product Development across various sectors. Proficient in Waterfall, V Model, and Agile-Scrum methodologies. Holds extensive onsite exposure in the US, Japan, the UK, and Qatar.

Krutika Patre, is an aspiring programmer and technology enthusiast, currently pursuing Engineering in Artificial Intelligence and Data Science. With a passion for learning, she is building experience in a variety of programming languages and technologies, including C, C++, Python, Data Structures (DS), HTML, CSS, and JavaScript, DBMS (My SQL). After learning this programming language, she has created interest in Full Stack Development. She had also attended an Arduino-Based Automation course at Dolphin Labs to improve my software knowledge. There, she learned how to work with sensors, microcontrollers, and circuit design. She has written review paper on Sustainable engineering on build environment. She is doing researching and learning many topics related to AI, Policy and governance and related to my interest. She has taken part in hackathons, workshops, and tech events to explore many fields. She is also working with a group on Hyperloop. Being part of this project has really helped her grow, especially in areas like teamwork, innovation, and systems thinking.

Rajkumar N is an Associate Professor in the Department of Computer Science and Engineering. He earned his Ph.D. in Information and Communication Engineering from Anna University, Chennai. With a rich experience of 15 years in the realm of technical education, he has made substantial contributions to the academic arena. His research background is highly commendable, encompassing over 20 publications in esteemed international journals, coupled with numerous presentations at both international and national conferences. Moreover, he actively engages as a member of prestigious professional societies such as ISTE, IAENG, and CSTA. His primary areas of interest comprise Software Engineering, Computer Networks, Internet of Things, and Machine Learning.

Sunil Sankathala is pursuing B. Tech Computer Science and Engineering at Ajeenkya DY Patil University, with a diverse range of interests that bridge technology, sustainability, and innovation. His academic focus lies in computer science fundamentals like programming, data structures, algorithms, and software development. He actively supplements this with hands-on experience in web development and robotics. Beyond the core curriculum, He has a strong research inclination in emerging and impactful fields. His current research interests include Artificial Intelligence in Healthcare, bioplastics, nano bioplastics, e-waste management, and solid waste management—areas where he believes technology can make a meaningful difference in solving real-world problems. He has been publishing research articles and book chapters in reputed national and international journals and books. He is also part of an ambitious Hyperloop project, which involves interdisciplinary collaboration and cutting-edge engineering aimed at revolutionizing transportation. Working on this project has enhanced his skills in teamwork, innovation, and systems thinking. In the tech domain, he has developed proficiency in web development using technologies such as HTML, CSS, JavaScript, and React. His interests in robotics further reflect building smart, responsive systems that interact with the physical world. Throughout his course, he has helped strengthen problem-solving and collaborative skills. He is proficient in languages such as Python, C, C++, MySQL, Ubuntu, Machine Learning and familiar with frameworks and tools like React, Git. He actively participates in hackathons, coding competitions, and tech events to challenge himself and learn from peers. He is also a quick learner and highly adaptable, with an eagerness to stay updated with the latest trends in the tech world. He aspires to become a skilled software engineer and contribute to building innovative solutions that have a positive impact on society. The long-term goal is to work in a dynamic environment where knowledge, grow professionally, and make meaningful contributions to the field of technology. Driven by a spirit of exploration and sustainability, he aims to contribute to technological solutions that address both human and environmental needs. The long-term goal is to become a versatile engineer and researcher, working at the intersection of computer science, environmental innovation, and human well-being.

Rizwan Shaikh is a distinguished academician, researcher, and software consultant with over 30 years of rich experience. He holds a Ph.D. in Computer Applications from Pune University, India. His doctoral work focused on the evaluation and analysis of e-Governance systems. Dr. Rizwan currently serves as Professor (Computer Applications) in prestigious D Y Patil Group of Institutes, Pune. He was Director (R&D, Science and Technology) at Anam Green Revolution (AGR) IT Solutions LLP. As a Board of Studies (BoS) member and syllabus designer, he contributed to curriculum reforms at RTM University and SPPU. He has authored and co-authored over 25 research papers on e-Governance, CRM, semantic web, and cloud computing. He has received research grants from BCUD, University of Pune, and holds a patent on electronic assessment systems. He has presented research at international conferences organized by IIM Bangalore, CSIR-IPR, and London Business School. Dr. Rizwan is an active member of professional bodies including INETA, CSI, ISTE, and the National Entrepreneurship Network (NEN). He played a pioneering role in establishing EDP cells in collaboration with IIM Bangalore and IIT Mumbai. He has served as coordinator for MBA online exams across 153 institutions affiliated with SPPU since 2013. As an educator, he has taught Computer Science, Management, Physics, and Engineering subjects. His contributions span academic leadership, accreditation processes (NAAC, NBA), and institutional development. He is a passionate advocate for value-based education and digital transformation in governance. With his cross-disciplinary expertise, he mentors students, faculty, and professionals in research and innovation. His vision is to create impactful digital ecosystems through governance, education, and technology.

Sneha Ashish Shirke is a dedicated and highly skilled mechanical engineer, currently pursuing her Ph.D. in Mechanical Engineering, with a focus on advancing her expertise in thermal engineering and heat power. Currently, she is working as an Assistant Professor in the School of Engineering, Ajeenkya DY Patil University, Pune, Maharashtra, India. Her academic journey began with a Bachelor of Engineering (B.E.) in Mechanical Engineering, followed by a Master of Engineering (M.E.) in Heat Power, laying a strong foundation for her professional and academic pursuits. Ms. Shirke is renowned for her exceptional soft skills, which have significantly contributed to her success in both academic and professional settings. Her technical acumen is complemented by a robust set of hard skills that underscore her engineering prowess. Ms. Shirke's technical skill set is extensive, reflecting her deep understanding and proficiency in various engineering tools and methodologies. Ms. Shirke's specialized knowledge in various areas (Thermal Engineering, Heat Power, Engineering Thermodynamics, Applied Thermodynamics, Thermal Management Systems and EV Battery Cooling Systems) distinguishes her as an expert in her field. Ms. Sneha Ashish Shirke continues to contribute significantly to the field of mechanical engineering through her research, teaching, and innovative projects. Her blend of emotional intelligence, leadership, technical expertise, and dedication to her craft make her a respected and influential figure in the engineering community. She has several years of teaching experience. She has published many research papers in prestigious national/international conference proceedings and journals.

Aditya Shrivastav is an aspiring technologist currently pursuing a Bachelor of Technology (B. Tech.) in Computer Science and Engineering at Ajeenkya D. Y. Patil University. He holds solid programming expertise in C, C++, and Python, alongside strong command over data and business tools such as Microsoft Excel and Tally software. Aditya is a member of Team Vac-Vectoor Hyperloop and participated with the team in the Global Hyperloop Competition organized by IIT Madras, contributing to cutting-edge transportation solutions. He actively engages in hackathons and various technical events to expand his skills and contribute to innovative problem-solving. He has authored and co-authored book chapters in the domains of solid waste management, bioplastics, nanotechnology applications, and artificial intelligence, showcasing his multidisciplinary approach and research acumen. Aditya is also working on an innovative project on predictive e-waste management. The project is targeted toward IT departments, schools, and colleges, aiming to support sustainable practices and resource optimization. In parallel with his academic journey, Aditya is serving as a faculty intern at Disha Computer Institute, where he teaches C, C++, basic Python, basic Java, Excel formulas, and Tally software. His dedication and teaching proficiency earned him a Letter of Appreciation and the opportunity to conduct a workshop on Advanced Excel at G. H. Raisoni College of Arts, Commerce and Science. With a strong foundation in technology, a passion for sustainability, and hands-on experience in both teaching and project development, Aditya Shrivastav is committed to driving impact through research, education, and innovation.

Rohini Vijay Tarade is pursuing her PhD in the field of computer science. She qualified NET and SET. She is working as an Assistant Professor in the School of Engineering, Ajeenkya D Y Patil University, Pune, Maharashtra, India. She has 18 years of experience in academics. Her areas of interest are machine learning and data mining. She has published research papers. She actively participates in outreach activities, workshops, conferences, short-term training courses and faculty development programs. She is deeply committed to education and has taught a variety of courses at both the undergraduate and graduate levels. She is known for her engaging teaching style, which combines rigorous theoretical foundations with practical, hands-on experience. Mrs. Rohini actively mentors students, guiding them in their academic and research pursuits. She has also worked on various Examination committees such as Paper-Setter, Moderator, and Senior Supervisor. Outside of academia, she enjoys singing and exploring new technologies.

Muhammad Usman Tariq has more than 17+ year's experience in industry and academia. He is a prolific author of research articles, case studies, book chapters, and academic books, with work spanning a wide range of disciplines. His contributions also include several patents. He is founder and CEO of The Case HQ, a unique repository for courses, narrative and video case studies. Additionally, he is President of Gulf Higher Education (Gulf HE) focused on advancing academic practice. He has been working as a consultant and trainer for industries representing six sigma, quality, health and safety, environmental systems, project management, and information security standards. His work has encompassed sectors in aviation, manufacturing, food, hospitality, education, finance, research, software and transportation. He has diverse and significant experience working with accreditation agencies of ABET, ACBSP, AACSB, WASC, CAA, EFQM and NCEAC. He is a Principal Fellow of Advance HE UK, Senior Fellow of SEDA UK, and Chartered Fellow of CIPD UK other than Senior Member IEEE.

Aryan Vasa is pursuing his B.Tech. in computer science in the School of Engineering, Ajeenkya D Y Patil University, Pune, Maharashtra, India. His research interests are AI, cybersecurity, and big data analysis.

C Viji holds the position of Associate Professor in the Department of Computer Science and Engineering. She accomplished her Ph.D. in Information and Communication Engineering from Anna University, Chennai. Dr. C. Viji's expertise in the realm of technical education has resulted in noteworthy contributions to the academic sphere. Her research background is indeed impressive, encompassing over 10 publications in esteemed international journals, along with numerous presentations at both international and national conferences. Furthermore, she actively engages as a member of renowned professional societies such as IAENG and CSTA.

Index

A

AI-Driven Business Intelligence 143
AI Governance 47
Algorithmic Bias 13, 29, 40, 54, 283
Artificial Intelligence 1, 2, 3, 4, 5, 6, 7, 8, 10, 11, 15, 17, 19, 24, 25, 27, 28, 29, 33, 34, 36, 37, 38, 39, 42, 45, 49, 50, 51, 52, 53, 54, 58, 59, 80, 88, 92, 103, 106, 111, 131, 136, 137, 158, 159, 160, 161, 163, 164, 166, 167, 188, 189, 190, 216, 221, 234, 235, 239, 240, 241, 257, 260, 264, 267, 268, 274, 276, 277, 278, 279, 281, 282, 283, 284, 285, 286, 287, 288, 289
Autonomous Pipelines 168, 177, 178, 187, 191

B

Big Data Ecosystems 136, 137

C

Chatbot 6, 10, 32, 180

D

Data Architecture 218, 225, 226, 228, 234
Data Engineering 57, 58, 59, 60, 61, 64, 68, 69, 70, 71, 73, 74, 75, 76, 77, 78, 80, 81, 130, 166
Data Governance 68, 73, 76, 122, 135, 136, 137, 138, 139, 140, 141, 143, 144, 145, 146, 147, 148, 149, 150, 151, 152, 153, 154, 155, 156, 157, 159, 160, 164, 216, 234
Data Leakage 241, 246, 254, 260
Data Orchestration 165, 166, 167, 170, 171, 176, 182, 184, 187, 191
Data Privacy 27, 29, 32, 46, 48, 54, 103, 122, 132, 141, 154, 155, 157, 194, 209, 213, 228, 259, 260
Data Quality and Compliance 150
Data Stream Processing 110
Deepfakes 14, 239, 244, 251, 252, 265
Deep Learning 5, 29, 30, 31, 32, 35, 36, 37, 39, 49, 60, 89, 90, 92, 102, 103, 106, 111, 112, 130, 131, 132, 190, 220, 221, 236, 249, 263, 264, 265, 278, 283, 287
Differential Privacy 123, 131, 162, 176, 187, 199, 239, 241, 246, 249, 253, 254, 260, 261, 263, 264, 265
Diffusion Models 1, 2, 4, 22, 27, 28, 30, 31, 32, 48, 49, 54, 60, 69, 81, 111, 119, 219, 242
Distributed Learning 198, 209, 260

E

Ethical AI 28, 222, 234
Ethical Governance 43, 54
External Audit 267, 271, 276

F

Fake News Detection 215, 217, 218, 219, 220, 221, 222, 223, 224, 225, 226, 228, 229, 230, 231, 232, 233, 235, 236, 237
Feature Engineering 83, 84, 85, 86, 92, 98, 100, 101, 102, 103, 116, 220
Federated Learning 80, 105, 123, 125, 129, 132, 176, 177, 193, 194, 195, 198, 199, 200, 201, 202, 204, 205, 206, 208, 209, 210, 211, 212, 213, 214, 239, 241, 260, 264, 265
Fiber Channel 193, 194, 203, 204, 211

G

GANs 1, 2, 4, 22, 27, 28, 29, 30, 31, 32, 33, 40, 43, 44, 48, 49, 50, 51, 52, 54, 60, 61, 69, 83, 84, 85, 86, 89, 90, 91, 92, 95, 98, 99, 100, 101, 106, 111, 112, 113, 127, 242
Generative AI 1, 2, 3, 4, 5, 6, 7, 8, 9, 10, 11, 12, 13, 14, 15, 16, 17, 18, 19, 24, 25, 26, 28, 29, 31, 32, 33, 34, 35, 36, 37, 38, 40, 41, 42, 43, 45, 46, 47, 49,

50, 51, 52, 53, 54, 57, 59, 61, 65, 69, 80, 81, 105, 106, 107, 108, 109, 111, 113, 114, 115, 116, 117, 118, 119, 120, 122, 124, 125, 126, 127, 128, 165, 167, 170, 171, 173, 175, 177, 184, 185, 188, 189, 190, 191, 215, 216, 217, 218, 221, 222, 223, 224, 225, 226, 227, 228, 229, 230, 231, 232, 233, 234, 239, 240, 241, 242, 243, 244, 245, 246, 247, 248, 249, 250, 251, 252, 253, 254, 255, 256, 257, 258, 259, 260, 261, 262, 264, 267, 269, 279, 280, 281, 286

I

Intelligent Analytics 165, 166
Interdisciplinary Collaboration 23, 55, 231, 234, 247

L

Large Language Models 2, 5, 6, 22, 28, 32, 34, 36, 37, 38, 40, 45, 49, 50, 60, 61, 80, 81, 116, 167, 172, 188, 215, 216, 220, 221, 223, 225, 229, 234, 235, 237, 263, 278, 286, 287

M

Membership Inference 248, 254, 263, 265
Metadata Management 149, 225
Misinformation 27, 29, 32, 46, 131, 215, 216, 217, 218, 220, 221, 223, 224, 227, 228, 229, 230, 231, 232, 233, 234, 235, 239, 240, 251, 255, 264
Model Inversion 239, 241, 246, 254, 261, 263

N

Natural Language Processing 5, 6, 32, 49, 51, 53, 64, 72, 103, 111, 220, 242, 277, 278, 279, 285, 286, 288

P

Privacy 14, 27, 29, 32, 39, 41, 46, 48, 50, 54, 59, 67, 69, 71, 73, 76, 77, 80, 85, 87, 88, 94, 97, 102, 103, 113, 116, 122, 123, 125, 126, 129, 131, 132, 141, 148, 152, 154, 155, 156, 157, 162, 163, 166, 176, 185, 186, 187, 194, 195, 196, 199, 200, 201, 205, 206, 209, 213, 228, 231, 239, 240, 241, 242, 244, 246, 248, 249, 251, 253, 254, 256, 258, 259, 260, 261, 262, 263, 264, 265
Prompt Injection 239, 241, 243, 244, 245, 254, 255, 261

R

Real-Time Analytics 106, 107, 108, 109, 110, 113, 114, 115, 118, 119, 122, 126, 127, 128, 136, 137, 138, 166, 225
Responsible AI 125, 159, 184, 221, 250, 287

S

SAN 193, 194, 195, 201, 202, 203, 204, 205, 206, 207, 208, 209, 210, 211, 212
Security 12, 14, 19, 33, 50, 86, 100, 102, 103, 114, 121, 131, 132, 135, 136, 137, 138, 139, 141, 146, 148, 149, 150, 152, 153, 154, 155, 157, 163, 166, 171, 176, 177, 187, 188, 189, 190, 194, 195, 196, 198, 199, 200, 201, 203, 204, 208, 209, 210, 211, 212, 213, 224, 239, 240, 241, 242, 243, 244, 245, 246, 249, 251, 252, 253, 254, 255, 256, 261, 262, 263, 264, 265, 282
Synthetic Data 22, 41, 57, 73, 75, 77, 80, 81, 84, 85, 86, 87, 88, 89, 93, 94, 100, 102, 103, 111, 112, 113, 121, 122, 175, 176, 179, 260, 265
Synthetic Data Generation 57, 75, 80, 88, 100, 103, 113, 265

T

Technology 2, 3, 4, 5, 6, 9, 11, 12, 15, 18, 24, 25, 29, 33, 36, 38, 47, 48, 49, 51, 52, 53, 62, 67, 69, 70, 73, 81, 91, 105, 107, 117, 137, 138, 139, 140, 142, 150, 153, 158, 160, 164, 166, 167, 183, 188, 189, 190, 193, 194, 198, 201, 202, 203, 204, 206, 208, 209, 210, 212, 216, 230, 235, 239, 240, 244, 251, 257, 260, 265, 267, 268, 274, 275, 283, 286, 287

U

Unsupervised Feature Engineering 83, 84, 85, 86, 98

www.ingramcontent.com/pod-product-compliance
Lightning Source LLC
LaVergne TN
LVHW081531300926
849161LV00006B/1375
9798337356167